S0-AEB-901

John Randolph Haynes

California Progressive

Tom Sitton

John Randolph Haynes

California Progressive

Stanford University Press
Stanford, California
1992

Stanford University Press, Stanford, California
© 1992 by the Board of Trustees of the
Leland Stanford Junior University
Printed in the United States of America

CIP data appear at the back of the book

Frontispiece photo: John Randolph Haynes, ca. 1905.
Seaver Center for Western History Research,
Natural History Museum of Los Angeles County

For Karen, Toni, and Suzi

Preface

While researching a doctoral dissertation in the early 1980s, I began a systematic examination of the papers of John R. Haynes, by far the richest collection of material in Southern California related to state and local politics. In an earlier and much narrower perusal of this treasure at UCLA a decade earlier, I had paid little attention to the myriad subjects encompassed within it. But now I wondered, who was this person who had been involved in so many organizations and crusades for so many years, supported so many philanthropies and political and social reform causes, and left behind a foundation bound to continue financing some of these interests?

A review of available secondary sources did not help much. Biographical essays in "mugbook" histories and references in textbooks and monographs repeated the same sketchy outline of his career, mostly based on information he supplied, on bits and pieces of his correspondence and speeches, and on errors of previous writers. Amazingly, a biography of this multi-interest activist did not exist. That revelation sparked the present attempt.

The individual who emerged from several years of research on this project is something of an enigma. Haynes amassed a fortune in his medical practice and in real estate, mining, and other capitalistic ventures yet spent a good portion of it in promoting a form of gradual, democratic socialism in the United States. To advance his social and moral ideals he never failed to work with political bosses he despised. Though a late-blooming reformer who became more active in social-reform politics as his medical career waned, he was no "letterhead liberal," as were some of his wealthy contemporaries, but a vigorous crusader as well as a noteworthy member of many reform organizations. Spurred by competition with elitist peers who resisted change, this arrogant altruist grasped for a distant utopia while accepting palliative increments of improvement. His reform career reached from the Progressive Era to the New Deal, four decades of persistent social and political reform activity in which he served as a bridge between the left and middle-class dissidents, helping to unite these factions at times to accomplish some measure of progress in his world. Especially in the controversial areas of direct legislation and public ownership of utilities, his legacy looms large in his adopted town and state.

Haynes was not a typical progressive. In fact he was much more progressive than his fellow reformers. In one way or another, he participated in all the major political issues and events that shaped California and Los Angeles in a most dynamic era of their development. In a broader sense, Haynes's life serves as a yardstick with which to measure others of his time and place, and as a key for understanding the motivation of those idealists who shaped our present political institutions.

Since this book is a political biography, I have only briefly mentioned Haynes's medical career and other facets of his very busy life that could be treated in much fuller detail. In fact, even some of his political, governmental, and philanthropic interests are ignored or given only scant attention herein.

Biographers are rarely (if ever) neutral, and I freely confess a reserved admiration for Dr. Haynes. I have, however, tried to identify his faults and shortcomings. The warts have been exposed when found.

Over the last several years I have accumulated a mountain of debts to many individuals who assisted in this project in some way. I am very grateful to the personnel of all of the research centers listed in the notes and bibliographical notes, especially to David Zeidberg and his staff at UCLA Special Collections, particularly Simon Elliott, Jeff Rankin, and Carol Turley, and a legion of students who schlepped hundreds of boxes of Haynes material across campus; to Nicole Bouchet and others at the Bancroft Library during several trips; and to Mary Wright and her associates at the Huntington Library, who made some of the research and most of the writing such a pleasure.

The John Randolph Haynes and Dora Haynes Foundation provided a research grant to defray some of the project expenses. President F. Haynes Lindley, Jr. graciously aided me in acquiring the grant and in securing family photographs, Diane Cornwell made Haynes Foundation files available, and both supplied encouragement and hospitality on numerous visits.

My colleagues in the History Division and others at the Natural History Museum of Los Angeles County assisted in a variety of ways: Harry Kelsey, the late Burt Reiner, and Marsha Hamilton offered encouragement early on; Errol Stevens critiqued earlier portions of this work; John Cahoon, Janet Evander, and dedicated volunteers unearthed important material and brought it to my attention; Mona Martinez took me through a not-quite-WordPerfect world in preparing the final manuscript; and Janet Fireman helped immensely by reading and insightfully commenting on one of the last drafts, eliminating many errors and suggesting more pleasing prose.

At Stanford University Press I received encouragement from Norris Pope, who diligently guided two drafts of this manuscript through the examination process. Professor John M. Allswang and an anonymous referee offered both corrections and constructive suggestions that improved an otherwise much longer and more narrowly focused study. Copyeditor Nancy Atkinson did an outstanding job in improving the grammar and style, as well as identifying mistakes and inconsistencies. And Ellen F. Smith carefully steered the piece through its final stages.

Permission to publish photographs, illustrations, and/or quotes from unpublished material has been granted by the following: Department of Special Collections, University Research Library, UCLA; Department of Special Collections, Stanford University Library, Stanford, California; Henry E. Huntington Library, San Marino, California; Bancroft Library, University of California, Berkeley; California State Library, Sacramento; Richard L. Lissner and the Lissner Family; *Los Angeles Times;* F. Haynes Lindley, Jr.; The John Randolph Haynes and Dora Haynes Foundation; Department of Special Collections, University of Southern California Library; and the Seaver Center for Western History Research, Los Angeles County Museum of Natural History.

Bill Deverell: what can I say? From the beginning Bill offered advice, discussed the issues, and read, commented on, and suffered through the most primitive drafts. Beer and pizza cannot adequately pay his invisible bill; my good friend and accomplice in the study of California politics will never be thanked enough.

Finally—my wife, Karen, and daughters, Toni and Suzi, sacrificed much more than they would admit in the precious years this project devoured. There is no way I can ever express my gratitude for their love and support. I hope proving that the book is finally completed is a start.

Contents

Photo sections follow pages 50 and 180.

John Randolph Haynes

California Progressive

Chapter One

"My Idea of My Biography"

I was born in the spring of 1853, entirely without my permission and [with] no responsibility for the results of that event.

I am a man of limited education; of mediocre intellectual ability; but with a certain amount of obstinacy and persistency which has enabled me to accomplish some of the things that are dear to my heart. I believe I am a fundamental democrat and I believe it is only through the proper physical, mental and moral education of the masses of the people who will be, and should be, the rulers of the government under which they live, that we will in time achieve the best known government.

With this self-proclaimed introduction, John Randolph Haynes began dictating vignettes and anecdotes of his life and political activities to his private secretary in the mid-1920s. These reminiscences were to be assembled and transformed into a biography, first by Native American rights activist John Collier, then *Sunset* editor Walter Woehlke, and later newspaperman Franklin Hichborn. The biography never reached fruition; some of Haynes's autobiographical notes are buried in the office files of the philanthropic foundation he created, others are scattered among his private papers housed in a university library.[1]

Haynes was persuaded to record his reminiscences by a number of his contemporaries, who had little difficulty convincing him that he had achieved much of importance. He was well aware of his role in shaping the twentieth-century social and political institutions of Los Angeles and California, and vain enough to covet an autobiography, yet humble enough to suspend it repeatedly when he believed his reform interests were more pressing. Indeed his short essays are as saturated with humility as with his utopian vision of society; they also reflect his optimism, even though he dictated them from his sickbed in his 70s and early 80s. His notes continually stress the necessity of citizen participation in civic affairs and the importance of using government to improve institutions for the "betterment of mankind," ideas still promoted by the foundation he established.[2]

In middle age, John R. Haynes had the bearing, manners, and wherewithal of a patrician, belying his simple upbringing. Both sides of his family traced their roots to England; one branch had arrived recently, whereas the other claimed several generations of American ancestors. On his mother's side, Haynes traced his lineage to William Fellows (1609–76), a shoemaker from Selsten, Northants, England, who sailed to the colonies aboard the *Planter* in 1635. With his wife, Mary Ayers (1607–1702), Fellows settled in Ipswich, Massachusetts, where he became a farmer and the town cowkeeper. His descendants had moved to Canaan, Connecticut, by 1720.[3]

One of Fellows's many great-great-grandsons, Abiel (1762–1833), distinguished himself as a soldier in the American Revolution, having joined the Connecticut militia at fifteen. Attached to a division commanded by his uncle, General John Fellows, Abiel fought at the battles of Freeman's Farm and Saratoga in 1777, and was mustered out of the service at the end of the war. He married Katherine Mann (?–1805), the second of his three wives, in 1791, and settled down on Fellowship, a farm of several thousand acres in western Luzerne County, Pennsylvania. There he raised nineteen children, engaged in farming and mercantile trade, and helped organize the Susquehanna and Tioga Turnpike Company. Commissioned a colonel in the War of 1812, he claimed to have served with Commodore Perry at Lake Erie. In 1829, Abiel ventured into what would become the state of Michigan, where he began farming near Praire Ronde. Three years later, at the age of 70, he volunteered as an aide to General Lewis Cass during the Black Hawk War. He died in Michigan in 1833.[4]

One of the six children of Abiel and Katherine, Anna A. Fellows (1794–1859), was born in Huntington township in Luzerne County. In 1819, she married John J. Koons (1795–1878), and the two moved to New Columbus in northern Huntington Township. A stern Dutchman, Koons became a prominent merchant, surveyor, and investor in several turnpike ventures, and was commissioned an associate judge of Luzerne County in 1846. The eldest of John and Anna's six children, Elvira Mann Koons, was born in 1820 and resided in New Columbus until her marriage to John Randolph Haynes's father in 1844.[5]

John Haynes was very proud of these sturdy pioneers, and just as proud of his father's English heritage, especially the family tradition of social reform, which he himself would carry on. One of his paternal ancestors was imprisoned in 1667 for publishing a tract on the prevention of poverty. Haynes's grandfather Joseph was born in Loughborough, near the coalfields of Nottingham, about 1785. Joseph married Mary Leader (1795–1869) in 1815, and the two raised a family of eight in Poplar in eastern London. Not far from Westminster Abbey, Joseph operated a law publishing house at Temple Bar, well known for its bookstores. Besides running this business he spent much of his time working with Major John Cartwright and other political dissidents agitating for parliamentary reforms and universal manhood suffrage. Joseph named his oldest son, Francis Burdette Haynes, in honor of one of these radical leaders.[6]

Joseph and Mary's third child, James Sydney Haynes, was born on March 7, 1819. James grew up in Poplar, where he occasionally played in a coach once used by Napoleon Bonaparte and subsequently owned by Joseph, a loyal Englishman but ardent admirer of the French emperor. Apparently, the family publishing business passed on to James's younger brother, Robert; hence James was left without a birthright. So, a decade after his father's death in 1831, James decided to seek his fortune in America. In March 1841, he arrived in Boston on the *Mediator* and made his way to eastern Pennsylvania. There he met and courted Elvira Mann Koons, and the two were married in Fishing Creek, Columbia County, on June 21, 1844.[7]

At first James and Elvira settled in her hometown of New Columbus, in a fertile agricultural region in Luzerne County, where James probably tried his hand at farming. The first two offspring of this marriage were born there; Mary Evaline in 1845, and Alice Anna in 1847. Three years later, Francis Leader Haynes was born to the couple in nearby Shickshinny, where Elvira's sister, Evaline, resided.[8]

In 1849, James began purchasing property in Fairmount Springs, at the foot of the Appalachians, directly north of New Columbus and about nine miles west of Shickshinny. Situated in the center of Fairmount Township, Fairmount Springs was described as late as 1866 as having "fifteen sawmills and one tavern but no church." This sparsely populated village in a township of about 950 souls at midcentury was surrounded by hills and rich farmland. James's property lay along what remained of the portion of the Susquehanna and Tioga turnpike stretching from Berwick to Towanda, a road Elvira's grandfather had helped to develop in 1806. The Haynes family had moved to this property by early 1852. On June 13, 1853, another son, John, was born.[9]

James and Elvira remained in Fairmount Springs for three years, then migrated in the spring of 1855 to Tamaqua, a mining town located in northeast Schuylkill County. By this time James was a coal operator, and it was here that a third daughter, Florence, was born in 1856. They stayed until 1859, when the family lost most of its Tamaqua property and moved to Yorktown, a small village in the northwestern corner of Carbon County. There James managed mining properties leased from the New York and Lehigh Coal Company. At Yorktown (since swallowed up by neighboring Audenried), the Haynes's youngest child, Robert, was born in early 1861. In the following year the family moved to Hazleton, another mining center located five miles north of Yorktown, before abandoning the coal-mining region in the autumn of 1863.[10]

Named after Virginia congressman John Randolph, the states-rights champion admired by his father, John Randolph Haynes seems to have experienced a typical childhood in the Pennsylvania coalfields. In his first decade the family made a succession of moves. His fondest memories were of times spent with his youngest sister, Florence, and his older brother, Francis. In Tamaqua he tried his first cigar, regarding which experiment he would later report that no one "was ever quite so sick before or since." An end of one finger was lost in an escapade with Diamond, the family horse. And initiation rituals took place on a number of occasions as John, Francis, and a few young male friends formed a "gang" to defend themselves from bullies as they fought or avoided the territory of other cliques. All in all, his childhood evoked many pleasant memories.[11]

Haynes was especially close to his mother at this time. He remembered her as "a peculiar woman, hard and cold to the world and the great sympathies of life but devoted to her family." Elvira Mann Koons Haynes, daughter of a Dutchman universally regarded as difficult to get along with, was a proud, self-sacrificing woman "of highly nervous temperament" exacerbated by chronic digestive troubles. Both John and his siblings witnessed numerous quarrels between Elvira and James Haynes, partially attributable to her having to make sacrifices for the children as a result of her husband's "lack of financial acumen," as John recalled.[12]

John portrayed his father as a vivid and occasionally incongruous character. Though an Englishman who hated slavery, James sympathized with the Confederacy during the Civil War. He worked hard to amass a small fortune and then squandered it on poor investments. His vain romanticism made him susceptible to the flattery of sales clerks. As a lover of good literature, he encouraged his children to read English classics and American history. He could also become highly emotional, instilling fear in his offspring; this disposition most notably manifested itself on the few occasions when he drank to excess and argued with Elvira. These scenes profoundly affected John, who pointed to them to explain his eventual advocacy of prohibition.[13]

But John also believed his father to be a man of courage. During a career as a coal operator, James worked in a region racked with ethnic, religious, and political conflict. The rapid development of anthracite coal for domestic heating and industrial power had converted northeast Pennsylvania, the world's chief coal region, into a booming land of opportunity. Coal mines and breaker buildings dotted the landscape of the four anthracite fields, reaching northeast from Dauphine (near Harrisburg) to Forest City (northeast of Wilkes-Barre). By 1860, hard coal was the major heating source of homes and industry in the Northeast, and the coal industry was vital to the growth and prosperity of that area.[14]

The bustling anthracite region was also a hotbed of ethnic strife intensified by abominable working and living conditions. The heavy influx of immigrants from the British Isles in the 1840s populated this area with English and Irish newcomers who fell into an ironclad pattern. Protestant Englishmen, like James Sydney Haynes, became coal operators and mine owners; Irish Catholics, formerly poor farmers who detested their British masters in Ireland, took jobs as miners. The ethnic rivalry was further strained by the economic structure of the mining region: English and American mine operators formed the social elite of these communities, while Irish working-class families occupied substandard housing near the mines, where husbands and sons toiled for long hours in dangerous conditions. In self-defense and to promote self-help, the Irish miners formed mutual aid societies such as the Ancient Order of Hibernians, which took on political functions as well. In the midst of a wave of anti-Catholic sentiment in the 1850s, the so-called "Molly Maguires" came into existence, a secret society preying on Protestant mining capitalists. The emergence of Irish miner opposition to the 1863 draft of Union soldiers in Pennsylvania, vigorously supported by the mine owners, incited a number of murders and other instances of terrorism. For over a decade the region was in turmoil.[15]

In this perilous situation, James Haynes worked as a coal operator. John recalled that his English Protestant father got along well with his Irish Catholic workers because he was brave and just. James never carried a gun and did not hesitate to criticize his employees, which seemed to gain their respect. But there were trying times. On one occasion James returned home with a bullet hole through his hat. On another he spoke of hiding from a group of drunken miners while transporting a substantial amount of payroll money. "Every time father was not at home on time mother was terrified for fear he had been killed. Shots frequently rang out in the wee small hours of the night." Finally, as John recalled, news reached the Haynes family that the man who replaced James as superintendent of the Yorktown Colliery had been shot to death by a Molly in the Haynes's former home. As soon as the reign of terror arrived in the family's new community of Hazleton, Elvira decided it was time to quit this violence-torn region. In the autumn of 1863, they departed for more genteel Philadelphia.[16]

The Haynes clan arrived in the City of Brotherly Love at the midpoint of the Civil War. With a fortune of $60,000 earned in the coal trade, James and Elvira purchased a three-story brick rowhouse on Wallace Street, a few miles northwest of the city hall. James established himself as a coal dealer, but soon decided to live off his investments instead. The 1867 city directory described him as a "Gentleman," a charitable appellation for a man whose investment savvy soon left him unemployed with a heavily mortgaged house and a depleted family treasury.[17]

To relieve the family's recent impoverishment, John left the private school he attended and went to work at the age of fourteen. At first he obtained employment with an oil company, where he painted barrels and performed other tasks until an accidental fire and exposure to the cold left him with inflammatory rheumatism. Next he tried the dry goods business on Market Street, but his deteriorating physical condition would not allow him to handle stockwork. Encouraged by noted surgeon D. H. Agnew, the family physician at the time, to work outdoors in the fresh air, John obtained a job as a carpenter's apprentice. His health soon improved.[18]

As the family fortune increased, thanks to John's job and Francis's work as a printer, John began thinking of a career. Initially he considered architecture, but soon realized he had little aptitude for drawing or math. Francis then suggested that John follow his lead in studying medicine at the University of Pennsylvania, and began informally tutoring the younger boy, who continued to work as a carpenter. In the summer of 1871, John was hired to build houses in Oil City, where he worked long hours and saved enough to finance a full year of study without having to work.[19]

Haynes attended the University of Pennsylvania Medical School from October 1871 to March 1874. At that time the regular course was two years, but John, like Francis, chose a three-year course "in order to get a more thorough knowledge of medicine." For his thesis he first decided to examine a claim that atropine was an antidote for morphine. Using himself as the subject of this research, he began taking doses of morphine and then small quantities of atropine. Rather than sobering up, however, he began to hallucinate, bouncing off hallway walls and "talking fluently of things of which I had never known I had any knowledge." With the aid of panic-stricken family members, who kept him awake with strong coffee, aromatic ammonia, and the five-block stagger from Francis's house to James and Elvira's home, John was pulled through his delirious ordeal. Abandoning this subject as a thesis topic, he then conducted experiments to demonstrate the effects of various methods of ligating blood vessels and stitching wounds after operations. This effort, not performed on himself, earned him first prize for best research in his medical class.[20]

While studying to become a physician John also enrolled in the Auxiliary School of Medicine. This short-lived institution at Penn granted the degree of Doctor of Philosophy, then a little-known German degree that seemed anomalous in a medical education. But the curriculum allowed John to attend classes in science—such as geology, botany, and zoology—and in world literature and history. The latter courses exposed him to ideas suggesting a sociological approach to healing. In this way and others, his training for the Ph.D. was important later both to his medical practice and to his social reform activities.[21]

When he received his medical degree in March 1874, Haynes was not yet 21. Since he was not required to serve an internship, he worked in brother Francis's medical office for a few months, until he could establish his own practice. On June 25, John hung his shingle at a house he rented with a loan from his father. The two-story brick rowhouse was situated near the Delaware River on Richmond Street, across the road from the Pennsylvania and Reading Railroad coal wharves and a block away from Anthracite Street. This district was known as Port Richmond, an "unattractive outpost of the city" inhabited by poor Irish and Jewish immigrants. In this ghetto the young physician filled his seven-day workweek with a steady stream of office patients and over a dozen house calls each day. Here he worked "as a galley slave," witnessing the poverty and other ills of this urban industrial milieu on a daily basis. Like Jane Addams, Walter Rauschenbusch, and many other Progressive Era social reformers who encountered poverty early in their careers, Haynes would be deeply affected by this experience for the rest of his life.[22]

In the meantime the family situation improved in the 1870s. Francis ran a thriving medical practice and was becoming a noted surgeon. Robert, the youngest Haynes child, became the third brother to graduate from the University of Pennsylvania Medical School when he received his degree in 1881. James Haynes developed social and political contacts and began a new career as a hospital administrator. About 1873 he was appointed steward of the Philadelphia Municipal Hospital, a city institution founded to care for the poor afflicted with smallpox and other contagious diseases. Elvira Haynes became the matron of this hospital, and the couple soon moved to a new home in the vicinity. But the family also experienced tragedy. John's older sister, Alice Anna, whom he admired for her literary aspirations, died at 35 in 1879.[23]

In the early 1880s, John married Dora Fellows, a not-so-distant cousin. She was the granddaughter of Andrus Fellows, a son of Abiel Fellows, who was the great-grandfather of both John and Dora. Dora's father, Alfred W. Fellows, was born in 1830 in Cambria, Pennsylvania, near Fairmount Springs. He married Susan Achenbach, of nearby Lime Ridge, in 1853, and they raised a family of seven. Like James Sydney Haynes, Alfred became a coal operator in Mauch Chunk (now Jim Thorpe). In 1859, he moved his family to Audenried, a community adjacent to Yorktown, where the Haynes clan lived at that time. Dora was born the same year and remained in this area until the Fellows family moved to Wilkes-Barre about 1872. In this coal capital her father was not among the social elite, but he did make a comfortable living. The family moved to Chicago in the 1890s.[24]

In 1880, Dora entered Wellesley College, in Massachusetts. As a "special student," she took courses in Bible study, history, English, German, French, and music. She attended only one year, as she probably planned, and in 1881 returned to Wilkes-Barre. There her relationship with John led to an exchange of marriage vows in her family home on March 14, 1882.[25]

Just prior to the wedding, John moved his Philadelphia residence and office a few doors down the street to a larger, three-story rowhouse. It was here that he and Dora began to raise their own family, which included Sydney, a son born to them on Christmas day, 1882. In her spare time Dora helped John in the office as his practice continued to thrive. John joined fraternal organizations in the city and even taught Sunday school at Messiah Episcopal Church. His younger brother, Robert, lived with John and Dora for a short time before establishing his own medical career.[26]

As John later recalled, his profession at this time required more than just medical skills: "The general practitioner is the father confessor, the attorney at large, frequently the religious advisor of those whom he knows intimately." House calls occasionally resulted in composing wills, or in baptizing babies when Haynes thought they might not survive long after birth; for the latter cases, the Episcopal doctor first consulted a Catholic priest. Under these conditions, and convinced that his patients frequently needed better wages and working conditions, rest, and health insurance even more than the medicine he prescribed, Haynes found that he was as much a social welfare worker as a physician.[27]

As a bright, young Philadelphia doctor, Haynes was soon introduced to municipal politics. Since he was the personal physician for many families associated in the 1870s and 1880s with the "Gas Ring," as the corrupt Republican city machine was called, Haynes received overtures from ward bosses to accept the position of coroner's physician and cooperate with the city machine. Instead, he supported the mugwump Committee of One Hundred in its campaign to smash the Ring and remove machine hacks from office. Because this corrupt organization was Republican, Haynes became a Democrat, campaigned for reformist gubernatorial candidate Robert Pattison (who was subsequently elected), and voted three times for Grover Cleveland.[28]

The tranquility of the Haynes household was shattered on May 4, 1886, when three-year-old Sydney died of scarlet fever. The trauma spurred the Hayneses to consider a more amenable climate, for almost everyone in the family had one serious disease or another. John suffered from chronic bronchitis, while his parents and siblings battled tuberculosis in the often cold and moist climate of Philadelphia. Dora also was often sick in these years.

John decided to investigate a removal to semi-arid Los Angeles, which was then publicizing its many resources for those in search of a healthier atmosphere. At that time the city and its environs were experiencing a real estate boom and railroad rate war, which already had made it the refuge of choice in the 1880s for middle-class immigrants from the East and Midwest.

In the summer of 1886, John and sister Florence journeyed to Southern California in search of a drier climate and new opportunities. They found more than they expected. Upon their return a decision was made to move to the booming city of Los Angeles. On March 12, 1887, John sold his medical practice in Philadelphia. Within two months, John and Dora, his parents, and all of his siblings were settling down in the City of Angels.[29]

Chapter Two

First Decade in the City of Angels

May 8, 1887, was both a common and unique spring day in booming Los Angeles. The thermometer reached 77 degrees that afternoon from a low of 47 the night before, and the air was clear. Real estate advertisements flooded the local newspapers, testimony to the frenzy of property transfers taking place throughout Southern California. In the previous week the all-time record for total sales in Los Angeles County had been shattered. In a town with a reputation as a cultural wasteland, the National Opera Company was preparing to begin a four-night stand at Hazard's Pavilion. The *Los Angeles Times* had just opened its new office in a re-creation of a medieval fortress at the corner of First and Fort streets. A temperance meeting that afternoon at Armory Hall preceded a rash of alcohol-inspired brawls and more rumors of altercations that night: "Bad whiskey seemed to fill the air," reported the *Times* the following morning.[1]

The day's events typified the experience of a postfrontier boomtown in the throes of urban expansion. In 1887, Los Angeles celebrated the 106th anniversary of its founding as a Spanish pueblo. After the cession of California to the United States and discovery of gold in northern California, Los Angeles's meager population became Anglicized by the 1880s, when the appearance of a second transcontinental railroad sparked a real estate boom that peaked in the summer of 1887. Before reckless speculation subsided early the next year, thousands of immigrants and visitors from the East, South, and Midwest poured into Southern California. These newcomers made their journey to buy property and build homes, to gamble in real estate, to improve their health in the mild climate, or just to visit. Los Angeles was the nucleus of this activity, the headquarters for real estate hawkers, eager buyers, and county property recordings, and the location of most of the new subdivisions. The city exploded from a population of 11,000 to over 50,000 in the 1880s, and this rapid influx overtaxed the city's private accommodations and public services, while creating endless opportunities for speculative gain.[2]

In the midst of this excitement John Haynes and his family arrived in the City of Angels, on May 8. The center of downtown at this time was Temple and Spring streets. Haynes later recalled that the St. Elmo was the leading hotel then, and much of the city south of First Street consisted of "barley fields, vineyards or vacant lots." John and Francis opened a joint bank account and purchased a lot with a large furnished house on Main Street south of Ninth for $11,000. Initially, John and Dora, Francis, Florence, Robert, Mary, and their parents, James and Elvira, moved into 829 South Main Street, where the three brothers would also run their medical practice. Within three years John, Dora, James, and Elvira moved several blocks west to Hill Street; Robert moved farther north to his own home on Hill. The Main Street house would remain the family medical office for quite some time.[3]

The three Haynes sons immediately established themselves as investors in Los Angeles real estate and other ventures. But after a short time they resumed their medical careers. They obtained certificates to practice medicine in California on September 7, 1887. Francis and Robert already had contributed articles to the local medical journal, and the three began working out of the Main Street house. In August, Francis and Dr. Walter Lindley, a prominent Los Angeles physician and former city health officer, founded the Pacific Hospital in an old abode on Winston Street between Los Angeles and Wall streets, and began their surgical practice.[4]

Two years later, Lindley and the Haynes brothers moved their hospital to a three-story brick structure on Sixth Street between Spring and Broadway, opening on May 1, 1889. Here most of the surgery was performed by Francis, while John, Lindley, W. W. Beckett, and Henry G. Brainerd also had offices on the first floor. The second floor, "Buzzard's Roost," was occupied by younger doctors who handled the overflow business of their mentors below. The top floor was the hospital—a modest affair of about eight beds. The Lindley-Haynes partnership quickly became one of the two most prominent medical groups in the city, the other being the rival "Bradbury Crowd" of physicians located in the Bradbury Building at Third and Broadway.[5]

In association with the Pacific Hospital, the Haynes brothers achieved reputations for their medical skill. Francis and John received appointments as professors of gynecology at the University of Southern California. John served in this capacity from 1889 to 1891, assisted by Dora, who drew charts and diagrams for classroom demonstrations. Both Francis and John published medical articles in the *Southern California Practitioner*, and Francis wrote *Primer on Surgical Nursing*, which became a textbook. Francis was especially noted for his contributions to antiseptic surgery, and he designed several surgical instruments. John administered the first dose of diptheria antitoxin in the city in 1894, and became an authority on nervous disorders. The two were personal physicians of the Otis, Newmark, Rindge, and other affluent families in Los Angeles. John was also the personal doctor of William S. Rosecrans, a retired Civil War general and the Hayneses' cousin by marriage. Robert, who did not distinguish himself to the same degree, opened his own practice as an otorhinolaryngologist (ear, nose, and throat specialist) in 1893.[6]

The partnership of John and Francis Haynes flourished until the latter's death, in 1898. A fragile man since a serious illness at age fifteen, Francis further deteriorated even in salubrious Los Angeles. He retired eighteen months before his death, and during his last six months suffered repeated attacks of angina pectoris. An embolism of the brain finally ended his life on October 18. The University of Southern California Medical School marked his passing by the cancellation of all classes on the day of his interment at Rosedale Cemetery, for he had been lauded as one of the most skilled surgeons on the Pacific coast.[7]

Francis soon was replaced in the medical office by Alfred Fellows, Dora's younger brother. Francis and John had encouraged Alfred to become a doctor in the early 1890s, while he studied civil engineering. After graduating with a medical degree from Northwestern University, Alfred came to Los Angeles and moved in with his sister and John in 1897, when Francis could no longer perform surgery. When Alfred started his own practice in 1901, his place at Pacific Hospital was assumed by John's nephew, University of Pennsylvania graduate Harry Haynes Koons, who had arrived in Los Angeles the year before. Harry did not perform well in the office at first, so John arranged a position for him as company physician of the Commonwealth Mine in Arizona. Alfred then returned to the Haynes office after a short experience on his own and remained throughout the decade. During the entire time Dora handled the bookkeeping tasks of the practice.[8]

John Haynes continued to work out of the old home on Main Street as late as 1904. He operated on and attended patients at the Pacific Hospital (also known as the Lindley Hospital) until he moved to the new California Hospital in 1898, where he had been elected a director the year before. This institution was conceived and promoted by Walter Lindley, who convinced a number of his rival doctors to join the venture. The hospital opened its doors at Hope and Fourteenth streets on June 11, 1898. Within four years Haynes accumulated the largest patient load in the hospital and had the highest income of any participating physician. His profits must have been impressive, judging from the comments of interns sorely disappointed by their scant remuneration from the Haynes medical group for anesthesia services.[9]

By the turn of the century John Haynes operated one of the most extensive individual medical practices in Los Angeles. Besides his essays in *Southern California Practitioner* describing Francis's and his own work, he published articles in local newspapers, pamphlets on miscarriages and "tuberculosis of the ovaries," and a short essay titled "Duty of Railroads in Transportation of Tuberculosis Passengers," which appeared in the *Journal of the American Medical Association.* He belonged to the American, California, and local medical associations and a number of national public health organizations, and was a director of several local sanitoriums and hospitals. In 1903, he helped to found and served as treasurer of the Los Angeles Academy of Medicine, formed to publicize new developments in pathology, medicine, and surgery. His reputation as a physician propelled him to the forefront of the Los Angeles medical community.[10]

Haynes's lucrative practice generated a substantial reserve to fund his investments. He and Francis arrived in Los Angeles with a joint savings account of about $150,000 and began investing in real estate. Throughout the 1890s and early 1900s, John purchased house lots in Los Angeles city, a brick business structure (the "Haynes Block") in nearby Monrovia, a 2,700-acre ranch in Riverside County, and other parcels throughout Southern California. In downtown Los Angeles Haynes owned partial interests in the twelve-story Braly Building (called the city's first "real skyscraper"), Majestic Theater, and the New Orpheum Theater on Broadway. He also owned whole or partial shares in smaller lots purchased in the 1890s. A shrewd investor, he continually sold various parcels at a profit and reinvested these earnings in more expensive holdings.[11]

Real estate was far from his only business interest. He invested heavily in a number of Los Angeles banks, the Union Oil Company of California, the Los Angeles Pacific Railroad Company, and the Conservative

Life Insurance Company, as well as land development ventures in Southern California and Mexico. He also became interested in mining companies in Arizona and in South America, where he lost a small fortune in 1906. As a founding stockholder of over a dozen new businesses, Haynes served on the board of directors of several of them, including the California Hospital Company, Conservative Life Insurance Company, Union Title and Trust Company, American National Bank, Quartette Mines, Simi Crude Oil Company, Sinaloa Land and Water Company, Pan America Gold Dredging Company, and the Los Angeles Investment Company.[12]

Haynes accumulated an additional small fortune—despite many losses along the way—in joint ventures and personal loans made to individuals. His financial ledger for the 1890s reads like a veritable who's who of Los Angeles business and society, with names like Chapman, Childs, Cotton, and Clover appearing among more than a hundred others. One of Haynes's most interesting "accounts" was H. Gaylord Wilshire, the "millionaire Socialist" developer of the Wilshire Boulevard area and publisher of the *Challenge* and *Wilshire's Monthly*. Although Haynes frequently donated money to Wilshire to support his monthly socialist journals, the physician had also loaned the publisher over $70,000 by 1902. In order to protect this outlay, Haynes helped to manage Wilshire's bill-posting business in Los Angeles while the publisher was in New York and later in Canada. Haynes's involvement resulted in a clash with the secretary-treasurer of Wilshire's company, but saved at least some of the physician's investment.[13]

Since Haynes's business activities depended on the economic expansion of Los Angeles, it is not surprising that he, like many other local businessmen, became a city booster and joined the Chamber of Commerce. He was accepted as a member in July 1893, and served as a director from 1895 to 1897, and again in the 1920s. In his 44 years as a member, he provided some medical expertise on the Health and Sanitation Committee, and served on various ad hoc committees to welcome distinguished visitors or to speak at special events. His participation in Chamber of Commerce affairs and in boosterism promoted by the city's industrial elite demonstrated his leadership in the Los Angeles "growth machine," which promoted the city's phenomenal economic development in the early twentieth century.[14]

John Randolph Haynes's reputation as an investor, lender, and business leader placed him in the ranks of the city's top businessmen, so much so that he was called a "capitalist" as often as a physician. His wealth made him a much-sought-after investor and joined him in partnerships with friends and business partners such as Frederick Hastings Rindge, Pacific Mutual president George I. Cochran, and banker Joseph F. Sartori. Ironically, much of the wealth Haynes gained in conservative Los Angeles business transactions he would later use to fund not-so-conservative social-reform ideas.[15]

Outside of his medical practice and financial activities, Haynes found time to join social, fraternal, and cultural organizations and to mix in Los Angeles society. In 1897 he joined the Los Angeles Country Club, and in 1898 the California Club, both exclusive social organizations for the city's elite. In the latter year he also became a founding member of the University Club, and six years later he was invited to join the Sunset Club; both of these were social organizations—for males only—devoted to the discussion of current affairs, but offering business contacts and recreation as well. By 1900, he had joined the Scribes, another discussion club composed of journalists and others who met weekly for dinner and outings. His fraternal affiliates in the 1890s included the Knights Templars (which he joined in 1889), Sons of the Revolution, Society of Colonial Wars (he was surgeon of the state chapter after 1895), and the Scottish Rite Masons. He also belonged to cultural organizations such as the Los Angeles School of Art and Design, for which he served as president of the board of trustees in the early 1900s. In all of these organizations he made additional contacts with business associates and patients, further binding his ties with social peers.[16]

Dora Haynes, too, was active in clubs when she was not managing the business affairs for the Haynes medical office or entertaining. Her most treasured social affiliates were the Ruskin Art Club and Friday Morning Club. The former, named for nineteenth-century English artist and radical John Ruskin, was primarily devoted to the study of art and architecture. The Friday Morning Club was a discussion and service club that gradually became involved in civic affairs. Dora was a charter member, served on the club's board of directors, and participated in its activities until poor health slowed her. In both clubs she met and worked with the more influential women of the city. And through her contacts John met many of the women who later aided him in his reform efforts.[17]

Membership in clubs and other organizations enhanced the position of the Haynes family in local society. Throughout the 1890s, John and Dora appeared in local blue books and in the social columns as guests of the city's elite. The couple also played host to local and state notables: future

U.S. senator Frank Flint, novelist Jack London, and Earl John Russell (older brother of Bertrand Russell), among others. John and Dora also traveled with Los Angeles society, though John's busy medical practice limited the number of trips before 1900. His standing as a parish leader at St. Paul's Episcopal Church and his selection as a delegate to the Los Angeles Episcopal convention in 1898 further complemented his social position with the more affluent religious members of the community.[18]

In local politics Haynes was not very active, but he made the right contacts. Having become a Democrat in Philadelphia because of the corruption associated with the Republican city and state machines, John remained ostensibly a Democrat in Los Angeles. In party circles he met local lawyer Stephen Mallory White, who served in the U.S. Senate in the 1890s, and the two became friends. The doctor occasionally made requests for the senator's help, as in obtaining a letter of introduction for a European trip in 1899. In 1901, Haynes served as an honorary pallbearer at the senator's funeral.[19]

But the doctor's partisanship was never very strong. Though still described as a Democrat in 1902, he was never wedded to any political party. In the 1890s, when he voted for Grover Cleveland and William Jennings Bryan, he was still on very good terms with General Harrison Gray Otis and other staunch Republicans, as well as Socialists like Job Harriman. Haynes's brother Francis, also a Democrat, was appointed a trustee of the Whittier State School by a Republican governor in 1891. This appointment no doubt was engineered by medical partner Walter Lindley, who had important connections in state Republican affairs. Like John, Francis also remained a Democrat in a predominantly Republican region because partisanship was never an important consideration for him.[20]

The melding of John Haynes's medical practice, business activities, and role in Los Angeles society and politics established his place in the elite of the city before the turn of the century. His medical practice was one of the city's largest, and his patients included many of the most influential Los Angeles citizens. His investments associated him with the city's wealthiest businessmen and promoters, who sought his capital and offered new profit opportunities in return. His reputation as a physician and capitalist left him firmly entrenched in the Los Angeles establishment within a decade after his arrival. Haynes's standing as a man of wealth and social prominence was important to adherents of both the political right and the political left as he gradually espoused his social philosophy in his second decade in the city.[21]

John and Dora Haynes lived in the two-story frame house on Hill Street south of Ninth from 1891 until 1893, when John decided to develop a lot on Pearl Street (now Figueroa) just north of Tenth Street. On this lot he built a two-story Victorian residence, another large house, and three cottages on the back of the parcel for income property. There at 945 South Pearl Street the Hayneses would reside until 1911, along with Dora's brother, Alfred, and a few servants.[22]

At the same time other members of James and Elvira Haynes's family also experienced changes. The entire clan lived in the Main Street house for a short while, but all of them gradually moved out. Elvira passed away on November 23, 1891, while visiting her sister in Shickshinny, Pennsylvania. James, who was retired, was residing with John and Dora when he died at the age of 80 on March 10, 1899, almost six months after the death of his oldest son, Francis. Mary, who never married, continued to live in the old Main Street residence until it was sold about 1905. Robert, the youngest son, moved out of this home to a new residence, where his wife, Lesbia, gave birth to a son in 1894. Throughout these years and after, Robert and John were never especially close since John resented his younger brother, believing that his father had favored Robert as the baby of the family.[23]

The youngest daughter, Florence, married almost two years after her arrival in Los Angeles. On February 7, 1889, she exchanged vows with Robert Hardie, an attorney from Canada and real estate investment adviser to Los Angeles physicians such as Francis and John Haynes. This marriage ended in tragedy a year later. On vacation with Francis in May 1890, Robert was shot by Apaches while riding a horse about 40 miles from Tombstone, Arizona. Francis, whose horse was shot beneath him, barely escaped and brought help to the crime scene, though Hardie was already dead. The murder became a major controversy when Hardie's sister in Canada suggested that Francis had murdered her brother. The matter was resolved only when one Apache confessed to the shootings and another was found with Robert Hardie's watch. Misfortune still haunted the family; Robert and Florence's infant daughter, Alice, died at the same time that the incident was settled.[24]

Four years later, Florence married Dr. Walter Lindley, her brothers' medical associate. Already prominent as a physician and editor of the

Southern California Practitioner, Lindley also was a rising political figure in the circle of his brother, Hervey, a leader of the political apparatus of the Southern Pacific Railroad. From 1890 to 1894, Walter served as the first superintendent of the State Reform School in Whittier, where his second wife had died after a long illness in 1893. On July 18 of the following year, he and Florence were married. When Walter founded the California Hospital in 1898 and became its general manager, Florence assisted him with the business matters of the institution. The couple had two children of their own; the youngest, Francis Haynes Lindley, born in 1899, would become John Haynes's favorite nephew and a community leader in Los Angeles.[25]

By the turn of the century John Randolph Haynes had established himself as a wealthy physician-capitalist, a member of the economic and social elite of Los Angeles. In the 1890s, he and Dora Haynes worked to build a family fortune and social standing envied by their peers. Their acquisitive impulse during this first decade in the City of Angels, however, would contrast sharply with their concerns during the period beginning in the late 1890s, when John Haynes, in middle age, suddenly became an avid social reformer.

Chapter Three

A Reformer at 44

In his first decade in Los Angeles, John Randolph Haynes worked hard to establish himself in the city's social and economic milieu. He declined to become deeply involved in political affairs until 1898, when he burst upon the scene and became a leader of Los Angeles and California insurgents, a role he would play for the next four decades. The timing of this conversion coincided with the early development of progressivism. Haynes himself became known as one of the city's foremost progressives, though his views were far to the left of those held by most Los Angeles reformers.

The progressives were only one of many types of "interventionists" who challenged outdated concepts of unrestrained individualism and an apolitical national market system at the turn of the century. Recent historians such as Robert M. Crunden and John C. Burnham have demonstrated how the amorphous progressive "movement" was propelled by a vast array of religious, economic, artistic, and other forces, and how it affected all American institutions at the time. The political aspect of progressivism has been examined by historians such as John Whiteclay Chambers II, who argues that these interventionists included Socialists, advocates of both women's rights and corporate reorganization, labor and agrarian leaders, and even conservatives. Responding to the effects of rapid industrialization, immigration, and urbanization in the late nineteenth century, these insurgents of many ideologies "formed voluntary associations and other private cooperation groups and, when necessary, expanded the power of government . . . to benefit their own particular group and at the same time be consistent with their vision of the national interest." The varied actions of radicals, moderates, and conservatives, which "sought on a nationwide basis to bring industrial change under control," did not represent a unified movement. In fact, progressive leaders disagreed on many specific issues and in their general assumptions regarding the nature of politics and the American electorate. Rather, progressivism was a "dynamic general reform movement composed of many specific social movements and shifting coalitions of self-interested groups uniting temporarily over different issues and behind different political leaders."[1]

Progressive leaders usually were middle-class professionals and businessmen who "mixed new methods with old visions." These "nostalgic knights of reform" felt pressured on the left by Socialists and radical laborites striving to overhaul the socioeconomic system, and on the right by anti-interventionists whose defense of the worst aspects of corporate capitalism threatened to increase the ranks of the radicals. In response, the progressives aimed to save capitalism by modernizing American institutions "while attempting to recapture the ideals and sense of community which they believed had existed in the past." Looking both forward and backward, the progressives set the agenda for modernizing American political, social, and economic institutions as the United States entered the twentieth century.[2]

In the center of the era's impulse for change, progressives generally divided into two camps. Social reformers, like John Haynes, were closer to the political left, more sympathetic to the plight of ethnic groups, the working class, and the poor. They were active in campaigns for such objectives as child labor laws, municipal ownership, modifications of the tax structure to transfer wealth from the rich to the less fortunate, and other goals related to human rights and equal opportunity. Political reformers worked to effect minor changes to the political structure—nonpartisan elections, the elimination of voting by district, and the like. With these measures the structuralists hoped to make government more efficient, moral, and responsive to the middle class by undercutting the power of immigrants and workers and placing the operation of government in the hands of experts. Political reformers rarely supported social-change objectives. Paternalistic social reformers, however, generally shared the moral outrage of the structuralists concerning corruption and fear of the lower classes. The two factions often worked together in "good government" campaigns to "kick the rascals out" and install middle-class efficiency experts. The union of these progressives was most apparent at the municipal level, where reform evolved on a massive scale just after the depression of 1893, and moved on to the state and national levels.[3]

John Randolph Haynes's limited interest in Los Angeles civic affairs in the 1890s introduced him gradually to the dynamics of structural reform. In the mainstream of the growing agitation for municipal reform throughout the United States, various Angeleno civic leaders founded organizations to restructure city government and remove undesirables from office. The Municipal Reform Association, created in August 1890, hoped to end the squandering of tax money by the Republican city administration. John Haynes probably joined this nonpartisan (predominantly Republican) organization. But his only public link was a newspaper interview in which he blandly exclaimed that he was "heartily in favor" of the movement, believing that "it is the proper way to conduct the city government." He apparently played no role at all in a similar group, the Citizens' Non-Partisan Reform Association, established in 1892 with intentions, which proved unsuccessful, to alter the city charter.[4]

A year after the demise of the latter group, another political reform organization blossomed. The League for Better City Government, whose list of members resembled a roll of the city's business and professional elite, included in its leadership *Times* publisher Harrison Gray Otis, lawyers Henry W. O'Melveny and Frank Gibson, and business tycoons William Kerckhoff, I. N. Van Nuys, and J. B. Lankershim. The mostly Republican group formed in the summer of 1896 as a response to the municipal administration of Republican mayor Frank Rader. Supported by most of the city's press, the league hoped to choose and elect the best possible candidates for city offices, and to secure a new city charter "which shall reduce the expenses of administration, definitely locate responsibility among municipal authorities, and which will apply, as far as practicable, the civil service system to employees of the city government." Haynes eventually joined the organization and even served as a vice president at one of its mass meetings in late 1897, though he did little else to advance its objectives.[5]

The league organized quickly and drafted amendments to the city charter calling for greater executive powers for the mayor, reduction of elective offices, and elimination of city council and school board wards. Most of the league endorsees for the 1896 municipal election won, but the charter amendments fell to defeat. The league existed for another two years, investigating alleged corruption in the school system, preparing new charter amendments, and acting as a watchdog on city government. But from an estimated membership of 4,000 in early 1897, the league shrank to a skeleton by late 1898. Internal dissension played a role: "A thing like that has a fascination for men of a certain impractical type who manage with the best intentions in the world to tangle things up for everybody else and make life miserable for us all," complained one of the league's founders. Defeat of its charter work also contributed to its demise.[6]

Through much of the 1890s, another "reform" organization—the Free Harbor League—worked ostensibly to limit corporate influence in civic affairs by preventing the Southern Pacific Railroad from gaining a virtual monopoly at a federally built harbor in Southern California. The controversy stemmed from an attempt by the railroad's president, Collis P. Huntington, to pressure the U.S. Congress to appropriate funds in 1892 for a deep-sea harbor at Santa Monica rather than San Pedro. Since the railroad owned (or was acquiring) much of the land surrounding the proposed Santa Monica harbor, some city leaders feared that the Southern Pacific would hold a monopoly on all trade through the port.[7]

Collis Huntington's tactics unified his opponents in Los Angeles who lobbied for San Pedro, considered the more appropriate site because of its sandy bottom. The coalition—christened the Free Harbor League—consisted of businessmen and community figures under the leadership of the Chamber of Commerce. The league publicly condemned the Southern Pacific for attempting to strangle future oceanic trade in the region, while claiming that the selection of San Pedro would assure free competition in transportation. Some of this opposition was rooted in hatred of the railroad and its record of high-handed tactics in California business dealings and politics. Something too may be attributed to the fact that more than a few league members had extensive financial interests in the rival Terminal Railway, which risked ruin if San Pedro lost.[8]

Cloaked in terms of "the Octopus versus the People," the controversy was viewed by league members as a reform campaign to rescue the economic and political development of the city from corporate greed. Many of the leaguers also belonged to the League for Better City Government, so this episode has been interpreted as an early skirmish in the progressive war with the Southern Pacific that came to a head in the following decade. The facts that some urban reformers supported the Southern Pacific position in this instance (or favored appropriations for both harbors), that many future opponents of the progressives were part of the "reform" coalition, and that Terminal Railroad stockholders, as well as any businessman with holdings at San Pedro, stood to lose if the Southern Pacific was victorious, all question the role of this coalition in the reform impulse of the decade. It is important, however, that the league did successfully oppose the single most influential political force in the entire state. Not surprisingly, John Randolph Haynes, who had no financial interests in either San Pedro or Santa Monica, played no part in this controversy. Although he was a member of the Chamber of Commerce, which orchestrated the league campaign, and was well acquainted with the league's Washington leader, U.S. senator Stephen M. White, Haynes was never a member of the Free Harbor League or its opposition.[9]

The harbor controversy was still raging when the League for Better City Government expired in 1898. Two years later, the Committee of Safety was created, at a time when police protection became suspect. Spearheaded by former League for Better City Government members, the new group of about 150 community leaders began investigating the police department to sever police connections with the underworld and find a better method to manage the department. One of several libel suits filed against the committee hastened its death in 1901, but meetings to discuss the continuation of its work led to the formation of the Municipal League of Los Angeles, a local chapter of the National Municipal League. This organization became the city's major vehicle for political reform for the next four decades as its members worked for a variety of structural and personnel changes in city government. By the time of its founding Haynes had gained political prominence in the city, and he was invited to help organize the league. He became a charter member, and served on its executive committee many times and as league president in later years.[10]

The more conservative wing of Los Angeles urban reform in the 1890s—the political/structural reformers—consisted primarily of shifting sets of businessmen and professionals concerned with rising taxes, crime, corruption, and inefficiency in government. To varying degrees these reformers, like their counterparts in major cities throughout the nation, wished to control public morals, increase public safety, lower tax rates, and conduct government like a business with strict accountability applied to its officers. The structuralists also praised the elimination of city council elections by districts, which dispersed power to ethnic and other group representatives in less affluent wards, as a sound measure of enlightened government that put the best candidates in office.

Structural and moral reform in the 1890s, then, embodied a constant

effort of the city's elite to strengthen its own economic and political position within the community, as well as to correct apparent problems in
the operation of government. John Haynes initially participated in this
effort to a limited extent, though he did not share all the objectives of the
structuralists. Working with the conservative reformers, he gained their
respect and sometimes their support for his less-conservative reform ventures in the years to come.

The left wing of reform in 1890s Los Angeles embraced a variety of
groups and individuals who sought to modify the social structure and
make government more responsive to the needs of all classes. The spectrum of social reform ranged from the radical Socialist Labor party and
its splinter groups to wealthy humanitarians and their discussion clubs.
In between were organizations formed to aid Socialist campaigns, advance leftist panaceas, or work for specific immediate measures such as
direct legislation and public ownership, considered part of the social-
reform agenda during the Progressive Era.

The radical end of this movement was represented by the local unit of
the Socialist Labor party. The SLP was formed in 1890 by socialist labor
leaders and some members of the local Nationalist clubs, groups of nonrevolutionary utopians committed to bringing about the socioeconomic
system described in Edward Bellamy's *Looking Backward*. The Los Angeles branch of the SLP followed the national party line in working for
the eventual replacement of capitalism with a socialist economy in the
U.S. By 1898, the competing Social Democracy organization had been
formed by non-Marxist followers of Eugene V. Debs. Los Angeles lawyer
Job Harriman, the SLP candidate for California governor in 1898, and
other dissidents who abandoned the SLP following doctrinal and personality disputes, soon joined the new party. The Debsites, Harriman's associates, and other leftist groups across the nation created the Socialist
Party of America in 1901, and the Los Angeles branch quickly became a
very active local. The party and its predecessor offered a program for
working-class and middle-class reformers to work for long-range and
immediate social changes in a nonviolent manner.[11]

Los Angeles also became the home of less-radical organizations for
social reform. Nationalist clubs flourished in the city in the early 1890s.
The middle-class membership worked toward a Bellamy utopia and such
nonrevolutionary goals as women's suffrage, direct legislation, municipal
ownership, and aid to the city's unemployed. The Single Tax Club was
formed in 1894 to promote Henry George's theory of taxing only the
unearned increment of the rental value of land. Led by Venice developer

Abbot Kinney and lawyer Frank Finlayson, the Single Tax Club accomplished little except to provide a forum for alternative taxation ideas and other reforms despised by doctrinaire Socialists. The Public Ownership Club, formed in early 1897, served a similar function for the advancement of government control of natural monopolies. The short-lived Civic Parliament, created in 1895, was a general discussion club offering a sympathetic forum for social-reform ideas ranging from evolutionary socialism to prohibition. Some of the city's social organizations, such as the Sunset Club and Friday Morning Club, also provided platforms for the debate of social-reform proposals.[12]

The membership of these reform-oriented groups embraced some of the city's more active and prominent citizens. Caroline Seymour Severance, a former abolitionist and suffragist, and founder of the first women's clubs in the United States and Los Angeles, belonged to several such organizations in the 1890s and early 1900s. H. Gaylord Wilshire, wealthy publisher, real estate developer, and Socialist party officeseeker, spent most of the 1890s in Los Angeles. Clergymen such as Dana W. Bartlett, Charles C. Pierce, Thomas Williams, and Robert M. Webster, lawyers Job Harriman, William Stuart, and William C. Petchner, editor William Andrews Spalding, and other professionals and businessmen who ranged from single-issue reformers to Socialist party members gave the entire social-reform movement in Los Angeles an air of respectability and legitimacy. This ambience, as Kevin Starr writes, was one "in which a middle-class Protestant community which had come to California out of incipiently utopian motivations in the first place found it perfectly natural, once there, to dream of shaping a political policy that would more completely express its collective desire for a better life."[13]

The interaction of these middle-class reformers manifested itself in a cooperative network of individuals on various ideological points along the spectrum of social reformers. Non–party members spoke at party meetings, while party representatives occasionally addressed gatherings of the discussion clubs. Less frequently, the members of these latter groups also included party members such as James T. Van Rensselaer, the SLP candidate for Congress from the Los Angeles district in 1898. Despite ideological differences, the social reformers often cooperated in campaigns for immediate objectives and together attended local addresses by national reform figures such as Lawrence Gronlund, George Herron, and Susan B. Anthony.[14]

The visits by such noted Easterners also served to keep the Los Angeles network abreast of evolving theories of prominent social democrats throughout the nation and Europe. As James Kloppenberg has shown, a "transatlantic connection" of two generations of European and American philosophers and political activists between 1870 and 1920 synthesized the theories of revolutionary socialism and classical liberalism that laid the basis for political action by social democrats of the early twentieth century. English Fabian socialists and U.S. Christian socialists such as William D. P. Bliss rejected Marxist revolution and argued that workers and their middle-class allies could operate within existing political systems to pursue democratic socialism gradually and concentrate on more proximate reforms. Visitors and some local leaders circulated these ideas within and without the social-reform network, keeping Los Angeles in touch with—for one moment in the forefront of—social democratic activism in the United States.[15]

Los Angeles in the 1890s, then, was a hotbed of social reformism. Enthusiasm and organizational activity seemed everpresent. One social reformer thought that on his tour of the United States, he received his warmest welcome in the City of Angels. Material achievements were few; these groups did not bring about a socialist state or even accomplish agenda items such as the single tax. But their efforts were important to the later success of direct legislation, women's suffrage, and other, less-radical ideas.[16]

In the midst of so much agitation for social reform, John Haynes initially declined to join the enthusiasm. He later recalled that he considered himself an evolutionary socialist when he arrived in Los Angeles in 1887, but did nothing while he "vegetated" for almost ten years. In that time he involved himself to a minor degree with the political reformers, and in 1896 joined a few community leaders hoping to expand the Young Men's Christian Association as a means of improving social conditions. Dora Haynes, as a member of the Friday Morning Club, participated in discussions of social problems and became acquainted with the club's founder, Caroline Severance, and other reform figures. But neither John nor Dora actively engaged in social-reform campaigns in their first decade in the City of Angels.[17]

The watershed in Haynes's gradual shift from passive observation to leadership in social-reform activism came in January 1898, when the 44-year-old physician attended a lecture on Christian socialism at his parish church delivered by Reverend William D. P. Bliss. Before he met Bliss, Haynes had considered himself "practically an anarchist" in that he could not see "any way out of the existing order of things except to throw everything over and start fresh." Increasingly alarmed by worsening social conditions and the accumulation of wealth in few hands, he could not imagine "how present conditions could be improved" and was willing "to try an entirely new form of government." Bliss's message, delivered in a revival atmosphere, transformed this pessimism into a realization that the world could be changed for the better without violent revolution, and supplied Haynes with a program to pursue that goal.[18]

Haynes's guru, William Dwight Porter Bliss, was born in Turkey in 1856, the son of Congregationalist missionaries. Educated at Amherst College and Hartford Theological Seminary, he became a Congregationalist minister in churches in Denver, Colorado, and South Natick, Massachusetts. At that time Bliss was influenced by the Christian socialist doctrine of Frederick Denison Maurice and Charles Kingsley. In 1885, he joined the Episcopal church, beginning a reform career that would mark him by 1900 as one of the nation's leading non-Marxian socialists. He also became a member of the Knights of Labor, which fused his theoretical socialism with experience in organized labor; founded the Society of Christian Socialists in 1889; and organized the short-lived American Fabian League in 1895.[19]

Bliss's social philosophy encompassed a Christianizing of secular socialism. He called for the church to embrace a "primitive Christianity" in which the teachings of Jesus Christ, particularly the Sermon on the Mount, would guide mankind in creating and governing a cooperative commonwealth, a "Brotherhood of Man" devoid of competition, where the community owned the means of production. This commonwealth would take form gradually, after workers were educated to its merits by middle-class Christian socialists spreading the gospel according to Bliss. While striving for this nonrevolutionary metamorphosis of the social system, these moderates would also work for immediate reforms—direct legislation, abolition of child labor, municipal ownership of utilities, and so forth—that would eliminate a few defects in the present system, as well as gain followers from among nonsocialists interested only in piecemeal changes.[20]

In the summer of 1897, Bliss arrived in San Francisco while on a lecture tour sponsored by the Episcopal Christian Social Union. There he launched the Union Reform League, a proposed national federation of all reformers, not only socialists; he also established local branches in Oakland and other Bay Area cities. The league platform called for the initiative and referendum, full employment, free state labor bureaus, municipalization of most public services, a graduated income tax and increased taxes on land, prohibition of child labor, women's suffrage, "rigid civil service rules," and other immediate objectives. Its principle function was to "work for the coming of the Kingdom of Heaven upon earth by organizing public opinion on lines of local, civic, state, national and universal co-operation; to prepare the way for a civilization, based upon fraternity and justice, where all men will co-operate as brothers for the common weal, as taught by Christ and by the great and good of every age." The league stressed its nonpartisanship and nondenominational character. No league member could be questioned "as to his religious or anti-religious views," although the league pledged to "work through and in churches" and to appeal "to the deep moral, ethical and religious sense of the community." [21]

In January 1898, Bliss came to Los Angeles under the auspices of the People's Club of St. Paul's Episcopal Church, the parish of John and Dora Haynes. Bliss delivered three lectures on current social problems, offering Christian socialism as an antidote. With the avid endorsement of Bishop Johnson, spiritual leader of the Los Angeles Episcopal Diocese, Bliss must have electrified his audience. A movement to aid his Union Reform League was established immediately, and soon the organization attracted many of the city's social-reform leaders. [22]

In the forefront of this crusade was John Haynes, who discovered in Bliss's message a nonrevolutionary cure for the ills of industrial America. After his childhood experience in the coalfields and years tending to medical and other needs of the victims of the economic order in Philadelphia, he already sympathized with those most in need of Bliss's program. With a fortune and position in the socioeconomic elite, he had the wherewithal and the influence to put his altruism into action. His own noblesse oblige extended much further than the "civic stewardship" charities of wealthy community leaders in cities such as Chicago, as detailed by historian Kathleen McCarthy. For Haynes, it was the system itself that needed the most attention, and Bliss offered a solution, an agenda for orderly, ethical social change. [23]

Like many of the leaders of the social-reform movement, Haynes experienced a conversion to activism akin to a religious awakening. Profoundly inspired by Bliss's sermons, the physician immediately turned his energies to advancing Christian socialism. He quickly organized and sponsored a banquet at the Van Nuys Hotel on January 20, attended by a number of clergymen and a few lay social reformers. Host Haynes introduced Bliss as the guest of honor, and the minister outlined his plans to form a Union Reform League chapter in Los Angeles. Most of the other guests agreed that Los Angeles was rife with problems and expressed approval of Bliss's remedy.[24]

Favorably impressed by Los Angeles, "where social reformers were almost as common as fruit flies" (according to one analyst), the minister decided to relocate his base of operations there. He continued to speak in local churches of different denominations, promoting the creation of his new league and Christian socialism in general.[25]

By early February 1898, less than a month after his conversion, Haynes had emerged as Bliss's first lieutenant. The doctor organized and presided over URL meetings as chairman of the Committee of One Hundred, which created the Los Angeles chapter of the URL. Located at Sixth and Broadway, this branch served as the national headquarters when it opened offices in March. The URL mission was to teach workers the benefits of Christian socialism, and its methods consisted primarily in publishing political tracts and scheduling lectures devoted to reform issues.[26]

The URL also lobbied local government as opportunities arose. When a Board of Freeholders was elected in 1898 to compose a new city charter, a URL committee consisting of Bliss, Haynes, and William H. Knight presented a memorial to the freeholders asking for the inclusion of civil service rules, a full-time school board, abolition of the contract system of labor on public works projects, acquisition of public utilities, and municipal direct legislation—the initiative, referendum, and "imperative mandate" (or recall). Several of these ideas were modified and accepted, but the final version of the document lacked features deemed vital by the URL, Socialist Labor party, organized labor, and other interest groups. Though the League for Better City Government and major business groups endorsed the charter, it was defeated.[27]

The Union Reform League was designed to be a national organization, and by January 1899, the elected officers reflected the proposed nationwide membership. Henry Demarest Lloyd, of Chicago, was chosen president, even though he was not a member. Vice presidents included George Herron, of Grinnell, Iowa; *Arena* editor Benjamin O. Flower, of St. Louis; Professor Frank Parsons, of Boston; Toledo mayor Samuel "Golden Rule" Jones; and Judge Walter Clark, of Raleigh, North Carolina. But the URL did not prosper except in California, where John Randolph Haynes was elected president of the state branch. The league was particularly strong in Los Angeles, the URL headquarters, where President Bliss was assisted by Haynes, Secretary William H. Knight, Treasurer Frederick D. Jones, and James B. Irvine, William H. Stuart, G. W.

Howes, and others, many of whom had belonged to Nationalist clubs or other social-reform organizations in earlier years.[28]

The failure of the URL to succeed nationally spurred Reverend Bliss to call for a national conference of all social reformers, an idea also contemplated by a few Eastern radicals. In July, the National Social and Political Conference in Buffalo "brought together Fabian Socialists, Single Taxers, Free Silverites, Free Traders, Direct Legislationists, Prohibitionists, Women's Rights Advocates, Republicans, Democrats, Populists, Social Democrats, Imperialists, and anti-Imperialists" intending to form a harmonious federation. The convention was racked by fiery debates over socialism and U.S. imperialism in the Philippines. But the delegates did agree to create the Social Reform Union, a more nationally oriented federation. Bliss, whose demand to "Unite or Perish" exaggerated the urgency of the conference, was selected president. The long list of vice presidents included H. D. Lloyd, George Herron, William Dean Howells, Eugene V. Debs, Michigan governor Hazen Pingree, American Federation of Labor leader Samuel Gompers, San Francisco mayor James D. Phelan, and Caroline Severance, of Los Angeles. The entire executive committee consisted of Chairman John R. Haynes, William H. Knight, F. D. Jones, William D. Stephens, Edward L. Hutchinson, W. C. Petchner, and others who resided exclusively in Los Angeles. The SRU platform contained five planks: direct legislation and proportional representation; public ownership; public revenue from increased taxes on land, income, franchises, and inheritances; government-issued currency only; and antimilitarism.[29]

The SRU absorbed the Union Reform League and operated for the most part in Los Angeles, where Bliss and Haynes directed it. The semi-monthly *Bulletin*, published from Bliss's home in nearby Alhambra, described SRU goals and activities. Haynes, as chairman of the executive committee, made plans to raise funds for the creation of new chapters, instruction of workers, and preparation of a strategy for the national election in 1900. He and his aides arranged for the writing and printing of additional tracts, urged Bible instructors to include certain topics in their lessons, and scheduled speaking dates for Bliss and other SRU orators.[30]

The SRU thrived in Los Angeles—by then one of the nation's major social-reform centers—but not elsewhere. Bliss decided that the headquarters had to be moved much further east. In December he journeyed to Chicago to establish the new main office. Haynes and the other executive board members resigned so a more representative body could be chosen. The move from Los Angeles, however, did not invigorate the

SRU. In the 1900 election year the SRU leadership divided over supporting Debs's Social Democracy organization or the Democratic party, and
the more radical members deserted. Bliss's removal from Los Angeles left
a leadership vacuum as Haynes and other local leaders pursued different
reform interests. In the sweltering summer of 1901, the Second National
Social and Political Conference opened in Detroit, where a dwindling
number of the members of the SRU and Social Democracy debated socialism and other issues. John R. Haynes, representing the California
branch, attended the meeting while on a vacation in the East. He delivered a paper on the need for direct legislation, his primary reform interest
by that time and the dominant topic of the conference. The Detroit meeting failed to revive the SRU since most of its leaders declined to attend,
and in a short time it ceased to function. Considering the tremendous
variety of radical and moderate social reformers who joined the organization, it is surprising that the SRU lasted as long as it did.[31]

Bliss's departure from Los Angeles coincided with the decline of the
SRU in the city, but it hardly dampened the enthusiasm of social reformers. As Bliss prepared to leave, Haynes and a few others—mostly Christian socialists—formed the Economic Club, a monthly dinner group to
meet and discuss "live subjects." Limited to a membership of 50, the club
was more an elitist social gathering than a reform organization. The
Union Reform League was well represented in the Economic Club's
membership with Haynes, W. C. Petchner, James Van Rensselaer, F. D.
Jones, W. H. Knight, E. L. Hutchinson, Professor A. K. Sprague, and
others. Topics included H. Gaylord Wilshire's argument for nationalization of the trusts, the municipal direct primary, public ownership, and
direct legislation, a subject on which Haynes addressed the club on more
than one occasion.[32]

The club's primary purpose consisted in discussion—not action. Its effectiveness was limited, although it did import prominent U.S. speakers,
such as Clinton Woodruff, of the National Municipal League, and Eltweed Pomeroy, president of the National Direct Legislation League. In
later years the organization included Abbot Kinney, Charles Dwight Willard, Reverend Robert Webster, and other social reformers. Some certainly were not as radical as others, but this diversity helped to make
club meetings a general forum for middle-class reformers of all types to
gather and debate other points of view. As one historian has noted, the
meetings also allowed John R. Haynes "ample opportunity to twist arms
and gain converts" for his favorite reforms.[33]

Since the Economic Club was open to members of myriad ideologies,

Haynes and others in Los Angeles decided that an organization devoted strictly to the advancement of Christian socialism was needed, particularly after the Social Reform Union had become a federation of so many nonsocialist groups. On September 25, 1900, a group of clergymen and lay people met in the offices of Haynes's attorney, George I. Cochran, and founded the League of Christian Socialists, with Haynes as president. Designed to be more activist than the Economic Club, the league emphasized its religious orientation, reflecting the influence of the large number of clergymen who helped create it. The league included many former URL members, such as Haynes and Caroline Severance, current members of the Economic Club, and social gospel ministers of a number of Protestant sects. Christian socialist speakers, such as Mrs. A. A. Chevaillier, of Boston, were brought in, and mass meetings resembling revivals were held at various churches. Promotional articles were placed in the city's newspapers, especially the *Evening Express*, whose editors sympathized with the social reformers. The Christian socialists even formed a nondenominational socialist church with Reverend Robert M. Webster as its pastor. In contrast to secular socialists, who appealed directly to workers, these Christian socialists hoped to convince local clergymen to preach its tenets to congregations throughout the city.[34]

As the League of Christian Socialists grew larger, its leaders reached beyond the Protestant clergy and proselytized among the city's Catholics. These efforts resulted in a local Newman Club's sponsorship of an address by Bishop George Montgomery in which he aired his views on Christian socialism. Haynes served as chairman of the event, held at the Elk's Club on January 29, 1901, and he and the other league members attending the meeting hoped for a positive statement. Bishop Montgomery expressed his approval of public ownership of utilities, but warned that under any form of socialism the family unit would disintegrate, and cited Karl Marx to support his case. The prelate instead preached arbitration as a means to satisfy the conflicting demands of capital and labor.[35]

The activists of the League of Christian Socialists continued their missionary work among the capitalist clergy while offering a forum to speakers of various philosophies. Haynes himself delivered one long address on the virtues of direct legislation, and participated in others. By late 1901, however, the league was fading. Some of its leaders devoted more of their time to individual endeavors, while the recently established Socialist Party of America siphoned off the more secularly inclined. The discussion function of the league, like that of the Economic Club, continued, and while activism waned, the free debate of radical topics did not.[36]

By the end of 1901, John Randolph Haynes had emerged as an important figure on the local reform scene. Though he rarely participated in the campaigns of the structuralist political reformers, his prestige as a leader in business and society made him a sought-after member of organizations such as the Municipal League. As a social reformer in the past three years, he moved from participant to leader, inheriting from Reverend Bliss an agenda for future activism. One of the few leaders to be found in both the social and political reform camps, Haynes represented a bridge between the two that could unite the distant factions on occasion to bring about success. In 1900, in fact, Haynes was considered as a candidate for the U.S. Congress by both political parties, which attempted to capitalize on his popularity with so many groups of voters. This stature in the eyes of his fellow reformers of all stripes would aid his reform campaigns and enhance his political effectiveness in the next three decades.[37]

Chapter Four

Direct Legislation:
The Means to All Reform Ends

In the first four years of the twentieth century, John Randolph Haynes rose to become the most significant reform figure in Los Angeles. Though no doubt interested in the eventual transformation of America into a Christian socialist nation, he expended most of his energy on the specific issue of direct legislation. With this device, Haynes believed, individual elements of his agenda for social democracy could be attained more rapidly.

Direct legislation consists of the initiative, with which citizens can propose laws, and the referendum, a device calling for a plebiscite to nullify or approve the actions of a legislative body. Both require the drafting of a petition to be signed by a certain percentage of voters, and placing the issue on the ballot. Considered integral components of pure or direct democracy, the initiative and referendum have been traced to ancient Greek city-states, through the development of cantons in Switzerland, seventeenth-century New England town meetings, and the national referendum of revolutionary France. A single use of the referendum has been in operation for centuries in virtually all state constitutions: most state constitutional amendments must be submitted to the voters for final approval.[1]

Closely associated with the initiative and referendum is the recall, or "imperative mandate." The recall is not technically considered direct legislation since it does not affect laws. It is often encompassed in the more general term "direct democracy," which includes the initiative, referendum, direct primary, and direct election of U.S. senators. The recall offers voters the opportunity to correct electoral mistakes by removing corrupt officials before the end of their elected terms. This power can be found in Switzerland's cantons, as well as in the Articles of Confederation, which preceded the U.S. Constitution. Many direct legislationists such as Haynes considered the recall inseparable from the initiative and referendum. Others, including Eltweed Pomeroy, president of the National Direct Legislation League, divorced the recall from the other two measures, arguing that it "involves the personal element in a manner allowing for reprisals and political revenge." The recall was so controversial that delegates to the 1896 convention of the league declined to add it to its platform. The additional feature of the recall of judges further heated the debate over this issue, leading some of those who favored the less radical initiative and referendum to question the wisdom of adopting any of the tenets of direct democracy.[2]

In the United States direct legislation became an increasingly popular panacea for the defects of representative government at the state and local levels. The decline in legislative effectiveness in the late nineteenth century due to legal, constitutional, and structural restraints, and increasing media attention on the subservience of corrupt lawmakers to wealthy special interests, spurred reformers to search for methods to make government more responsive to citizens and groups squeezed out of the legislative process. A concurrent flowering of direct legislation as a symbol of pure democracy in Switzerland led American writers J. W. Sullivan, W. D. McCracken, and others to offer the Swiss experiment as a solution. In 1892, the People's Power League was founded in New Jersey to promote the initiative and referendum. In the following year this organization became the National Direct Legislation League, and state branches began to appear throughout the West and Midwest. By the turn of the century, direct legislation had been adopted in a few states and cities, mostly in the West. These measures became mainstays of political reform for insurgents who claimed the devices would return government to "the people."[3]

The arguments for and against the initiative and referendum were based on divergent views of human behavior. Advocates claimed that direct legislation reduced the power of machine bosses and parties dominated by special interests in providing a method to pass or nullify laws in spite of these obstacles; that it served as a "safety valve" to force decisions on issues on which the legislature could not or would not act; that it educated the public on the pros and cons of the issue; and that it encouraged civic participation by making each voter a potential legislator. Opponents argued that only wealthy groups would use the process, which would thus result in special interest legislation; that the measures would dramatically lengthen the ballot with complex and crank propositions, thereby confusing an ill-prepared electorate and alienating voters from their civic duty; that the process was an unnecessary expense; and that this panacea was an affront to the American tradition of representative government, a slap at elected officeholders, who were much better prepared to balance the merits and defects of proposed laws. Direct legislation promoters touted the inherent goodness and intelligence of "the people," as well as the view that elected representatives rarely represented the electorate. Detractors, on the other hand, found themselves defending the status quo and appeared elitist in doubting that average citizens could make decisions as well as their chosen lawmakers. Proponents offered direct legislation as the solution to the deficiencies of government; opponents divided between those who denied that there was a problem to correct and those who believed that direct legislation was not the solution. The latter included a few Socialist thinkers who cautioned that direct legislation would be used as a weapon by wealthy capitalists to force uneducated workers into decisions that were anathema to their class interest.[4]

The left wing of reform, however, was predominantly in favor of direct legislation. Agrarian rebels, single-taxers, and organized labor led other interest groups in promoting the measures. The Populist and Socialist Labor party national platforms in the 1890s contained initiative, referendum, and recall planks, and labor leaders such as Samuel Gompers and John Mitchell appeared prominently in the campaign. Leaders of the national movement included moderate socialists such as Eltweed Pomeroy, editor of the *Direct Legislation Record*, and Reverend W. D. P. Bliss and other ministers of the social gospel. This leftist support was consistent with the nature of direct legislation as a potentially radical reform in the 1890s, giving conservatives another reason to oppose it. Opponents feared what proponents preached, that direct legislation unified social reformers who would use the initiative to bring about any of the various individual measures advocated by Populists, Socialists, suffragists, and others. With this in mind, John Haynes decided to concentrate on direct legislation as the vehicle for the success of many other reforms of Progressive Era America.[5]

Dr. Haynes first became a convert to direct legislation in 1898. Influenced by Bliss, who included direct legislation as an integral part of his Union Reform League platform, Haynes joined a URL committee that argued the case for insertion of URL reforms in the proposed 1898 city charter. The Board of Freeholders rejected the "imperative mandate" (or recall) but accepted the initiative and referendum, though increasing the percentage of signatures needed to qualify the initiative to an unacceptable level. Disappointed with these charter shortcomings, among others, the URL members joined organized labor, Socialists, city employees, and other affected groups—including those specifically opposed to the principle of direct legislation—in campaigning against the new charter and helping to defeat it.[6]

Haynes continued to study the intricacies of direct legislation through 1899. Initially, he rather passively supported the idea as a cardinal tenet of the URL and Social Reform Union, both of which included him as an officer. In 1900, however, Haynes's advocacy became highly visible when he spearheaded a new movement to place direct legislation in another proposed city charter.[7]

In the spring of 1900, Los Angeles mayor Fred Eaton summoned a convention of delegates from seven city organizations to nominate a ticket of freeholders to compose a more modern city charter. Representatives of the Merchants and Manufacturers' Association, Chamber of Commerce, Board of Trade, Board of Education, Bar Association, Socialist Labor party, and Central Labor Council met in early June and selected nominees for the special election. After two ballots, Haynes was chosen the at-large nominee of the assembled group, testimony to his standing in the business and social reform communities at the time. The Socialist Labor party, which had already demanded that the initiative, referendum, and imperative mandate be included in the charter, chose as its delegate the flamboyant H. Gaylord Wilshire, described by the *Times* as a "billposter by profession, golf player by preference and reformer by sufferance." Other freeholder selections included Assemblyman Nathaniel P. Conrey, *Times* executive Harry Chandler, and former *Herald* editor William A. Spalding, whose "socialistic views are extreme and depressing," according to the *Times*. In the special election on July 27, Haynes received the highest number of votes for any freeholder, and he, Wilshire, Chandler, Conrey, and Spalding were elected along with ten others.[8]

As the freeholders began their work, direct legislation emerged as a major issue. The Socialists already had made known their desires, and leaders of organized labor also stated their preference for direct legislation. With this support, Haynes began plotting. First, he exerted his influence in the selection of his friend Spalding as chairman of the Board of Freeholders. Next, he helped Spalding choose members for the various committees, making sure to have himself and two friends selected for the committee that would consider direct legislation. Haynes then congrat-

ulated Nathaniel Conrey on his appointment as chairman of that committee, and began selling the merits of the initiative and referendum. In
this conversation, Haynes proved to Conrey's satisfaction that in voting
on state constitutional amendments since 1879, the California electorate
had voted more intelligently than its legislature. Conrey promised to support the initiative, referendum, and recall measures to be drafted by
Haynes. With this approval the physician departed to try his case with
the third committee member, Richard J. Colyear. This merchant already
agreed with Haynes, and pledged to make the committee vote unanimous.[9]

Haynes then set out to prepare drafts of the three measures. He contacted William H. Stuart and W. C. Petchner, both local lawyers and
members of the Social Reform Union and similar organizations of the
late 1890s. These two friends (and patients) performed most of the legal
work in composing the drafts of the initiative and referendum. These
tasks were not too difficult since information was plentiful and a few
cities, such as San Francisco, already had adopted the two in some form.
The recall, however, did not exist at that time. Though the "imperative
mandate" had been an objective of the Populists and Socialist Labor
party, the measure had never been made part of a state constitution or
city charter in the United States. Unaware of its existence in Switzerland,
Haynes relied on a vague definition of the recall in Frank Parsons's *The
City for the People*. Stuart and Petchner then took Haynes's ideas and
drafted a recall provision for the charter, which Conrey and Colyear
slightly modified before presentation to the entire Board of Freeholders.[10]

While drafts of the measures were being prepared, Haynes lobbied in-
tensively for their passage. "I fear that I made life a burden to the other
members of the board," he confessed. He pursued freeholders at their
offices and homes "so that they could not eat in peace." On one occasion
he discovered that a freeholder whose vote was in doubt intended to
make a trip by train. Haynes recalled, "I bought a ticket to the same
destination, and having cut off all means of escape, I worked on him for
an hour, at the end of which time he surrendered unconditionally, fearing
perhaps, that if he did not I might follow him to his hotel further to
torment him." [11]

In late September the whole Board of Freeholders considered direct-
legislation measures as proposed by Haynes's committee. Haynes delivered a long address on the need for these measures and warned that
reforms such as civil service and more powerful mayors would be ineffective without direct legislation as tools to ensure good government.

Citing the experience of machine rule in Philadelphia, the record of voting in the 1892 California election, historical antecedents in the New England colonies, and recent laws concerning direct legislation in South Dakota, Oregon, and foreign countries, Haynes must have converted most of the freeholders he had not yet cajoled. With little opposition they approved the measures.[12]

This victory spurred further activism. On the day after the freeholders' decision, Haynes announced the creation of the Direct Legislation League of Los Angeles to boost the measures until they became law after the election. The league would be similar to its national namesake and would follow a short-lived 1890s organization of the same name. The *Evening Express* aided the campaign by printing editorials and articles, written by Abbot Kinney and others, favoring direct legislation. The campaign came to a halt in October, however, when the State Supreme Court ruled that the freeholders had no power to frame a new charter; modifications could be made only by amendment to the existing document. Since the freeholders had almost completed their work, they continued until their proposed charter was finished and forwarded it to the city council to be divided into separate amendments and voted on individually. The council, whose members were not terribly excited about laws allowing citizens to overrule their municipal representatives, declined the offer. All of the work for direct legislation, civil service regulations, and other reforms appeared to be for naught.[13]

Haynes's enthusiasm did not subside. Over the next year he continued his direct-legislation campaign in the press and on the platform. He wrote a short essay for the local *Saturday Post* in October 1900, followed by speeches to the Economic Club and League of Christian Socialists. In early June 1901, he delivered a well-publicized address on the subject before a joint meeting of these two groups at the Ebell Club hall, arguing for the initiative, referendum, and recall as the solution to the defects of representative government. Later that month he traveled to Detroit to address the Second National Social and Political Conference, where he told socialists, single-taxers, prohibitionists, and women's rights advocates that they should first secure direct legislation and then use it to bring about their individual objectives. At this meeting the National Referendum League was created, with Haynes as its first vice president and president of the California section. The doctor also corresponded with other reformers, such as Henry Demarest Lloyd, swapping information concerning direct legislation with a growing legion of its promoters throughout the United States.[14]

In 1902, another opportunity to place direct legislation in the city charter surfaced, and Haynes made the most of it. In December of the prior year, Mayor Meredith Snyder asked the city council to select a charter revision committee to draft amendments necessary for the modernization of municipal government. In March the committee finally began its work. Haynes was not among the members, but the group included his personal attorney, George I. Cochran, lawyer Joseph Scott, state senator Fred M. Smith, and a few others sympathetic to direct legislation.[15]

Working from outside the committee, Haynes influenced it with more than argument. In early April he approached Eltweed Pomeroy, the National Direct Legislation League president, who was in Los Angeles at the time, and asked him to speak to the committee. Haynes then arranged a banquet at Levy's Cafe on the evening of April 3, when the committee had scheduled one of its regular meetings, and invited the full committee to attend. The chairman consented, but stated that the committee must adjourn from the banquet by 8:00 P.M. and travel the short distance to city hall to conduct its business meeting. Haynes agreed, "inwardly hoping, however, that I might be able to persuade them to stay longer." [16]

The banquet commenced at six. Champagne flowed and a lavish dinner put the committee members in a jovial mood for the task at hand. Haynes briefly addressed the group concerning the need for direct legislation and then introduced Pomeroy, who delivered an eloquent speech in favor of the initiative and referendum. Nelson O. Nelson, a St. Louis plumbing manufacturer and wealthy socialist, echoed Pomeroy's remarks. Since the hour was getting late, committee member Frank Finlayson, a friend of Haynes's who had promised that afternoon to consider direct legislation, suggested that the meeting be conducted at the restaurant. The other contented members agreed. Finlayson then asked for a committee resolution calling for the initiative and referendum to be included in the charter amendments after consideration by his public utilities subcommittee. The resolution passed unanimously, and after discussion of a few other subjects the meeting came to a close, "when all drank to Dr. Haynes and sang 'For He's a Jolly Good Fellow.'" [17]

On the following day Haynes convinced Finlayson to propose as amendments the drafts of the initiative and referendum measures that had been prepared for the 1900 Board of Freeholders. Haynes then called on the two other members of the public utilities subcommittee, Walter F. Haas and attorney William M. Bowen, to obtain their approval. Up to this time Haynes had carefully avoided adding the recall to his direct-legislation package for fear that this more "radical and experimental" measure might jeopardize the success of the other two. Bowen found the recall draft in Haynes's papers, however, and decided to add it to the others. A short time later Haynes brought together the subcommittee members, who voted to submit all three measures to the committee as a whole. By the end of the summer the committee had completed its assignment and offered fifteen charter amendments—including the initiative and referendum (both in one amendment), the recall, and a civil service system—to the city council for submission to the voters in December.[18]

In the months before the regular municipal election, Haynes led the campaign for adoption of the two direct-legislation amendments. With considerable editorial assistance from the *Herald* and additional press cooperation from the *Express* and Gaylord Wilshire, he quickly lined up support. The mayoral candidates of the Republican, Democratic,· and Union Labor parties, anxious to gain Haynes's backing and the votes of his followers, endorsed the amendments. Socialists approved of the initiative/referendum and the recall amendments, and also the civil service amendment, but recommended a no vote on the other twelve amendments, which "were gotten up for the merchants and propertied classes and are not for the interests of the workers." [19]

Haynes also obtained the lukewarm support of the *Times*, the newspaper's last approval of direct legislation for more than half a century. As family physician and good friend of *Times* publisher Harrison Gray Otis, Haynes's influence was evident. Although Otis and Harry Chandler were "not very enthusiastic about direct legislation," Haynes and C. D. Willard convinced the editors to write a few mild editorials in favor of the initiative, referendum, and "Grand Bounce," as the paper referred to the recall. In November, a *Times* editor with no sympathy for Haynes's pet project printed a story inspired by a "nameless attorney" intimating that a 1901 State Supreme Court ruling already rendered direct legislation unconstitutional. Haynes immediately obtained opinions from three local attorneys—H. T. Lee, Charles Cassatt Davis, and George I. Cochran—and his associate George Dunlop, and all five composed a rejoinder. He visited Otis later that same day and convinced him to publish the retort the following week. Much longer than the initial attack, the defense by three respected (and "named") attorneys was an important antidote to the original charge.[20]

Haynes also tried to enlist the support of the Municipal League, but was only half successful. He spoke to his fellow league executive com-

mittee members and won their endorsement for the initiative and referendum. The league even printed a leaflet promoting the two, carefully
pointing out that the recall was not part of the single amendment that
included both the initiative and referendum. Two days before the election, Municipal League executive secretary Charles D. Willard phoned
Haynes and informed him that the league would oppose the recall. The
physician immediately printed "30,000 little yellow cards" calling for
passage of the direct legislation, recall, and civil service amendments.
Because of his already close association with organized labor, Union Labor party workers agreed to distribute the cards along with their own
literature.[21]

All but two of the fifteen amendments passed in December. The initia-
tive/referendum proposal won by more than six votes to one, while the
recall prevailed by more than four and a half votes to one. The measures
allowed citizens to enact an ordinance by first persuading at least 5 percent of the city's registered voters to sign a petition and then winning
approval for the measure from a majority of voters in a regular municipal election. An ordinance passed by the city council could be nullified
in a similar manner, the only difference being that the petition had to be
signed by at least 7 percent of the electorate. And any elected city officer
could be removed if first a petition was signed by a number of voters
equalling at least 25 percent of the entire number of votes cast for that
office in the last city election and then the officer was voted out in a
special election held within 40 days of the acceptance of the petition.
Approval of the recall moved Los Angeles into the forefront of national
civic reform, for the city was the first municipality in the United States
to adopt this device of "direct democracy."[22]

Though passed in the municipal election, the thirteen amendments still
had to be approved by the state legislature. Early in 1903, Haynes traveled to Sacramento to lobby personally for the new direct-legislation
measures; he was joined by C. D. Willard, who was in the capital to
lobby for the civil service amendment. With little opposition, except for
a few San Francisco legislators who questioned the legality of the recall,
the amendments were approved. Even representatives of the Southern
Pacific Railroad's political bureau, which opposed direct legislation at the
state level, acquiesced in the passage of these amendments, deeming them
a strictly local matter.[23]

The victory for direct legislation in Los Angeles elevated Haynes's reputation as a reformer to lofty heights. Writing in the *Direct Legislation
Record* late in 1902, Gaylord Wilshire labeled him "one of the best-

known advocates of Direct Legislation in the United States." On the state level, the physician already had initiated the drive to inject his pet measures into the state constitution by creating the Direct Legislation League of California in June 1902. League vice presidents included many of Haynes's prominent associates: E. L. Doheny, H. W. Hellman, Frederick Hastings Rindge, O. T. Johnson, M. J. Newmark, and other conservative businessmen; judges, attorneys, physicians, and clergymen; and social reformers such as Abbot Kinney, R. H. Norton, William Stuart, and C. D. Willard. The members (all from Los Angeles at this time) formed an impressive list, though most had lent their names only for display. Haynes and Secretary George Dunlop performed all of the league's duties.[24]

As he had at the municipal level, Haynes persuaded other single-issue advocates to push for a system of direct legislation at the state level as a mechanism for enacting reforms on a much larger scale. He recommended the initiative to prohibitionists as a means to outlaw old John Barleycorn and to suffragists, Socialists, and single-taxers as a way to secure voting rights, public ownership, a modified system of taxation, and other objectives. To labor leaders he proposed the referendum and recall as weapons against bad laws and anti-union officeholders.[25]

The 1902 state campaign of the Direct Legislation League began with Haynes's canvassing of candidates for state offices in order to identify those favoring direct legislation. He then organized a petition drive, from which he collected over 22,000 signatures of Californians favoring direct legislation. He lobbied the county and state conventions of the two major parties, convincing the Democrats to add a direct-legislation plank to their platform, but failing to sway the Republicans. Before departing for Sacramento, the Southern California delegation of the legislature listened to his address on the importance of passing bills for state-level systems of direct legislation.[26]

During the 1903 legislative session, Haynes launched his first biennial campaign to convince California's lawmakers to adopt direct legislation. With the aid of brother-in-law Walter Lindley, Haynes managed to meet Walter F. X. Parker, political manager for the Southern Pacific Railroad in the legislature. After a very long discussion of direct legislation, Parker finally agreed to support the measures in the assembly, but not in the senate, where they were subsequently defeated. Dejected but still optimistic, Haynes left Sacramento after the Los Angeles charter measures were approved. He began paying half the expenses of an Anti-Saloon League lobbyist who agreed to advocate direct legislation, and continued to work with Guy Lathrop, secretary of the State Federation of Labor, who coordinated the labor fight for the initiative and referendum in northern California. These efforts proved fruitless in 1903, but were only the beginning of Haynes's battle for state direct legislation.[27]

In the first few years of the twentieth century, Haynes devoted many of his spare hours to the fight for direct legislation, but he also found time to explore and promote his ultimate goal, Christian socialism. Though never a member of the Socialist party, Haynes subsidized local party organs and activities and became a close associate of party functionaries. He loaned money to some, such as Job Harriman, writing off the debt as a "gift to socialism."[28]

From 1902 to 1904, general interest in organizations such as the Social Reform Union waned, and local evolutionary socialists, such as Haynes and Caroline Severance, pursued their goals in other ways. Most worked informally within the local social-reform network and in correspondence with state figures, such as Reverend J. Stitt Wilson of Berkeley (whom Haynes met in 1901), and non-Californians like St. Louis manufacturer Nelson O. Nelson and soon-to-be Angeleno B. Fay Mills. Haynes, Severance, and other wealthy reformers were too aghast at talk of class consciousness and revolution to apply for red cards, but they did support the educational efforts of the new branch of the Socialist Party of America by helping to bring in speakers, donating socialist literature, and enriching the party treasury. This activity continued the work of the 1890s social democrats in keeping Los Angeles in step with the progress of the larger movement in the United States and abroad.[29]

Historian David A. Shannon has concluded that "millionaire Socialists" belonging to the party "probably had no more significance than as curious subsidizers of needed Socialist endeavors." Some of the wealthy individuals outside the party, such as Haynes, did contribute to the social-reform impulse of the era, however, especially regarding immediate reforms, and gave to the American socialist movement an air of interclass legitimacy as well as portions of their fortunes. As Kevin Starr indicates, rich radicals became conduits allowing social-reform ideas to flow from the far left to the reforming right unhindered by class antagonism.[30]

The anomaly of a wealthy reformer's working to overhaul the system that created his wealth was quite a philosophical problem for Haynes and fellow "millionaire socialists." Yet the physician did not mince words in expressing his belief about the system: "Both the accumulation of individual wealth and the system of competition that today govern the world, inciting labor troubles and international wars, are against the best interests and the destiny of the human race." He acted on this belief by means of the wealth he accumulated within the system he hoped to alter. Conservatives termed this hypocrisy. Even a fellow "millionaire social-ist" confided to another rich reformer: "I am wholly unable to under-stand the workings of men like Dr. Haynes, Wilshire and a great many such, who are intensely interested in getting the system changed that will cut off the rich and lift up the poor and yet go on and live high personally and accumulate all the money they can, only giving some to the cause. Should they not right now live according to their theory, what ever it be?"[31]

Hesitant to turn over all of his fortune to the party or the poor, Haynes preferred to spend some of it to advance his "theory" his own way. He retained his wealth and acquisitions in order to remain a part of the economic elite he wished to influence toward socialism. It was not until later in life that he searched for ways to dispose of the remainder of his wealth to aid this cause. In the meantime, he defended himself from charges of hypocrisy. As he later told an audience, he could manage his fortune more wisely by using it "to alleviate some of the results of the evil system" rather than giving it all away for the temporary care of the poor.[32]

For the time being, Haynes elected to help the party's educational ef-forts locally and to work with his nonproletarian associates. One of the latter, H. Gaylord Wilshire, aided Haynes during the last several years of the quest for direct legislation in Los Angeles. In 1902, the editor of the *Challenge* fled to Toronto, Canada, to avoid harassment by federal offi-cials who tried to increase postal rates for his publication. While in Can-ada (and New York just before that), Wilshire asked Haynes to oversee his Los Angeles bill-posting business. In 1903, the two men, who had become personal friends, decided to travel to England to confer with leading British socialists and other intellectuals. (Haynes had made a trip to London in 1899, when he met socialist leader John Burns in the House of Commons.)[33]

Early in July, Haynes rendezvoused with Wilshire in Toronto, and the two departed for London. Upon their arrival they arranged introductions to members of Great Britain's socialist Fabian Society. These meetings would be especially enlightening for Haynes, who would establish his own "transatlantic connection" with British social democrats whose agenda was similar to his own. On one evening Haynes and Wilshire dined with novelist H. G. Wells. On July 16, the visitors had dinner at the Hotel Cecil with H. M. Hyndman, "the grand old man of British socialism," and Anna Strunsky, a budding writer (and future wife of American socialist William English Walling). One morning the doctor had breakfast with George Bernard Shaw at the playwright's apartment. At this audience Haynes tried to enlighten Shaw on the merits of direct legislation. The arguments fell flat, however, as Shaw believed in the "rule of the intellect"; in other words, he much preferred that the Empire be governed by the Fabians than that the common people make their own decisions. Shaw "did not give up his point," Haynes recalled, "and I did not give up mine." [34]

Haynes and Wilshire also conferred with Lord Russell (older brother of Bertrand), *Review of Reviews* editor William Stead, historian and political observer James Bryce, and future prime minister J. Ramsay MacDonald. They also attended an international conference of socialists in Brussels before returning to America in early October. Haynes brought back to Los Angeles a heightened desire to hasten evolutionary socialism in the United States as well as a membership in the Fabian Society. Upon his return he was interviewed by local reporters. Startled by Haynes's sense of humor, which was amazing, "especially for a socialist," a *Herald* writer reported details and anecdotes of the trip. The *Times*, in one of its last positive stories concerning Haynes, printed a long statement in which Haynes complained that European laborers were woefully underfed. Describing conditions in York as an example, he argued that the physical and moral deterioration of the poor could only be improved by altering the system in which they lived and worked. Though he did not mention the word "socialism," it was obvious that Haynes was suggesting some such system as the solution to the problem. [35]

The doctor's interest in English laborers during his trip was comparable to his desire to improve conditions for the American working class, whether through socialism or immediate reforms. In the late 1890s, he had established ties with local labor leaders that made him one of the few progressive reformers over the next three decades to enjoy the confidence of the local and state labor movement. In 1898, he and several union leaders had served on the executive board of the Union Reform League. His socialistic sympathies and egalitarian outlook enabled him to cooperate even with radical laborites, though his concern for workers belied a strong paternalism. Advocating direct legislation and other immediate goals sought by labor gained him the respect of working-class leaders: in the 1902 municipal election, labor precinct workers gladly distributed his campaign literature; his speeches and activism were reported regularly in the Socialist and labor press; he received the enthusiastic endorsement of labor for the 1900 Board of Freeholders; and before the 1902 city election, labor leaders considered him as their mayoral candidate, though he again declined to run for office.[36]

In late 1901, Haynes attempted to assist local workers in a more material way. With a few moderate social reformers and friends the doctor incorporated the Los Angeles Co-operators, the aim of which was to establish a cooperative grocery. Based on the Rochdale Plan, which had been tried by American labor organizations since the 1840s, the Rochdale Store had attracted over 200 members by the time it opened on South Main Street in May 1902. Designed to allow working-class members to share in merchandise discounts and company profits, the store failed to attract enough capital to keep it going. Beset by financial and personal problems among the officers, the Rochdale Store disappeared by 1905. The experience had little effect on Haynes's desire to advance the welfare of working people, however, and his political involvement with labor increased over the years.[37]

Haynes's role as a political reformer, as well as his activities as a social democrat, accelerated at the time. Early on he found it expedient to promote reform with both political parties in the city, and he crossed party lines with ease. He clearly relished his role as a party chameleon. Gaylord Wilshire believed him to be a Democrat in 1902, while at the same time the physician's brother-in-law thought he was a good Republican. Local Democrats offered him the nomination for U.S. Congress in 1900, the year Haynes was reported to be joining the Fourth Ward Republican Club. Two years later, the Union Labor party wished to nominate him for mayor. Haynes refused all offers to run for office, however, having stated in 1900: "I am not, and have never been, and never will be a candidate for office. My only political ambition is to be one of a board of freeholders . . ." The description of his political affiliation as "Independent" in 1903 was a more accurate reflection of his disdain for political parties in municipal politics, though he later chose to be identified with the insurgent wing of the Republican and Progressive parties in state affairs. Haynes took the nonpartisanship of progressive politics seriously; philosophically, it helped to eliminate national partisan differences in strictly local politics, and pragmatically, it enabled him to cooperate with representatives of any party in advancing his favorite reforms.[38]

In local politics at this time, Haynes became involved both in campaigning for immediate improvements sought by social and political reformers, and in establishing ties with the city administration. Although not strongly in favor of a city council elected at large, he joined fellow members of the Municipal League executive committee in promoting most other progressive goals: direct legislation, municipal civil service, more stringent regulations in awarding utility franchises, and methods to make city government more efficient and honest. Outside of government he became a leader in the Municipal League's probes of unethical conduct on the part of city and county officeholders.[39]

In 1903, Haynes began reforming government from within upon his appointment to the first of many local and state commissions. In the previous municipal election he had endorsed Democratic incumbent Meredith P. "Pinkey" Snyder for mayor. Considered a reformer compared to many previous Los Angeles mayors, Snyder rewarded Haynes by appointing the doctor to the newly created Civil Service Commission. Haynes was an ideal selection to monitor health and medical standards for city employees. As a political appointee he was open to the usual pressure, even from the reformer Snyder, to work in the best interests of the administration by assisting in the hiring and protection of the mayor's friends. There is no evidence that the doctor complied with these requests, and his dozen years of service in this position proved to be beneficial to the city.[40]

Haynes's most publicized participation with both political and social reformers at this time was his role in the first application of the recall in the United States. In May 1904, the Los Angeles City Council voted to award the city's annual printing contract to the *Times*. The paper had the largest circulation in the city, but also proffered the highest bid by far of any other paper. The six councilmen voting for the *Times* (over Mayor Snyder's veto) stood accused of trying to curry favor for future political campaigns, and some observers protested the action as a criminal waste of public funds. Almost immediately critics began discussing the possibility of using the new recall device to remove all six and rescind the decision.[41]

The local Typographical Union, which would have suffered if the council had awarded the contract to the antilabor *Times*, took the lead in countering the council's action. Since the cost of recall campaigns in all six wards was prohibitive, labor leaders decided to demonstrate the power of labor and the recall by aiming the device at Councilman James P. Davenport, of the heavily unionized Sixth Ward. Davenport was the chairman of the Supply Committee, which had recommended the *Times*'s bid and already had a spotty record on the council. Haynes, a friend of labor who wished to protect the recall on its maiden voyage, joined the laborites early on. Another Direct Legislation League officer, retired businessman Richard H. Norton, formed the Good Government League to lead the campaign. Haynes, Norton, lawyer-businessman Thomas E. Gibbon, and *Express* publisher Edwin T. Earl, whose paper had the printing contract the year before, supplied the financial resources. Owing to technical errors the petitions had to be circulated three times, but the council finally set the recall election for September 16.[42]

The recall effort began as a dispute between organized labor and the "open shop" *Times*, but soon took on the trappings of a crusade waged by city reformers against elements of the dominant political organization. All of the city's other newspapers backed the recall, which was aimed at a defender of the adversarial *Times*. Davenport also was accused of receiving "contributions" to vote to extend slaughterhouses in his residential district, approving the abolition of streetcar transfers popular with his constituents, working for liquor dealers and voting for their interests, and representing a cigar firm whose products he sold to saloon keepers. The reform candidate was not much of an improvement. Dr. Arthur Houghton (whose real name was Howton) was actually chosen by an underworld figure who outfoxed the reformers at a mass meeting to nominate an opponent for Davenport. Although a union member, Houghton was revealed to be a "spiritualistic medium" who formerly operated the Electro-Hypnotic Institute in Chicago. The reformers defended Houghton's pseudomedical career, though Norton, Haynes, and the others later regretted having supported this charlatan, who soon turned against them. Houghton was, however, an effective speaker and campaigner, and with the backing of the Haynes group and the unions he defeated Davenport handily. The *Times* defended Davenport to protect its contract and attacked the recall device as an instrument of revenge. But the newspaper could not save the errant councilman, who was also supported by private city utilities and the regular Republican organization.[43]

Davenport challenged his ouster by suing the city to void the election on the grounds he was illegally removed from office. The State Supreme Court eventually ruled that the city owed Davenport his salary through the end of his regular term because the city clerk had not compared the petition signatures to the county's *Great Register of Voters* as prescribed in the recall ordinance. The constitutionality of the recall, however, was not considered; Davenport was awarded $400 in back salary but not allowed to return to his former office.[44]

Davenport's recall was a mixed victory for the reformers. The election elevated to the council an erratic character whom the *Times* unfavorably associated with Haynes and the recall measure. Reelected in the general election later in 1904, Houghton soon ignored the reformers and became an embarrassment. On the other hand, his victory in the recall election demonstrated how the recall could be used effectively, and stood as an example to officeholders. Though rarely used, the threat of recall became a political weapon for the reformers, as well as their opponents.[45]

The recall campaign also completed the break between Dr. Haynes and *Times* publisher H. G. Otis and his son-in-law, Harry Chandler. In the 1890s, Haynes and Otis had been good friends. The publisher was Haynes's patient, tried to interest the doctor in his business ventures, and even gave him a souvenir cane made from the wood of a Spanish flag-ship destroyed in 1898 during the Spanish-American War, in which Otis served. The *Times* glowingly endorsed Haynes for the 1900 Board of Freeholders and belatedly backed the recall amendment in 1902, after Haynes personally pleaded with Otis. But the relationship began to cool in 1903, as Otis became suspicious of Haynes's advocacy of socialism. When Haynes informed Chandler that he supported the recall of Davenport in opposition to the *Times*, both Chandler and Otis broke off personal relations with the physician. From that moment on, the *Times*'s policy regarding Haynes was consistently negative—for the next three decades it ridiculed the physician at every opportunity.[46]

After the 1904 recall election Haynes was a renegade of the *Times*–big business establishment, though he retained a personal friendship and business ties to a large number of the city's wealthy elite. And, while still a member of the local aristocracy, he had emerged as a leader of both the urban political insurgents and the city's more leftist social reformers. With his victory in the municipal battle for direct legislation and involve-ment in campaigns for social and structural change, he was well prepared to extend his activism onto other reform battlefields.

James Sydney Haynes (1819–99)
(*F. Haynes Lindley, Jr.*)

Elvira Mann Koons Haynes (1820–91)
(*F. Haynes Lindley, Jr.*)

John Randolph Haynes (1853–1937) in the 1870s (*Department of Special Collections, Research Library, UCLA*)

Mary Evaline Haynes (1845–1925) (*F. Haynes Lindley, Jr.*)

Francis Leader Haynes (1850–98) (*Department of Special Collections, Research Library, UCLA*)

Florence Haynes Lindley (1856–1949)
(F. Haynes Lindley, Jr.)

Sydney Haynes (1882–86) (*Department of Special Collections, Research Library, UCLA*)

Dora Fellows Haynes (1859–1934) in the early 1880s
(*Department of Special Collections, Research Library, UCLA*)

John Haynes in Los Angeles, 1899 (*Department of Special Collections, Research Library, UCLA*)

Haynes residence at Tenth and Figueroa streets at the turn of the century (*F. Haynes Lindley, Jr.*)

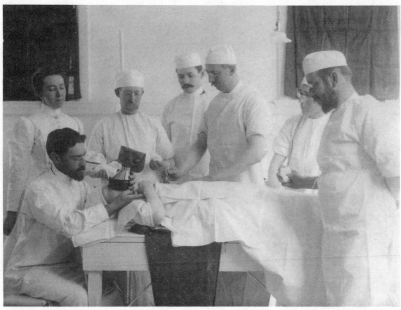

Haynes performing an operation in the 1890s; Walter Lindley is on the far right (*Department of Special Collections, Research Library, UCLA*)

Walter Lindley (1852–1922)
(*F. Haynes Lindley, Jr.*)

About 1903, Haynes sat for a portrait photographer who supplied the doctor with photos in half a dozen poses—most depicted Haynes very seriously; one did not (*Department of Special Collections, Research Library, UCLA*)

Haynes and the other original members of the Los Angeles Board of Civil Service
Commissioners, 1903 (*Department of Special Collections, Research Library, UCLA*)

Haynes and H. Gaylord Wilshire aboard ship during their trip to Europe in 1903
(*Department of Special Collections, Research Library, UCLA*)

ST' BOY!

One of many *Times* cartoons of Haynes, this one linking him to anarchy and violence (*March 3, 1908*; *copyright 1908*, Los Angeles Times)

Dora Haynes, about 1905 (*Hearst Collection, Department of Special Collections, University of Southern California Library*)

Caricature of a reformer (As We See U'm [*1904*])

Chapter Five

Less Than Socialism:
Municipal Ownership and Regulation

While Dr. Haynes worked to get a system of direct legislation established at the state level by early 1905, he continued to advance immediate reforms in Los Angeles. Among them was the municipal ownership of utilities. A far cry from the socialist goal of a nation that owned and controlled its entire means of production, municipal ownership was a halfway measure that appealed even to some conservatives as a method of improving utility services and attracting new industry.

Municipal ownership in Europe and the United States experienced a tremendous expansion in the late nineteenth century as major cities acquired private utilities or built and operated their own. Waterworks were the typical municipal operation, but some cities also managed their own electricity and gas plants, lighting facilities, and transportation systems. Frequently opposed by advocates of private enterprise, the municipal-ownership movement gained momentum in the 1890s, as it became an objective of Populists, Bellamyites, and moderate socialists.[1]

John Haynes came to favor the public ownership of all utilities but would accept municipal ownership of a few as a starting point. He had embraced municipal ownership as a tenet of the Union Reform League when Reverend Bliss founded the organization in 1898. Although the doctor appears not to have joined any of the several public-ownership clubs in Los Angeles in the 1890s, he endorsed the idea as a URL objective and approved the city's decision to operate its own waterworks in 1899. This impetus for municipal ownership in Los Angeles was not a triumph of the left. As Robert Fogelson has pointed out, the campaign for the city's acquisition of its waterworks, like future campaigns for city gas and electricity plants, was promoted by "thousands of ordinary citizens uncommitted to radicalism of any sort but dissatisfied with private service." Exorbitant water prices and frequent shortages convinced even the conservative *Times* to approve of municipal ownership in this instance since a cheap and plentiful water supply would attract manufacturers and developers. Municipal ownership aided industrialists by creating additional capital with which to improve the city's infrastructure and provide service at minimal cost.[2]

Haynes took several small steps in the direction of municipal ownership in 1902. Along with friends J. B. Irvine, Jr., Francis Kellogg, Charles H. Toll, B. R. Baumgardt, and others, he composed a petition to be forwarded to the city council relating to street railways. The group asked the council to consider a number of factors in granting franchises to those utilities: that the bidding be competitive, that the contract expire in 30 years or less, and that the service be strictly regulated. A year later Haynes, Irvine, and others refined this request to include a section in the franchise stipulating that the city might purchase the utility when the contract expired. These pleas were polite requests that the city consider regulation and future acquisition of utilities. For Haynes and others, they were also the beginning of a series of crusades to establish municipal ownership of Los Angeles utilities in addition to the waterworks, which were already city-owned.[3]

Haynes became more of an activist in late 1904. In his essay "Plea for Municipal Ownership," published in the *Graphic* late that year, the physician called for Los Angeles voters to begin catching up with those European cities far in advance of their U.S. counterparts. Pointing to the success of the Los Angeles waterworks, he encouraged voters to advance opportunities for municipal ownership by voting to shorten the duration of private utility franchises. This charter amendment, which limited franchises to 21 years, and another granting the city the right to acquire public utilities, passed in the December 1904 municipal election.[4]

Haynes increased his advocacy of municipal ownership the following year. In March 1905, the doctor and a few wealthy friends incorporated the People's Gas Company as a privately owned competitor to the Los Angeles Gas Company, which was also private. The People's firm was the first of two corporations formed by Haynes to establish a new gas plant that eventually would be sold to the city to become a municipal utility. The first company never accumulated enough capital to erect a plant, however. Two years later, Haynes induced over 50 wealthy friends and business associates to build a plant for the new City Gas Company. This firm survived only a year. Facing intense competition from the established Los Angeles Gas Company and constant harassment by the *Times*,

City Gas failed and was later acquired by the Southern California Gas Company.[5]

Haynes's interest in municipal ownership of hydroelectrical power in Los Angeles also began in 1905, and endured for three decades. In late July 1905, local newspapers broke the story that the city was considering a massive acquisition and construction project that would bring water from the Owens Valley over 250 miles to thirsty Los Angeles. The citizens overwhelmingly approved $1.5 million in bonds for the project, for they had suffered through a heatwave and heard that the city's principal source of water was an almost dry riverbed. The short campaign before the September election was a spirited affair that attracted little opposition to the project and a wealth of promotional pieces in the *Times* and *Express*. The publishers of both papers, General Otis and E. T. Earl, though personal enemies, were partners in the San Fernando Mission Land Company, which purchased vast tracts in the San Fernando Valley just before the plan was made public. This property would skyrocket in value when irrigated by the new source of water from Owens Valley. Ironically, Otis tried to induce Haynes to join the venture before Earl was included, but did not reveal the plan to import water. Unaware of the water opportunity, the physician judged it to be a poor investment at the time.[6]

Besides water for the city, the Owens Valley project offered the possibility of creating hydroelectric power where the aqueduct flow dropped dramatically at two points. Chief engineer William Mulholland proposed to use this power to aid construction. The *Times* and other private enterprises agreed, but demanded that after construction of the aqueduct the power it generated be sold to private electrical power companies. Haynes and municipal-ownership advocates protested, arguing that the power should be developed by the city for street lighting. In a speech at the University Club on September 14, Haynes warned that a plot already was afoot to capture the power and put it into private hands. In his talk he touched on many areas of municipal ownership but returned to the lighting issue as the perfect opportunity for the city to expand its own utilities with a minimum of effort. The final decision would not be made for several years, when construction of the aqueduct already was under way.[7]

Haynes's advocacy of municipal ownership sharply escalated at the same time that he became closely connected with the Hearst press. In December 1903, the *Los Angeles Examiner* began operation as a vehicle for the sensational promotion of its owner, William Randolph Hearst.

Aligned with the labor movement in Los Angeles, the paper soon began advancing municipal ownership as Hearst embraced this cause in his 1905 New York mayoralty campaign. In that year Hearst's Los Angeles paper promoted the municipal ownership of gas and electric plants, and the regulation of streetcars and saloons—all issues concurrently championed by Dr. Haynes. Like Haynes an ally of organized labor, the *Examiner* carried on a running battle with the *Times*, which in its more charitable moments labeled Hearst, as well as Haynes, only a socialist.[8]

With such a commonality of interests, Haynes and *Examiner* manager Henry Loewenthal quickly became political allies. Haynes provided civic leadership for campaigns that aided the *Examiner* in its competition with other publications, and Hearst's paper supplied the doctor with an abundance of favorable publicity. Haynes found ample opportunity to express his views and relied on the *Examiner* to defend him when attacked by rivals. Flattering biographical notes appeared in the *Examiner*, including one long piece exalting the physician as a civic patriot and an after-dinner speaker of "sufficient originality and individuality to make a few Romans howl." For the next 30 years Haynes usually could count on the support of the *Examiner*, depending on his own changing attitude toward Hearst.[9]

Promotion of municipal ownership was one of several bonds that tied Haynes and the *Examiner* to the organized-labor movement in California. The left wing of union leadership, which included a few Socialist party members, also touted municipal ownership as a reform goal and weapon against private utilities deemed unfair to labor. Another bond was labor's opposition to the "open shop" *Times*. In 1904 the *Times* enthusiastically promoted the creation of the local Citizens' Alliance, an anti-union organization financed by Henry E. Huntington and other employers. In January 1906, labor retaliated by establishing the Anti–Citizens' Alliance to combat the employer group both economically and politically; this group was backed both by Haynes and the *Examiner*.[10]

The Anti–Citizens' Alliance was additionally important to Haynes because it gave him the opportunity to pursue municipal ownership on an advanced level. In early 1906, Haynes and statewide labor leaders prodded the organization into direct political action when they met in Fresno and established the Public Ownership party. Founded "on the premise that private ownership of public utilities was the cause of all political corruption," the party was another fusion of labor leaders, Socialists who also favored immediate reforms, and public-ownership figures such as Haynes. The physician delivered the keynote address at the party's sparsely attended but enthusiastic convention held on February 21. The

Times, one of the infant party's chief targets, ridiculed the new organization, particularly its Los Angeles contingent, with barbs aimed at "Doc" Haynes and its guiding star, "Willie" Hearst. The Los Angeles branch of the party grew in numbers (principally union members) and influence with strong backing from the *Examiner.* Owing to a rift in both major parties in 1906, it had a chance for success in the state and municipal elections that year. But the failure of the *Examiner* to endorse the party outright combined with other factors to limit the party's electoral strength. Not long after the December balloting it withered away.[11]

Besides the Public Ownership party, Haynes found other forums for speaking and writing on the issue. The new party publicized him "as the most influential man in the public ownership cause," proof that the movement was also supported by men of property. In local publications, Haynes attacked critics of municipal ownership and fought new proposals to extend private franchise contracts or otherwise limit the public's opportunity to own utilities. In these years he shaped his advocacy of municipal ownership; this cause would later replace direct legislation as Haynes's most urgent reform objective, a status it would retain for the rest of his life.[12]

Years later Haynes recalled: "Socialists thought I was wrong in stressing public ownership and that I should go for the whole program." Socialist leaders did criticize Haynes for his halfway promotion of socialism through municipal ownership, but the local party press generally skirted the issue in commending his actions. This attitude, no doubt, was influenced by the party's dependence on Haynes's financial contributions as well as its concern to defend a sympathizer pilloried as a radical by the *Times.* Early in 1906, when novelist Jack London came to Los Angeles to speak in behalf of the local Socialist party, Haynes hosted a luncheon for him and author Julian Hawthorne at the California Club. Haynes purchased $50 and $100 "Socialist Libraries" for a number of colleges, became a member and benefactor of the Intercollegiate Socialist Society, and made many donations to J. A. Wayland's newspaper, *Appeal to Reason.* All of these contributions aided the Socialist movement in some small way, but the doctor's present and future work for public ownership had more substantial results. Though Socialist party hardliners argued that municipal ownership was merely a stopgap, this immediate goal provided at least some measure of gradual success.[13]

In situations where municipal ownership was not economically feasible, Haynes was not averse to joining or leading urban reformers in campaigns to regulate private utilities in the public interest. One such example was his role in the fight to require local traction companies to install lifesaving fenders on streetcars. This issue became a major concern in Los Angeles and other U.S. and European cities with the rapid growth of the urban population, expansion of downtown streets, and increase in street railway vehicles in the 1890s. These factors contributed to the rise in accidents in which streetcars struck down and often crushed pedestrians under the wheels and undercarriage. By the early 1900s, "basket" fenders had been developed, which literally scooped up and safely cradled the victim until the vehicle could come to a stop.[14]

Head-on collisions, of course, could not be eliminated completely. As historian John Stilgoe notes in the case of railroad accidents, the public was partially at fault in misjudging the long braking distances of such vehicles and not paying attention at grade crossings. But there were many more cases in which blameless children and adults were struck by speeding streetcars operated by poorly trained motormen on increasingly congested city streets. Self-interest in avoiding costly lawsuits brought by the families of accident victims motivated some trolley managers to install the clumsy-looking lifeguard fenders, which performed well on most occasions. Other managers opted for cheaper styles of fenders, which were also less effective. In still other cases, though, executives preferred to pay the claims and avoid purchasing the fenders.[15]

Traction safety became an issue in Los Angeles after a controversy sparked in May 1895, when the San Francisco County Board of Supervisors passed an ordinance requiring safer fenders on streetcars. Traction companies delayed complying with the law, so Hearst's *San Francisco Examiner* seized upon the issue to begin a sensational daily assault on Henry E. Huntington and the managers of the Market Street Railway Company, charging them with the murders of pedestrians crushed under fenderless cars. Los Angeles newspapers then began demanding similar appliances. The city council delayed action until passage of a state law in March 1899 requiring cable and electric cars to be equipped with "suitable fenders" prescribed by local authorities. With this stimulus the council decided that all city streetcars should carry safety fenders, and that the mere absence of fenders was sufficient evidence of the negligence of streetcar companies in the award of injury damages.[16]

Enforcement of the fender ordinance gradually slackened, and the subject again became an issue in 1905. Mayor Owen McAleer dispatched letters to local streetcar companies in March demanding compliance with the 1899 fender law. The mayor's order was diluted, however, by the city attorney, who admitted that much-improved mechanisms had become available. This view was echoed by a committee of the local Municipal League examining the operation of streetcars in Los Angeles. The committee concluded that streetcars traveled much too fast, and that the flimsy fenders in use were "worse than useless, and in fact add greatly to the danger of injury and death." The committee found that over 250 Angelenos were killed or injured annually by streetcars, and recommended that the city council end this "total disregard of public duty, and wanton negligence upon the part of the officers of the street railways of the city." [17]

In the confusion over whether to enforce an ordinance requiring outdated fenders, McAleer turned for advice to Dr. Haynes. Although the physician had supported McAleer's Democratic rival in the 1904 election, the mayor respected Haynes's judgment and appointed him to an unofficial "cabinet" of advisers. Haynes immediately distributed questionnaires to over 70 major cities throughout the world requesting information on streetcar accidents and the use of fenders. The results of this survey revealed that Los Angeles had the highest per capita mortality rate for street railway accidents of any major U.S. or European city. In fact, the rate in Los Angeles in 1904 was over three times that of Boston, Philadelphia, or Baltimore. Respondents assured Haynes that several available fenders had proved highly effective in reducing injuries and fatalities. So, he appealed to managers of the local street railways to install such fenders to stop both deaths and lawsuits. Rebuffed by the argument that most of those killed by fenderless cars or cars with unsuitable fenders were only "hobos," the doctor set out to convince a private-utility-oriented city council to compel traction companies to adopt safer fenders.[18]

While continuing his study of fenders to learn which were the best, Haynes joined forces with a cadre of activists to implement the Municipal League's recommendations on streetcar operations. In May 1905, the doctor and his younger friends created the Voters' League to campaign for safety fenders as well as progressive goals such as direct legislation, civil service, municipal ownership, and nonpartisan local politics. A Voters' League committee consisting of Haynes, Joseph H. Call, and Russ Avery prepared a fender ordinance after consulting the attorney for Henry Huntington's Los Angeles Railway Company (LARY). Unable to convince the city council to consider the proposal, the Voters' League made the ordinance its first priority and started a crusade to force the issue at a special election through the initiative process.[19]

During the summer of 1905, Haynes and his associates devised their strategy. The editor of the *Los Angeles Examiner* offered to step up the paper's already sensational reports of streetcar accidents and editorials in support of better fenders, duplicating the efforts of Hearst's paper in San Francisco a decade earlier. After further study of available fenders across the nation, the committee drafted a municipal ordinance that set speed limits and restrictions on freight as well as requiring fenders. On September 20, the Voters' League began collecting signatures in the downtown area.[20]

Several days before the petitions were circulated, Dr. Haynes delivered a speech on the subject of municipal ownership at the University Club. Citing the results of his fender survey, he pointed out that accidents were on the rise in Los Angeles and that the fenders in use were worthless in protecting lives when compared to newer devices that could safely catch and hold a victim until the car stopped. The address provoked an angry response from LARY counsel William E. Dunn, who claimed the best available fenders already were installed on LARY cars. Dunn then issued a challenge to Haynes, offering to pay $1,000 to the doctor's favorite charity—or his heirs—if Haynes would demonstrate his preferred fender by standing in front of it in a test. Haynes declined to offer himself as target but promised to supply in his stead a representative of the fender's manufacturer if LARY would equip each of its vehicles with the apparatus within three months of the test—providing, of course, that the test was successful. The fender company feared tampering by the railway, however, and declined to send its product to LARY, leaving the contest a verbal stalemate.[21]

By early January 1906, the Voters' League had collected over 4,000 signatures, only a few hundred shy of the requirement. With this ammunition Haynes and other league leaders once again appealed to the city council to pass the fender ordinance and avoid the cost of a special election. Haynes presented his argument, and the council appointed a five-member committee to investigate. On January 15, the doctor applied personal influence on the council committee as he wined and dined the five members at the California Club. The councilmen finally acquiesced. With a majority of the council in favor of the ordinance, LARY officials agreed to cease their opposition.[22]

In late March, four fenders were tested in the presence of witnesses representing the city, the railway, and the Voters' League. J. W. Range, an official of the Eclipse Life-Guard Company, manufacturer of the fenders, offered his own body in one test and escaped unhurt, a dramatic presentation that ensured the choice of his product by the judges. The city council passed the ordinance in May, requiring every streetcar operating within the city limits to be equipped with an Eclipse or comparable fender. By September LARY cars began to carry these fenders, and within a month Superintendent John Jay Aiken reported that the Eclipses had already saved the lives of a dozen pedestrians and one horse.[23]

The campaign for the new ordinance was only the first skirmish in the fender war. LARY, the city's major intraurban, complied with the new law, but the city's other two major street railways refused. Both contended that as interurbans operating within and outside of Los Angeles city limits, they were exempt from laws governing only one of the municipalities within their territory. The interurban dispute would erupt later that year; for the time being Haynes and the Voters' League celebrated their victory.

The fender episode was one of the few attempts to implement direct legislation in Los Angeles from the time the measures were adopted through 1906. Haynes was personally involved in another initiative campaign at this time, one to establish the Gothenburg System of saloon control in Los Angeles. After an ordinance to ban saloons was defeated in June 1905, the doctor and other upper-middle-class temperance advocates began educating Los Angeles voters about the advantages of the Gothenburg System, then in vogue in Scandinavia. This plan would reduce the number of saloon licenses from 200 to 70 and lease them to a private company operating under strict conditions intended to discourage consumption of intoxicating liquors, eliminate disreputable establishments, and remove the influence of barkeepers in local politics. Haynes, Abbot Kinney, Thomas Gibbon, and others joined banker William Mead in establishing the Gothenburg Association—a benevolent monopoly of elitist saloon owners—to campaign for the initiative and then operate the fewer number of saloons. The group failed to collect enough signatures by early 1906, and never filed the petition. The idea died but was briefly resurrected later that year and again in the next decade.[24]

The recall was unsuccessfully attempted twice against city councilmen in the two years after the 1904 Davenport recall election. Organized labor again initiated both efforts. Haynes apparently was not involved in either, though he received the brunt of the abuse by the *Times* for any such mention of a recall. Caricatured in political cartoons (frequently in company with the eccentric Councilman Houghton), Haynes was editorially speared whenever his "pet measure" surfaced. Once he was branded "that socialist demagogue, millionaire trouble-maker and self-boomer." On another occasion the *Times* vented its contempt for him as follows:

> If a petition were started on its travels today, and were industriously circulated, asking that Dr. John R. Haynes be drawn and quartered, hamstrung and crucified, it would undoubtedly receive within twenty-four hours, as many signatures as are required to give effect to a "recall" petition. Yet there is nobody in this municipality, so far as The Times is aware, who desires such a calamity to fall upon the misguided father of the "recall" iniquity.

The defense of Haynes by most of the city's other publications only pushed the *Times* to further attacks on the doctor's support of direct legislation and any other reform.[25]

At the state level Haynes campaigned for initiative and referendum constitutional amendments in the 1905 session of the legislature. As in 1902–3, he sent letters to all candidates for state office asking if they supported direct legislation. In December he hosted a banquet—"a marvel of gustatory delight"—for the Southern California legislative delegation that was departing for Sacramento. He again subsidized the expenses of a part-time lobbyist, mailed Direct Legislation League circulars requesting action to hundreds of unions and clergymen across the state, and traveled to the state capital to make personal pleas for the initiative and referendum. State Senator Cornelius ("Corney") Pendleton introduced the bills for Haynes, but cautioned against optimism. Satisfied that the Southern Pacific Railroad opposed them, Pendleton wrote to Haynes: "The great corporation which determines the affairs of state will, if necessary, issue orders against passage of these measures." Senator Pendleton, often accused of being a tool of that corporation, was correct; the measures again failed to pass.[26]

The most important news for Haynes concerning direct legislation in Los Angeles was the announcement of the Pfahler decision, which validated the city's initiative and referendum provisions. The case stemmed from the arrest of Andrew Pfahler, a butcher caught slaughtering pigs in January 1906 in a ward where that activity was prohibited after a 1904 initiative election. Pfahler's attorneys applied to the State Supreme Court for his release in a writ of habeas corpus on the ground that the initiative (and, therefore, direct legislation) was unconstitutional. The incident had been staged and the case financed by meatpacking and other interests to test the validity of the initiative. Since this occurred simultaneously with the circulation of the Gothenburg System initiative petitions, Haynes suspected that in fact the liquor industry had instigated the case in order to stop the saloon-reduction proposal.[27]

Haynes immediately leaped to the defense of the city's initiative ordinance. Although Assistant City Attorney Herbert Goudge was assigned to argue the city's position, Haynes went beyond the establishment and hired attorney E. W. Britt to help defend the initiative. The doctor then contacted all city attorneys in California cities that had adopted direct legislation and requested briefs to bolster the Los Angeles case. He made lobbying trips to Sacramento, hired additional attorneys to submit briefs, and organized support from around the state whenever possible. The final decision, announced in October, validated direct legislation and vindicated the efforts of its defenders.[28]

The year 1906 was particularly busy for Dr. Haynes. The first two months were mainly consumed by the streetcar-fender fight, the Pfahler case, and the organizing of the Public Ownership party. His medical practice still thrived with help from Dora Haynes and his partner, brother-in-law Alfred Fellows. By the summer of 1903, he had acquired an automobile, which ended three decades of buggy and horseback rides to visit patients. The following year he moved his medical office from the old Main Street house to the Herman Hellman Building at Fourth and Spring streets, while the family still resided at Tenth and Figueroa. He continued to pursue business opportunities and was active in social affairs. In 1904, he became a member of the Sunset Club, an organization limited to 50 prominent Angelenos who met for dinner, discussion of current events, and occasional outings. Haynes spoke before this group on many occasions and later became its president. In 1905, he joined the prestigious Commonwealth Club in San Francisco, an organization of noted social figures who studied civic problems in addition to attending social functions. Before and after his acceptance, Haynes addressed the club's members on the subject of direct legislation.[29]

By late 1906, Haynes's activities and influence were significant enough to warrant a number of biographical sketches in local newspapers and magazines. These tales of admiration frequently included portraits of Haynes in his early fifties. At six feet two inches, the physician was a tall and solid figure with blue eyes, a fair complexion, and thinning light-brown hair turning to gray. He always appeared very dignified with his well-trimmed mustache and wire-rimmed glasses.[30]

The hectic pace dictated by Haynes's many interests took a toll on the doctor's personal health, the primary reason for which he had come to

Los Angeles. Most of his family had been afflicted with bronchial diseases and various stomach disorders, and John seems to have inherited all of them. By the early 1900s, he was suffering frequent spells of severe indigestion and occasionally had to survive on a restricted diet of milk, toast, and scraped beef. The attacks limited his professional and political activities at some times, but the almost constant stomach pains did not stop his occasional banquets or sumptuous dinner parties. Dora Haynes's health also deteriorated, and by 1910 she had developed the condition that would keep her frequently bedridden for the rest of her life. In these years she managed the household, took care of some of the business and medical affairs, and still wrote much of John's correspondence until a private secretary was hired in early 1906. Most importantly, she lent a sympathetic ear and reassuring encouragement to her husband's reform interests.[31]

In mid-April 1906, John Haynes's busy schedule was interrupted by the catastrophe in northern California. On the morning of April 18, a tremendous earthquake jolted San Francisco, destroying thousands of buildings in the city's center and igniting fires that raged for three days. At 9:30 that morning, Dr. Haynes entered downtown Los Angeles and heard the first reports from a newsboy. Soon after he received word from the *Examiner* office that a special relief mission of doctors and nurses was being assembled to aid stricken San Francisco as soon as possible. At 6 o'clock that evening, about 25 doctors and 50 nurses departed from Los Angeles by train under the supervision of Haynes, who had been elected medical director of the mission. Arriving in Oakland the following morning, the contingent traveled by ferry across the bay and entered the ravaged city of San Francisco at 1 P.M. on April 19.[32]

"The sight that met our eyes when we got on Market Street will never be forgotten," recalled Haynes. "Men, women and children coming from all directions, some carrying blankets, some mattresses, some bird cages often empty, all bearing the impress of sleeplessness, grief, despair and horror." In the midst of this chaos Haynes and his cohort established five makeshift hospitals to provide medical and surgical attention to the injured and to distribute food supplied by the Hearst organization. Haynes took charge of a hospital set up near Golden Gate Park that became the headquarters of the Los Angeles expedition. There he cared for whoever came in, and occasionally ventured out into the streets and rubble in search of those trapped and needing attention. On several occasions he was warned that his Red Cross armband might not stop soldiers from shooting him as a looter if he was not careful. Late one evening he seized a well-worn automobile for a medical emergency from a man whose sister he had met in England. Haynes later asked the driver, Dick Tobin, to take to his sister "my greeting and apologies for so impolitely commandeering her brother at 1 A.M. in the streets of San Francisco with flat tires."[33]

With the fire finally under control and medical emergencies declining, Haynes turned over the supplies of the relief contingent to local authorities and arranged the group's return to Los Angeles. In the ten days this relief mission had been in San Francisco, it had accomplished noteworthy results. But the army of Los Angeles doctors and nurses no longer was needed because the anticipated outbreak of diseases did not materialize, thanks to quick and intelligent actions on the part of city health officers. Critical food shortages soon made the visitors' presence undesirable. Back home Haynes related the experience of this "Hearst expedition" in a talk to the Sunset Club and in an article in the *Examiner*, which played up its owner's benevolence while sensationalizing the tragedy.[34]

Almost immediately after his arrival in Los Angeles Haynes departed with fellow physician W. W. Beckett on a trip to Mexico. Upon his return in mid-May, he wrote of his observations of the nation's religious, economic, and cultural situation. He was particularly moved by the division of society into a wealthy few and the destitute many. The country possessed an abundance of resources and attracted investment capital from all over the world; but, he wrote, "Mexico can never become a great nation until it elevates the peons from the condition of worse than slavery in which they now live." Though he glossed over the Diaz dictatorship, Haynes managed to inject a segment in which he equated the treatment of these peons with racism and anti-unionism in a nation where child labor and low wages were the rule. He held hope for improvement only if the future development of Mexico included the uplifting of the lower classes and public control of its resources.[35]

A month after his return from Mexico, Haynes furthered the aims of local reformers who organized and elected him the first president of the Severance Club. Named in honor of Mrs. Caroline Severance—abolitionist, suffragist, founder of the first women's club in the United States, and a local Christian socialist—the club became a monthly dinner group offering a forum for discussion. It attracted wealthy social reformers, Socialists, and other civic figures, as well as visitors such as Clarence Darrow, Upton Sinclair, and Lincoln Steffens. Haynes presided over the first few meetings but eventually found it difficult to attend. Despite his absence, this discussion group prospered, and it still meets today.[36]

On the Fourth of July, Haynes and friend B. R. Baumgardt departed on another "pleasure trip" to Europe, ostensibly to study municipal ownership, transportation, civil service, and the Gothenburg System of saloon control. In three months the pair visited cities in Norway, Sweden, Russia, Germany, Austria, and England. Whether or not they collected significant data pertaining to all of Haynes's chosen subjects is uncertain, but the doctor did find additional evidence to support his continuing crusade for municipal ownership. Upon his return in October he reported that cities throughout Europe were buying back the utility franchises they had issued. One mayor he spoke to purportedly thought Angelenos "must be crazy; they are giving away practically for nothing, franchises worth millions, and which every city in Europe is striving to get back by paying millions." Haynes's story coincidently appeared in the *Examiner*, just as the paper was attempting to "stop the allied corporation machine plot to extend the life of twenty-one year franchises to thirty-three years." [37]

The highlight of the trip was a visit to czarist Russia in the throes of revolution. With great difficulty Haynes and Baumgardt obtained permission to enter the country, though they were warned of the gravity of the situation. While they were in St. Petersburg a bomb exploded in the home of Interior Minister Stolypin, who then escalated the government's campaign of repression. John Haynes's telegram to Dora in August, beginning "Terrorism rampant," did not exactly soothe Mrs. Haynes, but it did reflect the events witnessed by the pair as they journeyed to Moscow and back. At times the two had to avoid talking to certain Russian officials marked for death by revolutionary bombers. On the way out of Moscow they were stopped and searched by soldiers on several occasions. Baumgardt was "rather an anarchistic looking chap," so czarist troops "probably had their suspicion of him." As Haynes recalled:

> From the time we entered Russia until we crossed the Hungarian border I do not think I spent a half hour free from apprehension. Bombs were going off, officials were being murdered, and there was general unrest. . . . However, we had made up our minds to see Russia and Russian conditions for ourselves and were especially anxious to see it in time of trouble and terrorism. Our curiosity satisfied, we were certainly very happy when we safely crossed the border into Hungary.[38]

When Haynes and Baumgardt returned to Los Angeles in October, the physician had already experienced a very busy year. Besides his medical, business, social, and travel experiences, he had devoted much of his time to reform, especially the campaigns for municipal ownership that seemed to occupy the center of his activism in 1906. The year was not over,

however, and the final two months would be another busy season because of the coming state and municipal elections. In these campaigns
Haynes would continue to support social reform, but for him the time
would be better spent in cementing his bonds to the more conservative
wing of reform in Los Angeles.

Chapter Six

Godfather of Urban Reform

While John Haynes and companion B. R. Baumgardt dodged bombs and czarist soldiers in revolutionary Russia in 1906, a band of Los Angeles political reformers began to assemble elements of an organization that eventually took control of city government. Haynes never officially joined the group until it assumed power. But from the start he was godfather and inspiration to the insurgents, who shared some of his reform goals and used "his" recall process to capture the mayor's office. Though much further to the left than these structural reformers, Haynes nevertheless cooperated with them to accomplish some of his more moderate reform objectives.

On July 2, 1906, about 25 concerned citizens met in an assembly room of the Los Angeles Chamber of Commerce building to initiate proceedings for the selection of nonpartisan candidates for the coming municipal election. The group included Dana Bartlett and W. C. Petchner, both social reformers of the 1890s, and a few Voters' League activists such as Meyer Lissner, Russ Avery, and Nathan Newby. The majority, however, were prominent businessmen and professionals, including Harrison Gray Otis's attorney, William Hunsaker. Most of those in attendance were members of the Los Angeles Municipal League; in essence this convocation represented the formation of the political action wing of the league.[1]

The "businessmen's new municipal party," as one newspaper described it, had one primary aim—choosing a slate of city officials, regardless of party affiliation, to replace "machine politicians" in order to modernize and moralize city government. The new administration would be governed by members of the "better" element, middle-class businessmen and professionals who would limit the influence of large corporations, ethnic groups, and unionists. These reformers were especially concerned with restricting the political power of organized labor, whose leaders often were antagonistic in negotiations between municipalities and private businesses (especially regarding utility franchises and supply contracts). The situation in San Francisco, where Abe Ruef and the Union Labor party ruled, and the formation of the labor-dominated Public Ownership party earlier that year convinced otherwise apolitical businessmen to join the structural reformers in the nonpartisan movement.[2]

The quest for office was the adhesive that held together the variety of nonpartisans. While many of the businessmen wanted only to see their own peers rule local government for moral and economic reasons, a few of the reformers had additional motives. Municipal League leaders wanted structural changes made in the city's political system to eliminate parties and make government more efficient. More activist Voters' League members also wanted to protect and expand direct legislation, civil service, and municipal ownership, and tighten regulation of private utilities. The very few dedicated social reformers in this group could hope for slight improvements in the living and employment conditions of working-class Los Angeles. But the vast majority of nonpartisans were interested only in expanding their own access to city government and keeping the lower classes under control. As in many other U.S. cities at the time, the municipal reformers found in nonpartisanship an effective weapon with which to compete with the entrenched elite.[3]

Younger reformers saturated the nonpartisan leadership, infusing the crusade with enthusiasm and urgency. These upwardly mobile professionals hoped to penetrate the city's political establishment—an advancement denied to them by prevailing powers. Meyer Lissner, who emerged as the reform "boss," was described in early 1906 as "a young man who has made considerable money in real estate recently and is too rich to practice law, and too young to retire from active life." Lawyer Marshall Stimson was praised in a local journal: "[He] belongs to an element that is invading the political field in increasing numbers, much to the eventual betterment of conditions. He is young, a Harvard graduate, well off in this world's goods, and he believes that American citizenship means something besides following a corporation boss or a Federal 'bunch.'" Along with Russ Avery, an attorney working with Haynes in the Voters' League, and *Express* reporter Edward A. Dickson, the young progressive leaders hoped to make their mark in Los Angeles by defeating local incumbents and party leaders and stepping immediately into the void. Soon after the creation of the nonpartisan committee, they began devising strategy for the coming elections.[4]

The focus of nonpartisan wrath was the "SP machine" directed by Walter Francis Xavier Parker, "land and tax agent" for the Southern Pacific Railroad Company. Born in Ohio in 1864, Parker migrated to Southern California as a newspaper editor in 1886. After a few years in San Diego and Santa Ana, he settled in Los Angeles, where he sold real estate and immersed himself in Republican party affairs. Aligned with SP representatives in the city, Parker quickly became an important strategist in party campaigns both locally and statewide. By the turn of the century, he operated as the SP's chief political agent in Los Angeles. City newspapers claimed that this "Boss of California" dominated not only city and county government but also the state legislature, in which he became the SP's head lobbyist. Engaged in politics because he relished the challenge as "a substitute for golf or pinochle," the amiable Parker was an honest but shrewd and occasionally ruthless power broker.[5]

Parker's organization was not a "machine" in the traditional sense. Successor to the local SP organization of the late 1880s, which was headed by Hervey Lindley (brother of Dr. Walter Lindley), the machine was more a directorate of SP lawyers and other officials who used the corporation's wealth and influence to organize political support. Working with other corporations vitally affected by state and local laws, Parker doled out available patronage to reward key supporters, planned campaigns for nominees who were expected to follow his orders on important issues, and coerced city employees and railroad workers to provide manpower. Businessmen who were dependent on the railroad for transportation of their goods and interested in the continued domination of the Republican party found it expedient to cooperate. The organization offered a few amenities in the form of social mobility and jobs, but since Los Angeles was so largely middle class and native, the typical machine welfare system never developed. Instead, these functions were left to ward politicians who bargained with the SP or other political groups. In many cases it did not matter whether the ward organization was Republican or Democrat, since the Republican Parker collaborated with Democrats when necessary.[6]

Though Parker was the acknowledged leader of the machine, there was no rigid leadership hierarchy. In his circle of lawyers and corporation executives, he made decisions regarding Southern California as the subordinate of William F. Herrin, the SP's political manager in San Francisco. But disagreements between members of Parker's directorate did occur. Republican party leaders were never happy with Parker's pragmatic liaisons with Democrats. The SP and other transportation companies occasionally competed for the same rights-of-way or favored differ-ent candidates, with the result that rifts developed between Parker and traction counsel William E. "Billy" Dunn. Parker's choices for office did not always follow his orders; in fact, Mayor Owen McAleer was fre-quently at odds with the boss, and the city council did not always vote as instructed. "Boss Parker" was important, but his power was far from absolute.[7]

Although Parker's machine was no monolith, the nonpartisan reform-ers found it expedient to treat it as such in order to defeat it. The "Oc-topus," as the SP was known for decades in California, had a reputation for ruthless economic and political maneuvers in the state that reformers associated with Parker's allegedly corrupt machine. Making Parker the target of their crusade, the nonpartisans (mostly Republicans denied ac-cess to party decision making) attempted to remove all party structures in local government as a means of removing Parker.[8]

John Haynes was much more of a social reformer than any of the non-partisans, but he certainly sympathized with their aim to unshackle city government from corporate influence. Opposed to the SP as a corrupting force in California politics, he would support almost any attempt to re-duce its power and modify the structure of city government. Already acquainted with Walter Parker and well aware of his influence, Haynes hoped the defeat of this "boss" would remove some of the obstacles to political and social reform in Los Angeles and the state legislature, where direct-legislation bills failed in each session.[9]

The reformers hoped to curb Parker's influence by electing municipal officers who did not owe their victory to the Southern Pacific. Since most nonpartisans were Republicans, they planned to choose a slate before the regular party convention, which Parker usually controlled. In early Au-gust the insurgents considered a number of contenders, including Dr. Haynes, as their standard-bearer. Haynes's brother-in-law, Walter Lind-ley, was the favorite of many members of the group's city central com-mittee. But Lindley's close friendship with Parker, whom Lindley called "the logical leader of the Republican party at this end of the state," con-vinced the reformers to nominate Lee C. Gates, a corporation lawyer and former police commissioner. Selections for the rest of the nonpartisan slate were made and offered to the regular Republican convention, but only one found a place among the party's nominees. Although Parker had initially promised the Republican mayoral nomination to city coun-cil president George A. Smith, the SP "boss" compromised with H. E.

Huntington's counsel, William Dunn, on the choice of Lindley. Republican city council nominees included businessmen, ward politicians, and one nonpartisan.[10]

The Democrats convened at about the same time and nominated banker Arthur Cyprian Harper for mayor, Arthur "Spook" Houghton (of Davenport-recall fame) and three nonpartisan nominees for the city council, and a few nonpartisans for other offices. In late September, the city's Public Ownership party nominated Stanley Wilson for mayor, and E. L. Hutchinson, Fred Spring, and a number of workingmen for other offices. Haynes had been mentioned as a mayoral candidate for the new party at its founding, but he was still in Russia during this convention. The Socialists, who chose Frank Marek as their mayoral nominee, chided the public-ownership advocates for championing a halfway measure, even though Job Harriman and a few other party members were active in the Public Ownership campaign. The nomination of a Prohibitionist for mayor made the contest a six-way fight.[11]

During the campaign the *Times* vigorously backed Lindley, while the *Express* and *Herald* supported Gates. These papers, along with the *Graphic*, attacked each other's Republican more than they did the Democrat Harper. Most city publications, except the *Record, Examiner,* and union newspapers, used the threat of a Public Ownership victory as the chief reason to elect their endorsee. Regular Republicans and members of the Nonpartisan Committee of 100 both argued that voters who strayed from either camp would help to split the business vote, thus aiding the chances of Stanley Wilson and the "dangerous class element" that would destroy the all-important Owens Valley water project and virtually ruin the city. The organ of organized labor endorsed the Public Ownership party and Stanley Wilson, arguing that Harper and Lindley were tools of the SP bipartisan machine and Gates was only a lackey of traction magnate Henry Huntington. Imaginative campaign tactics of this era—printing phony straw poll ballots, deceiving one candidate into writing a "conditional" letter of withdrawal in support of a foe, tampering with the U.S. mail, and other strategies—kept the struggle amusing. The municipal campaign was also complicated by the concurrent elections statewide and in Los Angeles County.[12]

John R. Haynes was trapped in a peculiar dilemma. He had been a Democrat, and Harper was supported by a substantial number of labor leaders friendly to Haynes. The Republican Lindley was Haynes's own brother-in-law and former medical partner. Gates represented the reform movement's conservative wing, which included many of Haynes's associates and championed some of his reform ideas. Stanley Wilson was the nominee of the party Haynes helped to found, a fusion of organized labor and Socialists that reflected Haynes's own politics more than any other group. The Socialist party had been receiving some of his wealth in the past few years, and the Prohibitionist party stood for a principle he was beginning to support.

In this predicament the pragmatist Haynes declined to take a prominent role. It is almost certain that he did not support the Prohibitionist or Socialist, neither of whom had much chance of victory. The Democrats never claimed him as a supporter, nor did the nonpartisans, both of whom would have used his influence in attracting voters had he endorsed their candidates. The regular Republicans once claimed him as one of a hundred doctors planning to vote for Lindley, though Haynes quickly and vehemently denied it. In fact, he refused to contribute to his brother-in-law's campaign, and political disagreement caused quite a bit of tension between the two families. If he did support a party, it most likely was the Public Ownership party, an organization partially of his own creation. Composed of moderate socialists and labor leaders with whom he agreed on current political objectives, the Public Ownership party was supported by the *Examiner* and Haynes's other allies. Publicly, however, he decided not to alienate the other parties and kept both his contributions and ballot a secret.[13]

In the end, Haynes took the expedient (though not very courageous) course. Stanley Wilson and the Public Ownership party were buried in the election, as union laborites flocked to the Democrat Harper. Lindley and Gates split the Republican vote, allowing Harper to win with much less than half the total. Rumors of the last-minute switch from Lindley to Harper by Parker's organization appeared to be true, though they were denied by Republican officials. In the end, Harper was elected along with five Republicans aligned with Parker, but the nonpartisans, too, were successful. Four of their number were elected to the city council, as was another candidate who had been endorsed by the nonpartisans and one of the major parties. *Times* editors also were somewhat relieved by the outcome since the "labor union gang" was "completely routed in their political schemes," even though the Otis-Chandler candidate came in third.[14]

Except for the Public Ownership party, the 1906 municipal election held something for all of the city's major political groups. Rising labor strength was checked, and middle-class businessmen still ruled the government. Yet a party at least partially sympathetic to labor was represented in the mayor's office. More importantly, the event demonstrated the potential of the reform movement and gave insurgents added incentive to continue agitating and organizing in anticipation of capturing city hall.

The year 1907 was also busy for Haynes. Besides his continuing reform activities and new campaigns, he still managed a thriving medical practice, which included brother-in-law Alfred Fellows, brother Robert, and nephew Harry Haynes Koons. All four moved to a new office complex in the Union Trust Building in January 1908. John Haynes continued to speak at medical association meetings, hosted social events for noted physicians visiting Los Angeles, and again served as a clinical professor on the faculty of the University of Southern California College of Medicine from 1906 to 1908.[15]

In late 1907 and early 1908, Haynes attended to one of his most noteworthy patients, lawyer Clarence Darrow. While in Boise, Idaho, defending George A. Pettibone and "Big Bill" Haywood in the Western Federation of Miners bombing trial, Darrow suffered an attack of mastoiditis. He traveled to Los Angeles, where Haynes admitted him to California Hospital and took charge of the case. Haynes arranged for and assisted in an operation to remove the mastoid, and after a lengthy sojourn in Los Angeles the lawyer was cured. As Darrow later recalled, he was not able to pay the bill for this treatment at the time: "It was more than a year before these [debts] were liquidated, and my good friend, Doctor Haynes, waited until the very last." [16]

Haynes's own poor health at this time and his increasing political activity gradually convinced him that it was time to consider retirement from medicine. "After 1910 I found that I would have to do one of two things—either confine my efforts and energy to the practice of medicine; or give up medicine and devote myself to public work." Keeping up with recent developments in medicine had been sacrificed for his public interest activities, and Haynes came to the conclusion, "In the broader field of economics and its influence upon the health and welfare of the great mass of the people I could do more for society than I could by continuing my private practice." In January 1911, he and Alfred dissolved the practice and the associates vacated their medical office and scattered. Haynes moved to the Consolidated Realty Building at Sixth and Hill, where he continued to treat a few of his old patients until his complete break with medicine in 1914.[17]

While still busy with his practice before 1910, Haynes found ample time and resources to pursue his old political interests. One of these was the safety fender issue, which resurfaced when the interurban streetcar companies refused to abide by the May 1906 ordinance requiring fenders. Though the Los Angeles Railway Company, the city's major intra-urban, complied with the new law, the city's other two major street railways did not. The Pacific Electric Railway Company (PE, also owned by Henry E. Huntington) and the Los Angeles Pacific (LAP) insisted that they were interurbans, operating within and outside of the Los Angeles city limits, and therefore exempt from the laws of any single municipality within their territories.

Local court rulings upheld the ordinance in late 1906, but the LAP continued to claim that the law was unconstitutional. So in February 1907, the city's prosecuting attorney demanded that the interurbans install fenders on all cars running in the city within the two months that the LAP general manager judged possible. On the day of this deadline warrants for the arrest of the LAP and PE general managers were issued. But at the moment Mayor Harper, the city attorney, and a majority of city councilmen were away from the city. Hoping to avoid further conflict with politically influential traction magnates, the acting mayor ordered that the warrants not be served and scheduled a meeting with street-railway officials and the city attorney for May 4. At this meeting the full council compromised by instructing the city attorney to draft another fender ordinance more favorable to the interurbans.[18]

Dr. Haynes, who was on a trip to the East Coast in early May, missed these developments. Upon his return he resumed the Voters' League campaign for safety fenders. With abundant publicity from the *Examiner*, he wrote to each city councilman, imploring them to refuse to alter the ordinance. He reminded them that in the nine months the ordinance had been in effect, the number of fatalities involving LARY cars had dropped sharply. Before the council's final vote he personally appeared before the council, presenting data from fender manufacturers and citing statistics that compared local streetcar accidents with those of the entire state of Massachusetts. He again banqueted the city lawmakers to allow ample time to present his case. The result was almost complete victory: the council approved a minor adjustment, favorable to the railway companies, in the maximum distance between fenders and rails, but refused to exempt interurbans from carrying the fenders.[19]

With this defeat the LAP capitulated, while the PE continued the fight in court. In August, a police-court judge ruled the revised fender ordinance legal, and county officials conducted a number of sweeps in the downtown area, arresting over a dozen motormen in their fenderless cars. Joseph McMillan, the PE traffic manager, and LAP general manager Thomas Gabel also were arrested, prompting McMillan to threaten to stop all incoming PE cars at the city limits if arrests continued. The street railways then obtained a restraining order, creating a temporary cease-fire.[20]

While the cases of those arrested progressed, McMillan spoke to members of the Los Angeles City Club. He praised the investments and public-spiritedness of his superior, LARY and PE owner Henry Huntington, and defended the interurbans by questioning the statistics and motives of his opposition. The PE traffic manager claimed that even if it was possible to install Eclipse fenders on high-speed suburban cars, the devices would cause derailments and take many more lives than might be saved. He also charged that the ordinance was actually written by an Eclipse representative. Two weeks later, Haynes refuted these claims in his own address to the City Club with more statistics on street-railway accidents, more endorsements from trolley officials, and LARY's record of reduced fatalities since the installation of Eclipse fenders. The original ordinance was drafted by five Voters' League lawyers, Haynes asserted. As to the possible danger of the fender to high-speed suburban cars, he reminded the audience that the fender easily could be folded up at the city limits in about five seconds.[21]

McMillan also attended the second City Club meeting and offered Haynes $500 if he could produce a fender that fit PE cars and complied with the ordinance. Haynes quickly accepted, offered to donate $500 to charity if he failed, and shook hands with McMillan. The physician then contacted the Eclipse manufacturer, who designed an adjustment so that the fenders would properly fit PE cars.[22]

Testing of the fenders took place in November, and victory was claimed by both sides. The *Times* delighted in reporting that the Eclipse collapsed in every test, and the paper continued to caricature Haynes as a crank and troublemaker. Again he was accused of having a financial interest in Eclipse fenders, which the doctor denied, claiming that it was PE and LARY counsel William E. Dunn who initially had chosen that apparatus as the best. Haynes also defended the Eclipse, pointing out that it did fit properly and did not derail the car, even at high speeds. Most importantly, the tests failed to convince the city attorney that the fenders would not work if the car was moving within the speed limit of downtown Los Angeles.[23]

In early December, PE counsel Dunn again petitioned the city council to amend the fender ordinance for interurban cars. Haynes again ap-

peared before the lawmakers with testimonials from street-railway officials and victims who had been saved by the mechanisms. His star witness, seven-year-old Uki Sakabe, sat on a councilman's desk while
Haynes described how she had been scooped up by an Eclipse, and thus
saved from certain death under the wheels of a car traveling 25 miles per
hour along First Street. The council was very alarmed to hear this story,
particularly since the speed limit at First and Los Angeles streets was only
4 miles per hour! The lawmakers agreed with Haynes, and once again
refused to exempt the interurbans.[24]

With this defeat the PE and LAP agreed to install lifesaving fenders,
but asked to use what management thought to be a more efficient model.
Haynes again objected, and the council disapproved the substitution.
Several months later, Haynes was contacted personally by Henry Huntington, who invited the doctor to his estate in the San Gabriel Valley.
Huntington told Haynes that the railway had found a better fender than
the Eclipse. Would he object to the PE's equipping its cars with such a
device? The doctor agreed to witness a test, and McMillan arranged for
the demonstration. After seeing a Worcester in action, Haynes compromised and agreed to back the PE's request to incorporate this model in
the city ordinance. By early 1909, all PE and LAP interurban cars were
equipped with Worcesters. These devices remained on PE cars until the
company replaced them in the early 1920s with a more reliable and efficient fender—the Eclipse.[25]

The fender controversy further cemented Haynes's relationship with
the urban reformers who backed him and the regulation of public utilities. Another issue that tied him to reform was direct legislation. After
the announcement of the Pfahler decision, which validated the initiative
and referendum in California cities, Haynes attempted to form a permanent organization financed by contributions and able to invoke these
principles whenever necessary. He promoted the idea of a well-financed
direct-legislation organization ready to combat city officials and the actions of the city council, such as the passage in early December 1906 of
an emergency ordinance that made saloon permits easier to obtain.
Haynes charged, "Every councilman who so voted should be recalled
and probably would be if his term of office did not so soon expire." He
then joined the campaign to nullify this ordinance, which did not neces-
sitate a referendum since it was ruled illegal the next month.[26]

Haynes's fund for municipal direct legislation never came to fruition.
His activism in this field continued though, with biennial lobbying of the
California legislature in early 1907 and 1909. These efforts also failed,

as state lawmakers refused to pass constitutional amendments for the initiative and referendum. In August 1907, he traveled to San Francisco and asked the county's board of supervisors to reduce the percentage of recall-petition signatures that would be required by a charter amendment the supervisors were considering. After the speech the supervisors compromised on a lower percentage and placed the measure on the November ballot. This time Haynes won.[27]

Dr. Haynes also maintained his limited support for socialism in these years. Described by Gaylord Wilshire as "more of a Socialist after the John Burns persuasion possibly than after the Keir Hardie red hot revolutionary brand," Haynes continued his financial involvement with local and national Socialists. Eugene Debs sent him a special note of thanks for contributions to national Socialist organs in 1908. Locally, he became a stockholder in *Common Sense*, organ of the Los Angeles branch of the Socialist Party of America, and a major contributor to the fund-raising drive for a new building to house the newspaper and serve as party headquarters. Although still a prominent "capitalist" in the city, Haynes's reputation as a "millionaire socialist" was widespread, resulting in many requests for donations from party activists.[28]

Haynes's advocacy of gradual socialism and direct legislation exacerbated his personal conflicts with the city's more conservative elite, especially Harrison Gray Otis, Harry Chandler, and other officials of the *Los Angeles Times*. The newspaper did not let up its attack upon the physician in editorials, cartoons, and even in its supposedly objective news columns. In January 1907, the *Times* challenged Haynes to defend his support of the municipal recall to visiting muckraker Lincoln Steffens, then attacked the physician's response, which was published in the *Express*. In February, *Times* editors reported that Haynes was a very heavy cigarette smoker who distributed his favorite brand at civil service commission meetings. In March, Haynes was castigated several times when he received a subpoena from the San Francisco County grand jury to testify in the investigation of the Home Telephone Company's questionable ties to political boss Abe Ruef. The *Times* neglected to mention later that Haynes was only a stockholder in a subsidiary of Home Telephone, knew nothing of its San Francisco operation, and never testified because the prosecutor admittedly made a mistake in calling for him in the first place.[29]

In July, that same San Francisco prosecutor, Francis Heney, was investigating bribery charges against traction magnate Patrick Calhoun. When Heney charged that Calhoun had purchased a substantial number of copies of the *Times* in exchange for Otis's editorial defense during the investigation, Haynes seized the opportunity for vengeance. He composed a long diatribe branding Otis a blatant egotist, a fanatic in opposing union labor, a bully, and a coward "absolutely destitute of manliness." This lampoon, forwarded to Heney for background in the investigation, charged that Otis had assaulted one of his reporters, armed his employees and turned the *Times* building into an arsenal during a peaceful union parade, was literally kicked out of command in the Philippines for cowardice, forged election postcards in 1906, and blackmailed his advertisers, among other crimes. At the same time Haynes asked Lincoln Steffens for help in obtaining depositions from witnesses attesting to these charges because, at long last, the physician was planning to silence Otis once and for all with a libel suit, though he would not commence action right away.[30]

The *Times* attacks on Haynes, "a perennial and preposterous pretender," became so obscene that in early December, Caroline Severance urged him to sue Otis for libel. Her letter arrived at the time Haynes was defending the fender ordinance before the city council. The *Times* again belittled him as a crank with a financial interest in the Eclipse firm. In his speech Haynes was very adamant about the *Times*'s defense of Huntington and his traction company in defying the city ordinance, making the paper an accomplice in the injuries that could have been avoided. The paper, of course, did not print this attack on its editors.[31]

Three months later the *Times* moved beyond the limits of reason. On March 3, 1908, it reported on its cover an alleged plot by Chicago "Reds" and anarchists to assassinate the city's chief of police. On the front page of the local news section it brandished a warning against toleration of Socialist political activity by the Los Angeles police chief. The editorial page contained a cartoon of a policeman being shot by a crazed anarchist. Near the murderer was a "demagogue" holding an "incendiary speech," a figure obviously mirroring scores of *Times* cartoons of John R. Haynes. The editor of the *Graphic* immediately urged the physician to sue for libel, though the doctor apparently declined. Public and private outrage did have some effect on the *Times*; though it continued to attack Haynes at every opportunity, its most extreme criticism was that he "expresses the views of semi-socialistic populism."[32]

The milder attacks included an April editorial belittling Haynes and other "local cranks" who staged a filibustering crusade to oppose the Penrose bill, which would allow the postmaster-general "to shut out of the mails permanently any publication which he deemed improper." The

bill was offered at a time when anarchist plots were suspected throughout the nation. Senator Penrose, the *Times*, and others believed the law
was necessary to muzzle "the dangerous socialist and anarchist press"
they accused of fomenting such terrorism. Haynes and others disagreed,
and the doctor himself wrote to every Californian in Congress urging
defeat of this bill. Soon even Penrose dropped his support, and the proposal died along with predictions of subversion. In this episode Haynes
again had the last word, further infuriating the *Times* editors.[33]

Besides assaulting Haynes for his association with Socialists, organized
labor, and direct legislation, the *Times* continually attacked the doctor
in his capacity as a civil service commissioner. In his dozen years on this
board, Haynes twice served as its president. In the course of these duties,
complaints from those dissatisfied with their grades often called into
question the motives of examiners, and the *Times* pounced on every opportunity that might reflect badly on Haynes. During the summer of
1907, the paper tried to foment discord between board members and an
examiner, Henry L. Adams, who refused to supply board chairman
Haynes with a list of test questions. Another examiner later claimed that
Times managing editor Harry C. Andrews offered to pay him to write an
article listing "irregularities happening in the Board" to back up Adams's
criticism of the commissioners. Adams, however, refused to sign this
statement, and later wrote to Haynes to deny there were ever any problems, and insist that the board always acted correctly.[34]

When Haynes's tenure as chairman came to an end in February 1908,
the *Times* report on the event carried the headline "Scandals during the
freakish reformer's regime furnish material for grand jury investigation,"
and predicted that Haynes would be deposed. The Adams "controversy"
again was raised and a statement was issued by another examiner discharged by Haynes (the same one who defended him several months earlier), in which board members were accused of favoritism in testing applicants. These *Times* stories, along with an editorial demanding an
investigation, brought an immediate response. Four of the city's other
major newspapers and two local magazines reproduced letters by Adams
and board members debunking the *Times* story, issued a statement of the
actual facts, and printed a glowing account of Haynes's chairmanship of
the board, which report was read into the board's official minutes. Additionally, it was revealed that Haynes had informed his fellow commissioners at the beginning of the December nomination meeting that he
would not accept another term as president; he certainly was not "deposed."[35]

Without evidence of malfeasance, the *Times* eventually dropped its case. Most likely, its editors were not pleased to hear in May that Haynes was selected as the Los Angeles delegate to the Second Biennial Conference of the National Assembly of Civil Service Commissioners in Chicago, where he read a paper on the qualifications of municipal commissioners. Conversely, the *Times* was delighted to report that Mayor Harper would not reappoint Haynes to the commission in February 1909. The physician belonged to too many reform groups by this time, and had already approved of the mayor's recall. His departure was very conciliatory, however. The other commissioners unanimously adopted a resolution regretting his departure. The doctor, in turn, treated them to a farewell dinner at his residence. In December, the board chairman, accused of playing politics for the departed Mayor Harper, finally sent his resignation to the new reform mayor. This vacancy was filled by the appointment of Dr. Haynes.[36]

Haynes's experience in the Harper administration mirrored the relationship of the mayor to the emerging reform movement. Appointed by a previous chief executive, Haynes ably performed his duties on the civil service board but gradually came into conflict with figures in the new administration. This tension was intimated in a speech delivered by Haynes to other city officials in May 1908, when he thanked Mayor Harper for inviting so many city commissioners to the event because "I know a personal knowledge of one another will develop the fact that none of us grow horns." By the time Haynes's regular term expired in February 1909, Harper would not even consider a reappointment.[37]

Most of the nonpartisan reformers also had opposed Harper in 1906, but did not expect the battle that would come. Soon after the election, Municipal League secretary C. D. Willard wrote of the mayor, "While not our man, [he] is a member of this league, a merchant and a banker of good standing and he is very likely after the administration gets under way to come to us for help." Willard's optimism proved groundless, for Harper made his own appointments, some of whom were unsuited to their positions. He proved to the reformers that he would not be heeding their advice on two important issues, policing public morals and construction of the city's $23 million Owens Valley aqueduct. The latter offered vast possibilities for patronage to further entrench Harper in city politics, and both issues presented opportunities for graft to city officials associated with the underworld.[38]

Early in 1907, the urban reformers continued their organizational efforts, hoping to keep up the momentum gained in their 1906 municipal election victory. The first activity of the year was a dinner in honor of muckraker Lincoln Steffens hosted by Dr. Haynes at the California Club on January 23, 1907. E. T. Earl, C. D. Willard, and other reformers and businessmen were present, as well as the recently inaugurated Mayor Harper. Meyer Lissner apologized that many nonpartisans could not attend since they were exhausted after the long election campaign. Dr. Walter Lindley, the mayoral opponent of the nonpartisans, reportedly "leaned toward the speaker and said: 'For heaven's sake, Lissner, why didn't you have them take to their beds before the campaign began?'" Later in the evening Haynes introduced the guest of honor, who lauded the doctor's leadership and discussed the relationship of business to graft, arguing for municipal ownership to eliminate such possibilities. In another address to a much larger audience (an event also planned by Haynes), Steffens compared the situation of Los Angeles and San Francisco, where graft trials involving city officials and corporation officers currently raged.[39]

The Steffens addresses stimulated discussions leading to the creation of the Los Angeles City Club. This weekly forum and discussion group became a major force in uniting city progressives and educating them on current issues. Haynes was a charter member of the club, addressed the group on streetcar fenders and public utility franchises in the next two years, and remained a member for over two decades. Besides arranging speeches by noted progressives, the club held weekly meetings, which helped urban reformers keep in touch with the latest developments in local politics, especially important in the quiet periods between elections.[40]

The city progressives also enhanced their position by working to change the rules by which they competed for office. In 1907, reform agitators convinced the city council to ask leading civic organizations to choose representatives for an advisory committee to revise the city charter. Haynes was selected as a representative of the Voters' League, along with Meyer Lissner and C. D. Willard of the Municipal League. The committee produced a document including reform measures "as essential to the progressives' aspirations as they were subversive of the machine's operation." One objective was the municipal direct primary, which would eliminate conventions and party organizations at the city level. This nonpartisan measure was supported by most structural reformers and opposed by regular Republicans, Democrats, and Socialists, who argued that citizens would not really know which principles a candidate

stood for. Another major objective, currently the rage of municipal reformers throughout the nation, was the election of council members by
the whole city rather than by wards. Advanced both to allow the best
candidates to run for office, regardless of their residence, and to restrict
the power of ward politicians, it could also be used by elitists to eliminate
local control, which offered some amount of influence to ethnic minorities.[41]

Haynes participated in the drafting of these provisions. Though he opposed some of the committee's final recommendations, he voted in favor
of both nonpartisan politics and a council elected at large. His support
of the former was consistent with his opposition to the city's regular
Republican organization and Walter Parker's control of the nomination
process. Haynes's acquiescence to the citywide council, however, was a
glaring inconsistency. Years earlier he had opposed at-large council elections, believing that a machine could elect an entire slate of councilmen
as easily as representatives of individual wards. At-large elections would
also affect Haynes's municipal recall process by requiring that individual
councilmen be removed by vote of the entire city, rather than the much
smaller ward, a consequence promoting organized labor leaders to oppose this recommendation. In this instance, Haynes sided with the political reformers, ignoring the measure's effect on the recall and arguing
that an at-large council would result in "more efficient government." He
did not mention that it also would remove the power base of his city
council adversaries.[42]

The charter revision committee delivered its work to the city council in
the summer of 1908, anticipating the election of a Board of Freeholders
to frame the document. The council refused to call for this plebiscite,
however, spurring the reformers to offer 31 of their proposed changes as
charter amendments. At the election in February 1909, 10 of the most
important charter amendments were approved. One proposal extending
the life of city franchises to 35 years fell to defeat, having been opposed
by Haynes and the *Examiner*, while the proposals for the at-large council
and direct primary passed.[43]

While some reformers circulated the petition for the charter amendments in late 1908, others investigated the Harper administration's conduct of affairs related to public morals. Just after the election of Mayor
Harper, the *Times* had predicted that the Democratic administration
would signal a relaxation of vice and liquor laws: "We are to have a
Royal Arch and corporation Mayor, and a 'wide open town.'" In late
1908, the county grand jury verified that prophecy as it discovered that

top administration officials and insiders were involved in selling sugar and oil company stocks to saloon keepers in an alleged protection scheme. It was also revealed that the mayor and his police commissioners had accompanied policemen on inspections of brothels, where his honor and friends were observed frolicking with scantily clad women. Evidence that police segregated prostitution in one protected district also surfaced. The investigation into the administration's protection of prostitution, gambling, and illegal saloon activity was pursued by a politically ambitious assistant city attorney, whose bombastic style eventually resulted in his transfer to another job. His accusations were printed in E. T. Earl's *Express*, which charged that there was a "red light hanging from city hall." The mayor filed a libel suit against Earl, who hired a private investigator to verify the charges after a lengthy tour through the Los Angeles underworld.[44]

The reformers' concern for police policies was matched by their fears of official subversion of the city's $23 million aqueduct project. This enterprise offered an abundance of opportunities for graft in the planning and construction stages, and a wealth of patronage positions for aqueduct builders and support staff. It also threatened to destroy the concept of municipal ownership and the city's financial reputation if the project failed. For these reasons the reformers kept a close watch on Harper's handling of aqueduct affairs.

The mayor's motives became suspect early in 1908, when he rescinded a promise to reappoint James A. Anderson to the Public Works Board. A notable figure in the nonpartisan movement, Anderson was unacceptable both to Walter Parker and to the *Times*. To appease General Otis (who was believed to be blackmailing the mayor), Harper selected Adna R. Chaffey, a retired general and friend of Otis. The reformers grudgingly accepted Chaffey as a reasonable choice.[45]

The situation was much different the following January, when Harper appointed Police Chief Edward Kern to the board. A former Democratic city councilman believed to be a tool of the Parker machine, Kern was one of several political figures targeted for removal by an insurgent group of local Democrats. Kern's appointment triggered the publication of a series of daily exposés in Thomas Gibbon's *Herald* entitled "Is Vice Protected?," which identified gambling dens, "blind pigs" (unlicensed saloons), and the connections between administration figures and vice lords.[46]

The selection of Chief Kern for the Public Works Board fused the reformers' two chief concerns—police protection of vice and corruption in the building of the aqueduct—and propelled them to action. Rumors of attempts to recall Harper spread rapidly as reform newspapers continued to print articles damaging to the administration. Finally, it was reported on January 18 that when police raided the Apex Club the night before, gambler Eddie Morris told authorities to contact "A.C." (Harper's first two initials), who would verify that the club was protected. On January 20, the Municipal League held a mass meeting attended by over 200 members. After several speeches the crowd voted overwhelmingly to pursue the recall of Mayor Harper. Dr. Haynes, who more than anyone else was responsible for the creation of the city's recall law, was among those who voted in favor of the ouster.[47]

Immediately after this plebiscite, the Municipal League initiated the recall campaign. The league circulated petitions, raised funds, and searched for a candidate to oppose Harper. Many possible candidates, including Haynes, were consulted, and quite a few were offered the nomination, though all found a reason to decline. George Alexander, a 69-year-old former county supervisor who already had refused, finally agreed to run. The choice was made official at another mass meeting in February.[48]

Dr. Haynes was absent during much of the early activity of the recallers. After declining the nomination, he donated $200 to the petition drive and departed for Sacramento to lobby the legislature in favor of state direct legislation. He missed the lining up of political forces in the early stages of the campaign. The reformers, backed by Earl's *Express* and Gibbon's *Herald*, led the recall drive. The opposition included a variety of interests. The *Times* opposed any use of the recall and backed Harper and Kern's suppression of Socialists. The *Examiner*, *Record*, and *Evening News* backed Harper because his opponent was the tool of reform "boss" E. T. Earl, whose moralistic "class cult" would restrict personal freedoms of the working class. Democrats generally supported Harper, as did many Republican businessmen who opposed the recall because it would damage the city's reputation. Walter Parker's organization also favored retaining Harper since the SP had aided the mayor's election campaign and feared that his reform opponents might assume power. Organized labor remained neutral: since its leaders were not invited to the Municipal League meetings, labor made no official endorsement.[49]

The campaign was in high gear when Kern and then Harper abruptly resigned two weeks before the election. On the afternoon of March 11, the mayor visited Earl, who displayed some of the evidence his private investigators had collected in response to Harper's libel suit against the

Express publisher. Earl threatened to print the evidence if Harper did not resign. The mayor agreed after consulting Walter Parker, who advised him to quit. Parker hoped that the vacancy caused by the resignation would have to be filled by the city council and that the recall proceedings would thus be nullified. If this was correct, his choice for mayor would be selected by a sympathetic council majority and could complete Harper's term, which would last until the end of the year. But the city attorney ruled otherwise. William D. Stephens, a good friend of Haynes's and the reformers' first choice for mayor, was chosen to fill the interim period, and the election was to proceed.[50]

Left without a candidate, Parker and the regular Republicans were in a bind. Alexander was opposed only by Socialist Fred Wheeler. The *Record* switched its support to Wheeler, while the city's other nonreform papers made no endorsement. On a rainy March 26, fewer than half of the city's registered voters went to the polls. Wheeler attracted many protest votes so that Alexander won by a narrow margin, which encouraged the Socialists in planning for the regular election in December.[51]

As close as the election turned out, it still was a major victory for the city's municipal reformers. Using one of John Haynes's favorite political devices and beholden to him at many stages of their campaign, the progressives finally wrestled the mayor's office from their opponents. They had only a nine-month tenure before the next election and did not control the city council, but they occupied the critical executive office in city hall. Haynes did not always agree with their attempt at instituting limited reforms in city government, and he detested their constant attacks on socialism. But the progressives represented the opportunity to modernize and moralize city government and to create social welfare programs that Haynes favored on a much grander scale. And he was, after all, their hero.[52]

Chapter Seven

From City to State:
Haynes and the California Progressives, Phase 1

The victories of urban progressives in Los Angeles and other California cities spurred the reformers to advance their efforts to the state level. Since the Southern Pacific Railroad was the major influence in Golden State politics, the insurgents duplicated their methods and rhetoric in municipal campaigns both to alter the political structure and to obtain state offices. Dr. Haynes played a prominent role in nurturing the infant movement to maturity and eventually joined these reformers in reshaping California politics. In state progressivism he found a program encompassing many reforms he advocated, a large constituency, and the opportunity for immediate success.

The Southern Pacific Railroad (SP, or Espee) had been a major force in the California economy since the completion of its forerunner, the Central Pacific, in 1869. For two decades it dominated transcontinental and local rail transportation, oceanic shipping, and other means of conveyance in the state. This monopoly allowed it to manipulate freight rates, to demand concessions from budding cities as a price for establishing routes through them rather than through competing towns, and in other ways to wield enormous economic power as the largest single landowner, employer, and taxpayer in California.[1]

To protect this vast empire the company plunged into state and local politics. From the U.S. Congress to the state capitol to county courthouses and city halls, the SP spent money and employed lobbyists to influence government policies in its favor. Three events of the late nineteenth century—the publication of the private letters of a former SP financial director, the attempt by SP president Collis P. Huntington to avoid repaying the railroad's debt to the United States, and Huntington's attempt to coerce the federal government to build a deep-water port at

Santa Monica—graphically detailed the SP's involvement in national and state politics. The railroad's maneuvers in state legislative sessions and local elections furthered its reputation as a vile monolith, the corrupt "Octopus" of the Golden State.[2]

Some historians have argued that the SP suffered a multitude of defeats, thus debunking the idea that it had a stranglehold on state and local politics. In protecting the railroad's interests, however, top management was ever vigilant. In 1893, William F. Herrin ascended the throne of chief consul of the SP and director of its political bureau. From his office at Fourth and Townsend streets in San Francisco, Herrin managed a network of political operatives both in and outside of elective office. In San Francisco Herrin worked with Abraham Ruef, boss of the prevailing Union Labor party. For distant Southern California, Herrin relied on the leadership of his first lieutenant, Walter F. X. Parker, who was responsible for political matters south of the Tehachapi Mountains, particularly the SP political machine in Los Angeles, and for the SP state lobby in Sacramento.[3]

SP political power reached its zenith in 1906. After guiding the selection of U.S. senator Frank P. Flint, Parker managed the state Republican convention in Santa Cruz. There he dictated the choice of most of the nominees, including James Gillett for governor. With the help of a considerable payment from Herrin to Abe Ruef to support Gillett's nomination, and the desertion of Democratic candidate Theodore Bell by the Hearst press, the SP Republicans swept the election. Parker and his assistants set up temporary quarters in the state capitol in January, and "were in effect the 'people of California'" in the 1907 session. Reports of Parker's manipulation of the legislature were so widespread that he became a major tourist attraction for Sacramento visitors. His influence with legislators and the governor effectively killed all legislation deemed damaging to the Southern Pacific Railroad.[4]

Just as the Espee's economic power was buoyed by its status as the largest corporation in the state, its political clout was reinforced by the support of many businessmen and farmers dependent on its transportation facilities and of professionals employed to serve the SP's legal and medical needs. But businessmen and professionals without connections to the railroad resisted the SP's political influence. These independents were especially critical of its monopolistic development and what they saw as its "vast corruption of public life."[5]

John Haynes came to oppose the SP for both philosophical and practical reasons. He did not object to it as a massive business enterprise, for he owned substantial amounts of stock in many California corporations. He did, however, oppose it as a monopoly restraining trade, competition, and opportunity, which concentrated tremendous economic and political power in the hands of a few. As he gradually increased his own involvement in political affairs, he recognized that the SP wielded an inordinate amount of power in state and local politics, usually in opposition to what he thought were the best interests of "the people." Though he had a number of good friends—including brother-in-law Walter Lindley, SP traffic manager John A. Muir, and U.S. senator Frank P. Flint—who had close ties to Parker and the SP machine, Haynes became a staunch opponent of this group in the early 1900s.[6]

Haynes's personal crusade for a system of direct legislation at the state level was a critical factor in his opposition to the SP. Since 1903, he had made biennial lobbying excursions to Sacramento and paid lobbyists to convince state legislators to pass a constitutional amendment embodying the initiative and referendum. Witnessing the legislative proceedings, he was convinced that "no measure that Mr. Herrin was opposed to could pass either house," and "any measure, I believe, that the Southern Pacific R. R. Co. wanted could have passed both houses."[7]

This conclusion was based on the doctor's personal dealings with SP manager Walter Parker. Through Dr. Lindley and other friends, Haynes met Parker in Sacramento during the 1903 legislative session. After an all-night interview, Parker stated that he personally might favor direct legislation, but that he was paid by the SP "to watch their interests and to elect men favorable to their interests." He was "quite certain that they would not desire the passage of the initiative." But Parker gradually backed down and agreed to push the bill through the assembly. "I believe that he will do what he says he will—I may be an ass for so believing but I do," Haynes wrote to the skeptical assemblyman carrying the bill. The doctor was right. With Parker's blessing the bill passed the assembly by a vote of 65 to 1 before meeting death in the senate. Parker kept his promise, and the lopsided vote spoke volumes about his influence with state lawmakers.[8]

Haynes also witnessed other examples of Parker's power. One evening at the home of the speaker of the assembly, Haynes overheard him asking Parker for his opinion of a certain proposal. After receiving an answer, the speaker thanked Parker, adding: "You know the boys would not pass it unless you were willing." In 1910, Haynes and a few associates asked Governor Gillett to appoint a nonpolitician as state insurance commissioner. The governor regretfully declined: "Walter won't stand for it, and

I can't do it." According to the doctor's friends, Parker also claimed "absolute control" of the Los Angeles City Council and County Board of Supervisors, and a fair amount of influence over members of the State Supreme Court.[9]

It was in the state legislature that SP power most irritated Haynes. With corporate funds available not only from the SP but also from many firms that were its political allies, some legislators were amenable to following SP dictation. In 1905, Haynes convinced one of his patients, state senator Cornelius "Corney" Pendleton, to introduce a direct-legislation bill. Corney was considered a machine man, which explained the doctor's strategy. But as Pendleton predicted, the effort proved futile. While talking in the senate chamber, Corney treated the doctor to a political education. Pointing to the speaker pro tem of the senate, he related how the speaker had demanded $2,500 from the Santa Fe Railroad to allow it to take over a franchise of one of its subsidiaries. "Then the senator pointed out in the senate chamber $1000 men, and $500 men, and finally pointing to a small red-haired man coming in the door, he said, 'And that man takes the postage and the stationery from the senate chamber. You see what sort of a state government we have!' "[10]

With such an assortment of lawmakers willing to serve Parker, it is no wonder that direct legislation was defeated in every session. In opposing the initiative Parker protected the SP from attempts to regulate its rates and practices, and aided allied interests, such as the liquor industry, in thwarting attempts at regulation from outside of the state legislature. As Haynes wrote to Governor George Pardee during the 1906 state election campaign, Haynes had "very little influence with the Walter Parker gang." This understatement revealed his growing opposition to the SP machine and spurred him to work with others who opposed the railroad for similar reasons.[11]

The political influence of the SP inspired frequent opposition, particularly from Republicans seeking a railroad-free party. From the mid-1890s through the early 1900s, protests to SP domination resulted in attempts to elect independent Republicans. These revolts became an epidemic in 1906, as municipal reformers turned some of their attention to state affairs. Publicity concerning SP meddling in the local politics of several California cities was compounded by revelations of Parker's manipulation of the 1906 GOP state convention in Santa Cruz, where a full slate of SP candidates was chosen amid charges of raw political brokering and bribery.[12]

A coordinated statewide movement to rid the Republican party of SP domination developed in early 1907. During the legislative session of that year, *Express* reporter Edward A. Dickson and *Fresno Morning Republican* editor Chester Rowell covered the session for their respective papers. Observing the antics of SP lobbyists ringleading the legislative circus, Rowell and Dickson decided to organize an anti-SP faction within the party in their own halves of the state. The two contacted newspapermen and other professionals and assembled fifteen of them on May 21 at Levy's Cafe in Los Angeles. Besides SP influence, the group discussed regulation of public utilities, direct legislation, and other issues, and agreed to stage a much larger conference in the summer. On August 1, about 50 Republicans met in Oakland's Hotel Metropole and created the League of Lincoln-Roosevelt Republican Clubs. Referred to as the Lincoln-Roosevelt League, this group of insurgents planned to wrest control of the party from the SP in time for the 1908 national, state, and local elections.[13]

Dr. Haynes later recalled that he "was not an organizer of the Lincoln-Roosevelt Club and cannot remember when I was asked to join." But he was more instrumental in the founding of the group than he thought. An early historian of the league credited Haynes's dinner meeting with Lincoln Steffens in January 1907 as the spark that led Los Angeles progressives to begin discussing a state reform drive. This occurred at the same time that Edward A. Dickson, who attended the banquet, began his discussions with Chester Rowell. According to another banquet participant, Haynes's leadership and Steffens's speech spurred a few reformers to plan organizational meetings. Haynes attended the May 21 meeting at Levy's, where he tried to convince the other attendees to adopt a definite set of principles—including direct legislation—as the platform of the new organization.[14]

After the initial meeting Haynes removed himself as a league leader. He did not attend the August 1 conference in Oakland, and he turned down Meyer Lissner's request for a sizable contribution in early 1908. The doctor made it clear that he was reorganizing the Direct Legislation League and would divert all of his wealth to this revived organization. Aware of some opposition to direct legislation among Lincoln-Roosevelt members (particularly Chester Rowell), Haynes decided to pour all of his resources into his own concoction and watch to see if the Lincoln-Roosevelt movement was just another feeble snipe at the SP. More importantly, he knew that the new league hoped only to "redeem the Republican Party," of which he was not even a member.[15]

Haynes's impression of the Lincoln-Roosevelt League changed during the 1908 national election campaign. The insurgents were surprisingly successful in getting one of their own delegates chosen for the Republican national convention, and a number of league-endorsed candidates for the state legislature were elected. Impressed with the strength of the young league and hopeful that its adherents in the legislature would support direct legislation, Haynes promised financial aid, but did not officially join. At the same time he asked league leader Meyer Lissner to serve on the executive board of the revitalized Direct Legislation League. This association benefited both organizations.[16]

Like the Lincoln-Roosevelt League, the renewed Direct Legislation League needed as much of a boost as it could get. After a few years of carrying on the battle for state direct legislation by himself, Haynes had decided in late 1908 to resurrect the old organization and make it more active. He convinced a number of prominent progressives such as Lissner to allow their names to appear on the league's letterhead, though Haynes provided almost all of its financial support. League secretary Milton T. U'Ren, of San Francisco, managed its operation in northern California, while Haynes took care of the south. As opposed to the Lincoln-Roosevelters, the Direct Legislation League represented all parties; Haynes even hoped to place Socialists and Prohibitionists on the executive committee. The DLL was interested only in lobbying in the state legislature, an effort that required constant checks from Dr. Haynes. To make U'Ren's task a little easier, Haynes directed him to work for the initiative exclusively; the referendum and more controversial recall could be obtained later.[17]

The 1909 legislature was not as effective as the reformers hoped, but was considered a vast improvement over that of 1907. At the outset of this session Haynes, E. T. Earl, and Rudolph Spreckels, of San Francisco, financed the People's Lobby, operated by George Baker Anderson. The lobby monitored votes of the legislators and distributed the data to newspapers throughout the state in order to identify and publicize both reform and machine lawmakers. As usual, Haynes's initiative bill was defeated, but a law was passed that established a limited direct primary by eliminating party conventions. With this device the reformers hoped to restrict SP power in selecting Republican nominees for state offices in 1910.[18]

Toward the end of 1909, the Lincoln-Roosevelt leaders began organizing for the next state election. For all their pretentions to inject more democracy in politics, the insurgents very carefully handpicked their gubernatorial representative for the primary. Hiram W. Johnson, son of a longtime SP leader in the legislature, had established a reputation as a crusader for justice when he assumed the duties of prosecutor in the San Francisco graft trials in late 1908. Johnson also was aided by the SP leadership's indecisiveness in its maiden voyage with the direct primary. Czar Herrin hesitated until four SP-oriented officials entered the race. Johnson won the primary and shifted his attack to the Democratic winner, Theodore A. Bell. Though Bell had opposed the SP for years, Herrin backed him as the lesser of two reform evils. Conducting a single-issue campaign to kick the SP out of California politics, Johnson defeated Bell, and the Lincoln-Roosevelt League swept into office.[19]

Dr. Haynes played little part in the election. In late March he inquired whether or not Johnson, as a gubernatorial candidate, supported direct legislation. Johnson replied that he favored the initiative, referendum, and recall, so Haynes promised to publicize this support in DLL literature. It is most likely that he contributed to Johnson's candidacy, though he would do little active campaign work. In mid-May the doctor departed with Dora Haynes and Mr. and Mrs. Joseph F. Sartori on another voyage to Europe—a "vacation," although he planned to study mining safety and social conditions there. He arrived home in early November, just after Johnson's victory.[20]

Although Hiram Johnson campaigned almost exclusively on the single issue of Southern Pacific domination of California politics, there were other planks in the Lincoln-Roosevelt platform. When Johnson and the recently elected league lawmakers invaded the state capitol, these issues received immediate attention. The 1911 session of the legislature witnessed the passage of a number of reforms dear to the hearts of John Haynes and the league leaders. State constitutional amendments establishing direct legislation (including the recall), women's suffrage, workmen's compensation, regulation of railroads and public utilities, a state civil service system, and other important reforms were passed and presented to the voters for approval in a special election on October 10. All but 1 of 23 amendments passed handily. Other laws, which did not require a state constitutional amendment, included the eight-hour day for women and moral reform laws to close racetracks and establish local-option ordinances regarding the issuance of saloon licenses.[21]

The insurgent program was not far-reaching enough for Dr. Haynes, but since it moved in his direction, he participated whenever possible. He was especially active in the campaign for direct-legislation amendments.

Upon his return to Los Angeles after the 1910 election, he was appointed by the Republican State Central Committee to its Committee on Direct Legislation, which was assigned to draft amendments and devise a strategy to pass them. The original versions were composed by George Dunlop, a businessman and former mayor of Hollywood who had served as secretary of Haynes's original Direct Legislation League. The drafts were reviewed by Milton U'Ren, secretary of the DLL, and other members, and discussed with the committee chairman, Senator Lee Gates, and Governor Johnson. Gates introduced the bill in the state senate, and Johnson was instrumental in convincing recalcitrant reform legislators that the Lincoln-Roosevelt platform bound them to vote for it. With an insurgent majority in the legislature, the amendments were approved and signed by Governor Johnson.[22]

Since the direct-legislation measures were state constitutional amendments, they required approval by the electorate (appropriately enough, a form of referendum). Haynes's DLL began planning the campaign for ratification in the summer. Funds were raised (mostly from Dr. Haynes's checkbook), direct-legislation advocate Judson King was hired to run the league's publicity bureau, and literature was mailed to all points in the state. Noted speakers, including San Francisco graft prosecutor Francis Heney, Congressman William D. Stephens, and Governor Johnson, delivered speeches in support of these and other progressive amendments slated for the October 10 ballot. Haynes spoke in favor of the proposals at gatherings and debates throughout Southern California. His appearance on the cover of the September 9 issue of the state progressive organ, *California Outlook*, promoting his role in the "people's rule" amendment crusade, testified to his leadership in the campaign. Accompanied by Heney, the doctor began a "thirty-days' automobile tour of the State (using his own machine)" to stump personally for direct legislation in the month before the election.[23]

The initiative and referendum encountered little opposition in the legislature and on the campaign trail. The recall was another matter, since it included the removal of judges. Even progressives such as U.S. senator John D. Works, a former California chief justice who approved of the initiative and referendum, opposed the recall of judges as an affront to the theory of separation of governmental powers. Haynes argued most effectively that judges were not incorruptible, that powerful judges could undo the reform work of the legislature, and that many California judges owed their appointments or election to the SP, using Walter Parker's manipulation of the 1906 Republican state convention as an example.

"Why recall a Governor or other State official who is a drunkard, a knave or a fool, and not a judge who is equally culpable?" Haynes asked.[24]

As George Mowry has observed, the argument in favor of the recall of judges appealed to an electorate disenchanted with its judiciary. The controversial recall amendment was approved by a larger majority than the initiative and referendum amendment. After almost a decade of biennial journeys to Sacramento, organizational work, and a continuous drain on his wallet, Haynes finally witnessed the placement of direct legislation in the state constitution. This victory alone proved his association with Hiram Johnson and the California progressives to be a mutually beneficial marriage of partners with varying political convictions. The success of this decade-long quest earned him his most prized title, bestowed by national political observer George Creel: "father of the Initiative, Referendum, and Recall."[25]

Another state constitutional amendment considered on October 10 was that inaugurating women's suffrage. Haynes had always been in favor and hoped it could be achieved by means of a statewide initiative petition, which he suggested when trying to obtain assistance from suffragists for direct legislation. But his wife, Dora Haynes, was the family activist in this movement. Though she appears not to have been a leading member of any suffrage organization in Los Angeles or the state through the 1890s, Dora did engage in Friday Morning Club activities related to suffrage and probably belonged to the local Suffrage Club, formed in 1900. At any rate, she was considered to be one of the city's prominent suffragists by 1909.[26]

In the first decade of the century the state's women's suffrage advocates labored to educate the public to the injustice of withholding the franchise on the basis of gender. They challenged entrenched attitudes of both men and women who believed a woman's place was with her family, not in the sometimes seedy world of politics. Liquor and vice interests worked diligently to reinforce these age-old notions. It was a group of men, however, that sparked the final drive to success. Led by Pasadena businessman John Braly, a group of about 25 men, including Haynes and E. T. Earl, created the Political Equality League of Southern California in April 1910. At the first meeting Haynes and others made impassioned speeches and all agreed to use their influence to popularize the idea and agitate for its adoption.[27]

Almost immediately it was decided that the PEL should include women. By the time the Hayneses returned from their European trip in

November, Dora had been elected PEL treasurer and John was on the board of governors. Meanwhile, other members strove to include women's suffrage in the Republican state platform, and victorious insurgent legislators were reminded that they were bound to that position. In the 1911 session a women's suffrage state constitutional amendment was approved and placed on the October ballot with the other progressive measures.[28]

In the campaign, John devoted most of his attention to direct legislation, while Dora concentrated on the suffrage law. In Southern California, suffragists faced organized opposition from the *Los Angeles Times* and many influential men and women. Less than enthusiastic support by Governor Johnson and Marshall Stimson, who personally opposed the women's vote, did not help matters. But strong newspaper backing from Earl's *Tribune* and *Express*, the *Herald*, and other papers, and effective speaking engagements and publicity releases by Dora and her colleagues helped to sway Southern California voters. Though heavily defeated in the San Francisco Bay Area, the amendment carried in the south and rural areas of the state, and thus squeaked through by a few thousand votes. For Dora, John, and the suffrage advocates, this was a major victory in the larger struggle for the national franchise.[29]

The October election also validated the progressive legislators' bills establishing a state civil service system, facilitating municipal ownership in California cities, and regulating railroads and public utilities, among others. Haynes supported all of these measures, which were offered as constitutional amendments, besides a number of other laws passed in the 1911 legislative session. These included a stronger direct-primary system, the short ballot, and laws related to the conservation of natural resources. Of special importance to the doctor were bills protecting the rights of labor and a local-option law allowing county governmental units to restrict saloon licenses, a first step toward prohibition of alcoholic beverages.

Haynes had worked closely with labor leaders at the local level for over a decade to bring about reforms such as direct legislation and public ownership. With the progressives in office, he joined the drive to defend and extend the rights of working people, a drive that resulted in the passage of numerous pro-labor proposals in 1911. The most noteworthy were the eight-hour day for women and a constitutional amendment establishing workmen's compensation. Haynes supported the latter in the amendment election, though he concentrated on direct legislation while labor leaders championed the "employer's liability" law.[30]

Haynes's most active support for labor became conspicuous just after 1911. As one of the few Southern California progressives who consistently defended labor, the doctor was one of the area's major labor advocates from the ranks of the upper class. In 1911, he embarked on a decades-long campaign to improve working conditions in mines throughout the nation. The following year Governor Johnson appointed him a special state commissioner to investigate mining safety in the United States. During the Johnson administration Haynes worked with state industrial welfare commissioner Katherine Philips Edson to protect the workmen's compensation law and to establish a statewide minimum wage. In speeches and articles he argued for federal protection of the health of workers, more extensive employer-liability laws, and safety features to curb industrial accidents.[31]

Haynes was particularly concerned with lengthy workdays, which contributed to poor health, accidents resulting from fatigue, and an unjust ratio of leisure time between workers and the idle rich. He "kept the wires hot" in flooding Governor Johnson and legislators with information in support of the women's eight-hour day. Soon after the measure was approved, Haynes and others began agitating for the universal eight-hour day, proposed in the state assembly in 1913. Killed in committee, the measure was advanced by Socialists as a state initiative but defeated in 1914. The drive for a shorter working day would rise again after President Wilson signed into law the eight-hour day for railroad workers in 1916.[32]

In defending labor at this time, Haynes also contributed to the cause of strikers, both financially and vocally. In an address to the Los Angeles Women's City Club in 1914, he indicted John D. Rockefeller and the entire American industrial system in describing the massacre of miners' families by the state militia in Ludlow, Colorado. As might be expected, he offended business-oriented individuals with such rhetoric, as well as the most conservative progressives, who had little interest in protecting workers after 1911. His limited efforts to advance the cause of labor unions and workers did not wane over the years, even as progressivism did.[33]

Another law passed by the 1911 state legislature established local option. Despite this one success, and though many California progressives yearned for prohibition much more than for labor laws, the former fared nowhere near as well as the latter in 1911. In spite of the growth of the active Anti-Saloon League after 1898, little was accomplished at the state level. In 1907, liquor interests, supported by legislators primarily from the San Francisco Bay Area and wine country, defeated even the most basic of prohibition-related measures—regulation of saloon licenses by local government. But in the southern and rural portions of the state, prohibition sentiment voiced by civic leaders, clergymen, and even Socialist party figures became more prevalent.[34]

Most progressives were in favor of some degree of prohibition for a variety of reasons. Some considered alcohol consumption morally wrong; others were concerned with the consequences for the families of drinkers: economic deprivation and familial violence. Almost all progressives shared an aversion to the saloon, often the political headquarters of the working class, where machine voters were instructed and rewarded. Even "wet" progressives such as Franklin Hichborn supported the Anti-Saloon League as a means of limiting this institution. When reform legislators began their work in the 1911 session, there was considerable sentiment for some sort of prohibition law. Because of opposition from minority machine Republicans, Democrats, and even a few wet progressives from northern California, the only successful bill was a local-option law based on county supervisorial districts.[35]

Concentrating on other issues, Dr. Haynes took no part in the prohibition discussion in the legislature at this time. Like most progressives in Southern California, he favored limits on the availability of liquor. As a physician he frowned on the use of alcohol for medicinal purposes; as a social reformer he abhorred the devastation wrought by alcoholism on poor families; and as a political reformer he hoped to abolish the influence of saloons, bastions of antireform sentiment. Disturbed by his father's occasional overindulgence and the distressing reaction of his mother, Haynes participated in a number of temperance-related activities before becoming a major figure in the state's Anti-Saloon League in the 1920s. Earlier he worked with league officers in lobbying for the state initiative as a means of eradicating saloons, and twice was a principal in the movement to establish the Gothenburg plan of limiting and regulating saloons in Los Angeles. Though this plan was only a halfway measure, Haynes thought it "better than nothing." By the 1910s, he had moved beyond temperance and embraced prohibition by supporting statewide dry initiatives, speaking in favor of state and national prohibition, and otherwise lobbying to advance the cause.[36]

Despite what his public announcements lead one to expect, Haynes personally was more a temperance advocate than a prohibitionist. Though he did not consume hard liquor or beer, he was fond of good wine. According to a local publication, he "is a pronounced enemy of alcohol and will warn his patients that it is poison to their systems; nevertheless, the same evening, he may urge them to try a special vintage at his own table." He was noted for having a plentiful supply of fine wines located in a basement closet until the dawn of Prohibition. And in 1912, when confronted by a Women's Christian Temperance Union protest against the serving of wine at a National Municipal League banquet planned by Dora Haynes, the two decided to let the grape elixir flow for the banqueters.[37]

The doctor's pre-1919 stand on drinking revealed a deep-seated paternalism that dovetailed with his drive for social reform. A temperate wine drinker, he opposed alcohol consumption because it was unhealthy and made living conditions much worse for the poor, blocking their chances for economic and moral uplift. He smoked cigarettes but warned others of the dangers of what he called an "expensive, foolish and what is worse a deleterious habit," and he publicly opposed smoking on streetcars. Though he himself made an occasional bet, he opposed racetrack gambling "or any other gambling scheme that might be devised" because it was "inherently wrong," seemed always to be associated with crime, and bled the meager resources of the poor. This strain of elitist paternalism certainly was not uncommon among wealthy social reformers who expected the objects of their benevolence to conform to strict personal standards as a price for social salvation.[38]

The ever-increasing reform momentum, heightened by the 1911 legislative session and state constitutional amendment election spurred the California Republican insurgents to set their sights higher. Late in the year state progressive leaders, like their counterparts across the nation, began devising strategy to elect a Republican president who would champion their goals. Disappointed with President Taft's conservatism and close relationship with corporation leaders, progressives hoped to organize support for their hero, Theodore Roosevelt, whose previous terms had captured the imagination and reform spirit of the insurgents. By expressing displeasure in his handpicked successor, Roosevelt supplied the reformers with both legitimacy for their revolt from the regular Republican establishment and a candidate for 1912. TR initially refused to run, however, so the logical choice became Robert La Follette, whose progressive credentials while governor of Wisconsin and U.S. senator were impeccable. By November 1911, La Follette was a major contender for the insurgent-Republican nomination and the favorite of California leaders, including the now-Republican John Haynes.[39]

This situation changed in early 1912. Roosevelt suddenly decided to enter the contest, much to the delight of most Golden State progressives, who preferred him to La Follette. At the same time the Wisconsin senator fell ill, giving his supporters a convenient opportunity to switch to TR. Almost immediately, E. T. Earl launched his own crusade to obtain the nominations of TR and Governor Johnson for the 1912 Republican ticket. This "Hands Across the Continent" campaign appealed to most California progressives, who, like Haynes, joined the crusade with speeches and donations. Labeling President Taft a "weak, vacillating tool of special privilege," Haynes called for California progressives of both parties to concentrate on the nominations of TR and Woodrow Wilson and then join all insurgents in forming a new Progressive party. The physician was selected as an alternate delegate to the Republican national convention, and witnessed the Taft convention managers blocking the insurgent drive to nominate TR. Along with the other disgusted California delegates, Haynes joined Hiram Johnson in storming out of the convention hall in Chicago and was present when Johnson and other insurgents from across the nation formed the Progressive party the next night. Haynes was not a delegate at the Bull Moose convention that nominated TR and Johnson, but he was active in the presidential campaign. His candidate finished ahead of the regular Republican ticket but lost to the Democrats. Fortunately, as Haynes later believed, Democrat Woodrow Wilson was also a committed progressive.[40]

Historians generally have come to interpret "progressivism" as the conservative effort of a middle-class elite to modernize nineteenth-century institutions in the interest of preserving a capitalist economy. Hindsight lends some credence to this perspective: national and California progressive leaders advanced reform programs intended to ameliorate some of the most pronounced inequities of the economic system as a means of protecting it from attacks by Socialists and corporate monopolists. This view, however, ignores the left wing of the progressive coalition. A small but important group of reformers whose ideologies bordered on socialism, they pushed other progressives into accepting varying degrees of social improvement. California progressive William Kent thus interpreted his faction and socialism as "only two different phases of the same tendency," while another, Rudolph Spreckels, had no qualms about cooperating with Socialists if the situation required. These and other left-wing progressives nudged their more conservative allies to construct election platforms that almost mirrored those of the Socialist party; in fact, in sections of San Francisco, Socialists and progressives received votes from the same constituency in consecutive elections.[41]

John Haynes became recognized as the leading figure of the left wing of California progressivism. Though he delayed joining this movement, which he initially interpreted as simply a revolt against railroad politics, he gradually saw in its electoral success the opportunity to advance social reform from within the state and national governments. The Progressive party, he believed, would attract the left and moderates of both national parties and realign the old structure into progressive and conservative divisions. A quarter of a century later he would still be optimistic that this separation would come about.[42]

Haynes did not modify his belief, expressed in a well-publicized essay in 1913, that "the principles of Socialism will ultimately—in fact, I may say in the not distant future—be incorporated into the systems of government of all civilized nations." But the electoral success of California progressivism and the potential of the national Progressive party convinced him that progressivism could be a vehicle for advancing far-reaching social reform. It also had a much better chance of succeeding than the Socialist party. He believed, very optimistically, in "the Socialistic nature of the platform of the Progressive Party" of 1912, and thought it could become a blueprint for gradual reform in America. In a speech to the Women's Progressive League in May of that year, Haynes advised: "If our watchword is to be ultimate principles with present defeat, then our votes should go to the Socialist Party; if, however, we seek practical, tangible results now, we should vote for Roosevelt."[43]

In his quest for social reform, "practical" was Haynes's byword. Never a radical, he was a pragmatist, an opportunist in settling for reform increments along the path to a democratic utopia of equal opportunity and collective ownership of the means of production. Always "willing to accept a quarter of a loaf if I cannot get half and half if I cannot get a whole," he thought that he and other left-wing progressives could push the movement toward evolutionary socialism. He embraced it because it offered immediate, albeit limited, success. If there was such a specimen as a typical California progressive, it did not resemble Dr. Haynes. Straddling the nebulous border between the Socialist party and most progressives, he cooperated with both camps, acting as a bridge between the two to push a successful moderate movement toward the goals of the left. Considered a radical by the more conservative progressives, and a com-

promiser by Socialists, he was compelled by his pragmatism to collabo-
rate with the progressives to protect reforms already won and to advance
those yet secured.[44]

In the early years of the California progressive administration, Haynes
played only a limited role. After the 1911 election for state constitutional
amendments, in which he worked with Governor Johnson in campaigning especially for direct legislation, Haynes made few suggestions for
state appointments. Meyer Lissner, the governor's chief political adviser
in Southern California, conferred with the doctor, so Haynes only occasionally advised Johnson on matters relating to specific bills, policies,
and appointments.[45]

Over time, the governor and the physician became good friends, establishing a personal and political association that stretched into the 1930s.
The two occasionally disagreed, but Haynes believed Johnson to be courageous and effective during his tenure as governor. Haynes vocally and
financially supported Johnson in his 1914 reelection bid and 1916 campaign for the U.S. Senate. In the former year the doctor also defended the
governor from a personal attack in a national magazine. "He thinks
right, acts right, and fights right," Haynes claimed. In early 1916, he
advised Johnson to run for the Senate, "a better stepping stone than the
vice-presidency for the position which I would like to see you ultimately
occupy." And at the end of that year Haynes congratulated "the man of
destiny in the history soon to be making," encouraging the new senator
to run for president in 1920. Until Johnson's departure for Washington,
D.C., in 1917, Haynes was more than satisfied with the governor's political performance.[46]

Johnson appreciated the doctor's praise, advice, and campaign support
and hoped to appoint him to a position in state government to take advantage of Haynes's medical and political expertise. In late 1911, Haynes
was considered as a replacement for Walter Lindley on the board of the
Whittier State School, but several influential progressives persuaded
Meyer Lissner to recommend another Southern California candidate. In
January 1912, Johnson asked Lissner about appointing Haynes to a vacancy on the State Board of Charities and Corrections. After consulting
local intimates, Lissner replied that "we all agree" it would be a good
appointment; in April the governor made it official.[47]

In his eleven years as a member of the Charities and Corrections Board,
Haynes pursued his interests in prison reform and the state's care for its
dependents. His responsibilities entailed oversight of state prisons, refor-

matories, county jails, and homes for wayward girls. By 1913, he had also joined the executive board of the National Committee on Prison Reform, which searched for positive methods to allow prisons to pay their way without competing with private business. He inspected San Quentin and other correctional facilities to monitor progress on living conditions and made recommendations for improvement. These included the design of penal buildings to allow more sunshine and fresh air, and locating prisons on farms, away from "the urban environment of material possession which encourages theft" ("urbanitis," as he called it). As president of the California Prison Society during World War I, he recommended that some inmates—"victims of social or economic environment"—be allowed to fight as soldiers in Europe.[48]

His duties also included inspections of state and county hospitals, insane asylums, welfare departments, and almshouses. For these agencies he recommended, among other things, improvements in interior furnishings of buildings, patient care, sanitation, and procedures for state licensing of private institutions. In this capacity he came face to face with the state's insane and feebleminded population and searched for scientific methods to limit the propagation of such "abnormal individuals."[49]

Besides advising Governor Johnson and serving on the Charities and Corrections Board, Haynes worked with other California progressives to advance the insurgent program. He continued to monitor the legislature's proceedings, lobbying lawmakers and testifying in official state proceedings. In some cases he even helped to write "progressive" legislation, as in 1915, when he drafted a bill to regulate vivisection in medical schools.[50]

Protection of the state's new direct-legislation laws was one of his major concerns. Immediately after passage of the initiative law, a number of abuses of the initiative surfaced, which spurred antireform newspapers and spokesmen to call for its repeal. Even progressives such as Governor Johnson wished to modify the law by requiring more signatures and demanding that citizens sign the petitions in the offices of county clerks to prevent massive forgeries. Haynes admitted that a few abuses had cropped up, but argued against any but the most minor adjustments to the law since the abuses were illegal or just technical errors. Forgeries, misrepresentations by petition circulators, and use of the measures by "selfish and corrupt interests" could be remedied by more severe penalties, better enforcement, the addition to the petitions of a short synopsis of the proposal written by a neutral party, and a provision to ensure that voters received a handbook explaining the ballot measures at least 30 days before the election. More extreme suggestions—to prohibit payment to circulators, increase the percentage of needed signatures, and require that petitions be signed in offices of registering officials—would only aid special interests and render direct legislation useless for the average citizen, he warned.[51]

The recall law also posed major problems. In 1914, the device was used by former state senator Eddie Wolfe, a San Franciscan aligned with the old SP machine, to recall the progressive who defeated him in 1912. Wolfe won the special election and returned to Sacramento, alarming Governor Johnson and other progressives who feared future uses of the recall by the politicians it was intended to suppress. When a progressive introduced a bill in the senate to modify the recall, Haynes became irate, threatening to go on a "public rampage" to defeat it. When instructing Edward A. Dickson to lobby against the measure, Haynes warned the reporter not to let Johnson see the letter, explaining: "He'd snap that bulldog jaw of his and tell you to tell Haynes 'to go to hell' and we want to accomplish our end in an amiable and friendly manner." With Dickson's help and a written appeal to progressive senators, Haynes managed to sidetrack the bill into oblivion.[52]

The attacks on direct legislation by progressive legislators were indicative of the decline of progressive reform in California after 1913. Most of the 1910 Lincoln-Roosevelt platform had been fulfilled in 1911, and after the defeat of the Bull Moosers in 1912, reform efforts in California tapered off. During the 1913 legislative session a few social welfare commissions were established to aid workers, women, and immigrants. But the lawmakers spent as much time debating morality issues such as prohibition, gambling, prizefights, and prostitution, and passing an Alien Land Act restricting land ownership by Japanese nationals. This legislation, motivated by moralistic and racial values, demonstrated the more restrictive edge of reform, which overshadowed social-justice concerns by this time.[53]

Dr. Haynes hoped this trend would end and did what he could to reverse it. He warned his "Fellow Progressives" in 1914 that the old guard was creeping back into power in Los Angeles County and that it must be stopped throughout the state if the infant California Progressive party was to endure. The object of this attack, District Attorney John Fredericks, was the GOP candidate for governor that year and former associate of Walter Parker. So, Haynes contributed heavily to Hiram Johnson's reelection bid and the campaign of other progressives in order to stop the favorite of the *Los Angeles Times* and other antireform interests.

Johnson and a progressive majority won, but reform was not resurrected. The 1915 legislature, judged to be "stupid but honest" by one
progressive analyst, was even more ineffective than that of 1913. By this
time a substantial portion of progressivism's original upper- and middle-
class base had deserted it. That support was replaced by working-class
votes (especially in the case of Governor Johnson), but only when labor's
interests coincided with those of the progressives.[54]

Despite the receding of the state reform tide, Haynes remained optimistic. He believed that on the national level, President Woodrow Wilson
was proving to be as much of a progressive as TR. The doctor had written frequently to the White House concerning various issues, and on
most occasions agreed with Wilson's actions. In 1916, Haynes joined a
number of California progressives in supporting Wilson's reelection bid
in opposition to Republican Charles Evans Hughes. As treasurer of the
state's Woodrow Wilson Independence League, Haynes raised funds outside the Democratic party for its nominee. Speaking in support of the
president, Haynes praised Wilson's foreign and domestic policies and
leadership in the fight for a federal Labor Department, income and inheritance taxes, and other reforms. Conversely, Haynes opposed the "reactionary, negative, and critical" Hughes, whose term as New York governor proved that his "sympathies lie with the financially privileged." [55]

Wilson won the close national election with a surprising plurality in
California. This edge had been attributed to a lack of support by progressives who had returned to the Republican party but felt little enthusiasm for its nominee. The election campaign period appeared to reveal
a serious rift between these leaders and the Wilson independents like
Haynes who refused to back Hughes early on. But since both groups
deserted Hughes in fact or in spirit, the split was only a minor step backward for progressive unity.[56]

In the state election that year Haynes again supported Hiram Johnson
in his bid for a U.S. Senate seat. As vice president of the state Johnson-
For-Senator Club, Haynes contributed to the governor's finances and
worked with Meyer Lissner in running the campaign. Dora Haynes
served on the campaign committee of the Women's Johnson-For-Senator
Club. In publicly supporting a Republican senator and a Democrat for
president, John once again demonstrated that party labels meant little
to him in choosing the best candidate, a trait for which the California
progressives became known. Johnson probably did not need much of
Haynes's assistance in this campaign, however, for he won easily.[57]

The victories of Wilson and Johnson gave Haynes renewed hope that progressivism would again become the driving force for change in the United States. Writing just after the election, Haynes congratulated Johnson and, in no uncertain terms, expressed his confidence in Johnson's ability to "assume the leadership of the Militant Progressives of the Nation" in modernizing America. This process, according to Haynes, should include the organization of the "energies of our scientists, of our physicists, chemists, mechanists, into armies of research" to solve the problem of food synthesis from inanimate sources and increase the nation's food supply; the conservation of resources, especially water, to reclaim land for food production and to prevent floods; the development of hydroelectric power from that water; the modernization of railroads and street transportation; the organization and integration of the nation's factories; and the advancement of education. This "integration of America" should be followed by the integration of the world to rally all nations to "fight hunger and disease and ignorance and superstition." [58]

Believing that "nothing must be allowed to defy the people's will" in bringing about this change, Haynes demanded: "If the constitution interferes with the accomplishment of these tasks, it must be changed. If legislative bodies are inefficient or oppose [sic] obstacles, they must be reformed as radically as may be necessary. If courts interpose their power to defy the popular will, they must be compelled to bow to the people's desires." And Hiram Johnson, as senator and surely future U.S. president, was the man Haynes hoped would lead the nation in conquering world starvation and increasing opportunity for all socioeconomic classes. [59]

Haynes's optimism reflected both his own advanced thinking for organizing America and his misconception of Johnson as a statesman and reformer. Johnson had little interest in spearheading a far-reaching planned economy, especially as a freshman senator. America's war effort became his first priority.

Hiram Johnson's departure to Washington, D.C., contributed heavily to the decline of the initial phase of California progressivism. His absence left the insurgents without the movement's figurehead, whose personal popularity helped carry other progressive candidates. Another cause of the decline was the combination of personality clashes that fragmented insurgent leadership. The growing opposition of Lissner, Stimson, and Russ Avery to E. T. Earl's handling of reform affairs in Los Angeles, the split between an insecure Johnson and more-leftist reformers Fremont Older, Francis Heney, and William Kent in the north, and the distrust Johnson and his circle shared for Southern Californians he deemed too conservative and power-hungry destroyed the early unity so essential to establishing a political consensus. And with its original program completed and the World War assuming a higher priority, progressivism lost its initial relevance and fervor. By the beginning of 1917, the movement was mired in stagnation, even though its leaders occupied strategic positions in state offices and the dominant Republican party. Haynes did not lose hope for the resurgence of California progressivism, but many state progressives did.[60]

Conservatives claimed that the first wave of California progressivism went too far, while radicals charged that it did not go far enough. Considering its nature and goals, a major historian of the movement, Spencer Olin, Jr., has concluded that at least the social welfare program of the California Progressives was "an impressive effort, for its day and within its assumptions, to improve the living conditions and to increase the wages of urban and rural workers as well as to assimilate selected immigrants into American society." In protecting the framework of the American capitalist system, the movement sought to improve the stature of various groups in its coalition, as well as the unfortunates who required varying degrees of protection and social services. As a progressive, John Haynes was pleased with the success of the movement, though he personally wished it would move much further. For this opportunist, the limited but sure victories justified his partnership with the state progressives to advance important items of his own social reform agenda.[61]

Chapter 8

"The Rise and Fall of Goo-Goo"

In the decade before America's entry into World War I, John Haynes was deeply involved in the state progressive campaign to reshape California government. At the same time he was active with local urban reformers who worked to modernize city government and restructure the framework of political power in Los Angeles. Haynes was much more influential at the municipal and county levels than in state affairs, and he loomed as a major figure in local politics.

The progressives' overhaul of Los Angeles developed slowly. In the months following Arthur Harper's resignation, Mayor George Alexander and his advisers encountered numerous obstacles to reforming city government. Many of Harper's holdover commissioners refused to resign, and progressive leaders were reluctant to fill such positions of departmental oversight and policy-making. The new police commission began cracking down on liquor license violators and vice operations, raising protests from those who had warned that reformers really wanted to impose their puritanical morality on all city residents. While Alexander tried to strengthen the regulation of public utilities and depoliticize the civil service board, he failed to obtain support for his efforts from the city council.[1]

The period from late March through early November 1909, as the *Times* claimed, was a time of preparation for the coming municipal election. Under the direction of Meyer Lissner, "Goo-Goos"—as Otis's paper derisively called the reformists, playing on "good government," their pet cause—built their own machine by strengthening the Good Government Organization as a strategy and fund-raising body, electing Dr. Haynes and other prominent figures to the executive board. City commissioners appointed by Alexander filled patronage positions in opposition to the old Southern Pacific machine, and helped to expand the reform coalition. In token gestures Alexander even appointed representatives of organized labor and the *Times*, though he did not receive the endorsement of either.[2]

In the November primary election Alexander could not collect enough votes to escape a runoff. With party conventions for city offices prohibited by the progressive amendments to the city charter passed in February 1909, the Democrats did not nominate a candidate. The regular Republicans, however, called for a convention and chose Councilman George Smith as their standard-bearer, while several other Republicans ran for mayor independently. Without the management and resources of Walter F. X. Parker, who missed this election because of ill health (he was dying of Bright's disease), Smith fared poorly but placed second to face Alexander in the December runoff.[3]

"Next Tuesday, December 7th, a pleasant, little, home-like revolution is scheduled to come off in Los Angeles," predicted the editor of the *Pacific Outlook*. "Revolution" certainly was too strong a word, but Los Angeles voters chose to give reform a try. A GGO mayor, city council majority, and other city officers were swept into city hall.[4]

Dr. Haynes had contributed to the reform cause by donating money, loaning his automobile to transport voters to the polls, and speaking in favor of Alexander. Thus, he participated in the final defeat of the old SP political apparatus. Just after the election Haynes boasted in the official progressive organ:

> The victory of the friends of good government last Tuesday means much more than the release of our city from the long wasteful, debauching and demoralizing misrule of the political machine; more than placing in office honest and capable men; more than the saving of millions of dollars in the city's expenditures; more than the introduction of a genuinely businesslike government—it means something far greater than all these combined:—it proves that a majority of the people can be trusted to choose right rather than wrong—that democracy is magnificently triumphant.

With direct legislation, the direct primary, and "a civil service provision second to none," Haynes wrote, "the people have absolute power and, therefore, sole responsibility. They have done well; but let them see to it that they do not take their hands from the plough and look backwards."[5]

The progressive administration did not represent all of "the people" or only the aspirations of the upper-middle-class elite. Reformers made little attempt to include ethnic groups or working-class representatives in their coalition; in fact, the progressive city council soon passed an antipicketing ordinance that crystallized labor's opposition to the progressives in 1911 and 1913. On the other hand, the administration made significant gains in the area of municipal ownership and utility regulation when it created the Board of Public Service to operate its own water and power system and the Board of Public Utilities to regulate rates and operation of private utilities. During Alexander's first term a number of new police and fire stations and city parks were established, bond issues for power and harbor facilities were approved, and a movement was begun to streamline bureaucratic procedures.[6]

John Haynes generally agreed with the Alexander administration's policy decisions of limited reform, except in such cases as the antipicketing law. Dominated by Meyer Lissner and the structuralist reformers, the administration expanded some city services and moved further in the direction of public ownership. But to Haynes and other advocates of social reform, the city was not moving far or fast enough in providing more basic assistance for the underprivileged: adequate housing, improved sanitation facilities, antipoverty programs, and enhanced opportunities to earn fair wages. The social reformers pressured Alexander and the city council to adopt these proposals while the structuralists resisted in order to hold the support of a portion of the business community within the progressive fold.[7]

The structuralists printed a glowing tribute to Dr. Haynes immediately after the 1909 election. Playing down his socialist proclivities, *Pacific Outlook* editor C. D. Willard touted the doctor as the city's chief prophet of democracy. Willard recounted Haynes's work for direct legislation, streetcar fenders, and his favorite progressive structural reforms—"the direct primary, the non-partisan ballot, the council-at-large, the utilities commission law—all these had the guidance and help of the Doctor's hand." Haynes's social-reform objectives, however, were not a high priority for the administration, so he worked from outside city government to advance a few of them.[8]

In these years Haynes became involved in several new voluntary organizations to further political and social reform in Los Angeles. Even before the 1909 municipal election he helped establish a local chapter of the League of Justice, a national organization devoted to improving police procedures. Haynes served on the league executive board and made numerous donations to fund its operations.[9]

In 1912, Haynes and other wealthy humanitarians responded to the pleas of the city housing commission by creating the Municipal Housing

Association. Formed on the "basis of business philanthropy," this company tried to attract investors who could turn a profit of up to 6 percent while financing the construction of low-cost housing to replace slums. As founder, Haynes solicited numerous membership pledges, but a severe drop in the real estate market soon ended this venture. Also in 1912, Haynes launched programs to combat loan sharks throughout Los Angeles and saloon influence in city politics. He attempted to establish a pawnshop company to make temporary loans at 1 percent interest, but found few backers. In another attempt to establish the Gothenburg System of regulating city saloons, the doctor and friend B. R. Baumgardt convinced the police commission to ban the free lunches that were served in saloons to encourage drinking. The city council passed an ordinance prohibiting this practice, but the law was later nullified by referendum.[10]

Haynes was also interested in public health. As a member of the state's Charities and Corrections Board, he inspected sanitary conditions in local government facilities and lobbied for improvements. In 1915, he helped to found the Los Angeles Milk Fund, which supplied fresh milk to infants of the poor. This voluntary group of city health employees maintained milk stations financed by private contributions.[11]

Within the city administration, Haynes again served on the civil service board from his reappointment in December 1909 until his retirement in early 1915. Even though he worked for a reformed government, he again was pressured by "great influences" to "exempt or favor certain applicants." After Mayor Alexander's retirement in early 1913, Haynes's relationship with the city's new chief executive provoked the latter to search for ways to remove the old reformer. The mayor no doubt was surprised when Haynes announced that he would resign in early 1915. By that time he was too busy to serve on the board, but he continued to monitor board proceedings and made suggestions to the city council regarding department policy. As president of the Southern California Civil Service Reform League in 1917, he kept up with developments in this area within and outside Los Angeles County, while also serving on the council of the National Civil Service Reform League. Though not as dominant an interest for Haynes as direct legislation or public ownership, civil service reform was dear enough to him that he felt obliged to protect it at the local, state, and national level.[12]

While the Alexander administration showed only modest interest in social reform, its program of limited political changes and reliance on Haynes's advice was enough to merit the doctor's support. The city government did not curry the favor of the more conservative business community and regular Republican establishment, which opposed almost any reform. On the left, the progressives were opposed by the rising Socialist party, whose leaders saw little difference between the structuralist reformers and the class-conscious old guard formerly aligned with the SP. By 1911, the Socialists had joined a substantial portion of the city labor movement, which had been put off by the administration's reluctance to adopt social-reform measures and by the appointment of a *Times* reporter as police chief. After the administration's passage of an antipicketing ordinance in July 1910, both labor representatives in the administration resigned and union leaders forged an alliance with the Socialist party to contest the progressives.[13]

The Socialist-labor fusion coincided with the 1911 municipal election. In August the Socialist party and the Union Labor Political Club chose lawyer Job Harriman to run for mayor on the Socialist ticket. A former vice presidential and gubernatorial nominee and old friend of Dr. Haynes, Harriman was one party leader who consistently advocated collaboration with unionists to obtain immediate economic goals. David Shannon, historian of the American Socialist movement, concluded that Harriman was more a social-reform progressive than a true Marxist, except for his "occasional genuflection toward the cooperative commonwealth." In fact, the platform he pledged to implement was little more advanced than that of the social-reform progressives, calling for more municipal ownership, more city services and facilities, and other humanitarian objectives.[14]

Harriman's appeal to working-class voters was enhanced by his position as cocounsel for the McNamara brothers in one of the most notorious trials in Los Angeles history. After the dynamiting of the *Times* building in October 1910, Indiana labor leaders John B. and James B. McNamara were spirited to Los Angeles and charged with the murders of twenty workers who perished in the explosion and resulting fire. Defense of the two brothers against the antilabor newspaper and its allies became a national crusade for trade unionists, who retained Chicago attorney Clarence Darrow to lead the team of defense lawyers. As a cocounsel, Harriman was identified as a champion of the cause of organized labor, making the Socialist-labor fusion more palatable for unionists.[15]

The progressives approached the 1911 election without the unity manifested two years earlier. In 1910, Alexander and Meyer Lissner had disagreed over the staging of an advisory plebiscite to gauge approval for the city's operation of its own electricity distribution system. The dispute was well publicized, and the *Times* reported in December that a rumor was spreading to the effect that the "Lissnerites," Socialists, and union labor would forge an electoral coalition with Dr. Haynes as their mayoral nominee. But by early summer the Good Government Organization had regrouped and endorsed Alexander for reelection. The regular Republicans chose former city auditor W. C. Mushet, also endorsed by the *Examiner*.[16]

Haynes had a painful decision to make in the primary campaign. He sympathized with the Socialists and had known Harriman for many years and considered him "an honest, courageous and able man." On the other hand, he was on the executive board of the Good Government Organization, was an appointee of Alexander, and had some influence in administration policy-making. Reluctant to risk the loss of this power, he endorsed Alexander, whom the doctor believed to have done a good job as county supervisor and as mayor. But Haynes refrained from campaigning publicly for the mayor so as not to alienate Harriman and the city's Socialists.[17]

To the surprise of Haynes and most other Angelenos, Harriman won the primary, coming in only a thousand votes short of the number needed to avoid a runoff. Attacking the Alexander administration in general and E. T. Earl in particular, Harriman charged that the progressives were giving away city water to big business interests and had no intention of completing the Owens Valley aqueduct. Alexander, who had participated in the state campaign for women's suffrage the previous month, was not active in his own behalf. Standing on his record, with little assistance from the other reformers, he placed second. Mushet, representing the old guard, was a distant third.[18]

The results of this election were unlike any other for Los Angeles. The near victory of a Socialist in one of the nation's largest cities focused the attention of observers throughout the country on this cauldron of radicalism in the Southwest. Reaction to the primary vote in the city was swift—Harriman's opponents buried their differences and banded together to reelect Alexander. "It was very interesting to me to witness the zeal which the pocketbook class put into the campaign. They were thoroughly frightened and poured out money and volunteered for precinct work in large numbers," wrote reformer Marshall Stimson. "Boiled down, it was the town against the mob," thought Lissner, who immediately was drafted by his former editorial enemies from the *Times* and *Examiner* to save Los Angeles from the Socialists. "Of course the big interests are scared stiff," wrote Edward Dickson to Governor Johnson, as the Committee of One Hundred, composed of old-guard warriors and insurgents, assembled under Lissner's command. "A tremendous effort is needed to save us from the fate of San Francisco under Abe Ruef," C. D. Willard confided to Governor Johnson. These sentiments were bruited much more loudly and more widely in the *Times, Examiner,* and Earl's *Express* and *Tribune,* wherein predictions of the city's economic ruin appeared daily.[19]

Harriman, in the meantime, continued to campaign with increased momentum as his supporters sensed a victory in the December 5 general election. Four days before the runoff, however, the McNamara brothers confessed and changed their pleas to guilty as part of a deal with the prosecution and city leaders. This stunning news alienated some of Harriman's backers, who associated his campaign with defending organized labor. For those who tied his Socialist party to violence and murder, the revelation redoubled their efforts to defeat him. With the addition of the city's women, who cast their ballots for the first time, and many men who had neglected to vote in the primary, the Good Government ticket again was victorious.[20]

The temporary alliance of progressives and the old guard to counter a threat from the left quickly dissolved after the election. As conservatives reverted to criticizing reform, Mayor Alexander and his cohort initiated attempts to further both political and social reform. The former was most notably illustrated by the attempt to devise a new city charter incorporating the latest features of modern administrative theory. In this endeavor Dr. Haynes would play a pivotal role.

Haynes had had quite a bit of experience in revising the Los Angeles charter over the past decade. A central figure in the aborted freeholder deliberations in 1900, he was instrumental in the success of the major progressive changes of 1902 and 1909. In 1910, the city council appointed him to a charter revision committee that produced a few amendments strengthening direct legislation and municipal ownership, providing for the short ballot, and other reforms. Most of the amendments passed, but even the *Times* and Socialists complained that a new charter was needed.[21]

The progressives agreed. Soon after this election Lissner and Mayor Alexander requested $5,000 from the city council to pay expert consultants from the National Municipal League to help compose a new charter. The plan was part of a scheme for Los Angeles to host the annual meeting of the league in 1912, and it worked. In the following February, league secretary Clinton R. Woodruff announced that he was coming to

Los Angeles to organize the convention. In the same month the city council appointed a charter revision committee of fifteen to begin planning for the new charter. Haynes was selected chairman of the committee, which called for the election of a Board of Freeholders to frame the document. The board was elected on May 25, and at its first meeting he was elected president.[22]

The work of the freeholders began at the same time that details of the National Municipal League meeting were taking shape. Choosing progressives for various duties during the July meeting became a delicate matter because of personality and philosophical differences. One of the most important positions was that of presiding officer of the session on Friday, July 12, which entailed a general discussion of the proposed Los Angeles charter. Clinton Woodruff suggested Mayor Alexander, a conference host and chief executive of the host city. Lissner, growing cold to the mayor by this time, warned that Alexander "would only make exhibition of himself" and suggested five alternatives. Woodruff finally decided on the "dignified and effective" Haynes.[23]

The league conference lasted from July 8 through 12, and put the city on display for the nation's municipal experts and students. Daily sessions included papers on civil service law, the commission form of government, municipal finances, franchises, and direct legislation, the latter delivered by Haynes. The Friday session consisted of a critique of the proposed charter by noted experts. In addition, the participants were treated to a parade, entertainment, and excursions to local resorts. The conference was highlighted by a lavish banquet supervised by Dora Haynes. It was at this dinner that she faced the wrath of temperance advocates who, outraged by her decision to serve wine, protested that it was a "useless luxury."[24]

Upon completion of the conference, the freeholders resumed their work on the charter. It was generally agreed that the new document would stipulate the commission form of government, in which city government would consist of a number of department heads forming a legislative body with one of their number serving as mayor. There was much disagreement over the number of commissioners as well as details of other provisions, such as the elimination of most present boards, revamping of the civil service commission, and making the positions of city attorney and clerk appointive rather than elective. The final document consolidated municipal functions in seven city departments and fixed responsibility, while retaining progressive features such as nonpartisanship, municipal ownership, and direct legislation.[25]

The freeholders presented their compromise document to the city council, which set December 3 as the election date. Haynes led the campaign in favor of the charter, defending its provisions in speeches and essays for local newspapers. Arguing that it was based on sound business practices of organization, depended on the technical expertise of professionals, and would result in more efficient and democratic government, he carried the message throughout the city to business, labor, and other groups. In a debate at Labor Temple, Haynes became upset with the questioning of his opponent, Gesner Williams, charging that the "only people opposed to the new charter were those representing special interests and mossbacks." But Williams aptly countered that there were "two opposing forces which formed the proposed new charter. . . . The one led by Meyer Lissner represented centralized government and the other, represented by Dr. Haynes, throwing sop to the Socialists." In this debate the doctor appeared to be bested, at least as it was reported in the charter-opposing *Examiner* and *Times*.[26]

Haynes and John J. Hamilton, secretary of the Board of Freeholders, were joined in this campaign by Meyer Lissner, *Express* editor Harley Brundige, Lewis R. Works, and other freeholders, with the usual support of Earl's *Express* and *Tribune*. But opposition was formidable. The *Times* and its allies feared the document would further entrench the progressives in city government and attacked the "freak" charter "created by cunning politicians masquerading as civic patriots for the specific purpose of building a powerful political machine." The latest word from city hall, according to the *Times*, was this:

> Dr. John R. Haynes, president of the Lissner-Eddie Board of Freeholders who framed the dangerous instrument, subscribed $5,000 to the campaign fund raised by Boss Lissner and his sub-bosses. Haynes, who is a millionaire and a professional faddist of country-wide fame, is especially anxious to have the charter ratified for he is already being groomed as the Lissner-Eddie-Brundige candidate for Mayor in case the charter goes through. Haynes has nursed a Mayoralty bee in his belfry for many years and he sees an exceptionally fine opportunity to get rid of the buzzing creature if the charter is adopted.

Beyond this charge, the *Times* brought up the more reasonable issues of how responsive this new form of government might be and how much more it might cost the taxpayers.[27]

Haynes's opposition included many other forces. The *Examiner* opposed the charter as untested and inappropriate for a large city. The Socialist party remained neutral, but its leaders opposed the nonpartisan features and worked against it. Even a few progressives, such as Joseph Call, opposed it because it granted autocratic power to too few elected representatives and potentially opened the floodgates to favoritism in making appointments.[28]

To the shock of progressives, the charter was crushed by a two-to-one margin. The total vote was only a third of that cast in the tumultuous 1911 election, indicating that the new charter did not interest most city voters. The proposal was defeated in the home precincts of progressive leaders and corresponded closely with the vote on measures restricting saloons, leading one analyst to conclude that workers made the difference in defeating it. If the vote was a repudiation of the Lissner "Goo Goo clique," as the *Times* claimed, it appears to have been the protest of both labor and some of the city elite against more advanced municipal reforms.[29]

The defeat demoralized some progressives; for Haynes and others, it spurred them to work directly with Socialists to revise the charter. To avoid defeat of the many reforms contained within one proposal, they decided that amendments should be composed and offered to the voters individually. Within a week after the 1912 charter election, the People's Charter Conference, composed of representatives of the Socialist party and Good Government Organization, assembled. George Dunlop, former secretary of the Direct Legislation League, was elected president; other members included Haynes, former GGO president S. C. Graham, Job Harriman, and fellow Socialist Thomas W. Williams.[30]

The People's Charter Conference (PCC) began its work immediately. Still smarting from the defeat of the commission charter, Haynes was especially active in drafting the amendments. Sensing his dedication in composing the new proposals, Dora Haynes informed a friend, "He is very well and in a fighting mood so if you have any pet measures just let him know." In the next month the PCC produced eight charter amendments, including proposals to limit franchises to 21 years, move city elections to June, increase the salaries of council members, and make each of them a committee of one in charge of specific departments.[31]

The most controversial of the eight amendments established a system of proportional representation in city elections. This innovation, yet to be tested in any American municipality, was proposed by reformers in the late nineteenth century to give political parties representation in Congress according to the votes their members received in each state. Similar in many respects to European political systems, proportional representation had been endorsed by the Social Reform Union in 1899, the National Direct Legislation League, and the National Municipal League. Locally the idea was advanced by the Proportional Representation League, led by George H. Dunlop, also the president of the PCC.[32]

Proportional representation in Los Angeles was designed to aid Socialists, whose aggregate vote in 1911 was not reflected in a corresponding percentage of representation on the city council. Conservatives opposed it for precisely the same reason. Many structuralist reformers in the Municipal League contested it because it would bring back partisan politics since a candidate's party would have to be identified. Social reformers were more apt to approve it. George Dunlop hoped it would balance the city council with three conservatives, three radicals (Socialists), and three moderates (progressives). Dr. Haynes had worked unsuccessfully for the inclusion of this innovation in the 1912 charter, believing it a necessity to remedy the "present injustice" of denying Socialists any council seats after they had won 40 percent of the vote. "Sooner or later the Socialists through the oscillating pendulum of public opinion are certain to come to power," the doctor wrote. "It is much better that they first have a taste of the sobering influence of responsibility such as is afforded by minority representation." [33]

For the social reformers, advocating proportional representation was an admission that nonpartisanship already had outlived its usefulness, if indeed it had had any beyond its utility in removing the Southern Pacific Railroad from domination of the Republican party. Haynes asserted that Los Angeles politics had shifted from a Republican-Democrat alignment to that of "the Socialists vs. the Anti-Socialists," and proportional representation was needed to give the minority a voice in government. E. T. Earl agreed, "We are not going to secure effective city government under the non-partisan theory," and admitted that city politics was hardly nonpartisan in practice anyway. Both Haynes and Earl were afraid that the ward system would be reinstituted, returning Los Angeles to the days of the machine. Each agreed that nonpartisanship only eliminated the clash between parties of similar ideologies; it did not resolve the conflicts among the many disparate groups in the municipal political spectrum. [34]

The People's Charter Conference was not the only organization tinkering with the charter. The cry for revision was sounded by many groups after the 1912 election, including the Citizen's Committee of One Thousand, which was promoted by the *Times*, the *Examiner*, and business groups. Wary of the progress being made by the PCC to increase the power of Socialists, the Citizen's Committee framed its own set of eight amendments, calling for a return to the ward system, giving broad powers to a new harbor commission, and ending publication of a municipal newspaper editorially controlled by the progressives. These proposals were placed on the same March ballot with those of the PCC. [35]

In the short campaign the city's major interests lined up as expected. The social reformers, led by Haynes, Dunlop, and Earl, and the Socialists endorsed the eight amendments offered by the PCC, and opposed most of the eight composed by the Citizen's Committee. The *Times* and *Examiner* advocated the exact opposite. Lissner and the structuralist progressives favored a few offered by each side, but adamantly opposed both proportional representation and the ward system. In a light turnout the voters carried seven of the PCC amendments and a few of the rest. Proportional representation and the ward plan fell to defeat; hence the outcome resembled the moderate Municipal League recommendations rather than either of the extremes.[36]

Dr. Haynes's determination to modernize the Los Angeles form of government continued the following year. In 1914, he was selected as chairman of yet another charter amendment committee, which composed ten amendments calling for proportional representation, the city-manager form of government, and a regional division of the city into boroughs. The *Times* and *Examiner* opposed these changes, and the city council refused to submit them to the voters. In retaliation Haynes's group formed a more permanent committee to pressure the council to seek a new charter and call for the election of a Board of Freeholders in 1915. Haynes was elected to this body with a mix of progressives and conservatives who argued about the form of government the city should have and the best method of representation. As a compromise, a stronger mayor-council form was proposed and four alternative provisions were offered, calling for a city manager, proportional representation, shorter council terms, and council elections by ward.[37]

The charter election was set for June 6, 1916, and Haynes stumped for the charter and the provision for proportional representation. He defended the entire document, especially the section on civil service, an issue in which he always had a special interest. The Chamber of Commerce endorsed the proposal, but the *Times* and *Examiner* again opposed the "Socialist charter" and amplified opposition to its separate elements. On election day, the charter and three alternate provisions were defeated by a smaller margin than the 1912 proposal. Another disappointment for Haynes and his allies, this rejection cooled their enthusiasm for a few years.[38]

George Alexander's second mayoral term ushered in a number of city improvements, as well as a mild turn toward social reform to appease those who voted for Harriman in 1911. In his analysis of municipal reform in the United States, historian Martin Schiesl ranked Alexander as one of America's most notable reform mayors with respect to his quest for efficiency and humanitarian service. A municipal newspaper edited by progressives, to which Haynes was an occasional contributor, was created (though it was later voted out). The city's financial status was protected despite large bond issues for harbor and other improvements to its infrastructure. But these years also brought frustration for the mayor: an investigation of the construction of the Owens Valley aqueduct by Socialists who accused his administration of mismanagement and fraud; disputes both with Meyer Lissner over the city's distribution of hydroelectric power and with E. T. Earl over a probe of the Home Telephone Company; and continued opposition on some issues from the "progressive" city council. By early 1913, it was apparent that the aging mayor would not be seeking reelection.[39]

The 1913 municipal campaign began with the progressives in disarray. Already hampered by personal disputes, the insurgents divided early that year when social reformers cooperated with the Socialists in the People's Charter Conference. In March, a group of conservative leaders in the Chamber of Commerce invited the top structuralist progressives to a Municipal Conference to cooperate in choosing an acceptable mayoral candidate to run against the Socialist nominee. Fearing that social reformers were too close to Socialists and too willing to give labor leaders a voice in government, the political reformers again joined the old guard. Led by Lissner, Russ Avery, and Marshall Stimson, these progressives claimed that the editorial war between, on the one hand, Earl's *Express* and *Tribune* and, on the other, the *Times* and the *Examiner* made it impossible to convince a candidate "of the highest standing" to run for office. Shunning Earl and other social reformers, the Municipal Conference selected City Attorney John Shenk for mayor and chose a full ticket for other city offices.[40]

Earl interpreted the situation differently. He believed, he wrote to Hiram Johnson, that there was no immediate threat from the disorganized Socialists, that Lissner had simply renounced his progressivism and joined the old guard. The real issue of the moment was municipal ownership, Earl believed, and Lissner would follow corporate dictation because he favored regulation only. In a short time, Earl banded the social reformers into the People's Campaign Committee, consisting of Dr. Haynes and others who also endorsed Shenk but selected different candidates for other city offices.[41]

In the primary campaign the *Times* and *Examiner* railed daily against the Socialist threat and boosted Shenk and the Municipal Conference slate. Earl's papers backed Shenk and the People's Campaign Committee ticket, criticizing the Municipal Conference for nominating council candidates exclusively from the most affluent area of the city. The Socialists again nominated Job Harriman, who campaigned against an "Earl-Otis-Hearst combine," though the Socialist-labor alliance of 1911 was not reestablished. Also in the race was Police Judge Henry H. Rose, an independent backed by some elements of the old guard. In a surprising primary finish, Rose edged out Harriman with enough votes to face Shenk in the runoff.[42]

With the Socialist threat erased, the *Examiner* switched to the maverick Rose. So, too, did some disgruntled Socialists and workers dissatisfied with Shenk, candidate of both the antilabor *Times* and "progressive boss" Earl. Rose smeared Shenk as the stooge of Lissner and Earl, and won the general election by a few thousand votes. Earl blamed the *Times* and the Municipal Conference for Shenk's defeat; the *Times* and the *Examiner* returned the favor. Beyond the finger pointing, the second alliance of progressives and the old guard resulted in a reform fiasco as the mayor's office now was devoid of any type of progressive.[43]

The removal of the progressives from the executive branch of city government did not completely diminish their power to influence municipal policies. It is true that new mayor H. H. Rose had little in common with the reformers. The former police-court judge had been supported in the campaign by a variety of former machine figures and the city's liquor interests. In office, he frequently butted heads with Haynes and other progressive commissioners over policy matters. The defeat in 1913 and Rose's antireform actions as mayor became the primary evidence for the interpretation of Los Angeles politics that pointed to 1913 as the end of progressivism.[44]

The reformers lost the mayor's office but not complete control of city government. As Martin Schiesl has observed, by 1913, progressives were entrenched in the city bureaucracy. With civil service protection and diminished power for party managers, these civil servants became "semi-politicians" in policy-making. The city council also wielded enormous power, and usually contained a strong progressive element within its ranks. And the quality of city commission appointees, according to the *National Municipal Review*, was so superior that despite the poor quality of elected officials, the commissioners performed well and Los Angeles was advancing. Progressivism, at least in its most conservative sense, certainly was not dead after 1913.[45]

The persistence of urban progressivism was best illustrated in the crusade for municipal ownership and operation of hydroelectric power. This issue became the city's major political controversy over the next two decades, uniting progressives on both left and right with other groups in shifting coalitions formed to promote expansion of the city's water and power facilities. As a local application of the theory of public ownership, this campaign naturally appealed to Haynes, who took a leading role in organizing political support for it.

Municipal distribution of electricity surfaced as a major issue in 1910, when Mayor Alexander and the city council scheduled a special election to vote on $3.5 million in bonds to build a power plant along the Owens Valley aqueduct for street lighting and other municipal needs. The bonds were approved overwhelmingly, and it was only after the election that serious discussion ensued concerning what the city would do with the surplus power created by the project. While private power companies offered to buy all of the city's unneeded electricity, most progressive leaders favored the city's distributing the surplus power in competition with private firms. This position was ratified by the city's voters in a straw poll early in 1911 by a margin of ten to one.[46]

The stormy 1911 election and tight money conditions in the New York bond market delayed sale of the bonds, but by 1913 progressive leaders had forged ahead with plans to finance the distribution facilities for the soon-to-be-completed generating plant. City officials began negotiating with private power companies to purchase existing properties, while also planning a $6.5 million bond issue to build a distribution system. As negotiations with private companies bogged down, Dr. Haynes, former Public Works Board president James A. Anderson, E. T. Earl and his newspapers, Bureau of Aqueduct Power chief electrical engineer Ezra F. Scattergood, and advocates of the municipal power system planned and executed the political campaign to promote the bonds.[47]

For the first time, the city's expansion of its water and power program was opposed by more than just scattered opposition. The *Times*, which favored selling the surplus power to private companies, loudly championed the position of private power companies and other groups opposing the bonds. The 1913 Municipal Conference coalition and a Voters Educational Association worked for rejection of power distribution by the city, while the *Examiner* warned of the financial dangers of creating a duplicate power system. This opposition was buttressed by the confusion caused by a number of other bond proposals on the April 15 ballot and a belief by many that private power companies might purchase the surplus power at a great immediate profit to the city. These factors limited the affirmative vote to only 60 percent, when a two-thirds majority was necessary.[48]

The defeat sparked a lengthy struggle for supremacy of the electrical power market in Los Angeles. Haynes and his allies realized that a more concerted effort was necessary to establish a city power system. A few months after this election, the progressives lobbied the new city council to order a resubmission of the bond proposal for the next spring. Since the proposal included funds for both completing the plant and beginning work on the distribution system, opponents tried to divide the proposal into two bond issues in order to defeat the latter. When the matter came to a vote in the city council, the progressives had only five of the six votes necessary to keep the issues united. The absence of one sympathetic city lawmaker on sick leave provoked Haynes to exclaim, "We'll get Councilman Reed here if we have to bring him in on a stretcher." The doctor vowed to carry Reed back himself if necessary. Reed did return, and after a week's delay the council finally voted to resubmit the power bonds as a single proposal.[49]

In this election campaign the advocates of municipal ownership pulled out all the stops for approval of the bonds. The spearhead of the campaign was the People's Power Bond Committee (PPBC), representing the Chamber of Commerce, Municipal League, Friday Morning Club, City Club, Builder's Exchange, Central Labor Council, and other city organizations lobbied by the progressives. Haynes, who served as PPBC vice chairman and finance committee chairman, played a key role in obtaining the endorsement of the Chamber of Commerce, which became instrumental in deflecting opposition from the business community as embodied in the Merchants and Manufacturers Association, Realty Board, and the *Times*. Still a member of the Chamber, Haynes appeared at its meeting and, according to the *Times*, swayed a majority of its members to endorse the undivided bond proposal.[50]

Haynes also held chief responsibility for fund-raising (much of it from his own wallet), made a number of speeches, and helped devise campaign strategy. With his assistance the PPBC scheduled nightly speeches in local schools, printed and distributed election material, placed ads in city newspapers, and arranged to transport constituents to the polls. With editorial aid from the *Examiner*, the *Herald*, the Earl papers, and others, the PPBC refuted the *Times*'s argument that the bonds would ruin the city financially, and the two-thirds majority vote was secured.[51]

Soon after the bond election, Haynes recommended that the ad hoc

People's Power Bond Committee be made permanent. His associates did not think it necessary, but two years later the ad hoc committee had to be resurrected for another battle stemming from the city's attempt to purchase the distribution facilities of the three largest private power companies in Los Angeles. After completion of the first generating plant, the Power Bureau began negotiations with the private companies, which resisted until the city initiated condemnation proceedings against two of them and began construction of its own parallel system. Southern California Edison then offered to sell its facilities, and the city council appointed a committee including Haynes to work out details of the contract. The company gave up many of its demands but retained the right to operate its facilities until the city paid for them in full. This proviso meant that private companies could eventually purchase surplus power from the city to distribute through their own facilities, a feature that raised the opposition of previous backers of the municipal power program.[52]

To accommodate this purchase, about $12 million in additional bonds would be needed. In support of this issue, the People's Power Bond Committee was revived in late 1916, with Haynes again serving as vice president. In January 1917, he hosted a dinner for PPBC speakers and began delivering his own speeches in favor of the bond proposal to a splintering coalition. Some public-power advocates opposed the election date set in early June because the new operating agreement would only have been in effect a short time and voters would be influenced by developments in the World War. *Record* editors were upset that the agreement allowed private firms to sell surplus city power for even a short time. These dissenters echoed the opposition of the *Times*, which had campaigned long and hard in 1916 and early 1917 to defeat any new bond proposal for distribution of electrical power. Two months after the United States declared war, Los Angeles voters resoundingly defeated the bonds, one of the very few occasions when power bonds failed to achieve a simple majority. For Haynes and his fellow municipal power supporters, future expansion of the city power program would have to wait until after the end of the war.[53]

The municipal ownership issue demonstrated the vigor of urban progressivism after 1913. The success of reformers in these struggles reinforced their influence with officeholders and voters, and in the vacuum created by the departure of party managers after 1909, the reformers became the new political chieftains. Meyer Lissner was considered to be the city "boss" after the Harper recall until 1912, when he became more involved in state affairs and split with Mayor Alexander and the social reformers. When political reformers again joined the old guard in 1913, the mantle of progressive leadership fell upon E. T. Earl and Dr. Haynes, who became the "Goo-Goo bosses" in the years after 1913. In this capacity they mixed their political philosophies with hardball politics and significant outlays of their own money to elect officeholders and to influence municipal policies. They performed this function in a manner not unlike that of the deposed Walter Parker, except that they operated in the name of progressivism rather than stand-pat corporate protectionism.

Like Haynes, Earl had no aversion to dabbling in practical politics. A native Californian, he owned a fruit business when in 1890 he developed the first successful combination ventilator-refrigerator railroad car. This vehicle preserved fruit shipped eastward and became an immediate boon to the California fruit industry. In 1900, he sold the rights to this invention to the Armour Company of Chicago, which used the car for shipping meat. With the proceeds Earl purchased the *Los Angeles Express* and plunged into fierce competition with the *Times*. Upon moving next door to General Otis, Earl began a lifelong personal feud against the *Times* publisher, which kept the two at odds with each other in all matters except real estate speculation.[54]

As a progressive, Earl was slightly to the left of the structuralists. In favor of most political reforms, he also approved of some of the social reforms Haynes promoted. In 1907, Earl instructed his editors to counter the *Times* position in defending the open shop. "The fact is," he wrote, "the tyranny of organized capital in politics and industry is far more dangerous to the people than labor union tyranny." Five years later he campaigned for a guaranteed minimum wage in the platform of the Progressive party, and in the intervening years made his paper the most progressive in Los Angeles. It was the *Express* that sparked the anti-SP crusade in California after reporter Edward A. Dickson was hired in 1906. Earl's morning *Tribune*, established in 1911, combined with the *Express* to expound his views. This perspective had become closer to that of Dr. Haynes by early 1913, when Earl assented to giving labor and even Socialists more power in the city.[55]

Earl's motives were not entirely altruistic. His editorial and financial support of the 1904 Davenport recall was aimed at retrieving the printing contract lost to the rival *Times*. Earl broke with George Alexander in 1912, when the mayor refused to intercede with Public Service Commission members who denied a rate increase for a utility in which Earl owned substantial stock. His final break with Governor Johnson came in 1914 after Johnson agreed with state officers who ruled against construction of a state highway through Earl's property in Tehachapi, and who awarded a large state oil contract to a competitor of Union Oil Company, in which Earl was a stockholder. A major bankroller of local and state progressive campaigns, Earl expected that his financial support would be taken into consideration when progressives made decisions that affected his investments.[56]

With backing from Earl's newspapers, Haynes's personal following, and their wealth, these two reformers became "bosses" of the progressive forces after 1913. Neither ruled a "machine," but both were undeniably influential in election campaigns, appointments, and policymaking. In most cases their efforts were directed against the choices of the *Times* and the business establishment, which opposed the social reformers.[57]

The reform bosses did not always agree. In 1915, Earl reluctantly supported Police Chief Charles E. Sebastian for mayor. A Los Angeles policeman since 1907, Sebastian had been a Chinatown vice raider and allegedly a bagman for the Harper administration. He had joined the progressives by 1911, when he was appointed police chief, and tried to maintain a closed town devoid of vice operations. Haynes privately backed city council president Frederick Whiffen, a maverick progressive who responded to Earl's snub by promising to end the publisher's influence in city politics. In the primary, about a third of the registered voters appeared at the polls. Sebastian, at the time suspended and on trial for contributing to the delinquency of a minor, placed first, with Whiffen second. In the runoff, Sebastian, having been acquitted of the morals charge, defeated Whiffen.[58]

Sebastian later admitted that as mayor he had conferred with Earl on all important appointments and that Earl helped him write every message he sent to the city council. But this partnership did not last long. In the summer of 1916, the *Record* stepped up its criticism of the mayor by printing intercepted "Dear Lil" letters from Sebastian to his mistress in which the mayor referred to his wife as "the old haybag." Though he pledged to fight the *Record* editor, Sebastian acquiesced to business leaders who asked him to end the continued embarrassment of the city. On September 1, he resigned because of "ill health," and the city council appointed Harbor Commissioner Frederick T. Woodman interim mayor.[59]

Woodman had joined the progressives in 1909, and was appointed to the Harbor Commission three years later. More capable than his two predecessors, he was a political reformer who tried to improve the police and public utility departments and worked for more centralized authority in city government. Haynes usually cooperated with him, so much so that the doctor was accused of being Woodman's mentor. The *Times* reported in January 1917 that Haynes had decided he wanted to be appointed to the Public Service Commission, and Woodman would comply. The story prompted Haynes to ask the mayor to announce to the press that the physician did not visit the mayor's office to demand appointments for himself or his friends. A few months later, during the 1917 municipal contest, the doctor and political progressives such as Marshall Stimson served on Woodman's reelection committee.[60]

Haynes and Earl also were interested in Los Angeles County politics. Prior to 1910, Walter Parker had exerted considerable power at the county courthouse owing to his influence over the "Solid Three" of five supervisors and District Attorney John D. Fredericks. Reformers, most notably Haynes and Earl, hoped to assume control after Parker's political defeat in the city. In 1912, social reformer Richard H. Norton joined the board of supervisors, and in the next four years other progressives were elected to the board, though a progressive majority rarely existed.

Earl and Haynes did have some influence, however. Earl and Norton routinely conferred on county matters. Earl even boasted that he occasionally had the entire board of supervisors at his office to discuss county business and ordered them to follow his dictation. Haynes became Norton's patron, helped him survive a recall attempt in 1914, and served on his reelection committee in 1916. The reform bosses were also instrumental in the election of John J. Hamilton to the board. On the other hand, the two were unable to elect their own district attorney in 1916, or force the appointment of their choice for county counsel in 1914.[61]

Haynes's increasing involvement in county affairs resulted in his appointment to the Public Welfare Commission in 1915. Created at the end of the preceding year, the commission was responsible for overseeing the county's charitable institutions, including the county hospital, poor farm, and outdoor relief agency. The commissioners were charged with investigating "all charities and philanthropic institutions dependent upon public appeal" to decide which of them served the needs of the community, with encouraging the formation of new private charities, with enforcing county regulations regarding sanitary conditions in these institutions, and with issuing permits for child care and other agencies. Haynes was elected president of the commission and served for a decade. In this capacity he duplicated some of his concurrent work on the State

Board of Charities and Corrections by inspecting hospitals, orphanages, juvenile halls, and other facilities.[62]

In both county and city politics an underlying impetus for the progressive bosses was their enduring personal opposition to General Otis and Harry Chandler. Earl had been an enemy of Otis since taking over the *Express* in 1901. Their feud took on an additional intensity after 1906, when Earl became a leader of the anti-SP reformers, while Otis, who had opposed the railroad politicians for years, was not asked to participate because of this rivalry. The animosity reached its zenith when Earl filed a libel suit against the *Times* in 1916 and won.[63]

Haynes, meanwhile, was embroiled in his own feud with Otis and Chandler. From 1909 to 1917, the *Times* intensified its editorial attacks on Haynes. The paper regularly characterized the doctor as a "crank," a "professional faddist," and troublemaker who helped direct the "Earl-Haynes-Norton Ring" of grafters. In some cartoons Haynes was clearly labeled a "Red" because of his socialist sympathies, and editorials criticized his seeming duality: "He believes in the division of wealth in the evenings when he addresses ladies' clubs and parlor Socialist gatherings. During banking hours, the 'Doc' keeps his eye fixed on the main chance, with a padlock on his pockets. . . . He orates against 'the unearned increment,' and he got rich out of it." Other stories and editorials portrayed him as an opportunist, who on many occasions coveted the mayor's office.[64]

One morning in December 1910, Haynes found himself ridiculed as usual in the *Times*'s "Watchman" political column. That same day the doctor received a letter from the paper's librarian politely requesting a recent photograph, for the entire *Times* photo file had been destroyed in the explosion two months earlier. Apparently Haynes decided to ignore the request for a photo that no doubt would accompany future insults.[65]

Haynes responded to the attacks of the *Times* in different ways. In his speeches he criticized the paper and its publishers as reactionary tools of special interests. He wrote a few graciously sarcastic letters to Harry Chandler pointing out errors in *Times* stories or the inconsistencies of its publishers. On other occasions he became vindictive, once asking a California governor to investigate General Otis's pension and estate records to uncover fraud after the General's death. Most of the time Haynes simply retaliated with essays published by friendly newspapers. The feud with Chandler, fueled by years of personal animosity, would continue long beyond 1917.[66]

The Haynes-Earl alliance won many victories, but did not long survive the death of General Otis, in 1917. Late that year Supervisor Norton was tried and convicted of mismanagement of county funds and forced out of office. In October the *Times* celebrated with an editorial entitled "The Rise and Fall of Goo-Goo," heralding the demise of reform in Los Angeles. A few weeks later Earl's libel suit against the *Record* commenced. Charged with the malicious crime of branding Earl a "political boss," the *Record* publisher was defended by a lawyer who paraded a number of city and county politicians—former mayors A. C. Harper and C. E. Sebastian, supervisors Norton and Hinshaw—and others, including Haynes and even Earl himself before the jury, all of whom testified to Earl's contacts and influence with officeholders. After a short deliberation the jury agreed that Earl certainly was a political boss, and the suit was dismissed. This verdict could have enhanced Earl's reputation as a power broker, but instead it embarrassed him into withdrawing from politics. He died a little over a year later, leaving another power vacuum that necessitated a realignment of Dr. Haynes's political affiliations.[67]

While John Haynes dabbled extensively in state and local politics, Dora Haynes participated in social and political affairs as her health would allow. In 1911 she was active in the women's suffrage movement as treasurer of the Political Equality League, working for the state constitutional amendment to allow women to vote in California. The stress of this activity took a toll on her already fragile health. Late the following year she was hospitalized, and she spent most of 1913 "resting at home." On occasions such as the National Municipal League banquet in 1912 and a political rally for mayoral candidate John Shenk in mid-1913, she served as a hostess, but usually she took part in political affairs only by opening her home to such meetings.[68]

In general, Dora agreed with her husband's political philosophy. After a Friday Morning Club meeting in which a book on socialism was reviewed, she wrote to Caroline Severance: "[The club members] agreed with most that was written. They were also given women suffrage in a disguised form and now it is not a disturbing factor.... So it will be with Socialism when conservatives lose their prejudices against the idea." But like her husband, she declined to join the party, and in the 1911 and 1913 municipal elections, she publicly supported the progressive mayoral candidates.[69]

For the next few years Dora continued to advance women's suffrage as she could. In 1911, she hosted meetings of the suffrage campaign leaders to organize a state drive in support of the national movement. Two years later, she was elected a vice president of the Southern California Civic League, a nonpartisan group advocating this reform. In that same year she chaired a committee of Southern California women who assembled information concerning suffrage in the state and composed a lengthy essay that was entered into the *Congressional Record* as an address of Senator John D. Works. At her urging, John Haynes helped convince presidential secretary Joseph P. Tumulty to implore President Wilson to order the release of suffragist Alice Paul after her arrest for picketing the White House in 1917. In these and other instances of less notoriety Dora Haynes pursued her favorite reform until its legal realization in 1920, and promoted its social realization for many years after, urging women throughout the state to use their votes to win further reforms.[70]

While experiencing busy political schedules in the early 1910s, John and Dora Haynes's personal lives also were full. In 1912, they moved into a new home a dozen blocks south of the old Victorian house at Tenth and Figueroa. The new residence, built on the east side of Figueroa Street just north of Adams Boulevard, was located in the fashionable West Adams district. Adjacent to Chester Place, an enclave of mansions belonging to E. L. Doheny and other wealthy Angelenos, the new Haynes house faced a bevy of South Figueroa residences inhabited by the Barlow, Slauson, Solano, McNeil, and Sabichi families.[71]

Robert D. Farquhar, an architect of rising fame in Los Angeles, was commissioned to design the new structure. His plan, in the French Norman style, of two and a half stories with a steeply pitched roof and elegant window and door treatments translated into one of the city's most stately residences of the time. Even the *Times* touted the completion of the house in its real estate section, while national magazines illustrated its front elevation as a prime example of Farquhar's work. With matching garage, formal enclosed garden, and a richly appointed interior of fine woods, silk damask panels, and exquisite furnishings, the new house was a notable addition to the city's most affluent residential district.[72]

When the house was completed in 1912, John and Dora moved in with a chauffeur, cook Inga Swenson, and a maid. Dora's brother, Alfred, moved to his own house two blocks farther south. John's older sister, Mary, already lived in the home of their younger sister, Florence, and her husband, Dr. Walter Lindley, three blocks north of the new Haynes house. Lindley continued to manage the California Hospital and was a prominent member of the business, medical, and political communities, while Florence was active in social circles. John's younger brother, Robert, was divorced from his wife, Lesbia, in 1912, and later retired and moved to Long Beach.[73]

With his political activism increasing both locally and statewide, John Haynes found it necessary to hire a full-time personal secretary. In 1911, he replaced his part-time secretary, Florence K. Ingram, with Joseph W. Park, a local high school teacher. At one time a fellow of the social science departments at Princeton and the University of Chicago, Park was overqualified for the task of taking the doctor's dictation, typing correspondence, and filing letters, news clippings, and other literature in Haynes's rapidly expanding personal and research files. At one point in 1916, Park proposed that Haynes spearhead a national crusade for direct legislation with Park as the chief writer of campaign literature. The doctor apparently declined, preferring to employ his secretary in his original capacity until Park's death in 1919.[74]

In social spheres, the Hayneses were limited by John's busy political life and Dora's health. The new house offered more room to entertain and provided temporary living quarters for guests, but parties decreased as Dora's condition deteriorated. After the trip to Europe in 1910, she rarely accompanied her husband on vacations. John continued to spend leisure time in the California Club headquarters, while Dora attended social functions and meetings of the Friday Morning Club as she could.[75]

Dr. Haynes also attended meetings of the discussion clubs to which he belonged: the City Club, Severance Club, Commonwealth Club, and others. He spoke on numerous topics such as the proposed city charters and immigration to Los Angeles at meetings of the Sunset Club, and attended most of the social outings of this group. He had joined the Fine Arts League of Los Angeles by 1913, in time to help defray the commission of Julia Bracken Wendt to create a monumental bronze sculpture for the new Los Angeles Museum of History, Science, and Art. A year later he joined the newly formed X Club, a dinner and discussion club that met every two weeks. Based on an organization originally formed in London and later expanded to New York, the local branch was founded by William J. Ghent, a leading American Socialist at the turn of the century. This club became another forum for views on civic and national affairs, as well as for guest speakers such as Upton Sinclair and Roger Baldwin. Haynes would speak many times before the club members in the early 1920s.[76]

In financial circles at this time, Haynes expanded his fortune. He still was a director of several companies, helped to incorporate a few, invested in many more, and continued to transfer property at a profit. In 1915, he was elected a director of the Los Angeles Investment Company, a co-operative firm established in 1899 to aid prospective homeowners in purchasing a new house. The company was one of the city's "most flourishing enterprises" when it almost crashed during the real estate dive of 1913. The company appointed Haynes to the board along with his nemesis, Harry Chandler, in order to reassure thousands of stockholders that the enterprise could survive and prosper. After Haynes's friend former senator Frank P. Flint was elected company president, it did.[77]

It was at this time that Haynes made another major investment in a mining enterprise, Gaylord Wilshire's Bishop Creek mine in Inyo County. Since their trip to Europe in 1906 and Wilshire's subsequent move to England, Haynes and the Socialist editor had had little contact. Occasionally, the doctor loaned money to Wilshire, and Dora Haynes wrote to Wilshire's wife, Mary. During these years Wilshire developed gold mines in British Guiana and near Bishop in eastern California. The Bishop Creek operation gained the editor some notoriety when he offered stock in this capitalistic venture as a reward to those who sold subscriptions for his Socialist journal.[78]

In 1913, Wilshire convinced Haynes that the Bishop Creek mine had begun to produce an appreciable amount of bullion, so the physician made plans to inspect his holdings there. In the following year, Haynes and other investors paid a visit, and the doctor, who already owned a few shares, loaned Wilshire another $20,000 to accelerate output. The operation failed to make its anticipated profit, though Haynes did recoup his investment within a few years. Despite this setback, the friendship of these two capitalistic socialists would endure for another decade.[79]

As in California at large, in Los Angeles the political milieu changed markedly from 1909 to 1917. From partisan to "progressive" politics, the structure and operation of government and the methods of countervailing forces were modified by reformers who sought varying degrees of change in the status quo. In both the statewide and local movements seeking these changes, John Haynes played a prominent role. Although not the single, dominant force in either crusade, his participation was crucial to the success of each.

Chapter Nine

A Reformer's Passage Through World War I

Like many idealists of the Progressive Era, Dr. Haynes was deeply affected by the War to End All Wars. In a decade in which he broadened his perspective on national and local issues, the war expanded his reform consciousness to the international level and further modified his priorities in advancing social justice. The war interrupted Haynes's support for some reform activities and spurred his support of others. In these years his personal contradictions were most conspicuous, for his militant patriotism often overshadowed his belief in civil liberties.

By 1910, Haynes had already become concerned with conditions outside the United States. That year he made his fourth trip to Europe and observed living and working conditions, reporting on them in speeches over the next two years. Long before the outbreak of European hostilities in 1914, he warned of the implications of Prussian militarism. After the war began, he was shocked by the spectacle of Christians "drenching Europe with the blood of fellow-Christians." This threat to democracy and world progress hit home in April 1917, when the United States declared war on Germany. For many Americans the declaration demanded total commitment to the protection of their homeland by defeat of the Central Powers. For Haynes and many other U.S. progressives, this devotion became an obsession.[1]

As a patrician patriot, Haynes supported the war effort on a number of levels. Locally, he served as chairman of the Southern California membership drive of the Red Cross just before Christmas 1917. Stressing the gravity of the world situation, he exhorted his volunteer workers to enroll all of their neighbors in this humanitarian organization. Although he could devote little time to this crusade, he almost reached his assigned quota.[2]

Haynes dedicated more of his time to his duties as a member of the State Council of Defense. He was one of 33 prominent Californians appointed to this ad hoc committee by Governor William D. Stephens on April 5, 1917. He departed for Sacramento and the council's first meeting the next day and took part in initial proceedings to mobilize California's resources to aid the war effort. Over the next year and a half he promoted ideas to increase food production and provide for the dependents of servicemen.[3]

At the organizational meeting Haynes was selected chairman of the Relief Committee and a member of the Public Health and Sanitation Committee. The Relief Committee met right away to devise methods to improve the plight of families whose household heads were in military service, of those disabled while in the military, and of those forced to abandon their homes because of the war. Within a day Haynes submitted a report to the governor recommending the institution of daylight savings time to decrease utility costs for consumers and aid agricultural production. This innovation had proved to be very successful in England, Haynes asserted, and its only critics were private lighting companies. He also believed that a centralized relief agency like the one in Canada was needed to set standard rates of relief allotments and distribute aid to soldiers and their dependents.[4]

Besides these suggestions requiring government involvement, Haynes also argued for the role of volunteers in supporting the war effort, especially clubwomen who had tremendous resources for tackling some of the problems faced by Californians. He recommended that the state be carved into six districts—exactly as it was divided by the California Federation of Women's Clubs. The clubs then could be recruited to raise money, educate citizens on relief problems, and assist in the care of soldiers' families. A month later he was appointed to the new Committee on the Work of Women with his friends Edward A. Dickson and Mrs. Shelley Tolhurst.[5]

Because of Dora Haynes's involvement in club service and John's own past work with clubwomen in reform campaigns, he hoped to mobilize these women to aid his committee's relief efforts. In May 1917, he appeared before the state convention of the California Federation of Women's Clubs in Pasadena and beseeched the audience to follow the leadership of Mrs. Tolhurst in undertaking "in a systematic way" the education of mothers and training of children in matters of health, household administration and expenditures, and other domestic concerns as a first step in caring for relief needs. Alerting the audience to an array of deficiencies in the nation, both those brought on by the war and those already existing, he hoped his listeners would join him in whatever capacity they could.[6]

This speech also outlined Haynes's ideas for escalating support of the war effort. He was especially concerned that certain steps be taken to ensure adequate food for the Allies. First, the United States should avoid an early mistake of the Allies "in trusting to enthusiasm and voluntary organization" only, and instead rely on "the management of trained experts and national government organization." Federal administrators must be allowed to plan and implement programs for the most efficient use of resources in producing foodstuffs. Second, the nation's factories should not be raided for soldiers, a practice resulting in a shortage of trained munitions workers. Selective agricultural conscription should be implemented by Congress to create an "agricultural army" composed of both hoboes and men "who labor at present but produce nothing of value to society" (as examples Haynes offered real estate and stock salesmen and about 90 percent of the 3,000 lawyers in Los Angeles). Prohibition of liquor was also necessary to save the annual 1.5 billion bushels of grain used in processing alcohol. A larger, more equitable stipend for dependents of soldiers should be paid by the federal or state governments. These proposals were only the necessary beginning of the war effort.[7]

In carrying out his duties on the Relief Committee, Haynes also organized an advisory board of friends and experts to help inform and advise the committee. In May 1917, he reported to the committee that milk prices were so high that mothers on relief could not afford enough of it for their babies.[8]

Sometimes, however, he moved far beyond the scope of the Relief Committee in his devotion to defense. In one communication Haynes asked Governor Stephens to use his influence with federal authorities to remedy four matters only remotely associated with the committee. For one, the doctor urged inquiries into complaints about the inefficiency of a state military officer. Also needing investigation was a series of confidential reports that food was being wasted in soldiers' camps because it "was so wretchedly cooked that the boys could not eat it." Third, certain regulations at the San Francisco Presidio needed to be abolished, namely those allowing soldiers to leave the base after finishing their daily shifts. According to Haynes, this resulted in insufficient sleep and temptation to engage in "immoral practices," in that the doughboy "is unrestrained by his usual influences, and is filled with the recklessness of youth." Lastly, the doctor was incensed that the Hearst newspapers were "sowing sedition, discontent, and unrest in every issue" with pro-German propaganda. "I believe that Hearst has been paid by the German Government since the onset of the war in 1914, and I feel that his papers should not be allowed to help the enemy," Haynes wrote. "Surely there are some legal means of stopping this." A former political ally of the Hearst press in Los Angeles, Haynes, like progressives elsewhere in the nation, now looked for ways to silence what he considered to be the *Examiner's* traitorous viewpoint.[9]

Haynes did not limit his service on the State Council of Defense to the particular charges of the Relief Committee and the Public Health and Sanitation Committee. As a general council member interested in all phases of the war effort he investigated and made recommendations on matters such as the rescue of confiscated opium in San Francisco and its transfer to the war front for medicine. Haynes's activity on the council revealed a fervent, sometimes overzealous commitment to the war effort. He demanded personal sacrifice from all Americans, especially the wealthy:

> We must crush Prussian militarism. And in order to do it not only must every man and woman in the United States during the continuation of this war eat no more than is essential to maintain health, but we should wear our clothes until they shine like burnished steel; we shall spend no money for luxuries; we should desist from purchasing automobiles, both because of the waste of original outlay and because of the use of gasoline which passenger cars entail. No money should be spent for diamonds, jewelry, or furs, nor should we attend banquets.

The same sacrifice should apply to American industries, such as shipbuilding, which should be prohibited from amassing vast personal profits while Americans were conscripted into military and industrial armies. If not owned by the government, important industries should at least be managed by experts on a nonprofit basis. Minus the emphasis on government management, the State Council of Defense was relatively successful in convincing Californians to sacrifice for the war, and Dr. Haynes's role was apparent in the measure of success it achieved.[10]

Haynes also served the war effort as an official arbitrator of labor disputes. In the first decade of the twentieth century he had developed a close relationship with union leaders in political campaigns. His advocacy of direct legislation and other reforms sought by labor cemented a bilateral alliance in the quest for immediate goals for working people and established his local reputation as a friend of labor.

He broadened his concern to advance the status of workers from a state to a national level in 1910, when he began a crusade to improve safety conditions for miners. The doctor's interest in mining stemmed from his childhood experiences in Pennsylvania. His father, a mine manager and an Englishman, was a class and ethnic rival of the Irish miners. But the son sympathized with the plight of these laborers, whose working and living conditions he witnessed firsthand. He began investing in mining ventures in the late 1890s, at the same time that he embarked on his social-reform career. Closely associated with the problem of miner safety for a second time, Haynes began studying the frequency of mine explosions, raising the issue with colleagues, and assembling research files with statistics and reports of accidents and strikes in mines throughout the world.[11]

The doctor became more active in this area in 1910. Since he already had planned his trip to Europe that year, he asked Senator Frank P. Flint for an official appointment as a special investigator to study mining safety in Europe. By that time Haynes was convinced that a partial solution to the high mortality rate in U.S. coal mines would be the creation of an interstate mining commission with power to enforce safety regulations. Haynes's interviews with European mining officials and further research reinforced his conclusions that American mines were naturally safer than their European counterparts, but that the accident rate in the United States was much higher because of lax safety standards, unqualified superintendents, and greedy owners who expected huge dividends on their investments.[12]

In the following year he began agitating for his mining commission. He approached various political and media sources and was promised support by publishers, U.S. senators, and labor leaders. John B. Andrews, secretary of the American Association for Labor Legislation (AALL), was so impressed with the idea that he invited the doctor to present a prospectus on the mining commission to the annual meeting of the AALL, to be held in Washington, D.C., in December 1911. For this event Governor Hiram Johnson appointed Haynes a special state commissioner on mining accidents, enhancing the doctor's stature at the meeting.[13]

In the nation's capital Haynes convinced California Senator John D. Works to introduce a bill, written by Haynes and his associates, that would establish a federal mining commission. While the bill was being considered, the doctor pressed congressmen and others to support this legislation, distributing copies of his speech and additional literature throughout the nation. The bill failed to pass, so Haynes continued to agitate for it in later congressional sessions. His speech was printed in the *American Labor Legislation Review* and the *Western Comrade,* among other publications, and he spoke on the subject before groups such as the Los Angeles City Club and Socialist Open Forum. In 1916, he offered to donate $500 per year to the American Association for Labor Legislation if it would make coal-mining safety its top priority. At that time Secretary Andrews declined the request; years later he would reverse that decision. In 1918, Haynes resigned from his AALL membership to divert his finances to the war effort, but resumed his crusade for coal-mining safety the following year.[14]

As a result of his enhanced standing in the labor community and close relationship to Governor Stephens, Haynes was appointed, along with two other prominent figures, to a state arbitration board to help settle a wartime strike by Pacific Electric Railway employees in 1918. The dispute threatened to disrupt interurban transportation for workers in war industries and army and naval operations at the Los Angeles harbor. The company's anti-union militancy and immediate employment of strikebreakers raised the possibility of retaliatory violence. On the very afternoon they were appointed, Haynes, former senator Frank Flint, and Seth Brown, president of the Central Labor Council, met with representatives of the conflicting sides. Haynes reported to the governor that the workers had not demanded a closed shop as company officials had stated, that they pledged to go back to work, and that PE's representatives had not yet agreed to anything. In the ensuing months Haynes received information on the railway's tactics in countering the strike from a PE employee whom the doctor had delivered many years earlier in Philadelphia. The data aided these arbitrators and a federal mediator who eventually took over, but the dispute dragged on for years.[15]

Haynes was also involved in labor relations in a federal capacity in two instances during the war. In December 1917, he was asked by Labor Department officials to assist a federal mediator in settling a dispute between Los Angeles meatcutters and meat dealers. The conference resulted in an agreement on a minimum wage for meatcutters and averted a potential strike.[16]

In August 1918, the physician was appointed an industrial adviser for the federal draft board. His assignment was to compose monthly reports on the Southern California labor situation, documenting worker shortages and surpluses and recommending solutions for such problems. Haynes sent several reports to the U.S. Employment Service describing the local unemployment picture in Los Angeles. He recommended that a public works program be instituted before the return of servicemen from overseas aggravated the situation. But in February 1919, as the draft machinery was dismantled, the program was abandoned as otiose in peacetime America. Haynes and his fellow industrial advisers were thanked and their appointments terminated.[17]

Patriotism did affect Haynes's view of labor at one point during the war. Fearing work stoppages that would limit the war effort, he once admitted that American labor "from war causes has gotten somewhat out of hand." But he was more sympathetic to workers than to industrialists and played a small role in improving local labor conditions during the war.[18]

Outside of his state and quasi-federal duties, Haynes supported the war effort in a variety of other ways. On several occasions he wrote to U.S. Treasury Secretary William Gibbs McAdoo and U.S. senators, urging them to raise inheritance taxes, excess-profit taxes, and income taxes of the rich to better finance the war. Higher taxes would, of course, affect Haynes's own income, but he believed it necessary to bankroll the Allies and America's defense of democracy.[19]

The sale of liberty bonds was another of his wartime contributions. Early in the conflict he joined a team of businessmen who competed with other teams in soliciting friends and associates to purchase bonds. "We used to meet every day for luncheon at the Alexandria [Hotel] and read off the number of bonds sold by each team during the preceding twenty-four hours," he proudly explained later, "and we did very successful work."[20]

Also on the home front, he hoped to protect the nation's youth—soldiers and young girls—by clamping down on vice conditions. In 1917, he became chairman of the Morals Efficiency Association, a voluntary organization working with Los Angeles police to close down establishments offering gambling, liquor, and other pleasures to the large number of servicemen in the city. "One ruined young girl a day is brought to the police juvenile bureau," he noted, as a result of such conditions. The MEA hoped to restrain immorality by limiting opportunity and to combat social diseases by distributing literature provided by the American Social Hygiene Association to soldiers.[21]

Haynes's vigilance occasionally exposed a patriotic paranoia and the limits of his own tolerance of constitutional rights. In October 1917, he informed federal officials that he had been told that Germans at a Palm Springs resort were acting suspiciously (they spoke in German and refused a job offer). Two months later, after hearing of a Stanford professor's address arguing that Germany was not as evil as it was being represented, Haynes asked the Los Angeles superintendent of schools to dismiss "all teachers of pro-German sympathies" and eliminate the study of the German language in public schools. On two occasions in 1918, he wrote to the secretary of the Sons of the Revolution to report stories he had heard (not observed) of a man making derogatory remarks about the French army and of a Pasadena man who was said to have published pamphlets laudatory of the kaiser.[22]

From these activities, along with his diatribes against the "pro-German" Hearst press and other incidents, it is apparent that Haynes had little regard for civil liberties at the time. As he later explained to the Episcopal bishop of Los Angeles, he was "far from being a pacifist" then: "Had I been dictator of the United States on the third day of August, 1914, when Germany entered Belgium, I would have commenced to prepare for war. . . . Although abstractly I had sympathy with the conscientious objector, I believed he was a nuisance and interfered with the success of the war, and hence should have either been silenced or temporarily imprisoned." With such a view it is not difficult to understand why the doctor closed his eyes to free expression. As James Thompson and other historians have illustrated, many Americans, including Haynes's fellow patrician progressives, feared enemies from within and expressed intolerance of any conceivable form of dissent. Haynes willingly participated in this "American Reign of Terror," albeit not to the point of many zealots who physically harassed German-Americans, pacifists, and other dissidents. It was not until long after the armistice that he would relent by calling for an end to the prosecution of the war's political victims, petitioning the president to free conscientious objectors, and later asking friends to join him in this endeavor.[23]

The World War also tested Haynes's commitment to the American Socialist movement. Since 1913, he had been more open in his support of socialism at the national level. In newspaper articles and speeches he extolled gradual socialism as a remedy for the world's ills and predicted that it would eventually overtake the governments of the world. He called it "fundamental democracy" in one speech. In another, delivered at the 1915 World's Social Progress Congress in San Francisco, Haynes rekindled his old Christian-socialist beliefs as he argued for "economic democracy" based on Christianity as an antidote to urban problems in America and the catastrophe raging in Europe. "All of the forces for social betterment must unite in this common movement to Christianize our national and international, political, and social structures," ultimately "to Christianize war and slavery by wholly abolishing them." [24]

At this time Haynes found himself becoming more militant than he had been in the previous decade. Though abhorring violence suggested by syndicalism, he sympathized with those who resorted to violence in their war for social justice. In defending the acts of the Industrial Workers of the World (IWW), especially the general strike, he wrote to Gaylord Wilshire in England that he saw no reason why a man could not be a Socialist and a syndicalist at the same time. Wilshire claimed it impossible: "In both aims and methods the Socialist and Syndicalist disagree," for the former worked to capture votes while the latter tried to capture industries through the general strike. Haynes asserted that the majority of Socialists "would not object to sabotage if they felt that it would really advance the cause of socialism." He doubted that "burning the mill or smashing the skull of an unjust employer will really aid the workers." But if it could be proved "that the murders of some of the coal operators in England and the destruction of their property would benefit the coal miners and prevent these horrible accidents . . . I would say, 'go ahead, by all means and act.' For I consider the life of the poorest, most illiterate miner full as precious as that of the owners." [25]

In this light he could understand, though never condone, an act like that of the McNamara brothers, who bombed the *Times* building in 1910; twenty workers were accidentally killed in the blast. But this view on labor violence would not endure. In an address to workers on Labor Day, 1930, Haynes warned them: "Sabotage, murder and violence never succeed. . . . Such methods should never be used by any organization which has the welfare of the working man at heart." [26]

Haynes once declared, "To conserve my independence of action, I have never become a red card member of the Socialist Party." He did, however, financially support the local branch of the party. Nationally, he sponsored the Intercollegiate Socialist Society, the party's educational wing. In 1916, he pledged to donate $500 each year to the ISS, instead of his regular membership dues. He already had paid that year's pledge when a dispute involving free speech erupted that revealed his priorities during the war. [27]

The controversy evolved from the antiwar expressions of Scott Nearing, one of the "endorsers" whose name appeared on ISS letterhead. In 1915, Haynes had protested Nearing's dismissal from the doctor's alma mater, the University of Pennsylvania, in a dispute with the trustees. Nearing's ouster for "pernicious" and "seditious" utterances involving his criticism of child labor in nearby mines spurred his defenders to charge that this case was a denial of free speech and academic freedom. The university administration disagreed, explaining that the dismissal was based solely on the quality of Nearing's teaching ability.[28]

A similar situation appeared much differently to Haynes in 1917. Nearing was one of many noted Socialists who opposed America's entry into the war. When the doctor became aware of Nearing's close ties to the ISS, he canceled his yearly contribution and protested to the ISS treasurer:

> I am a Socialist and believe in collectivism democratically administered, with all my heart. Because of this I have been doing what little I could to help the cause. I feel, however, that if the Intercollegiate Socialist Society, thru its representatives, either orally or thru publications, fails to support vigorously the continuance of the war until the world shall have been freed forever from the menace of Prussian militarism, I shall not be justified in filling my pledge to the Society.[29]

ISS representative Harry W. Laidler answered this letter, asking Haynes to refrain from condemning or praising groups based on their position on the war. Laidler reminded the doctor that some "patriotic" groups supported the war while keeping workers in slavery. The retort fell on deaf ears; Haynes refused further contributions to the ISS until after the armistice.[30]

This episode revealed Haynes's priorities at a time when his socioeconomic philosophy collided with his national allegiance. But his motivation was more than just blind patriotism. Haynes believed that German militarism threatened not only the security of the United States but also world peace and the future of mankind. The war was "nothing less than a battle to the death between democracy and autocracy, between civilization and savagery." In this view he was in the company of a legion of Socialist intellectuals who broke with the party over its antiwar stance. Charles Edward Russell, Upton Sinclair, 1916 presidential candidate Allan Benson, former Berkeley mayor J. Stitt Wilson, and other highly visible party figures followed Woodrow Wilson into war. These bolters saw no hope for socialism in a world ruled by autocrats. Their disappointment with the "facility with which the German Socialist organization was delivered over to the Kaiser's military caste" and their repugnance of the worldwide carnage perpetrated by the Central Powers convinced them that Americans could not be neutral. Though the number of these idealists was small in relation to total party membership, their prestige made their defections especially newsworthy and contributed in a minor way to the party's concurrent decline.[31]

Some of these dissidents attempted to form a new organization for those who disagreed with the party. John Spargo, William English Walling, and others created the Social Democratic League of America to realign social-democratic forces in the country. But the objectives of the league—public ownership of railroads and utilities, abolition of child labor, direct legislation, and the like—revealed its members to be social-reform progressives rather than radicals. In 1917, league president John Spargo asked Haynes to join the budding collection of Socialists, Progressives, and even Prohibitionists, and to convince William Ghent, a former Socialist party figure then living in Los Angeles, to join also. Haynes had reason to accept the invitation, considering his agreement with all the league's principles and its emphasis on prohibition. But the physician was not inclined to support yet another national organization devoted to immediate reforms. Instead, he remained aloof from this league, which withered away in two years.[32]

During the war Haynes's major reform priority shifted from direct legislation to public ownership as the conflict proved to him that at the moment people needed to control their means of production more than they needed direct democracy. This change in attitude affected his social-reform activism for the rest of his life.

That is not to say that he curtailed his advocacy for direct legislation. In fact, after approval of the California initiative, referendum, and recall amendments in 1911, Haynes began working for the adoption of these measures in other states. At the same time he answered numerous inquiries into the workings of direct legislation in Los Angeles and California. Since direct legislation still was very controversial, his defense of the California experience with these laws was important to the spread of this doctrine.[33]

In 1913, Haynes and his Direct Legislation League became founding members of the National Popular Government League, a "permanent, central non-partisan organization to promote Constitutional and Legislative measures which will democratize our political machinery, and establish the control of government by the people." The NPGL—which was initiated by Senator Robert Owen, of Oklahoma, and Judson King, who became the organization's executive secretary—promoted the short ballot, direct primary, and other progressive goals. Its major interest was the advancement of state and local direct legislation, which attracted Haynes's immediate attention. The organization included a long list of noted national progressives, but it was Haynes and four others who kept it going financially in the early years. The doctor rarely attended NPGL meetings but did appear at its July 1916 convention in Washington, D.C. There he read a paper entitled "Direct Government in California," defending the use of the initiative, referendum, and recall in the state through the last five years. Impressed with this address, Judson King was able to have it printed as a Senate document in 1917.[34]

As the World War dragged on, Haynes revised his reform priorities. When federal authorities temporarily took control of various companies in this national emergency, the doctor recognized the opportunity for nationalization of major industries with minimal effort. Wartime government management demonstrated to him and other more leftist progressives the feasibility of public control of national resources and industry. In a letter to the NPGL three days after the armistice, Haynes recommended that the organization shift its major emphasis from direct legislation (though it was "no less important now than in the past") to government ownership, "the retention under government operation of railways, shipping, etc., and, further, the government retention and development of the oil, coal, and gas fields and water power sites that still remain in possession of the nation." Part of the battle would be won if currently government-operated facilities could be immediately taken over.[35]

At the same time Haynes urged support for nationalization of shipyards and packinghouses, and argued against returning the railways to their owners. He began a lifelong sponsorship of the Public Ownership League, founded during the war by former Socialist party official Carl D. Thompson, and took greater interest in local municipal ownership projects. Although it was only one facet of the overall program he hoped would one day guide the nation, public ownership in its many forms was a start. The World War, in the opportunities it presented for American public ownership and in its illustration of the effects of autocratic militarism in search of more markets and power, changed Haynes's reform emphasis from direct legislation to public ownership, though only by degrees. His defense of the initiative, referendum, and recall in local and state affairs still would demand much of his attention in the next decade and a half.[36]

It was during the war years that Haynes began his long association with Upton Sinclair. Haynes's first contact with the prolific novelist was in 1905, when the doctor agreed to help subsidize the publication of *The Jungle* so that the muckraking novel could appear "without mutilation" by publishers fearful of a suit by Chicago meatpackers. In 1906, Sinclair solicited from Haynes a contribution for the Intercollegiate Socialist Society, of which the novelist was a founder and officer. On both occasions the correspondence was formal since neither had met before.[37]

Sinclair moved to Pasadena in 1915 and quickly came into contact with local socialists. Within a short time he met and visited Haynes at his Figueroa Street residence. Haynes took an instant liking to the novelist, for the two had quite a bit in common: a commitment to socialism and prohibition, and absolute support of the U.S. war effort. In order to advance Sinclair's writing and activism, Haynes critiqued manuscripts of Sinclair's novels, supplied information needed by the author to complete other works, and gave him money for "pressing necessities." While admitting to William Ghent that Sinclair was prone to exaggerate, "sometimes makes entirely erroneous statements; is not judicial; is intensely egotistical and loves the limelight," the doctor believed that the novelist's work was crucial in promoting the cause of social democracy.[38]

This belief was well illustrated in Haynes's role in the republication of *Cry for Justice: An Anthology of the Literature of Social Justice*, which Sinclair had edited. First printed in 1915, the volume sold reasonably well, but Sinclair thought the retail price too high. In order to distribute it more cheaply to a mass audience, he decided to purchase the copyright and bookplates and print thousands of copies to be sold at bargain prices. Lacking the needed capital, he appealed to Haynes and others to subscribe to the project. In March 1917, Haynes agreed to become "one of a number" of subscribers, ultimately the only one. Negotiations between Haynes, Sinclair, and a printer produced a new edition in cloth and paper covers in 1921.[39]

The republication of *Cry for Justice*, with an introduction by Jack London, made this collection of essays and poetry available to almost everyone. Though Haynes never did recoup his investment (he never expected to), he did receive the gratitude of Sinclair in an acknowledgment at the beginning of the book:

> Dr. John R. Haynes, of Los Angeles, very generously purchased from the publishers the plates and copyright of this book in order to make possible the issuing of this edition. I asked Dr. Haynes if he would let me make acknowledgement to him in the book, and he answered: "Dedicate the book to those unknown ones, who by their dimes and quarters keep the Socialist movement going; to the poor and obscure people who sacrifice themselves in order to bring about a better world, which they may never live to see. Write this as eloquently as you can, and it will be the best possible dedication to 'The Cry for Justice.'"
>
> I decided, after thinking it over, to combine my own idea with the idea of Dr. Haynes.

Not exactly Dr. Haynes's words, this dedication reflected his intent, though not his request for anonymity.[40]

Another of Haynes's humanitarian endeavors at this time was his concern with child labor. He had been interested in this issue for years but did not become vocal about it until 1914. In that year he wrote an essay for *The Western Collegian* asserting that every child had a right to the highest possible level of education, no matter the economic status of the parents. In order to "perfect our democracy," he urged readers to contact their congressmen to support a bill to exclude interstate commerce of all goods manufactured by child labor.[41]

In the following year he joined the National Child Labor Committee and began agitating for "the two million little wage slaves who are toiling in the factories and mines of the United States." He implored the local Municipal League to investigate child labor and its relation to civic affairs in Los Angeles. He demanded that the children's bureau of the U.S. Department of Labor exercise more than just investigative powers. In 1916, he encouraged support for the national child labor bill, which superseded many state laws already enacted. The bill passed, but less than two years later it was declared unconstitutional by the U.S. Supreme Court.[42]

This ruling infuriated Haynes and exacerbated his growing distrust of the American judiciary. How could five men "override the will of a hundred million people?" he asked Hiram Johnson. America "has clearly no right to call itself a republic; it is definitely an oligarchy in its form of government as was Venice under the rule of the Council of Ten." Haynes wrote in similar fashion to the National Child Labor Committee, offering to "subscribe liberally" to the organization if it would "vigorously prosecute" a movement to curtail the power of the Supreme Court to nullify laws. The child labor controversy solidified his views of judges as servants of the nation's business leaders and of the necessity of the recall of the judiciary. In that same year he spoke of the Supreme Court as a usurper of power and suggested that a national initiative might be needed to put the court in its place. Like California jurists of the previous decade who, according to Haynes, were only tools of the Southern Pacific Railroad, the majority on the U.S. Supreme Court represented the same reactionary and greedy interests of giant corporations, in this case exploiting children for profit.[43]

Haynes's fulminations against the power of the court in this instance were obviously provoked by the fact that the court ruled in opposition to his own view. He did not, of course, oppose judges who agreed with him. He was one of many progressives who supported the nomination of Louis Brandeis to the Supreme Court in 1916. To Haynes, Brandeis represented the antithesis of the typical justice, a foe rather than friend of monopoly, and a champion of the rights of labor. After the nomination, Haynes encouraged President Wilson to promote Brandeis's confirmation in the Senate, to combat the "invisible government" that opposed democracy and would block Brandeis. More to the political point, Haynes warned the president that failure of confirmation would mean the loss of many thousands of Wilson votes in California. Brandeis became the doctor's single most noteworthy exception to his general estimation of Supreme Court justices for many years.[44]

World War I modified and clarified Haynes's views on a number of issues. Most importantly, it revealed a fervent patriotism occasionally bordering on fanaticism. It is ironic that he almost became a victim of the xenophobia that followed the war. In the short era of the Red Scare, when federal and local governments exacerbated fears of Communist subversion and violence with massive arrests of radicals and immigrants, Haynes's loyalty was called into question because of his ties to the American Socialist movement.[45]

The Red Scare of 1919 was ignited in the east, but swept rapidly westward. Spurred by Attorney General A. Mitchell Palmer's raids, in which thousands of suspected radicals were arrested, the frenzy hit Los Angeles, where the *Times* and its allies demanded similar actions to stamp out "Bolshevik conspirators." In the postwar era of economic instability, nationwide strikes, IWW activity, and terrorist bombings, the business community created the Commercial Federation to lobby for state and local action against suspected Communists, anarchists, and their sympathizers. At the state level it pressured the legislature to pass a law criminalizing syndicalism, aimed at the Industrial Workers of the World. At the county level, the federation and the *Times* fought for grand jury inquisitions of local "Reds." After investigating IWW activities and soliciting secret information from anonymous tipsters, the grand jury was able to indict citizens for "advocating the doctrine of syndicalism" or other offenses. The district attorney stated during the investigation of a Humane Animal Commission inspector accused of mouthing pro-Bolshevik thoughts: "We are attempting to make it impossible for a man to make this kind of utterance in the county and enjoy any degree of peace and happiness: we intend to make treason as unpopular as possible."[46]

Dr. Haynes was caught in the Red Scare web as a result of his continued participation in a loose network of social democrats. As in the years since 1898, he freely associated with socialists both in and out of the party. In the 1910s, this circle included party members such as Job Harriman, local ISS chapter president Rob Wagner, lawyers George Downing and J. H. Ryckman, and the newly arrived Upton Sinclair and William Ghent. They worked with individuals like Haynes in such groups as the Severance Club to aid social democracy outside of official party business. This activity included raising funds for lectures, utopian colonies such as Harriman's Llano del Rio, and other projects, and generating public approval from more affluent community leaders.[47]

The network also included Mrs. Kate Crane Gartz, a wealthy clubwoman from nearby Altadena, who became very vocal about her support for socialism and very generous to its leaders. She raised the profile of this group by bringing national figures such as Max Eastman and Floyd Dell to speak at her home, showered a fortune on the cause, and later published tracts containing her protest letters to local and national officials, newspaper editors, and apostate radicals. She and Haynes formed a mutual admiration society as they worked toward the same goals. He once confided to her, "That such women as yourself exist in the world is one of the hopeful signs of these reactionary times." She chastised a conservative for opposing the doctor, asking where else in Los Angeles is there a man "who gives his time and his money to the solving of problems that are to benefit humanity—no selfish interest dominates his activities."[48]

In December 1919, the county grand jury investigated "parlor radicals" and Socialist party members. Along with Mrs. Gartz, writer Rob Wagner, and others, Haynes was subpoenaed to testify concerning his knowledge of the subversive activities of the IWW. The doctor pleaded illness on the two days he was to testify, while the *Times* delightedly described his predicament.[49]

Haynes's dismissal from testimony followed his scathing protest to District Attorney Thomas L. Woolwine. The physician could not believe that his patriotism was being challenged and denied that he sympathized with anarchists. He demanded that Woolwine have local newspapers print the letter to give equal publicity to his many civic accomplishments. In that same month Upton Sinclair described Haynes's plight in an article in

Appeal to Reason, detailing how this philanthropist who contributed heavily to a milk fund for the city's children was required to leave his sickbed to be interrogated in a witchhunt. Upon further reflection the district attorney decided that the doctor need not appear before the grand jury.[50]

A major force behind the subversive hysteria in Los Angeles was the *Times*, which continued to take every opportunity to jab at Haynes. In an editorial concerning members "of the 'parlor Bolsheviki' cult," the newspaper expressed pleasure at having "had frequent occasion to sound a warning against vicious tendencies of the doctrines and causes which he has espoused." With this and other attacks in mind, Haynes was amused to find in 1920 that *Times* publisher Harry Chandler and a syndicate of his closest business and political allies had just signed a lease with the Soviets to develop oil and coal fields in northeast Siberia. Upon hearing of Chandler's ties with real Russian Bolsheviks, Haynes could not help but to pick up his pen and ask "Harry" how he could "conscientiously enter into a business deal with Lenin, a man you had been daily denouncing as a blood thirsty fiend desirous of destroying all property rights throughout the world." [51]

Chandler again took the offensive in 1921, when the *Times* learned that Haynes had donated $500 to the Intercollegiate Socialist Society back in 1919. The doctor made this contribution with the understanding that it would not be publicized, but the information was mistakenly released. The controversy died out quickly, although Haynes would be hounded again when the county grand jury discovered that he had paid the lawyer's fees for a Canadian serviceman who had published a "radical" paper after the war and was accused of treason against the United States! In this case the doctor was not required to appear and the incident was closed.[52]

Had the *Times* learned of Haynes's 1916 contribution to Max Eastman's *The Masses*, it would have had another opportunity to flay the doctor during the Red Scare. Socialist theorist William Ghent once ridiculed this magazine as a worthless publication financed by "rich men and women of that nebulous middle world which lies somewhere between the Socialist movement and the world of bourgeois complacency." To papers like the *Times*, Eastman's journal bordered on bolshevism, and Chandler missed this chance to connect it to Haynes. Nevertheless, the *Times* found ample opportunity to tie his philosophy of gradual, democratic socialism to the violence of anarchism and an IWW exaggerated to the extreme. Haynes might have been tarnished, but he survived the Red Scare with more integrity than his opponents.[53]

The World War impressed upon Haynes the need for an international organization of nations in which conflicts could be resolved to avoid future wars. Like many progressives he applauded President Wilson's efforts to establish the League of Nations. When a Republican group in the U.S. Senate led by Henry Cabot Lodge formed a united opposition to the plan, Haynes tried to convince Senator Hiram Johnson to lead support for the league, or at least endorse a national referendum on the subject. Johnson, who already had decided to run for president in 1920, was making defeat of the league his chief campaign issue. As he explained to Haynes, Wilson's league or any other such organization would force Americans onto battlefields to protect other nations who went to war—for example, Japan and Korea, or England and the many territories in her far-flung empire. The former governor refused to back any such plan, and made its defeat his top priority.[54]

Johnson's reply did not diminish Haynes's belief in American participation in the league. He continued to work for Senate approval of Wilson's proposal until it was defeated for a second time in 1920. The disagreement with Johnson caused a temporary strain in their relationship, as Haynes indicated to Meyer Lissner in 1921. Lissner wrote to the senator that Haynes was afraid to approach him about an unrelated matter because of their recent difference of opinion over the league, "as to which I think the Doctor has very largely seen the light." This observation of Haynes's wavering is further confirmed in a 1923 letter in which he stated that the League of Nations might not be the ideal way to encourage peace in the world. But by the mid 1920s, he again was solidly behind the idea, serving on the board of directors of the Southern California branch of the League of Nations Non-Partisan Association. The events of those years convinced him that it was vital for America to join the only organization offering at least the possibility of world peace.[55]

While the League of Nations controversy raged in 1919, the coming 1920 national election posed another dilemma for Haynes. He hoped that another progressive would follow Wilson, and was unsure which candidate to support in the primary. Privately and publicly he expressed admiration for Herbert Hoover's work on the Belgium Relief Commission and his service as national food administrator during the war, and the doctor seems to have been pulling for him. But Harry Chandler and his friends also were boosting the candidate at the time, and Haynes preferred not to be associated with them. Dora Haynes did endorse Hoover, calling him "one of the greatest men of the nation." She joined the Hoover Republican Club, which included progressives Russ Avery, Marshall Stimson, Harley Brundige, and Mrs. Florence Lindley, as well as the Chandler contingent.[56]

Haynes finally agreed to sponsor Hiram Johnson, even though he disagreed with Johnson's stand on the League of Nations (which alienated many California progressives). The doctor refrained from making public pronouncements, but contributed to Johnson's campaign and cooperated with Johnson's backers in the primary. Working with Johnson's new sponsors, who included some of Haynes's old political enemies, standpatters, and antilabor figures, was not a pleasant task, so the doctor remained aloof. His support of Johnson might have resulted from his having suggested in 1916 that Johnson run for president in 1920, but was more likely a ploy to secure the senator's help in campaigning against a state proposition limiting the initiative that year. For whichever motive, John Haynes unenthusiastically backed the senator, while Dora Haynes defended Hoover until the convention. Both were disappointed when Ohio senator Warren G. Harding won the nomination, and even more so when this conservative League of Nations opponent became president.[57]

In the aftermath of World War I, Haynes survived the Red Scare, during which his loyalty was questioned, and had to accept the defeat of the League of Nations, his hope for the future of world peace. These and other issues tested his beliefs in many tenets of democracy and found some of them as paradoxical as his status as a capitalistic socialist. In some cases stubborn single-mindedness prevailed over his usual pragmatism; in others he remained a gracious diplomat. Through it all, an unflagging patriotism dictated his actions and continued to shape his vision of how his society should evolve.

Chapter Ten

"We Cannot Afford to Permit the Reactionaries to Dig In"

The armistice enabled Dr. Haynes to devote more effort to his political and social causes. From the war years through the 1920s, he enhanced his role as a strategist of the state progressive forces in protecting reforms won in the previous decade and in promoting others. On the local scene he resumed his position as one of Los Angeles's most influential political figures, leading the fight for expansion of municipal ownership of electrical power. In both victory and defeat he displayed a fierce determination to combat the forces of retrenchment he believed to be threatening the limited accomplishments of two decades of progressive reform.

Historians used to accept the interpretation that World War I ended the Progressive Era in the United States. With the "Roaring Twenties" signaling a shift in national sentiment from reform to "normalcy," Americans abandoned efforts to improve their institutions and instead pursued wealth and material objects, loosened their social mores, and shifted their political views to the right. More recent studies have revised this view. Although presidential administrations of the 1920s were unsympathetic to further reform, the era witnessed renewed attempts by old progressives, Socialists, and other reformers to expand government ownership and regulation, and create new social programs for the underprivileged. The reformers failed in most of these campaigns for various reasons, but they did not give up their fight. "Progressivism" as an amorphous reform movement composed of many groups and issues was not as successful in the 1920s, but it was not dead.[1]

California is a classic example. With Hiram Johnson's departure to Washington, D.C., in March 1917, the state's progressives lost their fiery figurehead, and wartime emergencies leaped above reform measures on the priority list. But as Jackson Putnam has observed, "progressivism in the 1920s, while sharply challenged and perhaps overshadowed by contrary forces, did not 'die' but lived on in a different and possibly less attractive form." Progressives elected governors and state legislators, protected Johnson-era accomplishments, and even took the offensive to expand those reforms. At the same time many of them continued to display a lack of tolerance of perceived enemies ranging from leftists to Asians.[2]

In this second phase of California progressivism, Dr. Haynes played an even more prominent role than he had in the first. In the years of Johnson's administration, Haynes had only modest influence compared to Meyer Lissner and a few northern Californians. After Johnson's departure, the doctor's situation changed. The state's new chief executive, William D. Stephens, was a longtime personal friend and very receptive to Haynes's advice, both in medicine and politics. The governor had arrived in Los Angeles in 1887 (the same year as Haynes), was successful in the grocery business, and joined the nonpartisan reformers. His civic stature was such that Municipal League leaders made him their first choice to run for mayor in the Arthur Harper recall contest. After Harper resigned in 1909, Stephens agreed to serve as interim mayor. In 1910 he was elected to Congress as a Lincoln-Roosevelt candidate, and he won reelection in 1912 and 1914. Two years later he was appointed lieutenant governor by a reluctant Hiram Johnson, who bowed to the pressure of Haynes and other Southern Californians. When Johnson took his U.S. Senate seat in March 1917, Stephens became the state's twenty-fourth chief executive.[3]

Once in office Governor Stephens listened to Haynes's advice. The doctor made a number of patronage recommendations and frequently suggested that the governor take a certain stand on pending legislation. Stephens solicited and usually followed this advice and selected Haynes for various state positions to aid the administration. In his first year in office, Stephens appointed the doctor to the State Council of Defense and made him mediator in Los Angeles labor disputes. Haynes's influence in the Republican party grew when he was selected for the executive committee of the State Central Committee, an important post in which to help his friend Stephens remain in office.[4]

Stephens ran for governor in his own right in 1918, and Haynes took charge of the campaign. He advised Stephens to avoid seeking harmony with more conservative Republicans, who would not vote for him anyway, and to run as an unabashed "radical progressive." "I am zealous that you achieve equal or greater distinction by a program, if possible, even more comprehensive and aggressively progressive" than that of Hiram Johnson, Haynes urged. With his contributions and speeches, Haynes campaigned for the governor along with most state progressives. In the primary election the state's infamous cross-filing law eliminated Stephen's chief Republican opponent and the Democratic nominee. In the general election, with voter turnout limited by a tremendous influenza epidemic, Stephens handily defeated an independent candidate.[5]

During Stephens's regular term, he continued to seek Haynes's counsel, which the doctor was more than willing to offer. Stephens did not become the "radical progressive" Haynes had envisioned; indeed, the governor was viewed as a conservative in his overzealous stand against syndicalism during the Red Scare and in his support of Japanese exclusion. On these subjects, however, he stood with many progressive leaders, while on most issues he agreed with Haynes.[6]

With respect to governmental efficiency Stephens relied on Haynes's expertise by appointing him to the State Committee on Efficiency and Economy in 1918. This body of eleven civic figures was charged with examining the structure and operation of state government and recommending a plan to streamline departments for better bureaucratic control. Haynes asked to be appointed chairman of the subcommittee dealing with social agencies because of his experience in that field. This request was granted, and he also was assigned to subcommittees dealing with civil service and state defense and with public health and legal service. In this work he participated in public hearings and surveyed existing state agencies in regard to duties and operations. After several months the committee recommended that the 70 agencies be grouped into 10 departments. Stephens modified this plan and introduced it to the 1921 legislature, which passed a package of bills consolidating the agencies into 5 departments. This system was further modified in 1927, when several new departments were added.[7]

Stephens's administration, on the whole, produced more accomplishments than failures, but the governor's colorless and overly pragmatic style left many voters weary of reform. When he ran for reelection in 1922, conservative Republican leaders made every effort to defeat him in the primary, offering apostate progressive and former state treasurer Friend Richardson as an alternative. Haynes and his fellow progressives stood by their governor as the doctor assumed the duties of finance chairman of the Stephens campaign, coercing friends and associates to donate.

Richardson harped on government economy and spendthrift progressives, while Stephens ignored spending as the paramount issue. Thus Richardson narrowly defeated the incumbent in the primary, and moved on to crush Democrat Thomas Lee Woolwine in the general election.[8]

An outspoken opponent of Richardson by this time, Haynes was sure the new governor would sweep all progressives from appointive offices as soon as possible. "I do not like the idea of being fired by Richardson," Haynes wrote to Stephens, so he resigned his position on the State Board of Charities and Corrections in January 1923, just one week before Richardson's inauguration. In his parting shot, Stephens appointed Haynes a regent of the University of California with a fifteen-year term, well out of reach of Richardson's vengeance.[9]

The regental appointment was not strictly political since Haynes had had an interest in education policy for many years. He had praised public education and its opportunities for children of all economic circumstances, preaching that it would lead to a more democratic society. "Those who believe in plutocracy and plutocratic control of government have made a grave mistake in allowing the common herd to be educated," he believed. In 1902, he headed a committee pledged to establish a University of California extension program in Los Angeles. Through the years he remained interested in local education and the state's university, for which he lobbied the regents in 1919 to appoint someone like John Dewey to the presidency, rather than the "reactionary of reactionaries," Nicholas Murray Butler, of Columbia. In 1920, Governor Stephens appointed Haynes a delegate to the State Conference on Education, and in the following year the doctor assumed the lead in the campaign to give local high school teachers more input in administrative matters and to keep the influence of right-wing groups out of the schools. Also in that year he joined the executive board of the Committee for a National Department of Education, which he promoted in letters to all members of the U.S. Congress. The regental appointment, then, was not just a political plum but an opportunity for Haynes to act on his interest in higher education.[10]

The election of Friend Richardson appeared to Haynes and other social reform progressives as the triumph of a reactionary countermovement that gained momentum just after the war. Described by one historian as a "flamboyant conservative whose bristling mustache and rotund figure made him appear almost a caricature of the conservative, capitalistic 'fat cat,' " Richardson aptly represented the forces opposing continued reform. He demanded retrenchment in state spending and elimination of many progressive accomplishments. To Haynes and others, Richardson's victory marked the return to power of the stand-pat forces of the pre-1910 period.[11]

Richardson was elected at a time when the progressive leadership was splitting even further. The rift between Hiram Johnson and southern progressives in 1916 had worsened; many of the latter had refused to support him because of this division and his opposition to the League of Nations. Johnson, in turn, worked against Stephens's election in 1918, and backed conservative Samuel Shortridge for U.S. senator against progressives William Kent and James Phelan in 1920. In 1922, more state progressives deserted Johnson in the Republican primary to support C. C. Moore, also the choice of Harry Chandler and other conservatives. Even Haynes toyed with the idea of backing Moore if Johnson did not help in the campaign for progressive initiatives on the ballot that year. By late 1922, the old leadership of state progressivism was in disarray, dimming the reelection hopes of Governor Stephens.[12]

In the midst of this feuding, Haynes made several attempts to reverse the trend. In the period from 1916 to 1920 he tried to remain friendly with members of all factions. Always the diplomat in keeping progressives together, he was one of the few common friends of Stephens and Johnson. In September 1920, Haynes invited a number of state progressives—Franklin Hichborn, Chester Rowell, William Kent, Katherine P. Edson, and others—to a meeting in Sacramento, hoping to unite the quarreling reformers and renew their enthusiasm for the fight against "reactionary forces throughout the nation" that were trying to dismantle programs they had worked for so diligently. A year later he entertained the idea of reinvigorating progressivism by creating a new reform party. He envisaged a statewide version of the national party advanced by former Bull Moosers such as Amos Pinchot, a "liberal organization in California which will have in its platform, freedom of speech, press, and assembly and other fundamentally democratic principles. Not ultra radicalism but sane and safe liberalism would be the basis for the organization." He suggested this idea to Hiram Johnson as a way to arrest the "wave of reaction" sweeping the country. Johnson declined to participate, however, thus nipping the ambitious scheme in the bud.[13]

On another level Haynes contributed to the progressive defense by counterattacking its major organized opponent, the Better America Federation. This group of right-wing superpatriots evolved from the local Commercial Federation at the height of the Red Scare. Formed ostensibly "to continue the forcible suppression of radicals which had been a notable feature of the war effort," the group's "American Plan" program was a thinly disguised assault on organized labor, civil liberties, and progressivism in general. Centered in Los Angeles, its membership included a bevy of business leaders and politicians led by H. M. Haldeman and promoted by the *Times*. BAF activities included distribution of antilabor literature, encouraging students to spy on "disloyal" teachers, endorsing state and local candidates pledged to its platform, and lobbying in Sacramento. In its first year of existence, the BAF was tremendously influential, prompting Katherine P. Edson to admit to a confidant, "Even the judges are crawling to their chairman, Mr. Harry Haldeman, and explaining why they make the decisions they do." The organization remained an active though discredited force in Los Angeles beyond 1927, when Haldeman and five other leaders were indicted in the Julian Petroleum Company scandal.[14]

As the BAF grew, so did the ranks of its opponents. Organized labor, teachers, and progressive leaders were the first to realize the intent of the BAF and mobilized the progressive coalition to stop it. The YWCA, which incurred the BAF's wrath for endorsing the eight-hour day for women, carried out a lengthy fight with Haldeman over this issue. Even the Women's Republican Study Club attacked the BAF for its misogynistic literature. Despite its many allies, the BAF made many enemies, and gradually faded away in the 1930s.[15]

Haynes figured heavily in the fight against the BAF. The organization alarmed him because its membership included leaders of a group that attacked the state initiative process. More importantly, he opposed the hypocritical flag-waving with which the organization decorated its efforts to crush unions and progressive achievements. He wrote letters to BAF sympathizers and others to point out the dangers of accepting the BAF platform as an act of patriotism. In order to monitor the organization's progress, he even joined up; as a member he would receive its literature and learn its strategy.[16]

Haynes also fought the BAF in a more public manner. He inspired newspaper articles criticizing this new band of "Patrioteers" and its wellpaid speakers. In local educational circles he helped organizations that were trying to limit BAF infiltration of public schools. In initiative and legislative campaigns, Haynes contributed to and spoke for groups opposing the superpatriots. So active was he that Franklin Hichborn described the doctor as fighting the BAF almost single-handedly in the early stages.[17]

The BAF's anti-progressive attacks also had to be countered in the state legislature. In the early 1920s, Haynes subsidized Hichborn's expenses while the reporter monitored political activity in Sacramento. Mainly concerned with direct legislation and similar matters, Haynes kept tabs on all issues and frequently advised legislators on pending laws. One of the most important, he thought, was the 1923 Bromley bill, which would give Governor Richardson the power to immediately replace all state appointees with his own choices. Haynes helped to lead the opposition to this law, which would have removed nonelected progressives in state government. This bill passed in both houses, so Haynes and others threatened a state referendum campaign to rescind it. Fearing a possible defeat early in his term, Richardson declined to sign the bill into law.[18]

Haynes played a larger role in opposing Richardson's 1923 state budget. Keeping his election promise to cut spending, Richardson presented a spending plan with deep cuts in education and humanitarian services. The proposal virtually abolished several commissions created by the progressives, including the State Board of Charities and Corrections and the Immigration and Housing Commission. Haynes protested vehemently, urging progressive leaders to fight the cuts. Vowing "I certainly will not see my life's work destroyed under the false slogan of economy without making the hardest fight of my life," he warned that Richardson was intent on killing all "humanitarian, social service, and educational legislation that was put in the constitution and the state law by our good friend Hiram." Richardson's designs revealed him to be an "unconscionable brute of the ass variety," Haynes wrote to another commissioner, urging him to stop the governor and his BAF sponsors. Haynes's exhortations to progressives, statements to the press, and subsidizing of reports proving that the "economy measures" were actually aimed at gutting progressive achievements put him in the forefront of the battle. In the end, it was not enough. Richardson's budget passed, and with his veto power the governor blocked efforts to restore the eliminated programs.[19]

Richardson and his allies also took the offensive in a personal attack on Haynes via his midnight appointment as a UC regent by Governor Stephens. In May 1923, retaliating against Haynes for his role in the state budget fight, Richardson reappointed P. T. Bowles, of Oakland, to the regental position occupied by the doctor. The governor justified this action by arguing that Haynes's appointment had never received the requisite senate confirmation and thus was null. Stephens had in fact never requested confirmation, having been advised by the state attorney general that a change made in 1918 to the state law prescribing such appointments had rendered senate confirmation unnecessary.[20]

Richardson's move did not come as a complete surprise. The *Times* had predicted it in January, after publishing an editorial criticizing Stephens for appointing a "Socialist for Regent," in reference to Haynes's contributions to the Intercollegiate Socialist Society. Franklin Hichborn informed Haynes that the Bowles appointment was railroaded through the legislature late at night by state senator Arthur Breed at the behest of the governor. It was clear that Richardson wanted revenge.[21]

Haynes did not take this slap lightly. He wrote to each of the other regents, requesting their support, and asked secretary R. G. Sproul to have the regents' lawyer look into it. The regents advised Haynes that he had nothing to worry about, but the doctor hired his own lawyer anyway. At the June 12 meeting, Richardson personally introduced Bowles to Haynes and the other regents, and Bowles presented his credentials. Haynes "refused to yield to the demand" of the interloper, and the matter moved on to the courts. Before it could be legally settled, another regent died and Bowles assumed the vacancy. Richardson finally backed down, declining to pursue Haynes's removal until two years later, when he failed again.[22]

While defending himself in the regent controversy, Haynes joined a number of progressives in attempting to reinvigorate their ranks after the Bromley and budget battles. In late August 1923, they created the Progressive Voters League "to restore, maintain and promote a progressive state government." Branches were established in the north and south, with Haynes serving on the executive board of the latter. State senator Herbert C. Jones was elected president, and Franklin Hichborn and other noted progressives served in various capacities. Financed chiefly by Haynes and Rudolph Spreckels, with small donations from other individuals, the league established a network of sympathizers, disseminated information, publicly criticized the Richardson administration, and planned and executed progressive election campaigns. The timing was just right for the 1924 contest for the legislature; they picked up a few seats. With this victory the group decided not to disband but to plan ahead for the upcoming gubernatorial contest. "We cannot afford to permit the reactionaries to dig in. Now is the time to block them," wrote Haynes to a sympathetic legislator.[23]

Progressive Voters League leaders also participated in the presidential campaign of Senator Robert La Follette that year. With the major parties nominating two conservatives in 1924, many California progressives were pleased when La Follette entered the race. Like that of other states, California's political structure offered no possibility of placing his new Progressive party on the ballot in such a short time. "Fighting Bob" could only appear if he headed the ticket of a party already qualified, and the Socialist party was the only available opportunity. That label gave the opposition wide latitude in condemning the Wisconsin senator and his chief backers, including Rudolph Spreckels, state chairman of this campaign, and Haynes, treasurer of the Southern California Committee for La Follette. These two and other leftist progressives campaigned for "Fighting Bob" in the spirit of the Bull Moose crusade of 1912.[24]

Initially, Haynes had supported Hiram Johnson's bid for the Republican nomination, but he was sure it would go to President Coolidge. In a letter to William G. McAdoo in January 1924, the doctor admitted the futility of backing Johnson and promised to support McAdoo if the Democrats nominated him. After the conventions, Haynes refused to endorse Coolidge (a "moron" according to Haynes), or Democrat John W. Davis, whom the doctor believed to be an antilabor corporation mouthpiece. Although he turned down the opportunity to become a La Follette elector in California, Haynes entered the campaign and worked with Spreckels and Hichborn to raise funds, organize support, line up electors, and speak. He disagreed with La Follette's wartime pacifism and opposition to prohibition, but he would happily vote for "Fighting Bob" anyway. The United States was a plutocracy at the moment, he told one audience, and La Follette was the nation's only hope to kick Wall Street out of Washington, D.C.[25]

From the outset there was little chance that La Follette could win. But with progressive help he far outdistanced his Democratic rival in California while being swept away in the Coolidge landslide. Even in defeat this contest was a moral victory for Haynes and other California progressives of social-reform proclivities, who regrouped in 1925 to challenge Governor Richardson and his conservative allies once again.

The most important single issue in state politics for Dr. Haynes was the protection of the direct-legislation measures in the California Constitution. During the war several attempts were made to alter the initiative law in the 1917 legislature. One bill proposed the creation of a "counter petition" allowing opponents of an initiative to keep it off the ballot if they could gather signatures of 10 percent of the voters. Another prohibited the use of the initiative and referendum in matters concerning taxation. In both instances Haynes resurrected his Direct Legislation League to bombard legislators with letters urging defeat.[26]

In a different situation, Haynes refused to oppose an initiative that opponents claimed would restrict direct legislation. In 1918, he was asked to help defeat Proposition 20, which would establish a state health insurance system, because the proposal was written so that it could not be modified by referendum. A staunch defender of government-sponsored health insurance, Haynes attacked the argument that the "referendum-proof" feature would nullify the state law. In fact, he became a proponent of the measure, along with organized labor and other groups. Critics charged that it would create a medical monopoly, but the state's physicians opposed it, prodding Haynes to complain that his comrades by occupation would fight anything that adversely affected their incomes. Aligned with insurance companies, Christian Scientists, and fiscal conservatives, the doctors led the successful struggle to defeat Proposition 20.[27]

Far overshadowing any other state issue relating to direct legislation was the controversy stirred by the proposal for a single tax, a controversy Haynes feared might result in the virtual extinction of the initiative. For several years he marshalled the progressive forces of the state in a defense of the initiative against those who opposed either the single tax, direct legislation, or both. In this campaign he demonstrated the same determination he had shown in 1911 in the struggle to make state direct legislation a reality.

The conflict began as a reaction to proposals to establish the single tax in California. Henry George's call for a tax system based solely on the unearned increment in the rental value of land spawned a number of clubs in Los Angeles to advocate the idea in the 1890s, though nothing beyond discussion was accomplished. Aided by publicity surrounding the campaigns of single-tax advocates in Great Britain and Canada in the 1910s, agitation for a state single tax increased. The movement was boosted by the growing influence of Socialists, some of whom advocated it as a step toward the cooperative commonwealth, though doctrinaire Marxists opposed it as a halfway measure.[28]

The single tax, or "Home Rule in Taxation," was offered as a state initiative in 1912, 1914, and 1916, but generated an increasing number of opposition votes each biennium. The movement did not lose momentum, however. In fact, it prospered under the stimulus of competing advocacy organizations: the San Francisco-based Equity Tax League, led by former Berkeley mayor J. Stitt Wilson, and the more radical Great Adventure, located in Los Angeles. Both survived the defeats and began campaigning for yet another single-tax initiative in 1918.[29]

In the meantime, the People's Anti-Single Tax League (PASTL) was founded by representatives of the banking, transportation, oil, and real estate industries. In 1917, the group's leaders decided to take the offensive by restricting the initiative, the weapon of their opponents. The antis proposed to circulate an initiative that would limit the opportunity to submit certain initiatives to the voters: if a measure was defeated by a four-to-three margin, it could not be submitted again for eight years; if beaten three-to-two, it could not be submitted for twenty years; and if defeated two-to-one, it could never again appear on the ballot. The PASTL leaders decided not to circulate this proposal, however, but to defeat the 1918 single-tax proposition—and they did. The organization then began its crusade to curry legislative favor for restricting direct legislation.[30]

In the 1919 legislative session, PASTL lobbied for restriction of the initiative and referendum in matters of taxation. In concert with other opponents of direct legislation, the league supported a constitutional amendment raising the number of signatures required for initiatives from 8 percent to 25 percent of those who voted in the last regular election, a proportion unachievable by any but the very wealthiest interest groups. Haynes mobilized his Direct Legislation League to oppose the measure "fathered by E. P. Clark and his little coterie of corporation men called the Anti-Single Tax League." He warned all legislators and Governor Stephens that passage of the bill would "be hailed by Eastern reactionary journals as evidence that California, hitherto the leader in progressive movements, had become tired of direct legislation." Haynes personally appeared at the legislative session to argue against the bill and paid half the expenses of labor lobbyist Paul Scharrenberg to continue the battle. With the aid of various interest groups and Governor Stephens, the measure finally was killed.[31]

Not to be silenced by this reversal, PASTL leaders took the issue to the voters in the form of an initiative proposal. The petition was virtually identical to the defeated bill. In addition, the campaign leaders tried to link the initiative process to the controversial single tax so that the more radical backers of the latter would be seen as champions of the initiative as well. This intertwining of the initiative process with the disruptive taxation measure might turn advocates of direct legislation into opponents out of fear of the single-tax initiative, which was also scheduled to appear on the 1920 ballot.[32]

Dr. Haynes had to tread carefully through this controversy in order to protect the initiative process without being tied to a more leftist cause. As he explained to many correspondents, he was not in favor of the single tax per se. For years he had been a member of the Henry George Lecture Association, and in 1912 he had publicly advocated a heavy tax on vacant land rather than industry to help industrialize Los Angeles. During the 1916 single-tax campaign he wrote an essay for the Socialist party organ in which he defended the single tax in principle, but opposed its rigid application:

> I am not a "single taxer" in the strict sense of the term. Unlike Henry George I favor other forms of taxes. I oppose taxes on consumption, food, clothing and shelter, and taxes on labor, licenses, etc., for these are taxes on life. They take the food from the mouths of little children, the real assets of society. I favor taxes on wealth, on land with an exemption, perhaps, of say $1000 on land used as an actual homestead by the owner. I favor taxes on incomes and inheritances, graduated, with very heavy increases in the case of persons and estates of very large wealth.

And, in character, he believed the land tax should be introduced gradually over a period of ten to twenty years, "so that conditions can adjust themselves without disasters that come from sudden and violent changes."[33]

During the 1919 legislative session he explained to Governor Stephens, "I am just as much opposed to the single tax in the form in which it was submitted at the last election as are Mr. Clark and his followers." Haynes voted against the measure and would do so again, but he saw no reason why the initiative process itself should be modified as a means to prevent similar proposals. He wrote in the same vein to state senators, admitting that "large landed estates in California must in some way be broken up," perhaps with a graduated land tax like that in Australia. In any event, Haynes had established his own views on the subject long before the 1920 campaign, when PASTL tried to entangle direct legislation with the dreaded single-tax panacea.[34]

In early 1920, single-taxers circulated petitions for their proposal as PASTL gathered signatures for its proposition to restrict initiatives affecting taxes. Concerned that a more unified effort would have to be made to counter the expensive PASTL crusade, Haynes created the League to Protect the Initiative. In February he had mentioned his idea for the league to Franklin Hichborn, the Santa Clara writer closely associated with Rudolph Spreckels and other northern California progressives. Haynes suggested that it be "composed only of sane, safe professional, business men and women," explaining, "we do not want known single taxers or ultra radicals" who would alienate the group from middle-class voters. Within two weeks the LPI came into being, a virtual paper organization consisting of Haynes and secretary Bertha Cable in Los Angeles and Franklin Hichborn in the north. A headquarters was established in both regions (the Los Angeles branch in Haynes's own office), and stationery was printed with a long list of members on the reverse side. Numerous noted progressives agreed to join as honorary vice presidents, providing estimable window dressing: U.S. senators Hiram Johnson and James Phelan, Lieutenant Governor C. C. Young, several California congressmen, Herbert Hoover, and the presidents of the University of California and Stanford University. Additional well-known progressives served on the two regional executive committees. The president, of course, was Dr. Haynes, though he had initially thought he should not even appear as a member.[35]

In the 1920 campaign against PASTL's Proposition 4, Haynes used all the resources at his disposal. The major (almost only) financer of the League to Protect the Initiative, he spent thousands to pay Hichborn and other organizers, to bring in speakers such as Francis Heney, and to purchase and distribute a flood of literature. Individual appeals were made to Socialists, organized labor, teachers, single-taxers, and others to defeat Proposition 4 or lose the initiative as a political tool. He solicited the support of numerous state politicians, and immediately won over Governor Stephens, who asked the doctor to compose the ballot argument against Proposition 4 that would accompany sample ballots. Haynes appeared before as many audiences as he could throughout the state, accusing PASTL leaders of trying to strangle the initiative, not the single tax, because they knew the single tax would not pass anyway.[36]

On the day after the November election, Haynes expressed his gratitude to Franklin Hichborn for the "excellent work" done in northern California. A weary Haynes wrote: "I was very blue a week or two prior to the election and the night before I was fearful of the result. But the people have shown again that they can be trusted." Proposition 4 was defeated mainly through the efforts of these two progressives, while the single tax was buried by a margin of almost three to one.[37]

Victorious in its battle with single-taxers but defeated by direct legislationists, PASTL returned to the legislature. Various lawmakers were convinced to introduce bills prohibiting the initiative from being used specifically for the single tax, raising the signature total of tax-related initiatives to 15 percent, and amending the initiative to the point of impotence. Haynes relied on Franklin Hichborn to sound the alert when these bills surfaced. With publicity and lobbying of their own, the progressives stifled these proposals in committee.[38]

Thus again rebuffed in the legislature, PASTL turned once more to the initiative, ironically "the instrument they seek to destroy." Petitions were circulated to change the proportion of signatures required in tax matters from 8 to 15 percent, and the successful proposal became Proposition 27 on the 1922 ballot. Haynes and Hichborn conducted a campaign similar to that of 1920, encouraging progressives to speak out against 27, and arranging for a flood of literature. Haynes even convinced the Great Commoner, William Jennings Bryan, to become an LPI vice president. Owing to limited campaigning by the single-taxers and PASTL, Haynes and his allies did not have to work as hard as they had two years earlier. The results were similar; indeed the single-tax and anti-initiative propositions were buried by heavier margins than in 1920.[39]

In an article in the *National Municipal Review* early in 1923, Haynes briefly recounted the contest over the single tax and wondered if the "enemies of popular government will renew their attack" in the legislature. "If they should do so," he predicted, "there is no doubt but that they will be overwhelmingly defeated again." Anti–direct legislation measures were introduced in the 1923 and 1925 sessions, but none passed. Hichborn's observation of these sessions and immediate action by Haynes and other progressives thwarted the few attempts.[40]

Immediately after the 1922 contest, the single-taxers announced their intention to prepare yet another initiative for the 1924 election, and PASTL continued to solicit financial support for its opposition efforts. But the expected battle never materialized. With too many defeats and dwindling vote totals, the single-taxers gradually joined progressives in forming a new organization designed to modify the state tax system by raising rates on the holdings of large corporations currently taxed at rates equal to or lower than those of homeowners. Members of the old Equity Tax League, Great Adventure, and Single Tax League—such as David Woodley, George A. Briggs, R. E. Chadwick, and Staughton Cooley—formed the Tax Relief Association of California with progressives Haynes, Hichborn, Marshall Stimson, and Paul Scharrenberg, who desired tax reform based on assets besides land. This merger kept the single tax off the ballot, robbing PASTL of its strategy of attacking the initiative through the single tax. At the same time the new group attached a middle-class legitimacy to major tax reform for consumers. For Haynes, who orchestrated this compromise, the outcome reflected his usual politics of accommodation to achieve some degree of success.[41]

Another vital concern for Haynes and other California progressives at this time was the state's management of water and hydroelectrical power. In the early 1920s, the conflict between advocates of public ownership and private power companies became a national issue indicative of the persistence of the progressive movement in the United States. In California, Haynes and other public-ownership progressives moved beyond the defense of past accomplishments and took the offensive to obtain state control of water and power production.[42]

Already firmly established in the municipal water and power movement in Los Angeles, Haynes joined Rudolph Spreckels in 1921 to rescue a comprehensive state water and power plan defeated in the legislature. In the summer the two organized an initiative campaign to put the plan before the voters. Funds were raised (almost all from these two millionaires), petitions circulated, and supporters lined up. The Water and Power Act was placed on the 1922 general election ballot, and progressives such as Hiram Johnson were encouraged or coerced to campaign for the measure in return for the support of Haynes and Spreckels. But even with Haynes contributing over $13,000 and Spreckels well over $100,000, the proposal was soundly defeated.[43]

A major factor in the landslide, according to the vanquished, was the enormous difference in campaign funds expended by the opposing sides. Haynes suspected that private power companies spent a fortune in the opposition campaign. Soon after the election he asked Lieutenant Governor C. C. Young to investigate corporate funding of organizations involved in five initiatives on the 1922 ballot, including the Water and Power Act and the anti-initiative proposal. A legislative probe directed by Senator Herbert C. Jones began almost immediately, and Haynes provided as much information as he could to Jones's committee. In a short time this body discovered that Eustace Cullinan, leader of the opposition to the Water and Power Act and lawyer for the Pacific Gas and Electric Company, had collected over $500,000 for the campaign, mostly from private power companies. Furthermore, Cullinan admitted paying labor leader and former San Francisco mayor Patrick McCarthy some $10,000 to influence state labor organizations to oppose the measure. Outspent three to one, the advocates of this proposal were at a decided disadvantage. The committee hearings dramatized the hurdles Spreckels and Haynes faced.[44]

This episode seemed to illustrate a major problem of the initiative process—that the wealthiest interest group could buy or crush an initiative. This fear of both proponents and opponents of direct legislation assumed that the voters were swayed in direct proportion to money spent, but this was not the case with the anti-initiative proposal on the same ballot. The payment to McCarthy, however, was critical in influencing the large labor vote—and in tarnishing his reputation once news of the payment surfaced.

Disclosure of the private power companies' support for the progressives' opponents spurred Spreckels and Haynes to try again in 1924. A petition was circulated and another Water and Power Act was placed on the ballot along with the presidential choices. The leading backers were also supporters of La Follette, running on the Socialist ticket, so the opposition press painted them as Socialists who would expropriate the private property of the power companies. Again the proposal was defeated, and again Haynes and Spreckels set out to put it on the ballot, this time in 1926. In this third attempt Haynes was less sanguine, less energetic, and less generous. His suspicions were correct: the proposal was defeated by a margin of well over two to one. Not surprisingly, Haynes and Spreckels declined to try again.[45]

Control of water and power resources was one of the many state political issues of the early 1920s. In Los Angeles at the same time, it was the main issue. Since the power bond campaign of 1913–14, the question of municipal ownership of electrical power had become the catalyst of local politics, a much more substantive issue than the sex scandals and other events that grabbed the newspaper headlines at election time. Opportunities to expand or stifle municipal ownership cropped up from 1919 to 1925, stimulating new political alignments that kept Haynes in the forefront of local civic affairs as he strove to defend and expand the measures he had promoted for over two decades.

During and after World War I, Haynes was actively involved in local politics, though without his former partner, E. T. Earl, who died in early 1919. By this time the doctor had grown cold to progressive mayor Frederick T. Woodman. As a proponent of public health, Haynes demanded that the city take strong measures to combat a national influenza epidemic in late 1918 by requiring that flu masks be worn and by limiting public assemblies. This request was denied by Woodman and the city council. Haynes had privately surveyed the nation for antidotes to the flu and was surprised that city officials refused to take stronger steps to protect their constituents.[46]

But municipal ownership was the chief issue in Haynes's disagreement with Woodman. In 1918, the doctor protested to the mayor that his plan to abolish city commissions and replace them with one manager was unbusinesslike; all companies have a board of directors, not one autocrat. What Haynes really feared was that the probable director of the Public Service Commission, an unpredictable young man in the city attorney's office, would let private power companies block the city's attempt to gain control of electricity distribution. A short time later, Woodman tried to remove Power Bureau chief Ezra Scattergood, a leader of the municipal-ownership advocates. Haynes admitted that he had to blackmail Woodman to cease this effort by threatening to block the appointment to state office of one of the mayor's friends.[47]

As the 1919 municipal election approached, Haynes was as concerned with a bond issue for power expansion as with the mayor's race. As finance chairman of the Citizens' Power Bond Committee, he raised money for the campaign to approve $13.5 million in bonds for the city's purchase of the electrical distribution property of the Southern California Edison Company. The bond advocates obtained the endorsements of most city newspapers, the Municipal League, Chamber of Commerce, and other business groups that ordinarily opposed municipal ownership but were in favor of cheap power to attract manufacturing. The bonds were opposed by the *Times* and the Municipal Taxpayers' League, a group financed by private power companies, which claimed the bonds would necessitate higher taxes. The latter argument was neither true nor convincing, as over two thirds of the voters attested.[48]

In the 1919 mayoral campaign Haynes tried to remain publicly neutral to avoid alienating either of the "progressive" candidates, and he encouraged both to support the power bonds, which they did. But the doctor was not in favor of the reelection of Woodman, endorsed by the *Times*. Instead Haynes aided the campaign of Meredith "Pinkey" Snyder, a Democrat who had served as mayor early in the century and appointed Haynes to the Board of Civil Service Commissioners. Haynes contributed to Snyder's campaign without alienating Woodman, whose workers instantly agreed to mail cards promoting the bond election with their candidate's literature, as did Snyder's staff. After Woodman was flayed in the *Record* and *Examiner* for his alleged role in a vice protection racket, Snyder emerged as the victor in the general election.[49]

The 1919 election marked the rapprochement between Haynes and the *Examiner*, as both strived to elect Snyder. In the pre-1911 period, *Examiner* editors had cooperated with Haynes in his crusades for public ownership, direct legislation, and streetcar fenders. In the 1910s, however, the Hearst paper turned as conservative as the *Times*, and criticized "Boss" E. T. Earl and many of the groups to which the doctor belonged. During the war, the *Examiner*'s almost pro-German slant convinced Haynes that it should be shut down as disloyal. But near the end of the hostilities, the doctor and the paper's editors settled their differences. Throughout the 1920s, the *Examiner* again promoted his views. Haynes supplied information for the editors and was confident that he had considerable influence with them. The *Times* agreed, once referring to the *Examiner* as Haynes's "press agent."[50]

Cooperation with the *Examiner* paid off: the newspaper defended Haynes against attacks by the *Times*, as Harry Chandler continued his personal feud with the doctor into the 1920s. Previously championed by the *Herald*, the *Record*, and Earl's papers, Haynes was now consistently promoted by the *Examiner*. Occasionally the Hearst paper went on the offensive against Chandler, printing stories in which its political darling, Senator Hiram Johnson, chastised Chandler as "a greater menace than the Southern Pacific ever was [to California politics]." At one point Haynes wrote an anonymous letter to William Randolph Hearst, urging him to use his Los Angeles paper to gain revenge against the *Times* by printing exposés of Chandler's several misadventures: his indictment for inciting insurrection in Mexico, his alleged tax fraud, and his subsidizing of propaganda aimed at the city's Public Service Department. "If you show him up in the columns of your paper the fellow will stop attacking you," Haynes wrote; "if the batteries are turned on him he will shut up." Hearst did not take his anonymous correspondent's advice, and of course Chandler's editors did not shut up.[51]

Before Mayor Snyder took office Haynes contemplated serving on the city's Public Service Commission to promote the department from within government as he had from outside in the bond campaigns of the 1910s. Just after the election he asked John B. Elliott, a close political associate of Snyder's, to suggest that the mayor appoint the doctor to the commission when a vacancy arose. The first one surfaced in December, but Snyder reappointed Reginaldo Del Valle, a Democrat and staunch defender of the city's water and power program. When the next opening appeared in early 1921, Snyder chose Haynes, who was enthusiastically endorsed by organized labor. The city council confirmed the appointment, and he began his sixteen-year tenure on this board on January 4, 1921.[52]

As a public service commissioner, Haynes worked with Ezra Scattergood and other supporters of municipal power to expand the city's water and power program. Meeting on Tuesday and Friday afternoons, the board planned strategy and studied more mundane details of departmental operation. Haynes kept track of all the department's business, including public relations, advertising, finances, bookkeeping, and employment. Issues ranged from a departmental ruling advocated by Haynes that golf courses be charged residential water rates rather than less expensive agricultural rates, to planning the condemnation of private electrical facilities. For his service Haynes was rewarded with the admiration of many groups, abuse from the *Times*, and countless requests from associates to find jobs for friends and relatives.[53]

Shortly after his appointment, Haynes fell into a major controversy concerning the Public Service Commission's marketing of bonds approved in 1919 to purchase the electrical distribution facilities of the Southern California Edison Company. Following that election, Los Angeles Gas and Electric (LAG&E) sued to invalidate the bonds and delay the sale. The legal scuffle dragged on for two years, until the state Supreme Court ruled in the city's favor. By that time economic conditions changed, and selling the bonds at a low interest rate would prove difficult. Haynes was assigned to look into the disposition of the bonds, while another commissioner independently arranged with local banker Irving Hellman to solicit bids. Fearing that opponents of the sale were convincing eastern bond firms to avoid submitting reasonable offers, Haynes and the other commissioners recommended that the city council accept Hellman's bid.[54]

The *Times* immediately charged that the Hellman contract represented the giving away of over $500,000 in additional interest. Further, the secrecy surrounding the deal suggested collusion in that Haynes might have negotiated the deal to pay off Mayor Snyder's reelection debt to Hellman, the campaign manager. Haynes might advocate openness in international diplomacy, the *Times* asserted, but he conducted this bargain behind closed doors. The doctor denied any collusion: secrecy was needed to keep Edison and LAG&E from continuing to block the sale. Defended by other newspapers and the city council, the commissioners effectively argued that they had no other choice in protecting the city's welfare. Haynes replied on behalf of the commissioners: "Were the same conditions to arise again," they "would take precisely the same steps." [55]

The bond opponents then returned to the courts and obtained a Supreme Court ruling setting aside the sale. The court found no fraud but ruled that the bonds had to be sold at par value. Edison and LAG&E promised more litigation to hold up the sale, thereby inadvertently making the Hellman deal appear to be justified. New bids were solicited, and the one accepted by the council brought a premium, thus undercutting the argument of private power companies. Within weeks the suit was dropped and Edison gave up. In May 1922, the company sold its distribution facilities within the city limits to Los Angeles. [56]

In order to improve the department's chances for success, Haynes also worked outside of the Public Service Commission, as he had in the past. In 1921, he helped to create the Public Power League, a support group of city progressives and others formed to aid state and local power expansion. As public service commissioner, Haynes refrained from becoming a league officer, but he provided most of the operating funds for office expenses and the salary of PPL general manager John J. Hamilton by 1924. [57]

The Public Power League was chiefly interested in working with local publications to combat negative stories in the *Times* and promote power bonds. The league spearheaded the effort in 1923 to pass a $35-million proposal to develop generating facilities with the new resources on the Colorado River, but failed to capture the necessary two-thirds vote. It was more successful the following year when it campaigned for a victorious $16-million bond proposal to begin purchasing LAG&E distribution facilities. In the two drives Haynes campaigned actively both in and out of the Public Service Commission. [58]

One of several controversial issues confronting Haynes and the other commissioners at this time concerned the city's increasingly concentrated exploitation of the Owens Valley. Rapid population and economic growth in the early 1920s had created the need for more water, so Water Bureau chief William Mulholland again went searching for a new source. The Colorado River offered the long-term solution, but in the meantime Mulholland decided that all of the city's resources in Owens Valley should be exploited. The Public Service Commission authorized the purchase of land to divert water used for irrigation to the city's aqueduct supply. Friction between the commissioners and Inyo County residents developed quickly, as farmers requested high prices for their holdings while townspeople demanded that Los Angeles also buy their property, which would become worthless if the Owens Valley was depopulated. Mulholland advised against further negotiations, which broke down anyway, and valley residents resorted to violence to reaffirm their resistance, blowing up portions of the aqueduct system.[59]

In the fall of 1924, Haynes, who was president of the commission by this time, tried to bring all parties together. Promising Owens Valley residents a compromise, he devised a plan in which some 30,000 acres in the valley, though they would not be purchased, would receive adequate water year round. The valley leadership refused this offer, unwilling to accept anything short of the complete buyout of owners there. Negotiations between these leaders and a committee of businessmen appointed by the Los Angeles mayor could not resolve the differences, and the ranchers again turned to bombing. With this further resort to violence the commissioners held fast to their conviction that they had bargained in good faith with those who had sold their property to the city and that the dynamiters were trying to extort higher prices for their ranch land. The feud continued until 1927, when two valley leaders were imprisoned for embezzling the savings of their neighbors (and $40,000 from Los Angeles) and Governor Young finally brought both sides back to the peace table. By the end of the year Los Angeles had reestablished its hegemony in Owens Valley while spending more money to develop recreational facilities and improve the economy there. For Haynes and his fellow commissioners, the war was over, although the city's continued involvement in Owens Valley occasionally ignited further incidents. The legacy of this struggle is a never-ending parade of historical accounts, some expounding conspiracy theories and others staunchly defending Los Angeles in its quest for Owens Valley water.[60]

Haynes's Public Service Commission faced another major issue: the Boulder Canyon project. This undertaking of the U.S. Reclamation Service had a dual purpose. A high dam built on the Colorado River at Boulder Canyon would control constant flooding in the Imperial Valley and provide irrigation water by means of a connecting All-American Canal. The dam also could create electrical current, which the U.S. government could sell to finance construction. When the project was ruled feasible in 1921, advocates of both public and private power began battling to win this hydroelectricity source.[61]

Haynes, his fellow commissioners, and other proponents of municipal power recognized the opportunity presented by the project if they could convince the federal government to wholesale the electricity to Los Angeles and other cities. At first they hoped the Reclamation Service would allow Los Angeles to build the power-generating facilities at Boulder Canyon Dam. Failing at this, they set out to keep private power companies from grabbing a major share of the power or stopping the project altogether.[62]

In 1921, the League of the Southwest was formed by private power interests to dissuade government from buying this power. At its first conference Haynes packed the meeting hall with supporters of municipal ownership, who threw the proceedings into confusion and thus blocked any resolutions in favor of private power companies. This was one of many situations in which Haynes tangled head-on with political opponents, though one delegate remembered the confrontation in a more humorous light. The meeting having reverted to "struggling and haggling over who represented what, who was going to be allowed to speak, and all that sort of thing," there was a long delay before the final report. The wait was interrupted when "Dr. Haynes and the vice-president of the Southern California Edison Company got up to give [the audience] a little vaudeville show to kill time. They danced around and around and sang 'Ever Since We Were Boys' and told stories." The meeting finally adjourned without a vote, the "power companies being afraid they would be outnumbered."[63]

Haynes promoted the Boulder Canyon Dam in speeches, meetings, publications, and lobbying efforts throughout the 1920s. In 1923, he joined the Boulder Dam Association to support construction of the dam, and as a Board of Public Service commissioner he voted to initiate surveys of the area and studies of how his department would use these resources. He worked for Boulder Canyon plebiscites and bond issues in the 1923 municipal election, though the bonds failed to obtain a two-thirds majority. In 1924, he campaigned for the Swing-Johnson bill, the federal law that would authorize construction of the dam. The following year he lobbied the California legislature for the Finney resolution, which would commit California to participate in the Colorado Compact only if the high storage dam was built. Also in 1925, he helped to make the issue the centerpiece of the municipal election, which demonstrated the support of Los Angeles citizens for the project. It would be many years before the dam was approved and built, but without the activity of Haynes and fellow advocates of public power in the early controversial stages, the city might never have obtained Boulder Canyon power.[64]

Haynes was aided in his advancement of municipal ownership of water and power by his association with Kent Kane Parrot, chief political manager of Los Angeles in the 1920s. Born in Maine in 1880, Parrot came to Los Angeles at the age of 27 and graduated from the University of Southern California law school in 1909. Making all the right social and political connections, he aligned himself with the E. T. Earl wing of progressivism, though he was more a socialite than a social reformer. After Earl's death, Parrot further enhanced his reputation and associations with other figures, such as his USC law school professor, Judge Gavin Craig, and became Craig's chief lieutenant.[65]

Parrot demonstrated his political sagacity in the 1921 municipal election. Having been made campaign manager of mayoral candidate George E. Cryer upon Judge Craig's recommendation, Parrot constructed an odd coalition to oppose incumbent mayor Snyder. This alliance included the antilabor *Times* and Better American Federation as well as the Central Labor Council, a representative of the city's liquor interests and the chairman of the Anti-Saloon League, elements of the underworld and leading clergymen, and a few old progressives and officers of private utility companies. Parrot took advantage of Cryer's record as a progressive and Snyder's poor record with labor and failure to suppress vice. Though Snyder won the primary by a close margin, Cryer was the victor in the general election.[66]

As a loyal appointee, Haynes supported Snyder in the campaign, but he realized that Parrot was now the manager with whom he would have to work to retain his influence in local politics. The doctor had known Parrot and Cryer for years and was not afraid of their recent association with Harry Chandler and other opponents. On the contrary, Haynes repaired his relationship with Parrot and began cooperating with this new "boss" to support Haynes's own interests. In 1922, the two worked together in Governor Stephens's reelection campaign. This further association with state and local progressives brought Parrot and Cryer closer to Haynes's views on important issues. By the spring of 1923, Haynes was giving Parrot more than just advice; in certain instances Haynes "most respectfully" ordered Parrot to endorse certain candidates and tell the mayor what he should do for the doctor. Additionally, Haynes made recommendations for appointments to Mayor Cryer, who complied with many of them.[67]

In return for these favors, Haynes had to tolerate Parrot's constant interference in municipal government. In the early years this included Parrot's attempt to engineer his own appointment to the Public Service

Commission (which appointment the city council refused to confirm), his meddling in Harbor Department affairs, and perpetual meddling in the administration of the Police Department. The doctor also was expected to lend his personal influence and ensure the backing of public-power advocates for the Parrot coalition. As this "machine" evolved between 1921 and 1924, it cut its ties with the conservative *Times* by embracing municipal ownership and city progressives. Others in the coalition included leaders of organized labor (who usually opposed the *Times*), city employee organizations, some elements of organized vice, and various religious leaders and ethnic groups. The coalition won the tacit support of the *Examiner* (in return for votes for Hiram Johnson) and at various times other papers that supported municipal ownership. Parrot's "machine," rather a fragile and shifting collection of political allies, did not resemble Haynes's ideal of a good-government organization oriented toward social welfare, but it successfully defended his favorite reforms for at least a few years.[68]

Parrot's organization consolidated its support and influence in the 1923 municipal election. Revelations of Parrot's interference in the administration and Cryer's turnabout on the municipal-power question had not yet surfaced, so the *Times* endorsed the mayor. Cryer also had appeased Chandler and the business establishment with his use of the Police Department to keep industrial peace. In that a potentially violent IWW strike had erupted at the harbor, the *Times* editors saw no need to change mayors at the moment, even though Cryer's principal opponent was a champion of the open shop. With the backing of Haynes and other progressives, Parrot made municipal ownership—especially endorsement for the Boulder Canyon Dam—the chief issue, and Cryer came out in favor of the city's expansion of its water and power program. The resulting Cryer landslide in the primary enhanced the influence of both Parrot and Haynes in Los Angeles politics.[69]

The 1923 municipal contest also included the election of freeholders to rewrite the city charter. Afraid that opponents would use this opportunity to alter city laws regarding direct legislation and operation of the Public Service Department, Haynes decided to run for the position of freeholder. He immediately began planning his strategy, deciding which interest groups to ask for endorsements. Parrot was to put his "full machine in working order for a vigorous campaign" and pay all expenses with proceeds coming from the doctor. Haynes requested that Mayor Cryer issue a statement of support and appealed to newspapers to endorse his candidacy. He was backed by the *Examiner, Record, Express,*

Municipal League, and a host of civic organizations, even the National Independent Spiritualist Association.[70]

Haynes was only one of two candidates endorsed by organized labor, testimony to his long relationship with labor leaders in countless reform campaigns. Since the war he had improved his record with unionists by helping to mediate strikes, blocking the appointment of a *Times*-sponsored candidate for the Civil Service Board, subscribing to the construction fund of the Labor Temple, and loaning about $20,000 to Santa Fe Railroad strikers in 1922 to save their home mortgages from foreclosure. All of this was in addition to his usual lobbying efforts to protect legislation on behalf of working people. "Every trade unionist can, and should, vote for him," the editor of the *Citizen* advised. Many did, at least enough to help him win election.[71]

Once the freeholders began meeting, Haynes was elected vice president and requested that he be selected chairman of the subcommittees involved with public works, public utilities, the harbor, and water and power. For several months the freeholders discussed various tenets for the new city charter, and completed a document very similar to the old one. The mayor-council form was retained, although the mayor's powers were strengthened. Major changes included an executive budget and a centralized purchasing system, and longer terms for elected officers. The proposal did not please everyone; conservatives were unhappy about the retention of direct legislation and more red tape with new civil service procedures, and labor did not like the absence of district council elections. Haynes himself did not agree with the entire product, especially the sections on building heights, indeterminate franchises, and at-large elections.[72]

The charter encountered little opposition, except from those favoring a council elected by wards. Rather than oppose the document as a whole, the dissidents—labor unions, residents of the areas most distant from city hall, and even some of the old guard who never accepted the at-large reform—offered an alternative measure creating a fifteen-district council, to be placed on the same May 1924 ballot. Both the charter and the alternative passed, becoming effective in July 1925. This document, with subsequent modifications, is the framework of government that guides Los Angeles today.[73]

The majority of Haynes's crusades in local politics during this period concerned the expansion of the city's hydroelectric program; his work on the city charter was an exception, but not the only one. In 1919, he was one of several wealthy citizens who pledged to invest $50,000 in a city milk plant, an idea that never reached fruition. Throughout the early 1920s he was involved in other public health matters in his continued tenure on the county's Public Welfare Commission, for which he served as president in 1920. In this capacity he recommended changes in health procedures and helped to settle disputes among the many state, county, city, and private agencies over health and welfare practices.[74]

In 1920, Haynes again became entangled in a controversy over street-car fenders. The city's traction companies petitioned the city council to amend the 1906 fender ordinance specifically for "one-man cars," to allow a wheel guard to be installed under the car rather than a fender in front of it. Haynes protested that the proposed mechanism once again would allow pedestrians to be smashed by the front of the car instead of saved by the old projecting fender, which would trip and catch them. To protect the fruits of his earlier struggle, he mounted a lobbying effort to enlist the support of influential organizations and individuals, and personally appealed to the city council to keep the law intact. In this instance he again was victorious.[75]

The doctor was also interested in local school and police issues. In 1921, he became vice president of the Citizens' Better Schools Committee, which was promoting a slate of new candidates for the Board of Education. The group opposed the incumbents, who were backed by the *Times* and BAF. Haynes helped organize the campaign for his recommendations and contributed money and speeches to their success. On a less publicized level, he monitored the controversial Los Angeles Police Department and offered his help to a parade of police chiefs to improve the department. He regretted in particular that "Los Angeles has become the byword of the nation" regarding transgressions of civil rights by the police, such as the LAPD's arrest of peaceful demonstrators. But in this area Haynes had little influence since Cryer allowed Parrot to intervene at will in LAPD affairs.[76]

Kent Parrot's hegemony in the Cryer administration finally became public after the 1923 election, as the *Times* unleashed its attack. With the bonds between the "boss" and Harry Chandler completely severed, the *Times* began reporting Parrot's antics in police and harbor matters. The *Record* also printed stories about the city's newest boss as late as 1924, when its editors stopped criticizing advocates of public ownership until the Boulder Canyon project could be approved. Before then the *Record* called him "Mayor Parrot" or the "Defacto Mayor of Los Angeles." Describing him as "debonair and suave" as he sat through one of countless commission hearings reading the newspaper comics, or quoting him on his motives in politics ("I get a lot of fun out of it"), these papers characterized him as an amiable but cold-blooded strategist who considered himself "misunderstood" by reporters.[77]

Parrot intensified the activity of his organization in county and state elections in 1924. He also further entrenched his leadership in the Republican party and his commitment to the public-power program, thereby pushing his opponents to action. In early 1925, the *Times* and its allies selected federal judge Benjamin Bledsoe as their candidate to run against Cryer. A loose coalition of private utility companies, business leaders, reformers, and politicians left out of the Parrot organization rallied to Bledsoe's cause. Parrot, meanwhile, began planning Cryer's reelection bid.[78]

In the primary campaign Bledsoe and his supporters tried to make lax police enforcement of vice laws the major issue, just as Parrot and Cryer had done in 1921. But the boss once again turned the election on the issue of municipal power expansion. The Swing-Johnson bill authorizing construction of Boulder Dam had been introduced the previous December, and most in Parrot's coalition favored it. Parrot made sure that Swing-Johnson was the central concern, so Cryer virtually ignored the myriad attacks on his administration in other areas. Newspapers supporting Cryer—the *Examiner, Record, Illustrated Daily News,* and Hollywood *Citizen-News*—showed almost no interest in issues other than Swing-Johnson, the sole exception being Bledsoe's poor record with labor, at which they took occasional swipes.[79]

A more important exception was the issue of Harry Chandler himself. As the *Times* touted Bledsoe daily, the opposition press labeled the judge a Chandler puppet. Even though Bledsoe finally endorsed the Swing-Johnson bill, Parrot's papers claimed that once in office, Bledsoe would replace public service commissioners with Chandler's anti–municipal ownership favorites who would subvert the Boulder Canyon project. This charge was reinforced by stories documenting Chandler's opposition to the dam—for example, reports that the All-American Canal, a component of the dam projects, would irrigate the Imperial Valley and thus depreciate thousands of acres of land he owned in northern Mexico. In a stroke of genius, Parrot flooded the city with posters proclaiming that "Harry Calls Him Ben," in reference to Chandler's control of Bledsoe.[80]

Haynes played a pivotal role in this campaign. In urging Parrot to make Swing-Johnson the issue, the doctor early on expressed his confidence in Parrot's "honesty and ability" and believed he would "conduct an efficient honorable and legitimate campaign." This declaration, made for public consumption, was intended to reinforce Parrot's advocacy of municipal ownership. "I take great pleasure in assisting financially in the campaign," Haynes wrote to Parrot, in part to reassure progressives that Cryer's reelection was a worthy enterprise. This statement did not convince progressives such as Marshall Stimson, former mayor Snyder (a Democrat like Bledsoe), or even a few labor leaders to support the mayor. But it did keep most of Haynes's closest associates in line.[81]

Haynes also aided Cryer by making large contributions, soliciting support from friends, collecting information on Bledsoe's judicial record to enlighten the voters, preparing literature and statements for friendly newspapers, delivering speeches, and offering campaign tips. As a member of the Municipal League executive board since the late 1910s, Haynes also worked within that organization to gain an endorsement for Cryer. He would have done more had he not been sick at the time and also busy helping care for his ailing sisters, Florence and Mary.[82]

Additional help for Parrot and Cryer was not needed, however. Cryer routed Bledsoe and lesser challengers in the primary, while most of Parrot's city council choices were elected. The victory also crippled a potential Parrot foe, the Republican County Central Committee. Several of its members, having been deeply alienated by the Republican Parrot-Cryer administration, became a major force in the selection of the Democrat Bledsoe; they even tried to use the RCCC in Bledsoe's behalf. The group also alienated a chief source of financial aid, Henry E. Huntington, who complained that its methods of stressing the negatives of Cryer's administration made Los Angeles appear "a sink of iniquity." This mistake resulted in Parrot's further cementing his bond with Hiram Johnson and state progressives opposed to the county Republican leaders. For at least a short time, the alliance would prove valuable for Parrot as he entered the state political arena.[83]

"The Spring municipal primaries of 1925 marked the high water mark of the Parrot-Craig-Haynes machine, as the *Times* called it," remembered one observer. Fresh from his most stunning victory, Parrot consolidated his ascendancy in the city by having Cryer replace unsympathetic city officials with Parrot's favorites. For Dr. Haynes, the partnership with this boss served the municipal-power enterprise and enhanced the doctor's standing in local politics when his influence in state affairs was at a low point. The year 1925 was the best of times for his local affairs, the worst of times for his statewide fortunes. But all of that would soon change.[84]

While John Haynes was busy with state and local politics at this time, Dora Haynes, too, participated in political affairs. Although her deteriorating health confined her, for the most part, to the Figueroa Street residence, she remained active in local women's clubs. Occasionally she attended meetings of the Friday Morning Club, which had become more of a political forum in civic matters since the state women's suffrage amendment passed in 1911. By the 1920s, the club itself had become politicized, as various factions jockeyed to control the club's stand on important issues. One president, backed by the most conservative members, was even reported to have vowed that if victorious she would "get rid of the propaganda of 'old Doctor Haynes,'" referring to his advocacy of direct legislation and public ownership.[85]

Dora Haynes's primary interest still was women's suffrage. After the war she resumed her efforts in the campaign of local suffragists to aid the national drive. In June 1919, she hosted at her home a meeting of suffragists who followed the call of the National American Woman Suffrage Association by establishing the California League of Women Voters to promote the national suffrage amendment just passed by Congress. She was elected the first president of this body and helped to establish its permanent operation at a meeting in late June.[86]

Just after this meeting Dora Haynes assisted in the founding of the Los Angeles County League of Women Voters, the local wing of the state organization. In this capacity she hosted meetings in her home and avoided arduous trips north. Her group's public meetings and lobbying of Governor Stephens and state legislators paid off. California lawmakers approved the U.S. constitutional amendment in November, though it did not pass in three fourths of the nation's state legislatures until the following year. In September 1920, Mrs. Haynes, the acting chairperson of the California League of Women Voters, presided over the thanksgiving celebration of passage of the Susan B. Anthony Amendment.[87]

For the rest of her life Dora Haynes remained as active as possible in the league. After passage of the constitutional amendment she served on the executive council of the state organization and was treasurer and later historian of the Los Angeles branch. Stating in a newspaper article early on that many housewives knew more about political subjects than their husbands, she warned that women would not be swayed by their spouses. With this in mind she arranged for lectures and conferences to instruct women on politics and government, and for league discussions of local and national issues. She worked with other members to lobby congressmen on a proposed equal rights law and other legislation affecting women. Although physically limited, she did her best to transform the successful crusade for women's suffrage into an educational program to make sure women used their long-sought voting power effectively.[88]

In the postwar years, politics and civic affairs were not the only events in the lives of John and Dora Haynes. This period witnessed several personal tragedies as family members passed away. Dora's invalid mother died in Chicago in 1920, and her father less than a year later. John's brother-in-law, Walter Lindley, died in 1922. A prominent physician and civic leader for decades, Lindley had worked with John in many ventures, even though the two held widely divergent political views. His death made a widow of Haynes's sister Florence, and John responded by taking a special interest in looking after her son, Francis Haynes Lindley. In 1925, John's oldest sister, Mary, died at the age of 80 while in residence at Florence's home. His only other remaining sibling, Robert, lived in retirement in nearby Long Beach.[89]

John and Dora gradually withdrew from social circles. John humbly averred, "I live simply and have no interest in what is called 'society.'" He did, however, keep his memberships in social clubs and fraternal organizations such as the Masons, Shriners, and Scribes (he was president in 1922), as well as the prestigious California and University clubs. In 1920, he became a charter member of the Community Park and Art Association, which developed the Hollywood Bowl.[90]

His favorite club appeared to be the Sunset Club. Over the years he found ample opportunity to speak on civic topics at its meetings, and enjoyed the social atmosphere. He attended many Sunset outings to local mountain resorts where the members were free to engage in good-natured pranks and participatory entertainment. He hosted a dinner for Sunsetters near the beach at the Bolsa Chica Club in 1925, and the following year he was elected club president.[91]

The years from 1917 to 1925 also witnessed a never-ending string of illnesses for Haynes—bouts with flu, bronchitis, and other maladies that attacked his aging body. These infirmities barely affected his public work, though, partly because of his stubborn will to defeat political enemies, and partly because of his new personal secretary. After J. W. Park died, in 1919, Haynes replaced him with Anne M. Mumford, an able and loyal confidante. Born in Detroit in 1888, she graduated from Vassar College in 1910 and found her way to Los Angeles, where she accepted the position with Dr. Haynes. Mumford quickly familiarized herself with his interests and soon handled some of his correspondence on her own. Eventually she assumed considerable responsibility for the affairs of both John and Dora, which she would continue to bear long after their deaths. Her complete sympathy with most of the Hayneses' views became further evident in the next three decades in her devotion to the Haynes Foundation.[92]

Eclipse fender on a streetcar at the Orange Empire Railway Museum in Perris, California
(*Suzi Sitton*)

The California delegation to the 1912 Republican Convention in Chicago included Hiram
Johnson and Meyer Lissner (in center) and Haynes (sixth from right) (*Department of
Special Collections, Research Library, UCLA*)

Haynes, Gaylord Wilshire, and other investors at Wilshire's Bishop Creek Mine, 1914 (*Department of Special Collections, Research Library, UCLA*)

Haynes residence, and later Haynes Foundation headquarters, on Figueroa Street near Adams Street (1914) (*Department of Special Collections, Research Library, UCLA*)

The *Times* uncovers the secret Boss of Boss Kent Parrot; (*Nov. 12, 1925; copyright 1925,* Los Angeles Times)

Haynes and fellow revellers at a Sunset Club outing in 1915 (The Sunset Club of Los Angeles, *vol. 2* [*1916*])

Francis Haynes Lindley, John's nephew and a Haynes Foundation trustee for over four decades (*Department of Special Collections, Research Library, UCLA*)

The *Times*'s view of the 1927 municipal election results (*June 9, 1927; copyright 1927,* Los Angeles Times)

John B. Miller of the Southern California Edison Company, W. P. Whitsett of the Metropolitan Water District, and Haynes signing the Colorado River Power Agreement in 1930 (*Department of Special Collections, Research Library, UCLA*)

John and Dora Haynes in the early 1930s (*Department of Special Collections, Research Library, UCLA*)

Haynes signing a DWP contract in his sickbed; this photograph appeared in the *Examiner* in 1933 (*Hearst Collection, Department of Special Collections, University of Southern California Library*)

Haynes voting for a municipal bond issue to aid the Department of Water and Power in 1935 (*Hearst Collection, Department of Special Collections, University of Southern California Library*)

Boulder Dam hydroelectrical power illuminates Los
Angeles from City Hall, October 9, 1936 (*Hearst
Collection, Department of Special Collections,
University of Southern California Library*)

Haynes celebrates his eighty-fourth and last birthday on June 13, 1937 (*Hearst Collection, Department of Special Collections, University of Southern California Library*)

Chapter Eleven

Preparing for the Afterlife:
The Origins of the Haynes Foundation

As John Haynes approached his seventieth birthday, in June 1923, he contemplated the ultimate disposition of his fortune. He and Dora had no children, no wish to see the family treasury devoured by litigation and taxes, and much fear that their earnings might not be spent on the humanitarian goals for which they had labored so diligently. Noblesse oblige and half a lifetime of philanthropy dictated that the Haynes estate should not be wasted or allowed to reinforce the status quo of a society he thought to be regressing. Thus, the search began for a method to ensure that their wealth would always be allocated to the causes in which they believed.

In a letter to Dora written early in 1922, John outlined his ideas of how their money should be divided if he died before her. The family fortune, approaching some two million dollars, should be divided into thirds: one third for Dora, another third for John's sister, Florence, and the remaining third "for the advancement of democracy, industrial, political, and social." The latter included provision for their needy friends, up to $50,000 for the League for Industrial Democracy, funds for a new liberal party if one should start up, and money for the League of Women Voters, American Association for Labor Legislation, Child Welfare League of America, National Child Welfare Association, National Consumers League, and other organizations the Hayneses had been sustaining. A hospital for the poor of Los Angeles should be established under the direction of Episcopal bishop Joseph Johnson and Dr. Norman Bridge. The initiative and the state's Water and Power Act should be supported, and Franklin Hichborn, Haynes's political partner and "a great soul," should be given "five or ten thousand dollars." The Anti-Saloon League and Paul Kellogg's *Survey* should also be helped.[1]

The letter further advised that Dora and Florence provide generously for needy relatives and others they might "think it desirable to help," but that they not save a large amount for future distribution to relatives. "It would be foolish for Florence to leave her share of the estate to the children as it would undoubtedly ruin them both," John wrote. Rather, Dora and Florence should keep a portion for their own future, save a little for relatives and friends, and reserve the remainder "principally for the advancement of democracy." They should consult Upton Sinclair, John J. Hamilton, Franklin Hichborn, John Spargo, William English Walling, and others to decide on the best method, perhaps by "the establishment of community centers under the immediate direction of John Collier," a recent friend.[2]

Those were Haynes's general ideas for ensuring that after his death the family wealth would be spent on the people and causes he had cherished in his lifetime. The suggestion to his wife to consult with others indicated that he had not yet decided on a specific plan. In the next year he investigated the possibilities more intensely, conferring with Hichborn and with his new partner in public-ownership advocacy, lawyer Louis Bartlett, of Berkeley, about creating a trust fund. Bartlett suggested a private foundation along the lines of the Russell Sage Foundation or Edward Filene's Twentieth Century Fund, which promoted democracy through research and support grants.[3]

As Merle Curti long ago observed, Progressive Era leftists were wary of private foundations they believed to be "the creatures of nefarious 'robber barons,' " which "boded evil under the mask of doing good." The Carnegie and Rockefeller Foundations, they thought, allowed elitists to funnel money into pet projects that bolstered an unjust economic system. But the Sage Foundation and the Twentieth Century Fund, as well as the Phelps-Stokes Fund and Commonwealth Fund, had positive records in regard to financing studies and projects for low-cost housing, educational opportunities for minorities, and improvements in living conditions for the poor. In 1921, the American Fund for Public Service was established by an heir to the Garland fortune to provide seed money for experimental social movements. Directed by a board including Roger Baldwin and other leftists, this foundation promised to set an example of how private philanthropy could subsidize the quest for social justice.[4]

The foundation idea appealed to Haynes for several reasons. First, he could set its priorities and choose its trustees, thus ensuring that it would follow his dictates until his death. Second, though reform and social welfare organizations come and go, a foundation would endure to aid new agencies and to guarantee that older ones stuck to their avowed purposes. Finally, funds placed in the foundation treasury and the interest it earned were not taxable. This was especially important at the time, for it seemed to him that some of the wealthiest Americans, such as Secretary of the Treasury Andrew Mellon, were engaged in schemes to reduce the taxes of the very rich and use this bonus to subsidize reactionary ideals.[5]

Under Bartlett's legal guidance, a proposed trust document was drawn up in 1924. At first Haynes tried to interest other wealthy progressives, such as Rudolph Spreckels and James Phelan, of San Francisco, and William Kent, of Marin County, to contribute to the trust and become directors, since all had similar aims for social reform. The other millionaires declined, so John and Dora Haynes pursued the idea on their own. With further advice from friends, they had Bartlett revise the plan over the next two years and created the Haynes Foundation on September 2, 1926.[6]

As the foundation was established, the founders, John and Dora, selected nine other trustees to join them on the governing board, with John as president. The founders would endow the foundation with about $75,000 worth of stocks after the trust was ruled legal. In the meantime the trust would exist on a $4,400 loan from Dora Haynes, and few grants would be made until the legal questions were settled. The declaration of trust contained a myriad of other instructions as to the type of cause that would be supported, the scheduling of meetings, and the replacement of trustees; it even had a contingency plan for dispersement of assets in the event that a court of last resort decreed the trust instrument to be void.[7]

John and Dora set up the foundation so they could observe its operation during their lifetime and determine whether it would carry out their wishes in perpetuity. To ensure that it would, they chose for trustees some of their closest, most loyal friends. The group included two family members: John's younger sister, Florence Lindley, and her son, Francis. Florence had always been very close to John, possibly closer than his older brother and medical partner, Francis. The deaths of Dr. Walter Lindley, in 1922, and their older sister, Mary, in 1925, left a void in Florence's life that was not filled by her social and club activities, allowing time to devote to the foundation. More sympathetic to John's views than her conservative husband, she shared the humanitarian aims of the Hayneses and always freely offered advice and support.[8]

Francis Haynes Lindley, Florence's son, was a rising star in civic affairs. Born in 1899, Francis graduated from Harvard University and attended the law school of USC. He passed the bar in 1926 and became a deputy city attorney assigned to the Department of Water and Power that year, in which capacity he served until he enlisted in the U.S. Army Air Corps, in 1942. After Francis's father died, John Haynes treated the young man as a son. Their closeness was evident in 1926, when Kent Parrot tried to have Francis appointed executive secretary to governor-elect C. C. Young in order to curry Haynes's indebtedness. The doctor decided to keep his inexperienced nephew out of politics at the time, as well as to avoid owing Parrot a favor. Francis was not philosophically progressive like his uncle, but he was devoted and loyal, and served the foundation from the time of its establishment until his death.[9]

Two other close associates named as trustees were Anne Mumford and Franklin Hichborn. Mumford, Haynes's personal secretary since 1920, became his confidante and right arm as she coordinated his personal and business affairs. Being in general agreement with his social views, she also served as executive secretary of the foundation. Hichborn, Haynes's eyes and ears in Sacramento, was the doctor's most trusted political adviser. Still a newspaperman and political writer, Hichborn was one of the state's progressive strategists, always in touch with the leaders of this faction of the Republican party.[10]

Louis Bartlett, author of the trust instrument, was one of three original trustees appointed to a five-year term. He was the mayor of Berkeley from 1919 to 1923. A steadfast advocate of public ownership, Bartlett quickly became a friend and political associate of Haynes, whom he met in 1921. The doctor turned to him for legal advice in the trust matter, for he respected Bartlett's judgment. Haynes recommended him for state appointments and almost made him director of the foundation at its inception.[11]

William B. Mathews had been a friend of Haynes since the turn of the century. Elected city attorney of Los Angeles in 1901, Mathews had been involved with legal affairs of the city's Department of Water and Power since 1907—first with the Owens Valley project, later with the Boulder Canyon Dam. In this position he worked closely with Haynes and other advocates of public power. Mathews could be counted on to back Haynes's commitment to the expansion of water and power resources, a major concern of the foundation.[12]

Two clubwomen, both friends of John and Dora, were also selected. Mary S. Gibson was a former teacher, widow of a former Board of Education member, and mother of a future U.S. ambassador to Brazil, Hugh Gibson. She and Ethel Richardson both had worked with Dora in the women's suffrage and Progressive party crusades. Both Gibson and Richardson were interested in the adult education movement and very active with John in creating the local Indian Defense Association to protect Native Americans.[13]

The remaining trustee, Clarence Addison Dykstra, was a professor of political science and expert in municipal government. Appointed to the Board of Water and Power Commissioners in 1926, he became the DWP's director of personnel and efficiency. Thanks to his interests in government and municipal ownership, he became a friend of Haynes's and helped to shape the foundation. Dykstra remained a trustee until 1930, when he became city manager of Cincinnati. Later he held federal government posts and the position of provost at UCLA.[14]

The original trustees were charged with carrying out the purposes of John and Dora Haynes as specified in the trust instrument. These purposes consisted of support for several general and specific causes to which John Haynes had been contributing. The trust instrument was altered in 1934 so as to omit these specific interests and substitute less-activist pursuits. But an enumeration of the original categories of support is significant as a guide to the reform agenda Haynes had formulated by 1926.

The first category was the promotion of democracy. The trust instrument delineated this category in an omnibus package of measures designed "to assist in promoting and obtaining, maintaining and making improvements in the structure and methods of government, national, state and/or local." The first of these measures was the promotion of public ownership and operation of utilities, Haynes's first reform priority at the time. On the state level he personally was supporting the California Water and Power Act initiative for the third time. Locally he spent over $34,000 of his own funds to advance the city's water and power program from 1925 to 1937, most of the money being devoted to bond and charter campaigns. But to avoid conflicts with tax authorities over political uses of charitable donations, the foundation itself spent very little in this area during the same period.[15]

On a broader level, Haynes supported public ownership of utilities with his advice and contributions to national organizations and for major studies. The doctor was interested in the Institute for Research in Land Economics and Public Utilities, operated by Richard T. Ely, who solicited Haynes's financial backing for expensive statistical studies of taxation policies affecting public utilities. But in that the project developed just before the 1925 municipal election, Haynes decided that his money would be better spent on the campaign. Among the more direct ventures he supported was the publication in 1930 of *Public Ownership on Trial*, a survey of the operation of public utilities throughout California written by two political scientists from Occidental College. Haynes even helped them conduct the research. His membership in Gifford Pinchot's National Conservation Association in the 1910s and 1920s also related to public ownership in that the organization monitored federal legislation regarding development of natural resources used to produce energy.[16]

One of the chief beneficiaries of his patronage in this area was the Public Ownership League of America, founded during World War I. League secretary Carl D. Thompson enlisted Haynes's membership in 1918 and became one of the doctor's trusted advisers on the power question. The two corresponded frequently on issues of national and local hydroelectrical power, pondering methods to fight the national "power trust" and to help U.S. and Canadian cities develop their own power plants. Having "the utmost faith" in Thompson, Haynes frequently sent him extra checks to fund specific projects or to supplement his secretarial salary, and helped to arrange his tours and conferences in California. In return, Haynes expected Thompson to keep the organization at arm's length from more radical figures who might alienate moderates and conservatives who, while opposing public ownership in general, supported the doctor's water and power program. The foundation renewed Haynes's membership in the Public Ownership League for a short time after his death, but made no major contributions to Thompson.[17]

Direct legislation also fell into the first category of support. This reform was Haynes's primary goal at the turn of the century. Since he had been successful in establishing it in the Los Angeles city charter and state constitution, his charge to the foundation was to protect the measure from attacks and to encourage its adoption in other states and cities. To this end he financed and aided in the research for *The Recall of Public Officers in California*, a book by the same two political scientists who wrote *Public Ownership on Trial*. Haynes opened his files and downtown office for this study of the recall at all levels of California governments. The book criticized some of Haynes's political allies, specifically Mayor Cryer and the unnamed but unmistakable Kent Parrot. The doctor emerged as the hero, to no one's surprise, and the book's conclusion reflected his own view of the recall device: "Like all democratic political institutions it has failed to acquire automatic perfection, and its value in each instance of its use has depended upon the intelligence and judgment of the electorate which has employed it."[18]

Besides providing for additional expenditures of the Direct Legislation League of California and for Franklin Hichborn's lobbying expenses, Haynes supported the National Popular Government League, of which he had been the principal financier since its founding in 1913. The league espoused several "democratic principles," among them direct legislation. Through the 1910s Haynes corresponded with the league's secretary-treasurer, Judson King. Impressed with King's vast knowledge of the subject, Haynes agreed in 1921 to subsidize King's proposed book on the initiative and referendum. After spending several thousand dollars on the effort, Haynes finally gave up the idea (as did King) in 1928. He had kept sending the monthly checks for that long chiefly because King had obliged the doctor by changing the league's focus from direct legislation to public ownership, which Haynes deemed the more urgent cause. His trustees continued to support his membership in the organization into the 1940s.[19]

Other items in the first category included "improvements in the direct, popular nomination and election of public officials," "more adequate representation in government of the important groups," and "assisting in making, amending, and/or reviewing of city charters, county charters, and State and national constitutions." At a time when the direct primary was being attacked by conservatives throughout the state, Haynes considered it a necessary tool of democracy. Its defeat would bring back a situation similar to the rule of "the old Southern Pacific machine," in which bosses ruled through party organizations to protect special interests. "Such groups know that it is easier and cheaper to corrupt a majority of the delegates in the conventions of both parties, if necessary, than to control an entire electorate," Haynes reasoned. Although the California cross-filing law made the primary an easy target for critics, Haynes preferred to protect it rather than lose it altogether. Presumably another of his favorite reforms, proportional representation, fell into the realm of fair representation of political groups, though Haynes gave little to the Proportional Representation League in the 1920s and 1930s and the foundation made only token contributions in the late 1930s.[20]

Financing studies of charters and constitutions and of proposals for their improvement would become a very important function for the trustees. Throughout his reform career Haynes was active in composing and altering charters and state constitutions. In the 1910s and 1920s he lectured at local colleges about the need to revise, update, and otherwise improve existing documents to expand democratic principles and provide more services. Although it is not specifically mentioned in the original trust instrument, Haynes might have considered civil service reform a cause worthy of support, for he believed that competent government employees should be protected from political influence in the performance of their duties. At any rate, Haynes was and always had been a crusader for the merit system, and in later years he reminded the trustees of that fact.[21]

The second broad category of support was the improvement of the living and working conditions "of the working people" and encouragement of industrial cooperation. The latter reflected Haynes's experience as a labor mediator during the war, and the former his desire to see laborers and their families uplifted. Recalling his days as a doctor in one of the poorest areas of Philadelphia, he wrote: "As a physician I was obliged to depend on pills when I knew only too well that the real medicine my patients needed was good nourishing food, proper living conditions, freedom from financial worry, rest and change. All these were denied them because they belonged to the working class." In the intervening years he established an amiable relationship with Los Angeles labor leaders and hoped to move beyond his minor philanthropic efforts for workers to a major improvement in their living standard.[22]

The sections of the trust instrument concerning workers were generally broad, but specific features were mentioned. The Rochdale System of Cooperation was singled out for support. Haynes had helped establish such a system of selling and purchasing food and household goods in Los Angeles in 1902, but the venture folded a few years later. The prevention of child labor, though not spelled out in the trust instrument, could be inferred from its language. In the 1920s, he pursued this cause on his own: he offered to subsidize a civil suit in behalf of a child who had been injured in an industrial accident, lobbied for a child-labor amendment to the U.S. Constitution, and protested to those who defended the employment of children.[23]

Still another beneficiary designated in the sections concerning workers was the American Association for Labor Legislation. The AALL took up Haynes's crusade for better laws on mining safety in 1922, and he poured almost $20,000 into its coffers by the end of the decade. He considered mining safety his second priority in the 1920s, and took many opportunities to publicize the AALL campaign and preach the merits of "rock-dusting," which prevented explosions in the mines. John B. Andrews, AALL secretary, praised Haynes's work in the campaign for uniform mining-safety laws enforced by a federal commission, and the AALL was highly successful in convincing or requiring coal companies to rockdust their mines. With another $10,000 donation from Haynes in 1932, the

AALL continued its campaign, aided by additional support from the Haynes Foundation.[24]

Haynes's interest in improving the status of working people was also reflected in his support of major social-welfare organizations. One of them, Florence Kelley's National Consumers League, attracted the doctor's attention in 1914, and he became a member. The league took up the campaign for state and federal legislation to protect workers from mistreatment, lobbying on behalf of the consumers who purchased the goods those workers manufactured. Another of these groups, The Survey Associates, became a Haynes favorite. He joined the organization after the war at the request of its leader, Paul Kellogg, who published the *Survey*. This journal, initially intended for social workers, was devoted to the improvement of living conditions of the working class. Haynes tried to set up a support group for it in Los Angeles and contributed heavily to Kellogg's work in the 1920s.[25]

The third priority for the trustees was to "encourage and give educational opportunities" for the study of governmental, industrial, and social problems "with special reference to improvements" designed for "the working people." The intent of this section of the trust was to pay lecturers and instructors, furnish literature, and make donations to institutions "in furthering the causes already mentioned and aiding the enactment and protection of legislation for these purposes." As two of the foundation's later trustees (both of them academics) recalled, John and Dora Haynes intended that funds devoted to education be "used partly for the gathering of information and partly for the encouragement of desirable social action." "They were very critical of non-producing academic studies," afraid that "the search for knowledge might end in the search and not proceed to betterment." So, they believed, studies should be supported that "give rise to constructive, effective and concrete social legislation and a community will translated into community action."[26]

In the early years, however, this intent was not carried out by the founders or trustees. Haynes donated over $7,700 and the foundation almost $6,000 to colleges for scholarships and other programs from 1925 to 1937. A good portion went to Occidental College, one of Haynes's favorites, and to his alma mater, the University of Pennsylvania. A much smaller amount went to the California Association for Adult Education, an organization with which the doctor, Mrs. Richardson, and Mrs. Gibson had become involved by 1920. Although these donations did not fall within the actual intent of this priority, they did reflect Haynes's interest in higher education and in providing opportunities for young people of all economic backgrounds to attend colleges he supported.[27]

The fourth major support category, one of dubious distinction, was the "improvement of the human race by aiding and encouraging the science of eugenics." Since the early 1910s, Haynes had been a staunch booster of eugenics, which aimed to improve the human race by selective breeding and other means. The eugenics movement became a popular cause for scientifically minded U.S. progressives after 1900. Earlier it had taken hold in Great Britain, where it was embraced by Sidney and Beatrice Webb, George Bernard Shaw, and other Fabian Society acquaintances of Haynes's. The movement spread to Japan before declining in the 1930s, when the Depression pinched the movement's sources of revenue and when the rise of Nazi Germany, with its fanaticism about racial purity and the elimination of what it branded as genetically inferior groups and persons, cast a pall on all notions of human engineering. Although their aim of preventing the biologically inferior from contributing to the population was purportedly motivated by humanitarian and economic concerns, the eugenists consistently revealed class motives for restricting the procreation of the "feeble-minded" and other unfortunates of the lower classes. In boosting the idea that Darwinian natural selection applied to humans, eugenists "contradicted traditional Christian values of individual goodness and integrity and human equality," and stressed the dominance of heredity in determining character to the virtual exclusion of environmental factors.[28]

As a physician, Dr. Haynes believed society had a duty to improve its condition by preventing the unfit from procreating, for he accepted the "scientific" argument, advanced by eugenists, that unfit parents would bear unfit offspring. He likened this idea to dog-breeding practices "in celebrated kennels in England," where only those "fit to propagate are allowed to propagate." Extending this analogy, he wrote:

> What a wonderful change would occur in the welfare of man if the same principles were even approximately pursued in the breeding of human beings. That society shall allow the confirmed criminal, the degenerate, or the feeble-minded to propagate their kind is a criminal indictment and bespeaks for the eugenists of the day whose special duty is to instruct society as to good breeding, either abject cowardice or a lack of intelligence. Prevention of the breeding of the unfit surely is the first basic step in the breeding of a better society.[29]

Birth control was one solution, but Haynes was particularly enamored with "sterilization of the unfit" to eliminate all possibility that they would reproduce similar offspring. As early as 1898 he had stated his belief that marriage of those "physically, mentally and morally unfitted to become parents" should be prohibited. He supported the passage and implementation of a 1909 California law allowing sterilization of certain "unfit" persons. On the State Board of Charities and Corrections he advanced the notion that no patient should be discharged from the state insane asylum without being sterilized, and he surveyed over 500 state hospitals and prisons throughout the nation to compare sterilization practices.[30]

By 1918 Haynes advocated sterilization as a necessity. In a wartime speech entitled "The State Institutions of California," he argued that the presence of "abnormal individuals" in society was the result of their propagation by unfit parents and an unintelligent economic and social system. The latter could be remedied by political and economic reform, but the former could be eradicated only by sterilization.[31]

Haynes's view of eugenics was motivated by a genuine concern for the future of society, as evidenced by his past and future humanitarian endeavors. But this concern masked his own fear of the lower classes. In his most complete statement on the subject, an address delivered in 1922, the doctor offered as evidence for the utility of sterilization a number of examples of individuals whose descendents were "abnormal." The list included paupers and feebleminded people whose children became "criminals, paupers, inebriates or insane," conditions also attributable to economic and environmental factors. His argument that care of these unfit offspring put tremendous financial strain on governments and society sounded more like the justification of his political opponents, who demanded lower government costs, than of a humanitarian who consistently called for more government aid for society's unfortunates. Though he did care for these victims, he could, to a degree, ignore their humanity in his concern for the future of the human race.[32]

Haynes's advocacy of eugenics intensified in the 1920s. He contributed to organizations such as the Human Betterment Foundation of Pasadena, and supported national spokesman Paul Popenoe. Haynes even tried in 1922 to set up a $100,000 defense fund for state hospital directors who might be sued if sterilizing patients was ruled illegal.[33]

He continued to speak for sterilization in the 1930s, even defending it in the face of a similar policy being put into effect in Nazi Germany, which dampened the enthusiasm of American eugenists. Haynes was not one of the "sentimentalists who would allow the country to be flooded with degenerates, perverts, epileptics, the insane, feeble minded and others unfit to propagate." Haynes condemned the "wholesale edict of sterilization in Germany" by a "mad-man," and censured it as a political rather than scientific application of the method. But he failed to convince foundation trustees that eugenics was a worthy recipient of aid. While the doctor donated thousands to this cause, the foundation ignored it.[34]

Closely associated with sterilization was the issue of birth control, a highly controversial topic at the time Haynes began contributing to Margaret Sanger's crusade. He advocated limiting the world's population of even "fit" humans to eliminate starvation and wars sparked by the need for nations to expand beyond their borders to accommodate population increases. Locally he contributed to and served as treasurer for the Los Angeles Mothers' Clinic Association, Inc., a group he helped found in 1925, which counseled mothers on health and family planning. Also in 1925, he served as treasurer for the Los Angeles chapter of Sanger's American Birth Control League. He lobbied for national birth-control legislation as a vice chairman of the National Committee on Federal Legislation for Birth Control until Sanger dissolved the organization in 1937, declaring that it had achieved its goals. He remained active in the movement until his death, but his foundation made only minor contributions to Sanger in the 1930s.[35]

A frequent criticism of eugenists and advocates of birth control was that they were motivated by a belief in their own racial superiority. Eugenists' complaints of "the low birth rate among upper classes" as compared to the high rate among the lower classes (whose members were usually of a darker color), their recommendations regarding immigration restrictions, and their choice of certain racial features (their own) as traits to be preserved through eugenics left little doubt about their estimation of their own race and class.[36]

As a eugenist, Haynes eschewed the charges of racism, though he never championed racial equality. Growing up in Philadelphia during the Civil War, he accepted the prevailing view of racial segregation, which included prohibiting African-Americans from riding in streetcars. In 1923, during a particularly xenophobic period of anti-Japanese sentiment, Haynes, like many of his fellow progressives, admitted that he was "opposed to the Japanese owning land, being admitted to citizenship or intermarrying with other races." In his autobiographical notes dictated a little later, he claimed to understand both sides of the racial equality debate, but immediately remarked that a tribe of Native Americans in Riverside had not improved their condition after 5,000 years. This citation probably expressed his true feelings. He joined the NAACP and frequently was praised by local African-American leaders, but his interest in their community typically waxed at election time, when votes were needed for his candidates. Though he often expressed an affection for racial minorities, the feeling was rooted in his ethnocentric paternalism: he wished to see all races living in harmony—not necessarily together—for only such a world could assure proper care for society's less fortunate.[37]

The fifth category of support was the strengthening of "prohibition and other legislation" affecting alcoholic beverages and narcotic drugs. Haynes had always been in favor of anti-saloon laws, both to stem the tide of alcoholism and its damaging of families and society, and to quash the influence of the saloon keepers in politics. He also opposed the use of alcohol in medical treatments, and by the late 1910s he began to advocate outright prohibition. In 1920, he discarded his and his wife's supply of wine and began financing the defense and enforcement of national Prohibition. He took an active role in the state Anti-Saloon League and worked with Franklin Hichborn to change the league's leadership and strengthen its role in state politics.[38]

In 1926, Haynes delivered one of several Prohibition speeches to his fellow Sunsetters, concluding with the prediction, Prohibition "will never be repealed in your lifetime or mine." Probably most of his listeners were around to prove him wrong when Prohibition was repealed in 1933. By this time Haynes had stopped defending it with his money, though not in his public statements. But his trustees preferred not to support Prohibition in any manner.[39]

The foundation's sixth category of support also was very specific: the promotion of "justice for the American Indian." Haynes had been interested in the welfare of Native Americans since at least 1905, when he became a member of the Los Angeles Council of the Sequoya League. This national organization, spearheaded by Charles F. Lummis, sought to improve living conditions of California's first inhabitants until Lummis's death in 1928. After World War I, Haynes's interest in this subject grew when two of his friends and future trustees, Ethel Richardson and Mary A. Gibson, persuaded him to help them start the Indian Defense Association of Southern California. Founded in 1923, with Haynes as its president, this organization and a similar group in San Francisco became the state branches of the American Indian Defense Association (AIDA), established in the same year.[40]

The purpose of the national organization, which Haynes served as a member of the board of directors, and the local branches, was to lobby and otherwise campaign to protect the customs, cultures, and lands of Native Americans, and help them become more self-reliant. In its congressional lobbying and financing of aggressive legal action, the organization usually aimed at federal agencies, especially the Bureau of Indian Affairs, during the Coolidge and Hoover administrations.[41]

His endeavors in this field brought Haynes into very close association with John Collier, the AIDA executive secretary and a tireless worker for Native Americans. Haynes had met Collier in 1919, when the doctor helped bring Collier to Los Angeles as a leader in the field of adult education. This career lasted until 1922, when Collier agreed to assist Stella Atwood, Kate Vosberg, and other Southern California clubwomen in founding the national and local Native American defense organizations. Haynes, a major force in the movement in Southern California and one of the organization's chief sponsors, became one of Collier's closest confidants through their frequent correspondence. After moving to Washington, D.C., Collier often stayed at the Figueroa Street residence in his travels west; it was, he recalled, "my own home and office in Southern California." Haynes earmarked his donations to AIDA as contributions to Collier's salary. The doctor also paid tuition for Collier's son during the lean times and offered Collier additional financial support if he would compose a biography of Haynes. Collier agreed to this in 1925, and began assembling Haynes's reminiscences, which the doctor dictated to a secretary. But as Collier's other labors became more time-consuming, he finally had to bow out of this project.[42]

So high was Haynes's regard for Collier that the doctor not only invited him to become a foundation trustee in 1934, but also aided Collier's bid to be appointed federal Commissioner of Indian Affairs. Reformers had usually opposed the incumbent commissioner, and welcomed the election of Franklin D. Roosevelt as an opportunity for change. In September 1932, Collier notified Haynes and three others of his intention to obtain the position, and just before the election Haynes met with Collier and others to plan strategy. Soon after, Haynes initiated his own campaign on Collier's behalf. The doctor asked Senator Hiram Johnson and Senator-elect William G. McAdoo to line up support. Several candidates sought the appointment, but Collier was eventually selected. While not the determining force in Collier's victory, Haynes's lobbying effort was important.[43]

Haynes's voluminous correspondence regarding the defense of Native Americans, his hefty contributions to AIDA and similar groups, his leadership in the Southern California branch, and his effort to defend Paiutes in the Owens Valley while on the Board of Public Service Commissioners testified to his concern for Native American rights and welfare. Besides his personal friends, he encouraged the trustees to approve expenditures for AIDA and other groups in almost every year between 1927 and 1937, the year of his death. Although this crusade was not his chief reform concern, he took great pride in his work and earned notice in the field. One of his obituaries, an essay tribute to "one of Los Angeles' true pioneers," omitted mention of direct legislation and public ownership: the entire piece was devoted to his crusade to preserve the tribal rights of Pueblos and other Native Americans.[44]

The last specified category of foundation support was the protection of freedom of speech and other rights guaranteed by the First Amendment of the U.S. Constitution. During World War I, Haynes proved that he was not concerned about such rights, for he consistently recommended punishment for all expressions antagonistic to the war effort. After the war he relented and campaigned for the release of those jailed for such utterances. By 1920, he was contributing to the National Popular Government League's legal assault on the "Red Raids" orchestrated by Attorney General Palmer, and in 1921 he offered to finance a campaign by the Rand School of Social Service to challenge a New York law Haynes thought unconstitutional. Also by 1921, he had joined the infant American Civil Liberties Union.[45]

Haynes suffered his most profound experience in the area of civil liberties in 1923, when his friend Upton Sinclair was arrested for the heinous crime of reading the U.S. Constitution aloud. Early that year the IWW had launched an all-out attack on the state's criminal-syndicalism law which was aimed specifically at the labor tactics of IWW "Wobblies." A strike called by IWW dockworkers in San Pedro soon led to mass arrests, vigilante action, and protest marches. A sympathetic Sinclair and his entourage of friends and relatives received permission to stage a demonstration on Liberty Hill, a plot of private land. Sinclair warned Los Angeles city officials of his intentions and proceeded to the hill on May 15. When he began reciting the First Amendment he was arrested by the LAPD, along with three associates, and held incommunicado for two days while the police tried to decide what to do with them.[46]

Informed by a reporter of her husband's bizarre arrest, Mrs. Sinclair immediately phoned Dr. Haynes for help. "I will act at once, and do my very best," Haynes reportedly replied, and told her to call everyone she could think of to assist. He apparently contacted his political allies at city hall—Kent Parrot and Mayor Cryer—and demanded that Sinclair be set free. The police chief finally ordered the novelist's release. Haynes's intercession may have helped, but the chief realized that the operation had been bungled from the outset. Sinclair took advantage of the incident by publicizing his adventure as proof of the need for a local chapter of the ACLU. Less than two weeks after his arrest he wrote to Haynes asking for the doctor's money and support to help over 600 jailed strikers and to establish the Southern California branch. Haynes sent $500, keeping it anonymous to avoid further castigation as a "Red," as the *Times* had just labeled him in the controversy over his position as a UC regent.[47]

The local ACLU branch was established, though Haynes subsequently took little interest in it. He remained a member and made small contributions to it and the national office at times, but complied with few of the many requests from Sinclair and others for substantial donations. The foundation trustees followed this lead before and after his death by declining to support civil liberties organizations to any extent.[48]

These seven major categories for support represented John and Dora Haynes's intention for their fortune at the time the foundation was created. They were not the only causes to which John wished to contribute. As evidenced by early grants recommended by Haynes, he also hoped to advance the dissemination of literature related to social democracy, medical care for those who could not afford it, and certain religious organizations. In a broad sense these interests, although not specified in the trust instrument, reflected his commitment to improve the welfare of working people.

The foundation's grants to the League for Industrial Democracy were a pittance in comparison to what Haynes hoped to do for that organization. Formerly the Intercollegiate Socialist Society, the league was the American socialist movement's educational arm, of which Haynes had been a member since the early 1900s. Haynes once stated, "It is a wiser management of wealth to use it to destroy an evil system at the root than to use it to alleviate some results of an evil system," and accordingly he gave to the ISS and later the LID to facilitate its work in educating Americans in the operation of their economic system. He frequently corresponded with LID officials Harry Laidler, Norman Thomas, and Paul Blanshard, and entertained them at his house when they visited the West Coast.[49]

In 1926, Haynes contributed $500 to the LID for the purchase of books on socialism to be distributed to colleges throughout the nation, just as he had two decades earlier. He also began investigating a plan to donate $100,000 to an LID trust fund, a scheme that would have restricted his support of his own foundation at the time. The monetary consideration, which replaced his earlier idea of giving the LID a free 99-year lease on a building he owned, was made contingent on the donation of half that amount by another benefactor and an assurance that it would be tax-deductible for Haynes and not subject to an inheritance tax for the league. Negotiations between Haynes, his lawyers, Harry Laidler, and LID attorneys continued on and off for years, keeping the idea in limbo until the doctor's death.[50]

Though the $100,000 donation never materialized, the LID did receive thousands of Haynes's dollars, as well as some of the foundation's, in the period from 1925 through 1932. Since the LID's current priority was the "Social Control of Power," the foundation's donations fell into the category of support for public ownership as well as that of improvement of living and working standards for the nation's labor force. As Haynes desired, the foundation's contributions as well as his own were made anonymously to avoid linking his municipal-ownership activities to avowed Socialists. He even had to turn down his election to the LID board of directors for this reason. Privately, his faith in the advancement of gradual socialism remained firm throughout the 1920s and 1930s. As he wrote to a friend concerning the visit of British prime minister Ramsay MacDonald to the United States in 1929: "It tickles the cockles of my heart to see a socialist the most important man in the most important nation next to the United States receive such an ovation. Progress is certainly made."[51]

Medicine was not mentioned in the trust instrument either, but in providing for the welfare of "working people" the foundation made a few contributions to the Good Hope Hospital Association. The "Good Hope Hospital" was a service provided by the association in cooperation with the Good Samaritan Hospital of the Episcopal Church. Wage earners who could not afford regular medical treatment were charged for services at cost, up to a maximum of three dollars per day; the balance was paid by the Good Hope Association. Dr. Haynes had contemplated this venture as early as 1922, and in the next four years he induced several wealthy friends to join him in establishing the association, of which he was elected president. One anonymous woman donated almost $2,000,000 to the entity, while Haynes, Allan C. Balch, and others made much less substantial contributions. The institution opened in 1927, and judging from the enormous number of letters of gratitude sent by patients to Dr. Haynes, Good Hope was a tremendous success.[52]

The founding of this hospital expressed Haynes's continued devotion to medicine and his pride in his reputation as a doctor. This attitude also became evident at the time he was planning his foundation. His old friend Gaylord Wilshire had long before dropped his defense of socialism and by 1925 was promoting his "Ionaco," a belt device that transmitted electromagnetic energy to various parts of the body. Wilshire claimed it would cure a variety of ailments and advertised his invention as a "Short Cut to Health." The belt sold well but did not gain the endorsement of the skeptical Haynes. "In future please do not mention my name in any of your advertisements for Ionaco," Haynes wrote to Wilshire, wishing to avoid embarrassing his friend publicly. This appears to have been one of the last written exchanges between the two. Wilshire died not long after, in 1927.[53]

The Haynes Foundation also made early grants to religious organizations—St. Paul's Episcopal Church and the First Unitarian Church—although religion was not mentioned in the trust. In fact, Haynes's support for established religion in the 1920s was surprising since he considered himself an atheist. "The thought of there being a human, merciful and loving God became preposterous," he wrote at this time, and "to imagine that there is an entity outside the brain is illogical." Echoing Karl Marx, he states in an autobiographical note: "Religion is the opium of the people. It prevents them from seeing the wretchedness of the world and taking steps to prevent it." Described as a "systematic atheist" by John Collier, the doctor engaged his friend in "many a discussion far into many nights" with religion the dominant topic.[54]

Actually, Haynes always had had strong ties to organized religion. As a child he was "afraid of hellfire and damnation," although he claimed "this was only a temporary period of insanity." When he was a young physician in Philadelphia he taught Sunday school at Messiah Episcopal Church, though later he insisted that this function was more social than religious. In Los Angeles in the 1890s he was a leading member of St. Paul's Church, once representing the parish at an Episcopal convention. It was at that time that he launched his reform career as a Christian socialist, theoretically accepting Protestant doctrine as articulated by William D. P. Bliss and others who fused religious tenets with the economics of gradual socialism. And in the 1920s and 1930s he was an occasional officer in the Federated Church Brotherhood of California and Church Federation of Los Angeles. These interdenominational alliances of Protestants became important political interest groups, which would explain Haynes's participation: he wished to curry their support.[55]

In the chasm between his atheistic pronouncements and his work for and with religious agencies lay his agnosticism, which was based on a respect for Christ and some Christians but rejection of a loving God. In speeches he praised Jesus as a "Son of the common people," the "Palestinian laboring man" who "taught his followers to love their enemies." In exalting the Sermon on the Mount, which he, along with many other socialists, considered "the most important statement ever spoken," Haynes admitted: "During the long years that I have come into contact with thousands of people, . . . those who believe in and try to follow the teachings of the great Nazarene have done the most for humanity." These Christians, he believed, were altruists who attained true happiness by their unselfish service to their fellow man, "the fundamental purpose of life's work."[56]

But other Christians were responsible for the most cruel inhumanities Haynes could imagine. World War I was the watershed in his growing doubts about the existence of a supreme being. "Yesterday, a million men, calling themselves after the carpenter, Christians, drenched Europe with the blood of fellow Christians," he told a college class in 1922. And "today, in so-called Christian America, millions of men, women and little children are suffering from mental, moral and slow physical starvation in city slums." For him these facts demonstrated that a good God could not exist: "The very scheme of organic life logically disproves that theory." The facts of war and economic privation transformed Haynes into "a materialist believing that there is no hereafter when we die for we die like the butterfly." Christ might have been a "moral genius," but was not the God of John Haynes. Like the religiously unorthodox Socialists described by historian David Shannon, Haynes was not un-Christian in his ethics. His lifelong devotion to uplifting his fellow man expressed his adherence to the crucial principle of the Sermon on the Mount: "Thou shalt love thy neighbor as thyself." This commandment, he asserted, "should be impressed on the mind of every one of the children of men from the time of the awakening of reason to the end of life's span."[57]

Before Haynes transferred his property to the foundation, he wanted to be sure that the trust was a legal, tax-exempt entity. To do this he prodded John Collier to initiate a friendly suit against Francis H. Lindley and the other trustees to test the validity of the trust instrument. The suit was filed in Alameda County; Louis Bartlett (who lived there) and J. Wiseman Macdonald defended the foundation. According to Bartlett, the judge was hostile to the purposes of the trust, especially the eugenics clause, and allowed the case to languish for quite a long time. Finally, he approved the document, and Collier appealed to the state Supreme Court for a final verdict. The justices were unanimous in their criticism of this tactic of testing the legality of a contract by initiating litigation when "no real cause of action has arisen." In this case, however, "certain questions of public interest" needed to be examined. They also agreed that the Hayneses, who

> devoted a large part of their lives and a considerable portion of their fortune unselfishly to the promotion of the particular ideas of political and social reform which they are now seeking to have perpetuated beyond the period of their natural lives through this foundation, are to be commended rather than criticized for their desire to render permanent their life work. This method of achieving immortality is all too rare, and while we may not all agree upon the question as to whether or not certain details of these projected reforms in our political or social life are practical or even altogether desirable, we may not for that reason hold this foundation to be invalid by virtue of the defects in its creation which are urged by the appellant herein.[58]

This decision was reached in March 1928, while the foundation already had begun to operate. The first meeting of the trustees, on June 9, 1927, like most that followed, was held at the Figueroa Street residence. Anne Mumford took care of the business aspects of the foundation in Haynes's downtown office. In the first few years Haynes *was* the foundation: he decided which organizations to support and how much to give, and the trustees followed his recommendations. Occasionally he placed memorandums in the trustee files to remind them of his interests so that his wishes would be honored after his passing. Support for the prevention of maladies (e.g., for mining-safety laws to prevent accidents), he reminded them, should supersede support for alleviation of the results (e.g., for the care of miners' orphans), since there was little capital in the treasury. Few grants could be made, so the trust budget was miniscule in comparison to the budgets of larger foundations on the East Coast.[59]

Early grants were awarded to organizations to which Haynes already belonged: LID, AALL, AIDA, Survey Associates, and the like. Many requests had to be denied because of financial constraints or inappropriateness. One denial was meted out to Haynes's old friend J. Stitt Wilson, a Methodist clergyman and Socialist mayor of Berkeley from 1911 to 1915. At the doctor's suggestion, Wilson had requested a "Life Annuity" of $1,500 per year to support his writing and lecturing on democracy and social justice. The trustees denied the application on the grounds that grants would not be made to individuals. Instead, Haynes financed Wilson from his own funds as a personal favor.[60]

Wilson's request for an individual grant was one of many received and turned down by the trustees. Haynes was not so dogmatic. He once complained to Upton Sinclair, in reference to a common friend who was troubled by donation seekers, if she were besieged "any more than I am, she would have to have a man with a gun at the door. At least four persons a day come in with pleas for bare existence either for themselves or their organizations." (And this was in 1929, before the Great Depression!) But the doctor did accede to many of these pleas. Many individuals, such as Katie Mae Wilson, a poor black student at UCLA who eventually became a teacher, and Faith Chevaillier, an aging friend and former Socialist speaker, received money from Haynes to help them through hard times. Though he established the foundation to take care of his charities, he continued to spend thousands each year in this manner, beyond the aid he granted through his foundation and political organizations.[61]

The foundation entered the 1930s in dire straits. The stock market crash of 1929 had dramatically reduced its treasury, composed mostly of loans of securities from Dora Haynes, and the endowment plummeted in value. In the following year Mrs. Gibson died, C. A. Dykstra moved to Cincinnati to become its city manager, and a too-busy William Mathews resigned (he died less than a year later). Mathews was replaced by state senator Herbert Coffin Jones, leader of the progressives in the state legislature, who had worked with Haynes in many campaigns in the 1920s and 1930s. But the other two were not replaced immediately, since there was little for the trustees to do. The foundation's poor financial condition precluded the approval of many grants or even conducting business meetings. This situation lasted for over three years, putting the trust virtually out of business at a time the entire nation was coping with economic calamity.[62]

Haynes tried to remain optimistic about the future of his foundation. In 1931, he informed Franklin Hichborn that after the Depression ("if it ever will cease"), he intended to build a home in La Crescenta, about fifteen miles north of downtown Los Angeles, as a new headquarters. The house would include a "fire proof room which will hold all the archives we have, and such other as the Foundation may accumulate," notably the vast research and correspondence files. Personally he was worth almost $2,000,000 at the time, and most of this fortune was destined for the foundation treasury, the rebirth of which would have to wait for the infusion of more funds from its founders.[63]

In the midst of the Great Depression, the Haynes Foundation could make no headway in increasing "the happiness and well being of mankind," as Haynes had instructed his trustees to do. It survived its infancy, however, thus establishing a groundwork for future humanitarian service reflective of the values, priorities, and aspirations of its creator.

Chapter Twelve

"The Unfortunate Dr. Haynes": Young-Cryer Boom Through Rolph-Porter Bust

When John Haynes created his foundation, he wanted to be sure that his fortune would always sustain the causes he favored, regardless of changes in the political climate that might affect his reform and humanitarian interests. He knew the political atmosphere would fluctuate; his personal experience since the 1890s confirmed that apprehension. Such change was all too apparent to him in the period from 1925 to 1932. In both state and local politics, his influence rose and declined as new characters altered political alignments and tried to squeeze him from the political scene, and he fought back, limiting his losses and launching his own offensives. Opponents relished the decline of the personal power of the "Unfortunate Dr. Haynes," but would never see it eliminated.[1]

In state politics in 1925, Haynes and his progressive allies were planning the defeat of Governor Friend Richardson. After the 1923 budget fight and other battles, the newly formed Progressive Voters League made modest gains in the 1924 legislative elections and set its sights on the 1926 gubernatorial contest. Kent Parrot hoped to nominate his protégé, Los Angeles mayor George E. Cryer, as the progressive choice of the Republican party. Fresh from his impressive victory in the 1925 municipal primary, Cryer could catapult his mentor, Parrot, into a top position in state politics. Most state progressives, including Haynes, favored either Lieutenant Governor Clement C. Young or Superintendent of Schools Will C. Wood. With Parrot beginning to make his move in late 1925, a group of progressives met in San Francisco in October and chose Young as their candidate. At a similar meeting at the Alexandria Hotel, Haynes and other Southern California progressives selected Judge Robert E. Clarke as the U.S. Senate nominee to appease Parrot.[2]

The choice of Young did not impress Governor Richardson's backers. Harry Chandler called him a "weak kneed rubber stamp, 'all things to all men' nonentity." Young was not charismatic, but waged an energetic campaign calling for more progressive reforms and an efficient, business-like government. Richardson duplicated his primary rhetoric of 1922, branding his opponent as a radical bent on bankrupting the state trea-sury.[3]

Kent Parrot managed the Young campaign in Southern California with help from Haynes, who bankrolled both Young and the Progressive Vot-ers League. In San Francisco, Sheriff Tom Finn directed the campaign with contributions from wealthy northern Californians. Young's forces were aided by large infusions of funds from A. P. Giannini, president of the Bank of Italy, who was currently at odds with Richardson's bank commissioner. Seeking a new and more pliable administrator, Giannini also ordered his employees throughout the state to work on Young's be-half.[4]

Enthusiasm for Judge Clarke's Senate bid was not as strong as that for Young's gubernatorial candidacy. Indeed, Haynes tried to convince Ru-dolph Spreckels and others to back Clarke with but little success. Spreck-els argued that Clarke was not even 50 percent progressive, while Hich-born reminded Haynes that the candidate was formerly the personal attorney of Harry Chandler. Other progressives, and many conserva-tives, would rather have a northern candidate so that someone from Southern California would have to be nominated in 1928 (per an under-standing of party leaders in the north and south), thus eliminating in-cumbent Hiram Johnson. As a result of all this opposition, Clarke was defeated in the primary by incumbent senator Samuel Shortridge, who was easily reelected. Young, however, beat Richardson by a close margin, and in the general election defeated both his Democratic opponent and Socialist Upton Sinclair.[5]

Young's inauguration returned the progressives to power. With a sym-pathetic majority in the legislature, the Young administration restored some of the humanitarian agencies eliminated by Richardson and created others. Young completed the reorganization of state government begun by William Stephens, established programs for the conservation of state resources, and prodded the legislature to approve major water and power projects. In fiscal matters he improved the state budget process, and while increasing expenditures, his administration amassed a huge treasury surplus. In his only term in office Young personified one view of the progressive as a business-minded reformer with at least a minimal amount of compassion for the disadvantaged.[6]

Haynes frequently had worked with Young during legislative sessions in the 1920s, and was an important contributor and strategist in the 1926 campaign. After the election the new governor and the doctor continued this relationship, Haynes becoming one of Young's chief advisers in Southern California. Haynes soon began counseling the governor on state appointments. On many occasions he instructed Young on positions to be taken on pending bills, especially those concerning direct legislation. Some of these letters were addressed to Mrs. Young because the doctor feared that Lieutenant Governor Buron Fitts, whom Haynes never trusted, might intercept confidential letters to the governor and pass the contents along to the doctor's enemies.[7]

Sometimes Haynes's advice backfired. In 1927, he insisted that Young appoint Jack Friedlander as corporation commissioner. This Los Angeles city prosecutor was "honest and capable," according to Haynes, and the Southern Californians who had spent over $60,000 on Young's campaign might revolt if the governor did not appoint someone from the south. "We have to keep our forces together for the state water and power fight," Haynes wrote to Hichborn, so the southerners must be placated. Hichborn replied that northern Progressives were wary of the influences behind Friedlander—namely Parrot and motion picture magnate Joseph Schenk. Nevertheless, the appointment finally was made. To Haynes's chagrin, Friedlander became embroiled in a controversy over his ties to Parrot in a stock-manipulation scheme and resigned in March 1929.[8]

Haynes was not always successful in influencing the governor to his way of thinking. Beginning in 1928, the doctor tried on numerous occasions by letter, phone call, and visit to persuade Young to pardon Tom Mooney. This Socialist labor leader had been convicted of a bombing that took place in San Francisco during a Preparedness Day parade in 1916; the explosion had killed 10 people and injured 40 others. Mooney conducted his own campaign for a pardon from his jail cell, and his defense became a national cause for those convinced of his innocence. Haynes was among those who were sure that key prosecution witnesses in the trial had perjured themselves. Mooney asked him to persuade Young to grant a pardon, and Haynes made several attempts. In early 1929, he wrote to Fremont Older, who championed Mooney's cause, "[I have] used all the persuasive powers I have with the Governor to secure his pardon" but never succeeded. Mooney remained in prison until 1939, when Governor Culbert Olson pardoned him as the first act of his new administration.[9]

Out of loyalty to Haynes and respect for his judgment, Governor

Young appointed the doctor to three ad hoc state commissions. The first of these was the California Tax Commission, which, in addition to Haynes, included Chester Rowell, Lieutenant Governor H. L. Carnahan, State Controller Ray Riley, and four others. Formed in 1927, this commission was charged with recommending improvements for the state tax system. Haynes's special concerns were to prevent public utilities from being taxed, to block a possible retail sales tax, and to make sure that banks paid their fair share. The latter issue brought him into conflict with Bank Commissioner Will C. Wood. The controversy escalated when Haynes criticized Woods for allowing A. P. Giannini to change the name of one of his banks to a name closely resembling that of a bank owned by Haynes's good friend Joseph Sartori of Los Angeles. In fact, Haynes probably was not in good stead with any California bankers since he advocated an increase in their taxes. To prevent a sales tax, which he considered undemocratic and unfair to some industries, he appealed to single-taxers for help in fighting this assessment.[10]

The doctor's effectiveness as a tax commissioner was limited since for most of his two-year tenure he was ill and contributed little. At one point he reported to Chairman Irving Martin that a cold would keep him from an upcoming meeting: "As I am neither useful nor ornamental I know my absence will not be a severe blow to the Commission," he wrote. In his absence the other commission members endorsed taxation of public utilities, though the group refrained from recommending the creation of a sales tax. An increase in taxes on banks and corporations also was suggested, along with a personal state income tax and a business tax. The final report reached the governor in March 1929, and some recommendations eventually became law.[11]

In 1930, Young appointed Haynes to the California Constitutional Commission. Among his fourteen associates were ex-mayor George Cryer, Chester Rowell, and Irving Martin, the latter of the Railroad and Tax Commissions. This group was charged with examining the state constitution and deciding if a new one was needed. Haynes was especially interested in the sections on public utilities and direct legislation. He even created a "subsidiary confidential Haynes Constitutional Commission Committee," composed of his most trusted friends, to suggest new ideas. As a member of the committees examining the constitutional provisions for legislation, municipal government, and taxation, he attended many of the meetings and offered ideas for modifications and additions.[12]

The commission's final report was not adopted unanimously, but generally it was favorable to Haynes. The commission recommended revising the present document in many sections—their proposals would have cut its size by more than half—and suggested that it be further modified by use of the initiative. As Haynes had hoped, the section on direct legislation was altered to require a fixed number of signatures for the qualification of petitions. Previously, the section had required a percentage, which mandated more signatures as the population increased. Other major changes included the elimination of the governor's pocket veto and the creation of a permanent tax commission and state board of education. Its task completed, the commission delivered its report to the governor at the end of the year. Some of the changes eventually were adopted, although the entire document never was rewritten.[13]

The third of the bodies to which Haynes was appointed, the California State Unemployment Board, was created by Young in late 1930 as the Depression began to take its toll in the Golden State. The board was composed of two committees of fifteen—one in northern California and one in the south. Haynes served on the southern board with Automobile Club president Harry Bauer, Pacific Electric president David W. Pontius, Reverend Edwin P. Ryland, and others. Active in 1930 and 1931, the board wrote several reports for Governor Young advising that the state speed up construction of public works, monitor the number of unemployed, and initiate programs to encourage citizens to buy now and employ their neighbors with odd jobs. These recommendations were similar to those of local agencies dealing with the same problem. Haynes participated in the board's deliberations for a short while, but his poor health and other duties limited his service.[14]

While serving on these committees, Haynes continued his work as a University regent. His most important undertaking in this capacity was his aid in moving the Los Angeles branch to the Westwood campus. After its establishment in 1919, the southern branch had quickly outgrown its first home. Under the leadership of Edward A. Dickson, the other three Southern California regents—Haynes, George I. Cochran, and Margaret Sartori—and a few of their friends searched for a new site on which to build a modern campus. After several years of negotiations, the group settled on a tract in Westwood. The groundbreaking took place in 1927, and UCLA opened two years later. The four southern regents, especially Dickson, were involved in all phases of the project, and took special pride in the fruits of their labor.[15]

Over the years Haynes made many contributions to the University of California at Los Angeles to advance its development. Before the state acquired the Westwood site, he joined thirteen other citizens in signing individual notes for $25,000 each to guarantee a loan for the University to purchase the land. He and six others contributed $1,000 each to buy the library of historian John Fiske, comprising some 9,000 volumes. Haynes also purchased books for the Political Science Department as a favor to one of its faculty members, Charles Grove Haines. In 1931, the doctor offered to make up the difference in the building costs between the budgeted labor amount and the union wage scale for two new buildings, thus ending a labor dispute that had disrupted construction. In addition, he made many smaller donations for social events, academic improvements, and other projects.[16]

Regent Haynes also became involved in the politics of this state institution. He was very concerned about the composition of the Board of Regents and advised Governor Young on prospective appointments for vacancies. He protected favored administrators, such as UCLA director Ernest C. Moore, when alleged plots to remove them emerged. Controversial issues included the establishment of graduate study programs at UCLA (which Haynes was one of the few regents to approve), optional military training (which he favored), and student morals.[17]

As a member of the medical school committee and buildings and grounds committee for the southern branch, Haynes was busy with many details in addition to the general issues faced by the regents. He devoted quite a bit of his time to these local matters but missed many of the regular meetings of the regents (held in northern California) because of poor health. He was active, nonetheless, in meetings and events in Los Angeles, in lobbying for bills affecting the university, and in generating financial aid for UCLA from his acquaintances.[18]

During these years Haynes lobbied the state legislature for much more than just education. From 1925 to 1932 and after, Haynes continued to tell legislators how to vote. Civil service was one important issue he addressed in order to protect the state from meddling by "well meaning but misguided legislators." Other laws he worked to safeguard included the direct-primary statute, protective laws for women, children, and workers, and similar legislation of the early progressive years. He sought to prevent bills outlawing the teaching of evolution, requiring religious instruction in schools, and taxing public utilities, among others. Besides pouring forth a voluminous correspondence of protests and encouragement to lawmakers and governors, he still paid the expenses of Franklin Hichborn to monitor the progress of pending legislation and sound the alarm when a bill anathema to the doctor was introduced.[19]

Direct legislation, of course, was always his main concern in the legislature. In every session one or more bills designed to modify the initiative, referendum, or recall was introduced, sometimes by progressive lawmakers trying to correct what they considered to be abuses. Haynes appealed to legislators to kill these bills and to governors to veto them. This vigilance took its toll after three decades. Haynes admitted to Governor Young, "I must confess that as I get older I get more weary of continual and unnecessary strife." [20]

His major involvement in the defense of direct legislation at this time was his participation in the examination of these measures by the Commonwealth Club. Haynes had been a member of the San Francisco organization since 1905. Two decades later he considered resigning because of his belief that a "small clique of reactionaries" had taken control. He remained a member, however, in order to aid other progressives in arguing their points in the deliberations of this prestigious group. When the club added a direct-legislation section in 1928, Haynes asked to be appointed to it. Though he could attend few of its San Francisco meetings, he wrote to committee members expressing his views.[21]

The club became more involved in direct-legislation matters in 1929, when its members decided to study the state constitution to advise Governor Young and the California Constitution Commission, which included Haynes and other club members. Since the club's membership was composed of some of the most prestigious and influential jurists, lawmakers, corporate leaders, and other professionals in the state (especially in the north), the club's recommendations pulled a fair amount of weight in the final outcome of the constitutional analysis. As a member of the club's direct-legislation section, Haynes worked with Hichborn, Louis Bartlett, and other associates to present the positive aspects of the state initiative and referendum since their adoption in 1911.[22]

On November 20, 1930, the section met and members delivered a series of papers on the topic, most of them favorable. Haynes could not be there, so he had Franklin Hichborn read a critique entitled "Proposed Sponsor System and Other Suggested Changes in the Initiative." In this essay Haynes argued against a suggestion to require a $10,000 bond to be furnished by sponsors of a petition. According to the plan the bond would be forfeited to the state if the measure were defeated at the polls— a mechanism that would ensure that the initiators of a petition were serious and responsible. Haynes contended that this system would in effect turn the initiative system over to wealthy special interests who could afford the $10,000 deposit. He also advised against an idea to allow the governor to place initiatives on the ballot, arguing that such a power was too dependent on the whim of the chief executive. This essay, along with those written by Hichborn and others, represented a generally favorable interpretation of the system of direct legislation as it stood, which persuaded the section to recommend to the California Constitutional Commission that the initiative, referendum, and recall be left virtually intact. The meeting convened just before the commission issued its final report. But those of the Commonwealth Club's members who served on the state commission had certainly borne the club's deliberations in mind throughout its year-long study of the matter.[23]

Haynes also defended direct legislation in court. In 1932 he commissioned Haynes Foundation trustee and state senator Herbert C. Jones to assist Adolph Uhl in seeking to compel the San Francisco County registrar of voters not to allow petition signatories to withdraw their signatures after initiative petitions were filed. As Jones reported after the disposition of this California Supreme Court case, "we" (proponents of direct legislation) won the issue, but Uhl lost his plea on a technicality.[24]

Another arena of agitation was the local press, in which Haynes continued to counter the Times's diatribes against direct legislation. In a letter to the Times editor, which never was printed, the doctor advised him what to tell a reader who had written to say that he would oppose all 41 propositions on the 1932 statewide ballot because the initiative and referendum "fool the people more easily than the well-trained legislature." Tell the reader that only 5 of the 41 propositions were initiatives, urged Dr. Haynes. The other 36 were placed on the ballot by the "well-trained legislature," in accordance with the California Constitution of 1879.[25]

Haynes's relationship with other state progressives in the late 1920s was usually amiable, as long as they advocated his brand of progressivism. In the early 1920s he had warned associates that his good friend Edward A. Dickson had become quite conservative, inclining almost to Harry Chandler's way of thinking, so that Dickson should no longer be counted on to support the old progressive reforms. Haynes criticized Governor Young's appointment of Meyer Lissner, the doctor's old friend, to the State Industrial Accident Commission in 1928. Haynes reminded Franklin Hichborn, "Now you and I and everybody else know that Meyer was a very strong and influential progressive." But Lissner was "becoming more reactionary," as well as physically wrecked, no longer an asset to the administration. Expediency and self-interest dictated that a strong progressive be appointed to avoid aiding Young's political enemies and to add one more soldier to the army protecting progressive achievements.[26]

Haynes demanded political loyalty of progressives, but not necessarily unity, as is evidenced by his stand in the 1928 national campaign. Most prominent state progressives, such as Governor Young, Chester Rowell, and Hichborn, backed Herbert Hoover for president. By early August Haynes still had not made up his mind about whether to support the Republican Hoover or New York governor Al Smith. The question of where the candidates stood on public ownership of electrical power turned out to be the pivotal factor. Convinced by Judson King, Senator George Norris (of Nebraska), Rudolph Spreckels, and others that Hoover was against public ownership of power and that Smith was for it, Haynes endorsed Smith. "Hoover is a dyed in the wool reactionary," Haynes wrote to Hichborn, shocked that the latter intended to vote for such a "plutocrat." The "dry" Haynes's support for the "wet" Smith temporarily alienated some of the doctor's progressive friends. The rift was not too significant, however, since many progressive Hoover supporters also backed Hiram Johnson's reelection, as did the doctor. As the result of a compromise, anti-Johnson Hooverites, such as Friend Richardson, Harry Chandler, and Edward A. Dickson, were kept out of the Republican party limelight. Johnson again was reelected, but his adversary Hoover also was victorious.[27]

The state progressives were more united as they approached the 1930 California election. Most stood behind Governor Young, whose term had reestablished progressive hegemony. But the prohibition issue threw Republican politics askew. Young announced for his office early on, and so did two other Republicans. James Rolph, mayor of San Francisco, was a wringing wet and very popular in the Bay Area. Buron Fitts, the former lieutenant governor and current Los Angeles County district attorney, was a conservative and a dry like Young. Haynes and other progressives quickly grasped their predicament: the Republican primary vote would be split between wets and drys, and the dry vote again would be divided north and south. This situation spelled disaster for the lone progressive candidate. The doctor, still on the executive board of the California Anti-Saloon League, pressured its leaders to endorse Young right away to squeeze Fitts out of the race. But the league hesitated, allowing Fitts to consolidate his strength in Los Angeles, which was reinforced by the *Times* and the dominant municipal political organization. While Haynes and the progressives campaigned for Young, their worst fears were realized. Young and Fitts split the dry vote of the north and south, and Rolph won the primary.[28]

In the general election Haynes could not bring himself to vote for the wet Republican conservative or the weak Democratic rival, Milton K. Young. Instead the doctor seems to have cast his ballot for his old prohibitionist friend, Upton Sinclair, again running on the Socialist ticket. Haynes's vote did not really matter, as Rolph captured 72 percent of the final tally.[29]

The administration of "Sunny Jim" Rolph was not amenable to the advice of Dr. Haynes. Dedicated to business interests, the new government had little use for reformers. Rolph himself became more involved in the ceremonial trappings of his office as he crisscrossed California to appear at numerous functions, rarely providing leadership for a state in the throes of the Depression. When he did offer to lead, it was to recommend "that all Californians take a vacation to combat their depression blues." He "acted upon his own advice by going on a fishing trip." This suggestion might have brightened the outlook of some citizens, but not the financial condition of the state. Beset by mismanagement and a deteriorating economy, the Rolph government mired itself in scandals, embarrassment, recall threats, and economic chaos. It is perhaps fortunate for Haynes that he was shunned by this administration. He was not, however, shut out of the legislature, where he continued to lobby.[30]

Haynes's position in local politics in 1925 was the opposite of his situation at the state level. Though only one of many California progressives plotting the overthrow of their opponent in Sacramento, he cut a large figure in Los Angeles, aided by his association with Kent Parrot. After George Cryer's victory in the 1925 municipal primary, Parrot, the mayor's mentor, consolidated his influence in city affairs as Cryer replaced commissioners and department heads with officials more amenable to Parrot. Within months Parrot plunged into Los Angeles County politics, seeking to institute recalls of supervisors and replace them with his own choices in order to gain control of county jobs and contracts. He had some degree of influence over one or two supervisors and the district attorney, but no more. And in state affairs he gradually rose through the early 1920s to become the major strategist of the 1926 progressive campaign in Los Angeles, which gave him some leverage in the administration of Governor Young. By early 1926, Parrot seemed to be in control and gaining. A Republican party manager wrote at that time to his friend Herbert Hoover, "The city machine here is developing all the earmarks of the usual type of a large city political organization."[31]

Haynes's involvement with the Parrot apparatus assured its support for the water and power program, and the importance of this issue elevated the doctor's stature in Parrot's coterie. Rather than just offering advice and campaign funds to the "boss," Haynes asked for reciprocation, and occasionally demanded it. In one instance a copy of a note Haynes wrote to Parrot on June 29, 1925, mysteriously appeared on the front page of the *Times* the following November. In that letter, which concerned the appointment of a prospective commissioner, Haynes ordered Parrot: "I want you to get busy with the Mayor at once and have him appointed on the Public Utility Commission." The *Times* charged that this missive proved that Haynes was the real power behind Parrot's throne, the "Boss of the Boss" as he appeared in a front-page cartoon the next day.[32]

As usual, the *Times* was not quite accurate in the accompanying stories about Haynes. But its intimation of Haynes's position in city politics approached the truth concerning the doctor's power. He was a major figure in Parrot's coalition, which gave him tremendous clout in Cryer's appointments. He still held the respect of both political and social reformers: leftists consistently asked for personal and financial support, and the Municipal League, one friend recalled, "was especially under the influence of the most powerful local politician here, John R. Haynes." The doctor admitted that he still had considerable influence with at least one metropolitan newspaper, the *Examiner*. And as acknowledged leader of the public-power movement, he held the respect of citizens of all political stripes who were committed to the project. In his third decade of civic service, he remained passionately involved in many Los Angeles issues.[33]

Public ownership of utilities still was his major concern at the local level. He wrote in 1930 to Carl Thompson, of the Public Ownership League of America: "I believe in the public ownership of all public utilities and all natural monopolies." This included railroads, shipyards, and transportation, communication, and energy corporations. But a program to achieve this goal all at once was doomed because of political opposition equating it to socialism and because of lack of capital to effect the conversion of private to public property without resorting to outright confiscation. Contrary to Thompson's idea of initiating a statewide public ownership movement in California, Haynes believed that advocates should work individually with cities to build and operate municipal power plants. Once these enterprises proved successful and vindicated the principle, they could advance its application to other utilities. Haynes had followed this strategy for decades, offering advice to municipal officials regarding all aspects of production and distribution of public power.[34]

The doctor had to join the Public Ownership League of California anyway, to keep its activities from adversely affecting the city's power program. Established in 1930, the statewide organization was pledged to public ownership of all utilities. Thanks in part to Haynes, the league concentrated its efforts on electrical power. His contributions and influence were aimed at keeping the league from pressing its entire program. He exerted this influence at one point to keep Carl Thompson out of Los Angeles just before an election in November 1930 in which a major power bond was to appear on the ballot; Haynes feared that Thompson would alienate conservative backers of public power. Unfortunately for Haynes, after he convinced the local branch to stick to the power issue only, a rift developed between the national and state organizations. The issue concerned the accounting of monies involved in the 1931 annual convention held at the Alexandria Hotel, where Haynes himself served as toastmaster at the closing banquet. Thompson was convinced that the state director was inept or crooked, and cooperation between the two was never the same as it had been. The state branch made no further contribution to the cause after the national conference.[35]

Rather than promote public ownership of all utilities, Haynes persisted in his defense and advancement of the expansion program of the Department of Water and Power (formerly the Public Service Department). He continued to meet with the other commissioners twice a week to establish policy and oversee operation of the water and power bureaus. Haynes went far beyond expected devotion to duty in guarding the business, personnel, engineering, construction, and maintenance aspects of the department. He encouraged wealthy business friends to specify that municipal power, rather than private, be used in their buildings. Sometimes at his personal expense, he defended the department from accusations printed in local publications. He even went so far as to request that a neighbor instruct her gardener to sweep her sidewalk and driveway instead of hosing them off since water was scarce and "we must do our part to conserve it."[36]

Haynes defended the DWP in several major controversies, the most explosive of which erupted on March 12, 1928. Early that morning the city's St. Francis Dam, located northward in the Santa Clara Valley, burst and flooded the valley. The torrent raced 54 miles to the ocean in 5 1/2 hours, killing hundreds and causing over $15,000,000 in damages. The Times and others seized the opportunity to blame the DWP commissioners and Ezra Scattergood, chief of the Power Bureau. Haynes reminded reporters that the dam was used for water storage only, so there was no connection with the Power Bureau, which a grand jury ruled blameless in the catastrophe. The commissioners, however, were also responsible for the city's waterworks, whose chief, William Mulholland, was directly in charge of construction of the dam. Haynes and his fellow commissioners withstood a wave of angry reaction from newspapers calling for their resignations. The board eventually settled the claims of Santa Clara Valley residents and all commissioners survived the disaster. Water chief Mulholland's previously impeccable reputation, however, did not.[37]

Advancing the DWP program called for more than individual or official board action. Opponents continued to fight expansion, so proponents organized themselves into DWP defense groups. The Public Power League (1921–24) was followed by the Los Angeles Water and Power Protective League. Organized in late 1926 as a citizen's association unconnected to the DWP, the league was created, as Haynes admitted, by "a few of us." The few chose league officers and planned strategy for the 1927 power-bond election. President Shirley Ward and other league leaders raised funds to finance the campaign for two propositions that would initiate acquisition of the Los Angeles Gas and Electric Company's electrical system and purchase harbor property to build a standby steam plant. The forces against municipal ownership rained a torrent of opposition down upon the $40,000,000 "gas grab" and steam plant proposals. Both were defeated.[38]

Boulder Dam was another issue related to water and power that the doctor championed. Both water and electricity from this federal project would flow to Los Angeles if advocates of municipal ownership were victorious. Voters approved the city's quest for this power in a straw poll taken in the 1925 municipal primary. Afterward, Haynes continued to support passage of the Swing-Johnson bill authorizing construction of the dam, and hoped that all power generated at the dam would be made available first to municipalities. The Swing-Johnson bill passed in December 1928, and two years later was approved by six of the seven states in the Colorado River basin. In the meantime Haynes lobbied Hiram Johnson and others to let Los Angeles manage production and distribution of electrical power. "If I were you I would oppose any appropriation for Boulder Dam unless the city of Los Angeles had absolute control of the power plant," he advised Johnson. The final agreement was not what Haynes wished for, but not as bad as anticipated. Private companies in Southern California qualified for only 9 percent of the power, while Los

Angeles was entitled to 13 percent; other nearby municipalities could receive all of the remainder if Arizona and Nevada did not take their 18 percent each.[39]

Over one third of the power was allotted to the Metropolitan Water District, an agency created in 1928 to construct the Colorado River aqueduct, which would bring water to Southern California. Representing eleven cities in Los Angeles, Orange, and San Bernardino counties, the MWD applied for half of the available power for its members and received most of what it requested. Los Angeles was well represented on the MWD board by three DWP commissioners: John Richards, W. P. Whitsett, and Dr. Haynes. On this board the commissioners could safeguard the interests of the DWP, an effort that consumed much of Haynes's time.[40]

Besides public ownership, Haynes also took an active role in the regulation of city utilities whenever possible. He served on Mayor Cryer's Telephone Committee in 1925 in an unsuccessful attempt to improve service and lower rates in Los Angeles. In the same year he and City Attorney William Mathews followed up a report of the California Railroad Commission and the city's Board of Public Utilities by exploring the possibility of the city's purchasing of the Los Angeles Railway Company. Negotiations with LARY counsel Sam Haskins were amiable and an agreement was reached, but city officials declined to ratify it. After Haynes bowed out to allow others to pursue the purchase, the project fell through.[41]

Another municipal issue close to Haynes's heart was the functioning of the city's Health Department. As a physician he had always been concerned with the operation of this agency, particularly its care of indigents. In the 1920s, he continued to collect reports by the Health Department and followed its activities. He played a very active role in the hiring of Dr. George Parrish, former health commissioner of St. Louis and Portland, Oregon, as Los Angeles city health officer in 1925. Haynes and Parrish became friends and allies in that both were as intrigued with politics as they were with medicine. In the next decade Parrish became embroiled in many controversies with city officials and reformers as he worked with Haynes to elect candidates sympathetic to their interests.[42]

Parrish also was an able health administrator who reorganized the city Health Department and made it more productive. Haynes assisted this work by soliciting information on which to base health and building codes and improvement of health procedures, and by protecting Parrish from political interference. In 1927 the two unsuccessfully tried to consolidate the city and county health departments under Parrish's direction, for both believed that the county spent little for health purposes within Los Angeles city limits.[43]

Haynes's relationship with the Parrot "machine" had its advantages, but the tenuous partnership dissolved as Parrot's influence declined. Within months after the 1925 election two of Parrot's new city councilmen were convicted of accepting bribes and removed from office. Various Cryer-appointed commissioners were forced to resign owing to charges of conflict of interest and extortion. Parrot failed to win a majority of seats on the county board of supervisors, or in the local delegation of the state legislature. And since northern politicians directed the Young administration, Parrot had only marginal influence outside of the city.[44]

Parrot's power within Los Angeles ebbed dramatically in 1927. In the spring primary election he tried to reestablish his influence in the city council by running a slate of candidates pledged to municipal ownership. Haynes and the Los Angeles Water and Power Protective League entered the fray to defend the DWP's program by helping to elect sympathetic councilmen, and to carry two city propositions to further DWP objectives. Real estate entrepreneurs and opponents of public power formed the Los Angeles Protective Association to defeat these propositions and boost the candidates endorsed by the *Times*. The issues, therefore, were merged. Parrot's group was pledged to the DWP's expansion program, and again tried to make passage of the Swing-Johnson bill their battle cry. The *Times* and its allies smeared Parrot as a seedy manipulator in league with the IWW, a boss who promised "a sort of Bolshevik Utopia of municipal ownership of everything." This time Parrot's magic failed: both propositions lost, as did a majority of his choices for the council.[45]

The 1927 election was quite a setback for Haynes. Soon after, banker and *Times* political commentator Jackson A. Graves wrote that the election proved that Angelenos were fed up with Parrot, Cryer, and company, and disgusted with Haynes's management of the water and power board. The doctor replied to Graves that he could not "resist the temptation to prescribe" medicine for the banker's condition: "Your liver is undoubtedly in a very bad state and I am sending you some tablets which have a marvelous reputation for biliousness and as a gas eliminant." In reply, Graves advised the doctor to prescribe a remedy instead for his "political compatriots who are now mismanaging our City's affairs." Although Dora Haynes owned considerable stock in Graves's Farmers and Merchants Bank, her husband and the banker, one of the chief opponents of direct legislation in Los Angeles, continued their political feud.[46]

The 1927 contest shook Haynes's faith in Kent Parrot. The corruption episodes already had exposed the seediness of the administration, and the election demonstrated that Parrot could no longer protect the city's power program. By late summer Haynes grew colder to the "boss," writing to "Mr. Parrot" rather than "Kent." Early the following year the doctor was advised by a confidant to abandon the fading Parrot since his "power lies in the ability to give jobs and contracts. Civil service and a few of the councilmen have him blocked." In the state and county elections of 1928, Parrot proved equally ineffective, again manifesting his steady decline.[47]

When the Swing-Johnson bill passed in December 1928, Parrot lost the issue that united his forces, especially the advocates of municipal ownership, who no longer needed him or his scandal-ridden machine. For all intents and purposes, he was a dethroned political king. Several years after the 1929 election, which displayed his impotence once more (although he was in New York during the campaign), he moved to Santa Barbara, though he retained an office in Los Angeles. He remained the reformers' favorite whipping boy, various insurgents accusing him of aiding their political opponents in the years that followed. Haynes had cut his political ties to Parrot by early 1929, but kept in contact and probably sought his political advice from time to time.[48]

With the Parrot apparatus in shambles in early 1929, leaders of the components of this alliance began preparing for the upcoming municipal election. A personal dispute between Parrot and Cryer ended Cryer's chance for reelection, and he finally bowed out. Parrot decided to back automobile dealer Perry H. Greer, little known in local politics. Greer was also promoted by the *Examiner*, which reported that he was avidly endorsed by New York Yankee slugger Babe Ruth, a figure not celebrated for his incisive knowledge of Los Angeles politics.[49]

Dr. Haynes belatedly decided to back city council president William G. Bonelli, a former *Times* choice who had become a staunch supporter of the DWP. Bonelli was "absolutely incorruptible," "one hundred percent American," and "has stood like the Rock of Gibraltar ever since he became councilman against the most pressing opposition to the municipal power department," Haynes wrote to a friend. (Fortunately, the doctor would not live to see the day in 1956 when Bonelli, a member of the state board of equalization by then, fled to Mexico to escape arrest for bribery.) Haynes was very sick at the time and did not assemble a coalition to back Bonelli, but did provide money and publicity for the candidate.[50]

The *Times*, meanwhile, endorsed American Legion national commander John R. Quinn, who had no experience in government and later admitted that it was a good thing for both himself and Los Angeles that he lost the election. These three major candidates, along with several lesser ones, were joined by John Clinton Porter, foreman of the crusading county grand jury that had indicted Parrot's district attorney in 1928. An automobile salvage dealer, Porter also had no experience in elective office, but had a strong following among the organized Protestants of the city. One observer predicted at the time, "The moral forces are united on him, and these fellows win in certain cycles, widely separated, but now due, in my opinion." [51]

Porter's mentor was the newest political kingmaker in the city, Reverend Robert "Fighting Bob" Shuler. A fundamentalist Methodist minister who arrived from Texas in 1920, Shuler soon became a major religious force in Los Angeles. Through his publication, *Bob Shuler's Magazine*, and later his own radio station, he curried support from his flock by railing against Catholics, Jews, African Americans, the teaching of evolution, and criticism of the Ku Klux Klan. At first he backed the Parrot organization and respected Dr. Haynes, once telling the doctor, "There is no man in Los Angeles whose good opinion I prize more highly than your own." But Shuler broke with Parrot in 1924 to join the *Times* and private power companies. Over the airwaves he castigated Cryer and Parrot and took part in an aborted movement to recall Cryer in 1927. With a plentiful supply of money and spies from his congregation, Shuler titillated his listeners with tales of debauchery in civic affairs, which enhanced his own reputation. Certainly not a political "boss," this revivalist-reformer nevertheless was thought to control about 60,000 votes. By 1929, he stopped cooperating with the *Times* and became the third major force in municipal politics. Early that year he found his candidate and launched Porter's campaign. [52]

Porter surprised almost everyone by placing first in the primary, followed by Bonelli. In the general election campaign the *Times* remained neutral, rather than backing the candidates of Haynes or Shuler, and the *Record* threw its support to Porter. Since both candidates spoke in favor of the city's water and power program, the chief issue became morality in government and police protection of vice. Porter's opponents also accused him of being endorsed by the Ku Klux Klan (Porter admitted his past membership). Evidently this mudslinging backfired and alienated most voters, as Porter emerged victorious. [53]

The 1929 election placed the bombastic preacher Bob Shuler and his moral reformers in power in the official guise of John C. Porter, "a dull, rather uninteresting fellow." With and without Shuler's direction, Porter managed to disappoint many of those who had supported him. His early official acts included appointing his son as his secretary, changing the locks on city hall doors (to keep out Parrot politicians, no doubt), and appointing "super snoopers" to city positions to spy on enemies of the administration. Since he based appointments on religious and ethnic qualifications, WASPs soon dominated the city commissions. Within the city work force he promoted only his favorites—always WASPs—thus demoralizing city employees who interpreted this as a religious purge. To top off his record of diplomacy, Porter first insulted the president of France in the company of several other American mayors by refusing to toast the dignitary in Paris in 1931 (this was during Prohibition, after all, and Porter was a teetotaler), then neglected to welcome Franklin D. Roosevelt officially to Los Angeles during the 1932 campaign.[54]

Porter's administration of the Police Department was similarly embarrassing. Reformers were deeply concerned with vice, but Porter's new police chief did not stop payoffs to policemen or political contributions from underworld figures in return for protection. Furthermore, the moral reformers, who insisted on restrictions of personal liberties of others, were hardly interested in civil rights. As a sop to Harry Chandler and other conservatives, Porter allowed the LAPD "Red Squad" to continue unchecked. A prime ingredient in the reputation of Los Angeles as national capital of police "Cossackism," the Red Squad broke up meetings of liberals and leftists, antiwar demonstrations, political speeches, and any other gathering it branded subversive. The unit also functioned as a strikebreaking force for the city's business establishment, so it was only logical that its headquarters be located in the Chamber of Commerce Building. "Civil liberties in Los Angeles were at their worst during the administration of John C. Porter," concluded the local ACLU director, another testimonial to Porter/Shuler government.[55]

Even in defeat, Haynes and other advocates of municipal ownership hoped for a sympathetic ear from Mayor Porter. Initially Haynes and Porter seemed to get along. The doctor made two suggestions for appointments to the DWP board, and the mayor followed this advice, selecting Harlan Palmer and E. M. Scofield. Porter remained aloof from an internal conflict among DWP officials that resulted in the temporary demotion of Ezra Scattergood and the promotion of Water Bureau chief Harry Van Norman to general manager of the entire department, which infuriated Haynes. When the doctor managed to nullify this demotion and reestablish the two bureaus of the department in December 1929, Porter decided to adopt Reverend Shuler's advocacy of private power companies and crush the political influence of the DWP commissioners. He claimed that he needed to bring balance to the board with a combination of advocates and adversaries of municipal ownership, while Haynes argued that all five commissioners had to favor city power for the DWP Power Bureau to survive.[56]

Within days of Scattergood's reinstatement Porter filled a vacancy on the board with longtime DWP opponent Frank H. Brooks. Hailed by the *Times* and criticized by the Municipal League, the *Record*, and other newspapers, the appointment was the first shot in Porter's war against Haynes and the department supporters. For his next step the mayor demanded in January 1930 that Haynes and W. P. Whitsett, both members of the DWP and Metropolitan Water District boards, resign from one or the other to avoid intimidating smaller cities in the MWD that feared domination by the DWP. Haynes did not agree, but followed the mayor's wishes by resigning from the MWD, while Whitsett quit the DWP board. This compromise did not satisfy the *Times*, whose editors had hoped that Haynes, the "political wire-puller and a trouble-maker," would resign from both boards:

> Dr. Haynes has been actively antagonistic to Mayor Porter, and, while remaining as an ostensibly loyal member of the Mayor's official family, has intrigued and lobbied to a pernicious degree in his efforts to nullify the Mayor's efforts to improve the standing of the water and power administration.
>
> The spectacle of a bureaucrat attempting to keep a stranglehold on two public offices long after his absence of qualifications has been demonstrated and when public opinion generally approves his removal, is not inspiring.[57]

Whitsett was replaced on the DWP board by A. B. Prior, a choice acceptable to Haynes, Harlan Palmer, and E. M. Scofield, the three commissioners advocating public power. In May, when Palmer resigned for personal reasons, Porter replaced him with O. T. Johnson, Jr., a wealthy businessman who owned considerable stock in the Edison and Los Angeles Gas and Electric companies. Johnson's father had been a patron of the nonpartisan reform movement along with Haynes, and the doctor was a business acquaintance of the son. But "Junior" was a vocal opponent of the DWP and his selection and confirmation by the city council raised a storm of criticism. Johnson and Brooks became the minority bloc, opposing expansion and, according to Haynes, intentionally mismanaging department affairs. When the *Times* began making charges of irregularities, such as the destruction of department records, Porter decided to step in again. He removed commissioner Scofield to end the disharmony and reappointed Haynes to another term. This compromise allowed Haynes to remain on the board at the expense of giving Porter the chance to name another member. When the council confirmed the removal of Scofield and the appointment of Arthur Strasburger, Porter and Shuler finally had control of the board.[58]

The reconstituted Water and Power Board reflected the position of both Haynes and the city-power constituency in late 1930. While still president of the board, Haynes could only count on one other vote, and the two were frequently outvoted. In October a friend cautioned Haynes that he was compromising too much with Porter and was not the old fighter he used to be. In November the defeat of another power bond, this one for $13.3 million, set back the DWP program and tarnished Haynes's leadership. The *Record*, which praised and condemned Haynes to extremes at different times, claimed in December 1930 that he was no longer the leader of the city power forces: "Dr. Haynes, once a spirited fighter for municipal power, has grown weary and flabby, and more than once has permitted himself to be cajoled and trapped into betrayal of the department's best interests."[59]

The year 1931 promised more problems for Haynes as Porter's board majority continued to block departmental expansion. In January the board restored Van Norman as the department's general manager, meaning another demotion for Scattergood. Four DWP employees were dismissed because of "gross political activities" in hiding the department's involvement in a bond election. Outside of the board, political gadfly Andrae Nordskog, a former singer and paid publicist for Owens Valley bankers in their battle with the DWP, lampooned Haynes through a polemical newspaper, the *Gridiron*. In the mid 1920s Nordskog had worked with Haynes in the regulation of public utilities, and the doctor had even suggested his appointment to the Public Utilities Commission. But the two differed while serving on the Cryer Telephone Committee: Haynes advised the city to delay considering the purchase of the phone company while he was negotiating the city's purchase of the Los Angeles Railway Company, but Nordskog demanded immediate acquisition of the telephone property. Nordskog had opposed the DWP and Haynes consistently since that time. In 1931, Nordskog began assailing Haynes's defense of the department and demanded a response, which the doctor thought unnecessary. The barbs, including attacks on the Haynes Foundation, were additional thorns in the doctor's thinning skin.[60]

While Haynes suffered at the hands of the board majority and others, he and a few friends organized a new group to rescue the department's expansion program. In December 1930, the Municipal Light and Power Defense league (MLPDL) was created by Judge Leslie R. Hewitt, E. M. Scofield, John B. Elliott, and other proponents of city power. Haynes contributed to it but preferred to keep his name out of its affairs to avoid charges by Porter and the *Times* that the doctor created it to fight the administration. In April a MLPDL delegation accompanied a Municipal League committee to Mayor Porter's office to protest the firing of four DWP employees by the board majority. When Porter refused to reverse this action, MLPDL leaders decided to take action.[61]

With the 1931 municipal elections on the horizon, the league entered the campaign to elect a city council majority to thwart Porter's domination of the DWP board. The league chose a ticket of candidates and raised money for them. The opposition was headed by Mayor Porter and Reverend Shuler, financed by private power companies, and promoted by the *Times* and the *Illustrated Daily News*, published by E. Manchester Boddy. In the campaign the *Examiner* and *Record* were especially adamant in their support of city power, and the result was a close victory for the league. Eight of its choices formed the new council majority to oppose Mayor Porter on the power issue.[62]

The ballots hardly had been counted when warfare reignited. Porter immediately appointed a committee of citizens to investigate the Department of Water and Power in order to recommend further reorganization for efficiency and end its political activities. The council majority created its own committee to carry on the investigation, so the mayor's appointees declined to serve. The five-month study by the council committee included testimony by Haynes and others concerning the operation of the commission. Haynes personally supplied information concerning the DWP board majority to one councilman and even advised the committee on how widely it should probe and what questions it should ask its witnesses. The final report recommended a return to dual management with separate water and power bureaus, the appointment of commissioners sympathetic to municipal ownership, and continued expansion of DWP facilities. Two additional organizations—the Los Angeles Lawyers Club and the Affiliated Improvement Association—conducted their own probes at the same time and reached similar conclusions.[63]

During these investigations Haynes worked with the MLPDL to advance the department. He contributed some $400 monthly to help finance the MLPDL's publication, *Power*, which printed his statements refuting accusations by other commissioners. He supported its efforts to coerce Porter to choose power advocate Albert F. Southwick to replace

Commissioner Prior, whom the mayor refused to reappoint. And Haynes tried to recruit additional sponsors for the league. On November 19, 1931, he delivered an address for the MLPDL at the Alexandria Hotel, in which he defended Ezra Scattergood's record and demonstrated how the present board majority worked in concert with private power companies to scuttle the city's Power Bureau through intentional mismanagement. Porter's scheme would be made easier if he could fire another member of the board, Haynes predicted. "Modesty prevents me from mentioning his name." [64]

This public criticism of the mayor prompted Porter to unleash one of his "super snoopers" to attack Haynes over the airwaves. Dr. Martin Luther Thomas, a Presbyterian minister and Porter administration investigator, began broadcasting attacks on Haynes, painting him as a radical to smear the reputation of the city's foremost advocate of public ownership. Thomas accused the doctor of many instances of helping Communists raise funds and contributing to radical causes during the 1920s. Haynes refuted each charge and praised the work of the ACLU, League for Industrial Democracy, and other groups he sponsored. He also contributed to the church of Reverend Gustav Briegleb, a Presbyterian clergyman who defended Haynes on another radio program against Thomas's further charges in 1932. The general secretary of the Church Federation of Los Angeles tried to calm Haynes by telling him that no one believed Thomas anyway, but the personal attacks were irritating nonetheless. [65]

From August 1931, the new city council majority blocked Porter's efforts to further cripple the DWP. When O. T. Johnson, Jr., resigned from the board for health reasons, the council refused to confirm three consecutive selections of Porter adherents as replacements. Other Porter appointments, such as Shuler confidant John Buckley and Joseph Berkley, both named to the Health Board, also were rejected. With this council opposition and the MLPDL campaign appearing as a resurgence of the forces for public power, a recall movement was initiated against Porter to rid the city of his obstructionist tactics once and for all. [66]

The recall idea was circulated as early as August 1931. It went nowhere until October, when Porter fired city health officer George Parrish because of constant bickering with Bob Shuler and certain health commissioners. Parrish organized the petition drive the following month with advice, and perhaps funding, from Haynes. Signatures were gathered and the election was set for May 3, 1932. [67]

The recall campaign unleashed a flood of candidates to oppose Porter.

William Bonelli, the loser in 1929, and seven less-known contestants trailed Assemblyman Charles Dempster, who patriotically advertised that he was "born in a log cabin in Fremont County, Iowa." Dempster was backed by the MLPDL and advocates of city power, the Municipal League, and most city newspapers. Porter was supported by the *Times* and *Illustrated Daily News*, private power interests, Bob Shuler, and the LAPD hierarchy. The recall alliance initially justified Porter's removal because of his "inefficiency and incompetence," citing his appointments, electrical power and police policies, and administration spying, among others. When the recall was certified by the city clerk, Porter, anxious to defuse the power issue, appointed another city-power advocate, John Baumgartner, to the DWP board, thereby restoring a majority of three to two for the public-power program. Amid this confusion, the voters decided not to dump their mayor. One writer noted, "After all, dumb as Mayor Porter is, he is not an unfitting representative of the majority of the voters of Los Angeles." [68]

Buoyed by the victory, Porter seized back the offensive. Haynes and Southwick already had begun to implement the recommendations of the city council's report in restoring Scattergood to the dual management of the department as chief of the Power Bureau. Porter responded by demanding Haynes's and Southwick's resignations, and six days after the recall election the mayor removed them from the board. This action provoked instant protest from the Municipal League, League of Women Voters, and advocates of city power. Three U.S. senators—George W. Norris, Bronson Cutting, and Edward P. Costigan—also wired their displeasure. The removals required confirmation by the city council, however, which voted ten to five against Haynes's release and nine to six against that of Southwick. Porter was now stuck with a majority opposition on the board. [69]

The council vote spurred Haynes, Southwick, and Baumgartner to strengthen the Power Bureau further. Another fired employee was rehired; influential lobbyists were enlisted to aid the DWP's effort in Washington, D.C., to secure a federal loan for the Boulder Canyon power transmission line; and construction of a steam plant was begun. In opposition to all of these projects, Porter again tried to remove Haynes and Southwick, along with Baumgartner, citing a "riot of wastage of public funds." Haynes defended himself and his two colleagues, arguing that they actually were saving the city money. The council rejoined even more vigorously than it had before. A committee assigned to study the attempted ousters reminded the mayor that he had now labeled six of his nine appointments to the Board of Water and Power Commissioners as incompetent, concluding that the mayor must be "mentally and temperamentally unfitted to select commissioners." The present attack on the personal integrity of the three board members was deplorable: "In the case of Dr. John R. Haynes this attack is particularly lamentable. Here is a great and good man who has actually devoted over 32 years of his life to public service in Los Angeles. . . . In all this long period of public service he has never taken a dollar in compensation for his labors. And now in the closing years of a highly honorable career he is made the target of a man of no achievements." The council accepted the report and voted ten to four to refuse to sustain the removals.[70]

By the end of 1932, the Porter-Haynes battle had reached a standoff. The mayor could impede the progress of the DWP board by interfering with its plans and opposing its bond proposals requiring voter approval, but the board still established policy in favor of public power. For Haynes, the situation was better than it had been in early 1931, but a far cry from the height of the Cryer-Parrot regime in 1925. The doctor still held out hope for improvement since another mayoral election lay only months away.[71]

The period from 1925 to 1932 was one of boom and bust for Haynes's political fortunes. His health deteriorated steadily as he suffered attacks ranging from lumbago to the flu. A resurgence of bronchitis necessitated frequent trips to warmer and drier Palm Springs. In November 1927, he underwent a prostatectomy at Good Samaritan Hospital. Into the 1930s he was frequently bedridden, though he carried on his political and DWP business from his bed. Future county supervisor John Anson Ford described a visit to the doctor at this time: "Ascending the broad staircase to a large bed chamber, I found Dr. Haynes propped up with pillows, a telephone, and a mass of papers all within reach beside his bed." The *Examiner* even illustrated its story on the approval of a DWP contract with a photo of Haynes signing the document while sitting in bed.[72]

Haynes's physical condition in 1930 is illustrated in a letter he wrote to Dr. T. H. Althausen, of the University of California Medical School in San Francisco. Impressed by an article that Althausen had recently published, Haynes requested advice for a "patient" who, not coincidentally, matched the doctor in age and physical condition. Besides his recurrent problems the patient suffered from high blood pressure. He was "slightly overweight probably because he tires easily and therefore does not exercise very much." The patient was "actively interested in civic matters and in order to carry on spends about twelve hours out of the twenty-four in bed." It is apparent, though, that the twelve hours in bed included both sleep and work.[73]

Dora Haynes was also frequently ill at this time, indeed much more so than John. She was bedridden for long periods, which curtailed most activities. She did manage to continue her work for the Los Angeles branch of the League of Women Voters, serving as its treasurer in 1927, as vice president thereafter, and as historian and auditor by 1934. In her spare time she assembled data on the organization, which she used to compile an outline history of the league, and kept a scrapbook of articles and clippings tracing several years of the women's suffrage movement in Los Angeles. She attended all Haynes Foundation meetings held in her house, and Friday Morning Club meetings when she felt up to it.[74]

Failing health did not diminish John's political activity, but it did force retrenchment in other areas. In 1926, he resigned from the Celtic Club and National Liberal Club of London. Two years later he resigned as a director of the City Club both because of time constraints and his belief that this club was becoming too conservative; he did, however, retain his membership. Three years later, he resigned from the Annandale Golf Club, to which he had belonged for social, not athletic purposes. This event caused quite a stir: the club's director refused to accept the resignation and claimed that Haynes was required to continue paying dues. The doctor sued the club to release him from financial obligation, and the case eventually reached the California Supreme Court, which ruled in his favor in 1935.[75]

Haynes remained a member of the Masons and some other social and fraternal societies, though his involvement was limited. He had lunch almost every day at the California Club and stayed to play bridge and dominoes. He continued to enjoy the meetings and outings of the Sunset Club, though his club activity declined after 1926.[76]

He also retained his membership in the Los Angeles Chamber of Commerce, to which he had belonged since 1893. Over the years he had served on various committees and had occasionally been selected to greet visiting dignitaries. The positions required little work yet kept him in touch with business leaders. These contacts were helpful in business affairs but even more important in lobbying for political goals. It is not surprising that almost all of Haynes's reform campaigns included some of the city's top businessmen and professionals, many of them personal friends who served with him as directors of such organizations as the Major Business Center Association.[77]

The doctor also read much more than just mountains of DWP reports and contemporary articles in newspapers and journals regarding his favorite political and reform topics. He favored current literature—especially American and world history, Upton Sinclair's rapid succession of novels, and the works of his favorite poets. But time for these pursuits was scarce, and his training in consulting medical books made him a careful, slow reader.[78]

In 1930, Haynes was still very active for a not-too-healthy reformer of 77. He traveled daily to his downtown office in the Consolidated Realty building at Sixth and Hill streets, where he met countless visitors to discuss investments or politics. Considering the number of phone calls he made and accepted, and the volume of correspondence typed by Anne Mumford, his retirement from medicine in 1914 had marked no transition to a more leisurely lifestyle. His schedule is documented in a series of articles appearing in late 1929 in the *Record*, which traced the doctor's family background, career, and "the progressive causes to which he gave his heart."[79]

In this series, devoted to the "doctor of sick politics," Haynes was described as a "fighting millionaire progressive," not a millionaire socialist, as he was labeled in more conservative journals. This choice of terms might have reflected the more radical outlook of the story's author, former Socialist Reuben Borough, for whom "progressive" would more aptly describe Haynes's concept of gradual socialism. Or it could have stemmed from Haynes's aversion to being publicly linked with radicalism, which he feared would destroy his rapport with conservatives. For whatever reason, the rubric "progressive" was one he accepted proudly, for it placed him in the realm of fellow reformers who worked so hard to transform America's institutions in the late nineteenth and early twentieth centuries.[80]

Like his own health and that of his wife, John Haynes's political stature declined from 1925 to 1932. But national developments in the latter year would change the direction of his fortunes. Another wave of "reform" politics would offer another opportunity to advance his ideas of social betterment on several levels.

Chapter Thirteen

New Dealer Haynes

For John Haynes, the national scene in 1932 was even more bleak than his position in state and local politics. The Great Depression had devastated America for three years. Since the stock market crash of late 1929, the nation's economy had been wracked by plant closings, business failures, empty savings accounts, and property foreclosures. By 1932, unemployment reached 40 percent in some urban areas, while farmland lay idle for want of capital. President Hoover's administration made limited attempts to meet the crisis, but was not financially or philosophically capable of stemming the tide of economic disaster. Meanwhile, homeless families moved into ramshackle "Hoovervilles," and breadlines snaked along countless city blocks. Remnants of a "Bonus Army" of unemployed veterans marching in protest to Washington, D.C., were chased out of their temporary tent city by heavily armed U.S. soldiers.[1]

The local situation was just as bad. Financial crises usually took some time to reach the Pacific coast because of the lack of heavy industry and the predominantly regional economy of the West. But by early 1931, the Depression hit hard in Southern California. Unemployment in Los Angeles reached 20 percent; homeownership in a realtor's paradise declined for the first time; tourism and service jobs, the backbone of the local economy, dropped sharply; retail trade and building construction declined; and both private and public charities were taxed far beyond their means.[2]

To Dr. Haynes and others the situation looked grim. The calamity required drastic change in national leadership before worsening conditions sparked a revolt led by extremists at either end of the political spectrum. The opportunity to revamp the failed economic system dominated by a self-serving oligarchy was at hand, Haynes believed. The nation needed a messiah committed to transforming the system in accord with principles of social justice. The leader who emerged in 1932 was New York governor Franklin D. Roosevelt, a patrician bearing little resemblance to a leftist reformer. But with his promise of a "New Deal" to turn the nation around economically, FDR presented the main alternative to the present direction of America.[3]

Haynes was not quite sure about Roosevelt's "New Deal" in 1932. In fact, much of the doctor's support for FDR lay in his opposition to Hoover, especially the latter's policy on hydroelectric power. Since this issue was Haynes's top priority at the time, he might have backed any candidate who opposed the incumbent administration's favoring of the "power trust." The promise of an active federal government working to end the Depression was additional incentive. Haynes's view was shared by other proponents of public power, such as his friend Judson King. Active in FDR's campaign, King arranged to have the National Popular Government League temporarily reverse its nonpartisan policy by endorsing FDR because of the candidate's position on the power question.[4]

To be sure, FDR was not as progressive a candidate as Haynes wished to see in the contest. As the doctor wrote to an old friend, he would vote for the Socialist candidate did he "not think that a vote for Norman Thomas would be half a vote for Hoover." The incumbent had to be defeated at any price, and FDR at least appeared safe on the power issue. In addition he pledged an administration bound to fighting the economic catastrophe that Hoover seemed to ignore. Haynes declined to allow his name to be publicly associated with FDR's campaign at the time, since the doctor was trying to negotiate a federal loan for the DWP. But he did support the Democrat with donations and personal politicking among his friends.[5]

Historical interpretations of the New Deal increasingly have portrayed it as conservative in nature and relatively unsuccessful in reaching its objectives. Roosevelt did not establish economic stability. Some of his programs did not work, others were ruled unconstitutional. Many social, economic, and ethnic groups were overlooked as an elitist administration preoccupied with building a political coalition appealed to large organized groups and virtually ignored unorganized Americans. And in saving the present system by correcting a few defects, the New Deal did more for the wealthy than the underprivileged. But critics admit that such programs as social security, the Wagner Act, and other measures that have endured were positive accomplishments. "Even a cursory inspection of the New Deal shows that it reshaped American institutions and gave material sustenance to millions of people who had been thrown out of jobs and into various states of misery by the Depression," wrote historian Bradford A. Lee. Though it may not look like a revolution to historians blessed with hindsight, the New Deal certainly appeared to many contemporaries, among them John Haynes, as an upheaval by comparison to the past decade of limited government activity. With so many new programs and agencies created in the first three years, many in the first "Hundred Days," the New Deal promised sweeping changes in American life, even if it did not deliver.[6]

As one citizen vitally interested in the success of a national program committed to major reform without revolution, Haynes was pleased to find New Deal policies geared toward his own goals. Legislation that created new agencies to regulate the stock market and business practices, established collective bargaining and protected the rights of labor, expanded federal development of energy sources, and created jobs and a social welfare system were welcomed by an old reformer who had advocated these same objectives for decades. He seemed satisfied with decisions relating to these programs except in certain instances, such as the inclusion of municipal power plants in the National Recovery Act codes proposed by the electric light and power industry. Haynes was also happy to see his friend John Collier appointed U.S. Commissioner of Indian Affairs, for Collier shared the doctor's own views on the treatment of Native Americans.[7]

In some cases Haynes worked with New Dealers, especially local Democrats in Congress, on specific issues. On other occasions he contacted administration officials and offered his advice on various topics such as foreign policy. In a letter to FDR in 1933 he urged that the United States finally recognize Russia and avoid negotiating with Adolph Hitler, "a madman, a brute and a menace to the world's peace." Haynes warned, "Any attempts to compromise will increase [the Germans'] audacious attempts to arm themselves in preparation for another war." Four years later he reiterated his revulsion for Hitler in a letter to Secretary of State Cordell Hull, while asking that the government change its neutrality policy by sending aid to the victims of the Spanish Civil War. His worries regarding the rise of Mussolini and Italian fascism were just as strong, especially when he saw growing support for this movement in the United States. As in the 1910s, such threats to world peace and the security of America triggered patriotic fears of yet another world war.[8]

FDR's New Deal fell short of the national direction that Haynes would have preferred, but was far superior to the policies of the previous administration. Always the opportunist willing to accept small advances on the road to larger reforms, Haynes embraced the New Deal as one step in the right direction. He also feared that by not supporting FDR, he would aid his enemies' return to power and thus help legitimize the cause of radicals who promulgated a violent overhaul of the economic system. For this reason he avoided backing the American Commonwealth Political Federation, a third party promoted by Wisconsin representative Thomas Amlie, which promised a more leftist government. "I believe that the efforts of President Roosevelt are intended to help correct, to a certain extent, the evils that confront the nation," Haynes wrote to Amlie. A third party might prevent FDR's reelection, "thereby allowing the Republican Party to get possession of the presidency. This would not only continue the disastrous regime of Harding, Coolidge and Hoover but would probably mean the election of a man more reactionary than any of the presidents mentioned." FDR fell short of Haynes's ideal, but he might avert a national tragedy. Haynes told a reporter in 1934, "I worked for Franklin D. Roosevelt and I believe in upholding his hand to the utmost in his efforts to save the nation from revolution." [9]

This view carried into the 1936 national election campaign. Still a registered Republican, Haynes could not think of supporting Alfred Landon, a "tool of special interests" and "a man in whom I have no confidence." The Socialist candidate, Norman Thomas, was closer to the doctor's ideal leader. He wrote to Thomas in response to an appeal for funds, "I think I realize as much as you do that civilization can only survive through a radical change in our capitalistic condition." But the doctor believed the Socialist had no chance and further that his presence might aid the Republicans: "I fear that with a third party in the field which may attract the support of the various wild-eyed masses, enough votes may be taken away from Roosevelt to permit the election of Landon." Although FDR's program of state capitalism did not go far enough, it did move some of the distance. Again Haynes declined to have his name publicly linked with FDR's campaign, not wishing to alienate Roosevelt's enemies in Los Angeles who might then turn against the city's power program. But Haynes did back FDR from behind the scenes. [10]

Haynes's continued support of Roosevelt after the election was most notable in his defense of the 1937 judicial reform bill. FDR's plan to stop the nullification of New Deal laws by appointing additional justices for each member of the Supreme Court over the age of 70 gained Haynes's immediate approval. For decades the doctor had distrusted judges who ruled unconstitutional the reform legislation he favored, calling them pawns of a corrupt oligarchy ruling the nation. He was especially incensed with California jurists who upheld the interests of the Southern Pacific Railroad and Supreme Court justices who struck down child labor laws in 1918. He was furious when the Supreme Court nullified the National Recovery Act in 1935, and he advised federal officials to retaliate by legislating the requirement of a seven-vote majority in Supreme Court decisions and by carrying out a campaign to publicize the negative results of the court's actions.[11]

When FDR announced what critics would call his "court-packing" scheme, Haynes even volunteered to help finance a nonpartisan group to sponsor the plan if such a group emerged. From Haynes's perspective, the measure aimed at "unpacking the Supreme Court, which now has a majority of corporation attorneys." Tired of seeing the United States "continue to be a plutocracy as it has been for many years," he hoped the administration would push the bill without compromise. The doctor's view, like FDR's, was in the minority; the proposal not only failed but contributed to the cause of the New Deal opposition.[12]

As historian Otis L. Graham, Jr., observed some time ago, Haynes was one of the few old progressives who supported the New Deal. By the 1930s, most of these reformers of an earlier generation had become more conservative; those who stood pat merely revealed the differences in how far progressives and New Dealers would go to reshape American institutions. Most progressives believed the New Deal overstepped the proper limits of governmental power and exceeded the needful in reform. Only a minority of progressives embraced the New Deal; even fewer tried to push it further. Haynes was among the latter; had he lived longer he would have been disappointed by its eventual failures.[13]

In the early years of the New Deal the doctor lost his "silent partner," Dora Haynes. Her health had deteriorated through the 1910s and 1920s, and she continued to be bedridden for long periods. According to her husband, about 1929 she developed Hodgkin's disease, a disorder of the lymphatic glands that causes them to enlarge and press against vital organs. She took X-ray treatments to reduce the size of the glands, but side effects developed. In and out of the hospital in early 1934, she was confined to her bed in April, and nurses attended to her around the clock. By October her condition worsened. On the evening of November 23, she died in the Figueroa Street residence. Three days later she was buried in the family plot at Rosedale Cemetery. For weeks John was flooded with cards and letters from friends and national figures expressing sympathy.[14]

Dora's passing robbed the doctor not only of his spouse of 54 years but of his colleague in social betterment. She had supported his many reform efforts for three and a half decades. In her own right she was a leader in the local struggle for women's suffrage and a founder of the Los Angeles branch of the League of Women Voters. Active in women's clubs, she took part in state politics as a leader of progressive women when she could. The arrival of the New Deal pleased her as much as it did her husband. She prayed for the success of the federal Muscle Shoals power project and the passage of minimum wage and collective bargaining legislation now that FDR was in power. Her enthusiasm for FDR was high owing to the national leadership of the past dozen years: "How I despise Harding, Coolidge, Hoover, et al.," she wrote. But she lived to see only eighteen months of the new administration.[15]

Another family loss occurred four months after Dora's death, when John's brother, Robert, passed away. Youngest of the three Haynes boys who graduated from the University of Pennsylvania Medical School and moved to Los Angeles in 1887, Robert had retired about 1915 and moved to Long Beach, where he lived with his second wife, Mae. In March 1935, he died in his home at the age of 75. John's only remaining sibling, Florence Lindley, would outlive Robert by fourteen years.[16]

Dora Haynes generously remembered the Haynes Foundation, which was revitalized thanks to her bequest. Although over $200,000 worth of her estate was placed in a trust for her brother, Alfred Fellows, and sister, Maysie Miller, of Chicago, much of the balance was transferred to the foundation, bolstering the fund to finance grants and operating expenses. By mid-1935, Haynes had settled the estate and set up a trust of about $140,000 of this fortune for the foundation so it could resume its philanthropic ventures.[17]

Prior to Dora Haynes's death, the foundation had been in a state of suspension. In the early 1930s, its income shrank as stocks decreased in value. Grants were curtailed, and most meetings were canceled for lack of business to conduct. In February 1934, the economic picture looked brighter and a regular meeting was once again held at the Haynes residence. Vacant positions on the board were filled and the trustees looked forward to better times.[18]

Two new trustees approved at this meeting were John Collier and Dr.

Remson D. Bird. Collier, an old friend and confidant of Dr. Haynes and then U.S. Commissioner of Indian Affairs, joined the foundation to make it a "pioneering and shock troop agency" for social reform, as he understood Haynes's wishes. Bird, a former professor of theology and current president of Occidental College, was more interested in directing foundation funds toward academic pursuits—especially at Occidental. Although he later admitted that John and Dora disdained academic research that did not result in action, Bird consistently proselytized for strictly academic programs. In his tenure on the board, he championed this view in opposition to Collier, Louis Bartlett, Franklin Hichborn, and Herbert Jones—the old "battle warriors with Dr. Haynes in many progressive movements"—who favored direct action. This disagreement led to many lively discussions in board meetings and lobbying of the doctor by the two factions.[19]

The February 1934 meeting also was the convocation that approved a major change in the Haynes Foundation trust instrument. In 1933, Haynes had come to the conclusion that because of the "rapid changes in economic conditions," it might be wise to alter the wording of the foundation's statement of purpose. After studying compacts of the Rockefeller, Russell Sage, and Carnegie foundations, he decided to omit mention of individual purposes—eugenics, protection of prohibition laws, public ownership, and so forth—and substitute a general purpose that would allow trustees more flexibility. The proposed section instructed the trustees to support "appropriate research, discovery, instruction, and education, relating to civic, economic, social, industrial, educational and living conditions (and particularly of working people)," and allowed them to "apply all knowledge so gained to the improvement of all or any of the said conditions." Trustees should "publish and disseminate" this knowledge so that "the people of California and of the United States may be suitably educated, advised and informed thereupon," and should aid charitable activities in any variety of ways. Hichborn protested that this general purpose only addressed the results of present conditions, not the causes, as Haynes had originally intended. Jones and the other trustees thought it wiser to go along with the change, especially considering potential problems with the tax-exempt status of the foundation. The motion was approved.[20]

This gathering was followed by another string of canceled meetings for lack of money. Since the small amount of income was being used to retire Dora Haynes's loans, little remained for grants. Donations for the year consisted of small stipends to Paul Kellogg's Survey Associates, the American Indian Defense Association, a University of Pennsylvania medical scholarship, the Industrial Committee of the Federal Council of Churches, and UC Berkeley to support the Western Summer School for Industrial Workers. Similar grants were made in 1935, although no meetings were held until the end of the year, after Dora's estate was settled. With more income the trustees planned new projects—paid lectureships, a part-time employee, scholarships, conferences, and additional grants to organizations. The foundation's contributions to humanitarian causes rose to $4,750 in 1936 and almost $9,000 in 1937, and promised to get much larger.[21]

Recipients of grants continued to be those Haynes favored, including the American Association for Labor Legislation for its mining-safety program. Some of the doctor's other pet projects could not be funded. One was the Pacific Broadcast Federation, established in the late 1920s by Gross B. Alexander. The federation received a broadcasting license and aired programs advocating "civil liberties, social justice, world peace, genuine public service"; Haynes described the operation as "the greatest educational plan I have ever heard of." The doctor sponsored the PBF early on, and tried to induce Rudolph Spreckels, Upton Sinclair, and other friends to finance it. The foundation declined to take it on, however, so Haynes contributed from his personal funds.[22]

Another such project was the Institute for Social Discovery, promoted by Theodore P. Gerson, an old friend of Haynes's and founder of the Hollywood Bowl Association. In 1934 Gerson and a group of like-minded friends—Haynes, Sinclair, Ernest Caldecott, and others—had been part of a committee promoting the appearance of another newspaper in Los Angeles "to coordinate and disseminate liberal thought." In 1935, Gerson and UCLA professor Ordean Rockey organized a group of professors and others as the Institute for Social Discovery to study and advance social welfare programs. Haynes was very interested in this group, and three of its members attended the trustees meeting at Haynes's house in December, in which the grant application was considered. The request was too much at the time, however, so the trustees denied it. The institute did not apply again, apparently having ended its efforts to form under that title.[23]

One project the foundation did pursue was the hiring of a research specialist. Assemblyman H. Dewey Anderson, a former Stanford professor of economics, was hired on a part-time basis after the end of the 1935 legislative session at the suggestion of Hichborn and Jones. Anderson was to organize the Haynes library and correspondence collection, continue Hichborn's work in monitoring the legislature during its sessions, and provide information to the public on issues in which the foundation was interested. Anderson began working on an eighteen-month contract in June 1936, and devoted much of his time to researching and writing a book on state taxation practices, on which he was considered an expert.[24]

Haynes initially was satisfied with Anderson's performance, but problems developed early in 1937. Anderson's work consumed over a third of the foundation's budget, not counting his projected expenses for the coming legislative session. More importantly, Haynes believed a federal audit of the foundation's disbursements precluded paying Anderson because it might result in the assessment of a hefty tax on the doctor's settlement of Dora Haynes's estate. Anderson's contacts with lawmakers surely would exacerbate this problem by involving the foundation in lobbying activity. Anderson's record as a New Dealer in the 1935 legislature, which made him many enemies, would make matters worse, thus jeopardizing the foundation's charitable status. For these reasons, Haynes believed, Anderson should be kept out of Sacramento to avoid the appearance of lobbying.[25]

Anderson did not attend the session, but Haynes's continued fear of losing the tax-exempt status led him to consider cutting Anderson's ties to the foundation. The doctor liked Anderson personally and was pleased with his work, but decided that the foundation should not publish the book on taxation ("on account of its obvious bias in a number of points"). Instead Haynes offered to help subsidize its publication by another press. Later he even suggested that Anderson should resign. Jones and Hichborn were very disappointed by this decision and counseled the doctor instead to make Anderson a full-time director. "The Foundation needs Anderson worse than Anderson needs the Foundation," warned Jones. Ultimately Haynes chose to keep Anderson on without further discussion of the full-time appointment. Anderson remained with the Haynes Foundation until late 1938, when he was appointed director of the State Relief Administration by incoming governor Culbert Olson.[26]

By 1937, the Haynes Foundation was again functioning, albeit with many internal conflicts. The infusion of money from Dora's estate enabled the foundation to make more and larger grants. But the trustees had to conduct most of their debates by correspondence that year, since no meetings were held between September 1936 and December 1937. John's consistent illness postponed each regularly scheduled meeting until the first one of the new era, when the Haynes Foundation had to carry on without either of its founders.[27]

The controversy concerning Dewey Anderson's lobbying in Sacramento was only one of several facets of Haynes's involvement in state politics during the New Deal years. In the early 1930s he had been effectively shut out of the state executive office. Governor Rolph listened only to conservative advisers, while his administration bumbled through the Depression. The doctor, nevertheless, sent a few recommendations for appointments to Rolph, who thanked him for his interest. Haynes still had some influence in the state legislature as long as Senator Herbert Jones led the progressive faction.[28]

The doctor's relationship with the executive office improved slightly in June 1934, when Rolph died and was succeeded by Lieutenant Governor Frank F. Merriam. This former assemblyman from Long Beach, a favorite of the Times's, had been endorsed by the Better America Federation as speaker of the assembly in the 1920s. Haynes had consistently opposed Speaker Merriam while diplomatically requesting support for certain measures and thanking him on the few occasions he voted Haynes's way. Soon after taking office, however, Merriam asked Haynes for advice in making an appointment to the State Railroad Commission. Haynes was later informed that the governor would appoint anyone the doctor suggested, "provided the party came from the North." Merriam also selected Haynes for the Citizen's United Highway Commission of California, formed to enhance the governor's plan to substitute taxes on county roads with gasoline taxes and motor vehicle fees. Haynes agreed with this plan and accepted the appointment since it entailed no work; only his name and prestige were needed for the undertaking.[29]

The timing of Merriam's consultation of Haynes regarding the Railroad Commission was no coincidence: the governor had just launched his campaign to win this office in his own right. As a state Republican party official, the doctor apparently contributed to Merriam's campaign after the primary, but never actually endorsed him. Early in the year Haynes officially backed the candidacy of Herbert Jones, a Haynes Foundation trustee and leader of the progressive forces in the state senate for two decades. But Senator Jones, who was little known in Southern California, dropped out of the race by mid-June to avoid splitting the progressive Republican vote.[30]

Haynes then switched to the leading progressive candidate, a friend of Haynes's, former governor C. C. Young. Another "progressive," Raymond Haight, remained in the competition, diluting Young's strength, so that Merriam easily won the primary. Haight had already come to Haynes for advice, and the doctor urged him to make a strong stand for regulation of public utilities. But Haynes distrusted Haight, feared his backing by "Fighting Bob" Shuler, and knew he had no chance to win anyway. When Haight created the short-lived Commonwealth party in order to run in the general election, Haynes avoided it.[31]

The major alternative in the general election was the Democratic nominee, none other than Haynes's friend and political comrade Upton Sinclair. On four occasions Sinclair had been a Socialist candidate for governor or U.S. congressman in the Golden State. He rarely campaigned, making only a few speeches, but did spend time raising funds for his party. Many times Sinclair requested support from Haynes, who occasionally agreed, though the doctor tried to distance himself from Socialist party functions. These appeals were only one of many kinds of requests Sinclair made of Haynes.[32]

In the late summer of 1933, Sinclair changed his Socialist registration to Democrat and embarked on another campaign for governor. At this time he wrote *I, Governor of California, and How I Ended Poverty*. This tract outlined his program for economic recovery: the plan was to turn bankrupt factories and idle farmland over to the unemployed to produce food and goods for their own use. The twelve-point program, called End Poverty in California (EPIC), fell somewhat short of radical considering the problems it proposed to deal with, but it appeared utopian to some and frightfully communistic to others, while it was dismissed by leftists as a halfway measure that left basic economic inequities unaddressed. In fact, many EPIC points on old-age pensions, income taxes, and aid to the disabled eventually were adopted by the legislature.[33]

Sinclair's platform gained immediate popularity, and an EPIC campaign sprouted with a central organization staffed by ex-Socialists such as Richard Otto, H. Jerry Voorhis, and Rube Borough, editor of *EPIC News*. Hundreds of EPIC clubs formed throughout the state to promote the plan and Sinclair's candidacy. The movement demonstrated its popularity in the Democratic primary, when Sinclair defeated eight other candidates and marched on to his showdown with Merriam.

Sinclair's primary victory shocked his opponents and unleashed one of the most frenzied campaigns in the state's history. Major Democratic leaders repudiated their nominee, prevented FDR from endorsing the novelist, and encouraged Democrats to vote Republican. Individuals and business groups, fearing bankruptcy of the state, poured millions into the Merriam campaign. Newspapers twisted Sinclair's writings to paint him as an atheist, Communist, and advocate of free love, and daily prophesied the catastrophe awaiting California if he was elected. Hollywood motion picture moguls produced short films depicting movie extras dressed as bums descending on California to take advantage of the EPIC "free ride" and forced theater operators to screen them. Clergymen preached against this devil, and industrialists threatened to abandon California if Sinclair won.[34]

In the midst of the hysteria Haynes found himself without a candidate. He was almost sure Sinclair could not win, questioned the wisdom of the EPIC plan, and did not think much of Sinclair as an administrator. On the other hand, Sinclair had promised the doctor that he would appoint only those whom Haynes approved, an arrangement that would give him and adviser Franklin Hichborn considerable power in Sacramento. Many of the doctor's longtime associates—Hichborn, John J. Hamilton, Louis Bartlett, and others—believed that only a major change could pull California out of the Depression, and that, with proper assistance, Sinclair might be able to effect it. Besides, the alternatives, Merriam and the distrusted Haight, left little choice.[35]

In the end Haynes remained publicly aloof from the campaign, contributing a small sum to Merriam to satisfy his party and business associates. He also made small contributions to EPIC to support its newspaper, but apparently no large donations. He even voted for Sinclair and most of the EPIC ticket. One ballot was not enough to help his old friend, though; Governor Merriam won. But he was elected with little less than half the vote, while Haight captured almost 13 percent, much of which might have gone to Sinclair. Quite a few EPIC candidates won legislative seats, a result that infused the legislature with a strong dose of social-reform Democrats who were to shake up the political milieu in Sacramento.[36]

Though the doctor's gubernatorial choice was defeated, his friend Hiram Johnson succeeded again. In fact, by cross-filing in the Democratic and Republican contests, Johnson became the first U.S. senator from California to win election in the primaries, thus avoiding a runoff. His campaign was boosted enormously by the support of the Democratic president who returned the favor of Johnson's endorsement in 1932. Johnson again asked Haynes to serve as one of his sponsors in 1934, and Haynes was "delighted" to help his old friend and political ally.[37]

After the election Haynes turned his attention to the legislature, continuing to pay Franklin Hichborn as a lobbyist during the 1935 and 1937 sessions. Haynes wrote to individual legislators, asking them to support or defeat certain bills, and had very receptive contacts in Senator Culbert Olson, Assemblyman Frank Waters and H. Dewey Anderson, and other EPIC-endorsed lawmakers. Some even looked to Haynes for advice. As Waters wrote concerning a bill dealing with condemnation suits, Assemblyman Wilbur Gilbert "will drop it if you think best." [38]

Direct legislation, as usual, was Haynes's chief concern. In the 1935 session several bills were offered to alter the state initiative, referendum, and recall. Haynes fought them all. He resurrected the Direct Legislation League of California—merely by updating its letterhead—to lobby lawmakers and governors to defeat all attacks on his favorite reforms. DLL stationery displaying the names of many state supporters of direct legislation reminded lawmakers of the influence of its backers, especially Dr. Haynes and old progressives such as Edward A. Dickson and Judge Russ Avery, and social reformers like Rob Wagner, Mary Workman, and R. E. Chadwick. The campaign was worth the effort, for none of the offensive bills became law. [39]

In 1936, Haynes again witnessed a state controversy concerning the single tax and direct legislation. Three years earlier the state had adopted a sales tax for the first time. Haynes opposed such a "tax on poverty," believing, "Only luxuries which are not essential for food, shelter, and clothing should be taxed." Rather, he thought, the state income tax "should be graduated up to not less than 60 per cent upon the largest incomes" during the Depression. But he lost this contest in the state legislature since Governor Rolph and others approved the tax. [40]

In response, single-taxers of the previous decade devised a state initiative measure to abolish the sales tax and replace it with a tax on land values. The Citizens Tax Relief Association, headed by Jackson H. Ralston and David Woodhead, circulated petitions, and the measure was placed on the ballot of the 1936 general election. Haynes did not publicly support the proposal, but hoped it would pass. In a reply to the secretary of the California Committee Against the Single Tax, he explained that he did not want his name used in opposition to the measure because of his commitment to the Department of Water and Power. In order to advance DWP expansion, he stated, "we must have all factions behind us, irrespective of political, religious, or economic views; therefore, no difference what my individual preferences are, I have refused to allow my name to be used as sponsor for any organization." This justification, which he used frequently for all types of causes, helped to distance the "father of the initiative" from the issue, as it had in the 1920s, when he tried to keep foes of the single tax from attacking the direct-legislation process.[41]

Californians never had a chance to vote on the new proposal. The State Supreme Court agreed to hold a hearing on a suit in which the plaintiffs argued that the petitions lacked an accurate description of the proposal. The divided court ruled in favor of the challenge, infuriating Haynes and inflaming his distrust of the judiciary. As he wrote to Hichborn, this case established a precedent in which a court majority could void any direct-legislation measure. The court had no jurisdiction in the matter, he believed, and no power to keep the measure off the ballot. The ruling stood, on the basis of a technicality, and Haynes declined to challenge it. Two years later, a similar proposition did make the ballot but was soundly defeated.[42]

On the level of municipal politics, Haynes began the New Deal era in a position slightly better than his situation in state affairs. He was in command of a majority on the Board of Water and Power Commissioners and could count on a slim edge in the city council. His strained relationship with Mayor John Porter, though, precluded any influence with the administration and gave Porter added impetus to foil the DWP's progress. Electrical power was still the major issue, and as the 1933 municipal election approached Haynes was afraid that Porter or another would win and continue to obstruct the DWP. "If the power companies get control of the mayor and council," he wrote to Judson King, "we shall be in a bad way. It would be a national calamity if this should happen." Before the end of 1932 Haynes already had been "spending some money preparatory to the campaign lining up forces to aid the election of a mayor and council that will prevent a savage attack being made on our municipal plant."[43]

By early 1933, Haynes had found a suitable candidate to oppose Porter in the spring primary. Frank Leslie Shaw, a county supervisor and former councilman, had worked with Haynes and Kent Parrot since 1925. Shaw had consistently backed the DWP program and had cultivated a reputation as a Depression fighter among politicians who preferred to wait until the calamity had run its course. According to rumor he had been seeking the mayor's office since 1931, and considered running in Porter's 1932 recall election. In January 1933, Haynes arranged for Shaw to obtain the endorsement of the public-power leaders and influential figures such as "Queen Helen" Werner, a crafty political manager and wife of the city attorney. Shaw was on his way.[44]

In contrast to the bumbling Porter, who could only promise more of the same—an administration dominated by Bob Shuler, beset by internal bickering and bigotry, incapable of dealing with the Depression—Shaw offered a "New Deal for Los Angeles." As the campaign progressed, the Municipal Light and Power Defense League attacked Porter and his endorsement by the *Times* with a mass of literature, speeches, and radio broadcasts, which also praised Shaw and the MLPDL's slate of council candidates. The Municipal League, labor unions, and other groups backed Shaw, who won the primary. Four of the top five major contenders defeated in this contest then endorsed the supervisor. In the spirited general election race, highlighted by accusations that Shaw was not a U.S. citizen, he again emerged victorious, although the new city council contained many sponsored by the *Times*. Haynes was jubilant over the mayoral results but disappointed by the defeat of a few councilmen pledged to the expansion of city power. Nevertheless, ever the diplomat, Haynes congratulated his enemies on their victory (as he frequently did) and pledged to work with them in the city's best interest.[45]

The administration of Frank Shaw has long been considered the most corrupt in the city's history. Reformers had a field day accusing Shaw-appointed commissioners of incompetence and outright crimes; grand juries indicted and other juries sometimes convicted administration figures, including the mayor's brother, on charges of extortion, selling jobs and promotions, and offering protection to underworld kingpins in return for campaign donations; and the LAPD was exposed as a political weapon used to spy on administration enemies and trample civil rights. It was the conviction of three police officers who tried to kill a private detective snooping on the administration that finally convinced voters to recall Shaw in 1938. His removal brought national attention to Los Angeles and became the decade's most stirring incident of municipal malfeasance. In the meantime, Mayor Shaw initiated programs to fight the Depression, acquire federal aid to curb unemployment and finance municipal construction projects, consolidate city and county functions to eliminate duplication, and provide a centrist government in which all interest groups were represented. He was not entirely successful, but he did try to improve financial and social conditions in times of economic distress. His poor choice in some appointments, and his brother's involvement with underworld figures and covert political practices overshadowed the limited achievements of his administration.[46]

Haynes did not live to witness the downfall of the Shaw regime and had no involvement in its seedier side. He dealt directly with Shaw and steered clear of his secretary and brother, the notorious Joseph Shaw, even to the point of avoiding the mayor's downtown office. "I have told you that if I wanted anything special I would send it to your house and not to your office," Haynes wrote to the mayor.[47]

The relationship between Haynes and Shaw was mutually beneficial. Without Haynes's backing in 1933 and 1937 (though his support was more limited in the latter years), Shaw easily could have lost the very close elections. In return Shaw entertained countless suggestions from Haynes on policy matters and appointments. Even before Shaw took office Haynes recommended as commissioners such friends as James Irvine and A. B. Prior, both of whom had worked in the campaign. He proposed the very political George Parrish for reappointment as city health officer and put forward numerous other possibilities for positions over the next four years. In some cases the doctor advised a plan of attack: "Let us make up our minds as to the three members and when the time comes shoot them in." He also provided the mayor with political information at times—on the activities of some city employees in support of a recall attempt in 1934, for example—and advice on positions to take on certain issues. Many of Haynes's candidates were confirmed, for the mayor frequently followed the doctor's advice. It quickly became apparent to all that Haynes again was an administration insider, and job applicants requested his aid in obtaining commission appointments.[48]

Haynes's partnership with Shaw also afforded the doctor free rein in the Department of Water and Power. The mayor appointed only those commissioners approved by the doctor, and usually left the operation of this department to Haynes and Ezra Scattergood. The *Times* reported in July 1933 that Shaw had selected A. J. Mullen as his personal representative on the DWP board, but that the mayor would "need more than one man to keep track of the devious machinations of [Commissioners] Haynes, Southwick, and Prior." Shaw rarely interfered in DWP business as long as Haynes and Scattergood advanced the department's power expansion program, supported Shaw's policies, and found a few jobs for his campaigners.[49]

The change in the city administration's attitude toward municipal ownership was observed even before Shaw took office. One week after the city election, the DWP staged a party celebrating Dr. Haynes's eightieth birthday. Participants included many of his old friends and political allies: DWP stalwarts such as Scattergood, Will Anderson, John Baumgartner, William Mulholland, A. F. Southwick, and John Gray; Municipal League secretary Anthony Pratt and past president J. O. Koepfli;

B. R. Baumgardt and Fred Alles, both friends of the doctor's since the late 1800s; reverends E. P. Ryland and Gustav Briegleb; labor leader J. W. Buzzell; and many others. Haynes received a city council resolution congratulating him on his birthday and twelve years on the DWP board. The festive occasion shared with his closest friends was personally rewarding for the doctor. It also marked the beginning of a new era for him and other DWP supporters, for the affair celebrated not only the birthday of the city's most prestigious power advocate but also the launching of a new offensive to give the DWP a monopoly on power generation and distribution within Los Angeles.[50]

The city's power program would be complete upon accomplishment of two projects: bringing power from Boulder Canyon, which would end the city's need to buy electricity from private companies, and acquisition of the electric properties of Los Angeles Gas and Electric. In early 1933 the department negotiated a 10-year federal loan of $22,799,000 to build a power transmission line to the Boulder Canyon Dam, and construction began as the dam itself was erected. The original agreement called for the city to refinance the loan, so in 1935 the DWP board offered the voters a bond proposal to obtain a lower interest rate with a 40-year loan. This would save the city millions in interest, reduce power rates, and create jobs in businesses locating in the city. The board campaigned for the refinancing proposal in a special election in September 1934, and the measure passed handily.[51]

The refinancing of the bond was the last major hurdle in the quest for Boulder Canyon power. The dam, "one of seven modern engineering wonders in the United States," dedicated as Hoover Dam in 1930, was completed in 1936. In the same year the power transmission line was finished. On October 9, amidst a gala celebration organized by a group led by Haynes, electricity from Hoover Dam lit up Los Angeles City Hall. The beaming Dr. Haynes smiled from the platform as the light switch was turned. Two more power plants were completed before the end of 1936, enabling the city to generate all the electricity it distributed. On January 1, 1937, the Power Bureau terminated its contract with Southern California Edison, ending the DWP's reliance on private companies.[52]

During this same period Haynes and Scattergood worked to acquire the electrical properties of the Los Angeles Gas and Electric Company. Haynes had opposed this corporation for decades, hoping the city would compete with it by producing its own natural gas, as well as electricity. In the early 1920s, he fought the company personally when his own gas bill, for such a "wretched" product that he had to supplement his gas heaters with electric stoves, jumped over 50 percent from the previous year. In the later 1920s he supported the city's suit against LAG&E to compel the company to obtain a franchise to distribute gas, which it had not done since 1916. The suit, which finally reached trial in 1930, revealed LAG&E's political maneuvers to block the city's power expansion efforts over the past twenty years. During these same years the DWP board had offered to purchase LAG&E's electrical properties, to no avail.[53]

In 1934, LAG&E tried to obtain a proper franchise for its gas facilities by placing on the ballot a charter amendment for a franchise of 40 years, far longer than the normal 21 years. The DWP board opposed the franchise and offered ten proposals to advance the department's operations, three of which would prepare the way to buy LAG&E electrical facilities. The *Times* backed the franchise and condemned the Power Bureau's "gas grab" proposals, while advocates of municipal ownership and DWP employees did precisely the reverse. In a sparsely attended turnout, the franchise was defeated and the ten-proposal package passed.[54]

LAG&E again tried to obtain a gas franchise in 1935, this time for 35 years. A Municipal Affairs Committee, headed by two of Mayor Shaw's health commissioners, circulated an initiative petition for the franchise, which was placed on the April primary ballot. Power Bureau forces opposed the franchise as a strategy in bargaining with LAG&E for the purchase of the company's electrical facilities. The *Times* contended that Haynes and Scattergood were trying to "blackjack" the company "into selling its properties at less than fair price." The Municipal League again protested the length of the franchise. Opponents were especially concerned with LAG&E's expensive political campaign, predicting that the city soon would be saturated with speakers from the gas company offering their services "at $5.00 per speech," the "usual pay of prostitutes." Finally, Haynes advised Mayor Shaw to forsake his health commissioners and publicly oppose the franchise, which he believed would be defeated anyway. Shaw again followed the doctor's orders and denounced the measure a few days before the election. It was defeated by a margin of two to one.[55]

As the *Times* predicted, Haynes and Scattergood immediately approached LAG&E again to discuss the sale of its electrical properties. After its second defeat, the company resigned itself to negotiating in order to obtain its gas franchise. By the summer of 1936, a compromise was reached: the city could purchase LAG&E's electrical facilities for

$46 million if it would grant the company a 35-year gas franchise. The deal was offered to the voters in a special election in early December, and was approved two to one. At the end of January 1937, the city took over LAG&E's electrical properties, gained about 185,000 new customers, and finally won its monopoly of electrical power distribution in Los Angeles. Within three months the Board of Water and Power Commissioners approved a rate decrease made possible by the purchase. It was fitting that the *Times*, a decades-old foe of this moment, refused to join in the celebration. Harry Chandler ordered that the *Times* building be powered by a gas-fired steam plant in its basement, which would cost him annually about $12,000 more than the Power Bureau would have charged.[56]

For Haynes, the LAG&E compromise was won at the cost of alienating the leadership of the Municipal League. A founding member and former president, Haynes had been a hero of the league's political reformers since its creation in 1901. By the mid 1930s, though, he had grown weary of the arrogant behavior of the league's secretary, Anthony Pratt, whom the doctor once described as a "law unto himself." When Pratt and the increasingly leftist and intransigent league officers began criticizing DWP commissioners and other old friends, Haynes took offense, cutting off his financial aid and refusing to make further $500 donations to the national organization. When the Power Bureau agreed to the LAG&E franchise of 35 years, Pratt attacked Haynes and Scattergood for selling out the city. The Municipal League opposed the charter amendment to approve the compromise, to no avail. As a result of this episode Haynes distanced himself from the league, and the breach widened as the organization increasingly criticized the operation and political involvement of the DWP.[57]

Haynes's contribution to the success of the power program extended far beyond administrative care and politicking in bond campaigns. He had to operate on several levels, besides his official capacity as DWP commissioner, to promote the department's goals. One level was purely political: helping Scattergood to direct the loose coalition of department supporters, including advocates of municipal ownership, DWP employees, leaders of organized labor, and others—the "Scattergood-Haynes machine" as the *Times* called it. In return for allowing Haynes and "Scat" to run the department, Mayor Shaw expected them to support him in a number of ways. Shaw's campaign workers needed jobs, and the DWP was the city's largest department. (Councilmen, too, asked for positions for their constituents in return for voting for Power Bureau necessities.) Candidates allied to Shaw needed additional campaign workers, and the DWP had an abundance of employees with political experience. Occasionally the administration asked for certain favors, such as the donation of Power Bureau revenues (some $2.6 million in 1935) to the city's general fund to help balance the budget. Haynes also worked with associates such as DWP commissioner Alfred Lushing, a Shaw crony who followed Haynes's dictates while secretly involved in a protection racket on the side.[58]

Haynes supported the department in other ways as well. On many occasions he declined to be associated with organizations pledged to individual goals—such as FDR's court-packing scheme, academic freedom, or FDR's reelection—in order to avoid antagonizing certain backers of the city's power program. He wrote to one of his correspondents in 1936, "We must have as many supporters as possible in order that we may establish the principle of water and power in Los Angeles." He would not publicly sponsor an individual, party, or cause if it might jeopardize that support.[59]

Lobbying state legislators and the federal government was another of Haynes's methods of promoting the department. So too were his articles, which appeared in local publications, pointing out the good work of the DWP. And of course working with the Municipal Light and Power Defense League was crucial. In 1933, he was its major financier, a role that he felt justified him in ordering the organization's staff to perform certain tasks "and make it snappy." He did not direct the MLPDL but expected more than just cooperation for his donations.[60]

In return for this dedication, Haynes received special tributes from the DWP Employees Association. One was another birthday party, his eighty-third; more than 6,000 employees were invited to show their appreciation for his service. These events represented expressions of gratitude from those most directly affected by the prosperity of the power program. Bond elections served the same purpose for Los Angeles citizens, who ratified his work and that of his partners by approving completion of the DWP program in the Depression decade.[61]

Water and power certainly dominated all other municipal issues for Haynes, but it was not the only one that concerned him. Always interested in the administration of police affairs, he suggested several months after the election that Shaw send an investigator to Milwaukee to study its police and court system. Haynes was repulsed by the strong-arm tactics of the LAPD and its "Red Squad" and hoped Shaw would select someone unaffiliated with the *Times* who would not whitewash the LAPD in order to continue its use in labor conflicts. Haynes reminded Shaw that Milwaukee had had a Socialist mayor for fifteen years and a model police department; even the *Times* admitted that. But Shaw declined to follow the doctor's prescription in this instance. The LAPD remained a bastion of "Cossackism" and contributed directly to Shaw's downfall when its political activities became known.[62]

The creation of a municipal bus system also surfaced as an issue in 1935. Haynes had always been in favor of additional city-owned utilities, especially low-cost transportation. He campaigned for a municipal railroad to the harbor in 1912, and tried to negotiate the purchase of the Los Angeles Railway Company in 1925. But protecting the power expansion program required shelving such interests. In order to convince civic leaders, such as Mayor Shaw, to continue supporting the DWP's expansion program until it was complete, the doctor had to persuade them that he would not favor immediate takeover of the telephone system, street railway lines, or the gas department of LAG&E, because of the consequent financial strain on the city. In the same vein, Haynes considered making a substantial donation to Carl Thompson's Public Ownership League of America in 1935, but only because the league was concentrating its efforts on electrical power at the time.[63]

The bus plan, a measure intended to decrease downtown traffic congestion and provide cheap transportation for city workers, envisioned a network of city-owned buses charging a nickel fare. The Municipal Bus League promoted the plan as a charter-amendment initiative, which was supported by the Municipal League and United Organizations for Progressive Political Action. Opponents included the *Times* and *Examiner*, which claimed the plan was too expensive and would unfairly compete with the established railways. Municipal Bus League president H. Gale Atwater asked Haynes for his personal blessing and a donation, and intimated that the doctor had approved of the project. But in this instance Haynes declined to support it publicly in deference to advocates of municipal ownership such as Will Anderson, Marshall Stimson, and Shelley Tolhurst. They opposed it as a poorly conceived system promoted by those with a financial interest in its success, not to mention that its failure would blemish the principle of municipal ownership. Anthony Pratt, of the Municipal League, chastised the Board of Water and Power Commissioners for almost unanimously panning the project, telling them they did not really understand municipal ownership. But Haynes and his fellow commissioners did not change their minds, and the bus proposal was defeated in 1935 and again in 1937. The old progressives refused to back a new bus system at a time when street railways already were in decline. They held firm to their support of city utilities that could earn a profit, not incur a deficit.[64]

Direct legislation at the city level proved to be a minor issue for Haynes at this time because of the weakness of his opposition. The *Times* continued to criticize the initiative, referendum, and recall, and Haynes as the father of these "abominations." But Harry Chandler seemed more interested in his investments—including real estate ventures in which Haynes was his unfriendly partner—and the paper rarely moved beyond editorial wrath. The *Times* did support one crusade to alter the recall amendment to increase the number of signatures required, shorten the petition circulation period, and give the city council the right to choose the successor of a recalled official. This amendment, placed on a special-election ballot in September 1934, was opposed by Haynes and his Direct Legislation League, and was buried in defeat.[65]

By early 1937, Haynes had experienced almost four years of tremendous political influence in the city. He had a say in Mayor Shaw's appointments and policies, and presided over the victorious forces for city power. In view of this influence, he decided to support Shaw's reelection bid, though rather half-heartedly. Haynes played no part in the campaign other than to make a modest donation and to appear to endorse Shaw in a letter circulated by the mayor's campaigners (which the doctor had written much earlier, not for election purposes).[66]

Haynes's qualified support for Shaw (or lack of support for his chief opponent) was a devastating blow for mayoral contender John Anson Ford. Ford and Haynes had been friends for years. The doctor had helped to finance Ford's 1934 victorious bid to become a county supervisor, helped get him a DWP job when he needed one, and cooperated with him while Ford was president of the Church Federation of Los Angeles. Haynes agreed with many of Ford's actions as county supervisor and as leader of the New Deal Democrats of Los Angeles County.[67]

But the 1937 election was a different story. Haynes was suspicious of the reform alliance that backed Ford. The reformers—including the increasingly hostile Municipal League and its irascible secretary, Anthony Pratt, the religious forces of "Fighting Bob" Shuler and ex-mayor Porter, and everyone else who opposed Shaw for one reason or another—formed a strange coalition of leftists, fundamentalists, and everyone in between. The group embraced many of the doctor's old and new political enemies, as well as some friends. Proof of the shenanigans of the Shaw organization had not yet surfaced, so Haynes decided to defend his administration partner loyally and avoid offending Ford by remaining aloof from the contest. The final vote in this election was close, with Mayor Shaw coming out on top.[68]

The summer of 1937 should have been a high point in Haynes's life. The city power program had been completed early that year. His principal ally in municipal politics had just been reelected, an outcome ensuring another four years of Haynes's influence in city hall. State political affairs had improved as EPIC-oriented Democrats worked to expand social programs as Haynes wished. And in Washington, FDR was still in command, although New Deal activism was waning. At all levels of government things appeared to be going the doctor's way.

But he could not enjoy this prosperity. His health gradually declined in the 1930s, and by late 1936 he had reached a low point. Anne Mumford wrote to John Collier at the end of October, describing Haynes's condition. He was showing some improvement after a near collapse: "There is a pulse again in the wrist though the doctors said it might never be restored. I am afraid however that he is beginning to realize that he cannot get back to his old basis, for he has been wanting to sit up in a chair and the doctors have not been willing for him to do it." A month later he could sit up for a while but could see no visitors. In early 1937, he felt a little better and began attending DWP board meetings, but still slept for most of the day. His health remained fragile through the summer.[69]

This incapacity cut short his participation in his last political crusade, a brief attempt to defend the city's requirement of safety fenders for streetcars. Since leading the fight to require such fenders three decades earlier, he had kept watch on the city council and railway companies to prevent any attempt to change the ordinance. Another challenge surfaced in 1937. With the rising popularity of the automobile and motor bus, streetcar patronage declined steadily after 1923. In order to recapture former riders, the traction companies developed the "Presidents' Conference Car," a streamlined model sporting a curved front body that could not accommodate the standard Eclipse fender. LARY officials quickly moved to change the city's fender ordinance for the new cars.[70]

News of the imminent arrival of the streamliners spurred the sickly Haynes to alert John Baumgartner, his confidant on the city council, to prepare for an assault on the fender law. The doctor's fears were realized in July, when LARY management officially petitioned the city council to alter the law to allow simple wheel guards on the modern cars. City officials were sympathetic to this attempt to revive the declining street railways, and since automobile accidents far outnumbered streetcar mishaps, Haynes had lost much of his ammunition.[71]

The doctor's efforts in this episode recalled his crusade of the early 1900s. In February 1937, he contacted the Eclipse manufacturer and suggested that fenders be redesigned immediately to fit the new cars in order to undercut LARY's argument that no suitable fenders existed. He then conducted a very cordial exchange with LARY president Lucius Storrs, who agreed to test the fenders and sent blueprints of the streamliners to Haynes to forward to the Eclipse manufacturer. After two months Storrs gave up waiting for the Eclipse modification and asked the city council to accept the simple wheel guard approved by the State Railroad Commission earlier that year. Haynes then lobbied the council by letter to deny the request and began gathering testimony from other California cities attesting to the effectiveness of the old fender. The 84-year-old reformer, now physically unable to pursue the matter, hired an attorney to carry on the fight in the city council chamber.[72]

On this occasion Haynes's arguments were not as persuasive as in the past. The council voted ten to five to exempt the streamliners. The sick and disappointed Haynes thanked those who voted in his favor and began considering another initiative to require the old fenders on all streetcars within the city limits. His declining health postponed such action, however. An Eclipse fender never touched the streamliners, although older LARY vehicles continued to carry the mechanisms for another decade.[73]

The fender fight was Haynes's last political battle. In late September 1937, in the midst of a prolonged case of influenza, he suffered a cerebral hemorrhage and was taken to Good Samaritan Hospital. By the first of October, four nurses were attending him and no visitors were allowed in his room. His doctors gave him little chance of recovery. In the middle of the month he began to feel better but then suffered a relapse. The doctors again gave up hope. The end came at 2:30 in the morning on Saturday, October 30.[74]

Chapter Fourteen

A Reformer's Remembrance

On the morning of October 30, 1937, the flags "on all city buildings and other public edifices were ordered lowered to half-staff" in homage to Dr. John Randolph Haynes. Later that day, Mayor Frank Shaw, individual city commissioners, and Power Bureau chief Ezra Scattergood issued statements eulogizing the president of the Board of Water and Power Commissioners. On the afternoon of Monday, November 1, funeral services were held in an overflowing St. Paul's Cathedral. Interment rites followed at Rosedale Cemetery, where Haynes was buried in the family plot. Earlier that day, the Los Angeles City Council passed resolutions extolling one of the city's most valuable residents, and adjourned that afternoon in his memory.[1]

Newspapers listed Haynes's survivors as sister Florence Lindley; her son, Francis Haynes Lindley; her daughter, Mrs. Hawthorne K. Dent, of Seattle; and nephew Robert Eugene Haynes (son of John's brother, Robert). A few days later details of the will were released. Anne Mumford and Francis H. Lindley were appointed executors, and the family lawyer, J. Wiseman Macdonald, would serve as their attorney. Modest shares of the estate were to be dispersed to relatives and the remainder was to revert to the Haynes Foundation. Legal details for the estate were completed in 1939, and the personal affairs of John Randolph Haynes were closed.[2]

The legacy of Dr. Haynes, the fruits of a busy life of political and social-reform activism, survives in several areas with which he was especially concerned. One is the Los Angeles Department of Water and Power, which operates the world's largest municipal water and electrical power generation and distribution system. The DWP was the doctor's top priority after 1920. He hoped it would shine as a glowing example of public ownership of utilities, so it received much of his attention for more than just the nearly two decades in which he was a member of its board of commissioners. He lived just long enough to see the results of his labor, the completion of the DWP's power expansion program in 1937. Less than a decade later the water and power "machine" Haynes helped to build was dismantled by Mayor Fletcher Bowron, for it was no longer needed by that time. Since then the expanding department has continued to serve the needs of an ever-growing metropolis as well as Haynes might have expected.[3]

As a tribute to the doctor, the DWP employees' publication devoted the front page and some text to Haynes's achievements in the issue appearing just after his death. "The Department of Water and Power has lost the best friend it ever had," began the story. "Always loyal, forever aggressive in his fight for development of the City's citizen owned enterprise, he was a most important factor in its successful growth." With the assistance of old friend John Collier, Haynes's efforts in behalf of Native Americans in the Owens Valley, who were adversely affected by the DWP's operations there, were recognized in 1939, when the "John R. Haynes Re-settlement Project in Owens Valley" was initiated. This federal program sought to move Paiutes to more productive lands, recognizing the doctor's efforts to make them self-supporting. In 1963, the DWP dedicated its Haynes Steam Plant, located near Seal Beach. Designed to generate more power than Hoover Dam, this facility became an integral component in the department's power system. The dedication of this plant in the doctor's name at a gala celebration paid apt tribute to a man who played a crucial role in the advancement of the DWP in its formative years.[4]

Haynes's favorite interest for all of his reform career was direct legislation, and his contributions in this area are even more significant. Proud of his unofficial title, "father of direct legislation," he was the individual most responsible for the adoption of the initiative, referendum, and recall in the state in 1911 and in the city in 1902. His creation of the Direct Legislation League of California in 1902, his personal lobbying at every session of the state legislature from 1903 to 1911, his leadership in the crusade for direct-legislation provisions in the city charter, his vigilant protection of these measures thereafter, and his promotion of direct legislation throughout the nation testified to the validity of the moniker.

Although his role in the adoption of these measures is sometimes obscured in favor of more visible figures such as Hiram Johnson, Haynes's leadership can be traced in the basic study of direct legislation in California by V. O. Key and Winston Crouch, in monographs examining the use of such measures, and in almost any textbook devoted to the history of the Golden State. In the year after Haynes's death, noted political scientist Winston Crouch detailed some of the doctor's activities in the quest for direct legislation. Since then, nationally oriented studies of the subject have consistently reiterated his role as chief crusader for these objectives in California and Los Angeles.[5]

Over the years direct legislation has been attacked by opponents for a variety of reasons. Some claim it is a tool of wealthy special interests, though grass-roots organizations use the initiative to protect the environment, regulate industries, and create laws the legislature will not pass. Other critics flay the devices precisely because they are used by those harboring contrary political points of view. And the extremely long and complicated ballots that increasingly frustrate voters are often blamed on direct legislation, though unfairly so since most propositions on the California ballot are placed there by the legislature, not by initiative or referendum petitions.[6]

Abuses of direct legislation do of course occur. California's population and its political milieu have changed over the last eight decades, and media campaigning has altered the manner in which decisions are made. Suggestions for improvements have been offered to make the process less susceptible to manipulation by vested interests and to give the legislature a larger role while still allowing voters to retain control of these measures. But, as Thomas Cronin has recently concluded, direct legislation "has worked better at the state and local levels than most people realize." In the final analysis, the measures play an integral part in the reformed system of California politics. The legislature does not always resolve political issues, and not all officeholders prove to be fit for office.[7]

Since 1911, the direct-legislation amendments to the state constitution have not been altered to any major degree. The same can be said for the direct-legislation provisions in the Los Angeles city charter which were added in 1903. For better or for worse, the survival of this concept commemorates the convictions and tenacity of the person most responsible for their adoption, the physician who championed the belief that the voters should have the opportunity to overrule their elected servants.

Haynes's legacy is most visibly evident in the development of the Haynes Foundation. After his death, the foundation's treasury swelled with the lion's share of his estate. Some of the trustees—notably Herbert

C. Jones, Franklin Hichborn, John Collier, and Louis Bartlett—hoped
the windfall would be dispersed for the projects the founders would have
favored. Soon after Haynes's death, Jones reminded his fellow trustees:
"Dr. Haynes indicated repeatedly, both in writing and verbally, that the
Foundation should exist as an active force, whose program should influence public action for human betterment. It was not intended to be, nor
should it become, a passive agency possessed only of vague and diffused
ideas of how to affect general welfare."[8]

But the foundation would not in the future travel in the direction indicated by Haynes. The trustees elected the doctor's nephew Francis
Haynes Lindley as the new president, the first of his many terms in the
next four decades. An able attorney, Lindley did not share his uncle's
more advanced views on social reform. Along with Anne Mumford and
others, he feared that continued involvement with quasi-political organizations would jeopardize the foundation's tax-exempt status. Lindley,
Mumford, and Remson Bird coalesced in opposition to the old progressives, and steered the foundation toward support of research and community forum programs rather than advocacy grants. Foundation funding for such groups as the League for Industrial Democracy and Public
Ownership League of America was dropped. John Collier bowed out
because he had little opportunity to attend meetings, and Herbert Jones
and Franklin Hichborn resigned after disputes with the non-activist faction. (Hichborn was convinced to reconsider.)[9]

In 1942, the foundation began a major expansion program. Its headquarters was relocated from Dr. Haynes's old office at Sixth and Hill
streets to the mansion on Figueroa Street near Adams Boulevard. A
"think tank" was established for social scientists and research assistants
working on studies in sociology, economics, demography, city planning,
political science, and other disciplines, with particular reference to the
Los Angeles metropolitan area. Charles W. Eliot, director of the National
Resources Planning Board in Washington, D.C., joined the institute as
director of research. The investigators benefited from the expansion of
the Haynes library, which included the doctor's correspondence and research files, reports and monographs acquired by the librarians, and files
of trustees and others serving on various governmental committees. The
private papers of Franklin Hichborn were added in 1948. The library
provided research materials for a mass of literature published by the
foundation in the 1940s and early 1950s, including *Metropolitan Los
Angeles: A Study in Integration*, a series of sixteen monographs directed
by noted Stanford political science professor Edwin A. Cottrell.[10]

While operating this private research institute the foundation continued to support scholarships and fellowships at local universities, a vigorous lecture series featuring historian Arthur M. Schlesinger and other distinguished scholars, a number of conferences relating to the foundation's purposes, and even a short-lived radio program, "The American Way," which served as a broadcast forum for discussion of current issues. For a time, the Pacific Southwest Academy, a West Coast branch of the American Academy of Political and Social Science, was headquartered in the foundation office (Haynes had been an officer in the late 1920s, and Mumford and other trustees became officers and directors). New trustees on the board included Cottrell, former DWP Power Bureau chief Ezra F. Scattergood, architect Reginald Johnson, and UCLA professors Charles Grove Haines and Gordon Watkins.[11]

In 1952 the foundation took a new direction as a result of its eviction from the old Figueroa Street residence. Standing in the path of the planned Harbor Freeway, the foundation headquarters was slated to be razed and a new location had to be found. This circumstance prodded the trustees to rethink the entire operation, and the consensus determined upon dramatic change. The internal research program was discontinued in favor of projects carried out by outside organizations. The Haynes library was given to UCLA, and the headquarters reestablished in a downtown office.[12]

Overhead costs recouped by this change in operation were converted into more available funds for grant programs. Scholarships and fellowships were increased, and many more grant applications were funded. Numerous notable projects were awarded grants. On the recommendation of Haynes trustee Paul Fussell, the American Bar Association received funding to examine the trial-court system in Los Angeles County; this study led to a number of reforms in civil and criminal procedures. The Chamber of Commerce won support for its program, spearheaded by industrialist and Haynes trustee Harold C. McClellan, to create more private-sector jobs for the disadvantaged. In the 1970s, the Los Angeles County Bar Association received a grant to examine county government; this project resulted in the adoption of ballot measures designed to modernize county administration. Continued support to Town Hall, an organization dedicated to the improvement of local government and whose leadership frequently included Haynes trustees, funded studies of ballot measures and charter reforms. Examinations of segregation in residential neighborhoods and schools, natural resources management, distribution of information detailing the region's economy and history, and other subjects were also funded. Besides McClellan and Fussell, the board of trustees in this period included Occidental College president Arthur G.

Coons, Pomona College president E. Wilson Lyon, UCLA political science professor Winston W. Crouch, and attorney Maynard Toll, son of an old friend of the founders.[13]

Over the course of six decades the Haynes Foundation changed its focus from the many specific reforms espoused by John R. Haynes at its creation to a general purpose of supporting research in the social sciences and dissemination of the results of such inquiry. In that time it expended over $18 million to study some of the basic ills of modern America and examine the causes of these problems rather than to alleviate the effects temporarily. As Haynes instructed his trustees in 1928, the foundation should above all foster conditions for social betterment, for "our aim has been to increase the happiness and well being of mankind." This directive has been carried out by the entity that bears his name.[14]

The man who left such an imprint on his adopted state and city is something of an enigma. This reformer certainly does not fit the stereotype of the "typical" progressive—a middle-class professional trying to establish his place in the social and political structure, advance his profession, control the lower classes, and modernize American institutions. Haynes was a middle-class professional who advocated the transformation of the nation's economy and government, worked with reformers to alter political structures, and campaigned for morality laws that limited personal freedom. But his program of social change moved far beyond that of the more conservative progressives. Contrary to most of them, who hoped to keep the lower classes under control, Haynes tried to elevate the status of the less fortunate. He consistently worked with labor leaders to improve the lot of miners and other working people and made this a top priority of his foundation.

Haynes's motivation was not social status; he had that before his conversion to social reform. It was not money; he already was a wealthy man who spent a fortune on his reform pursuits. Nor was it political power; he never ran for office (except as a temporary freeholder) or created a personal political machine. His primary motive was an arrogant yet honest desire to aid in the creation of a more just society by improving the living and working conditions of the less fortunate. This altruism was reflected in his major reform interests: direct legislation, which he hoped would give all groups an opportunity to participate in the legislative process; public ownership, which wrested the nation's major utilities from private control; occupational laws for women, children, miners, and others who needed special protection from industrial oppression;

and aid to Native Americans and others at the mercy of opportunists and bureaucrats. All the money he spent on these objectives was aimed at improving life for the underprivileged and giving them some access to decision making. Four decades of social-reform activism in which he spent his fortune with no tangible personal return and placed himself in the position of a class turncoat attest to his commitment to the gradual attainment of an American utopia.

John Haynes was a man of many contradictions. He invested his vast sums of money to make more, but spent much of his wealth on ameliorating the effects of capitalism. He lived in material luxury and moved in wealthy social and business circles, but tried to convert his rich associates to his idealistic way of thinking. Though he styled himself a "collectivist," he was more an individualist in his quest for reform, often working alone (he declined to join the Socialist party because it would limit his independence, he once claimed). Though a staunch advocate of positive government, he championed the initiative, referendum, and recall precisely because he distrusted the politicians who embodied such governments. Though a church member with close ties to clergymen and established religion all his life, he professed atheism because he believed a loving God would not allow such suffering in the world. He began his idealistic crusade for social reform in middle age, rather than in youth; he increased his activism as he became wealthier and had more to lose if his redistributive program won out; and he remained committed to reform regardless of the mood of the nation.

All of these characteristics diverge from those of typical reformers whose commitment to more advanced reform values cooled or vanished altogether in their later years. Yet in some ways Haynes's motivation was not dissimilar to that of major reformers of the time. His altruism was formed early, in the coalfields of Luzerne County and the slums of Philadelphia, where he witnessed poverty firsthand. His sense of noblesse oblige emerged after he reaped a bounty from his socio-economic position and considered ways to pay some of it back. The solution—a Christian socialist utopia—appeared in the guise of a religious awakening. And he sustained his crusade with a determined arrogance aimed at his peers who resisted change. In these respects he was not unlike many U.S. and European reformers of the Progressive Era who tried to uplift the bottom of society from a position near the top.

Haynes's least paradoxical aspect was his blend of idealism and pragmatism. His utopian dream would not be achieved in one stroke without a violent revolution. It could only come about peacefully in gradual increments, spurred by piecemeal reforms that would reduce suffering and remake institutions slowly, without bloodshed or chaos. This vision, shared by many social reformers, made him a mere compromiser in the eyes of more dogmatic radicals, but a realist in the eyes of those sympathetic to his more limited reform goals. This tendency allowed him to work in a variety of ways to advance reform. He cooperated with bosses and other political manipulators in a manner anathema to more elitist reformers. He used his money as did his opponents: lobbying legislators, bankrolling campaigns to win votes, and wining and dining politicians to his point of view. In some situations he had to be crafty, in others secretive; sometimes he actually deceived people in his pursuit of victory. All of this was done, he believed, in the name of the betterment of mankind.

His practical approach took the form of diplomacy in occasionally uniting conflicting groups to support his objectives. His standing as a wealthy capitalist and political reformer helped him gain support from conservative friends and businessmen for reforms such as direct legislation and municipal ownership. His position in the camps of both social and political reformers enabled him to unite leftists and progressives at times to achieve more advanced reforms. In fact, he served as a bridge between the two groups, limited only by the fears of each that he was more committed to the designs of the other. By overcoming these fears, he succeeded in uniting a wide variety of reformers in many campaigns throughout his career.

For the last four decades of his life, John Randolph Haynes fought unwaveringly for his reform agenda. Though not unique in this respect, he is a prime example of the few insurgents of the Progressive Era who remained true to the more altruistic reform aims of the early 1900s. As such, he embodies the spirit of social reform activism that endured from the 1890s through the New Deal. The "father of direct legislation" in California, he was among the most prominent progressives who modified the political system of the Golden State. In Los Angeles, he was the most significant individual political force of the period from 1900 to 1937, the city's most effective and consistent activist in the quest for political reform and social justice.

Reference Matter

Notes

The following abbreviations are used in the notes and bibliographic notes:

Bancroft	Bancroft Library, University of California, Berkeley.
HF	John Randolph Haynes and Dora Haynes Foundation Office, Los Angeles.
Honnold	Special Collections, Honnold Library, The Claremont Colleges, Claremont, California.
HP	John Randolph Haynes Papers, Special Collections, University of California, Los Angeles.
Huntington	Henry E. Huntington Library, San Marino, California.
LC	Manuscripts Division, Library of Congress, Washington, D.C.
Lilly	Lilly Library, Indiana University, Bloomington.
Seaver	Seaver Center for Western History Research, Los Angeles County Museum of Natural History, Los Angeles.
SHSWA	State Historical Society of Wisconsin Archives, Madison.
Stanford	Special Collections, Stanford University Library, Stanford, California.
UCLA	Department of Special Collections, Research Library, University of California, Los Angeles.

CHAPTER ONE

1. William Allen White was contacted twice about writing the biography, and Oscar Lewis and Lawrence Clark Powell were recommended for the project after

Haynes's death. The 1926 attempt at beginning the biography was put off because of Collier's hectic schedule. The 1942 project was dropped after several Haynes Foundation trustees apparently opposed publicizing some of the founder's views on social reform. Mary Gibson to William Allen White, Jan. 19, 1926, White to Gibson, Jan. 26, 1926, Anne Mumford to White, Mar. 30, 1942, John R. Haynes to Walter V. Woehlke, Feb. 27, May 4, 1926, Haynes to Franklin Hichborn, Nov. 1, 1926, Correspondence files, HF; "Minutes of Meetings of the Board of Trustees, Haynes Foundation," 1: 191 (May 16, 1942), HF; personal interview with Winston W. Crouch, Oct. 5, 1988, Los Angeles.

2. Haynes's autobiographical notes are filled with inaccuracies and exaggerations but do illustrate his personal views and provide much information that is not available in other sources.

3. Ralph Arthur Watson, *Ancestors and Descendents of John and Hannah (Goodwin) Watson of Hartford, Connecticut and Associated Families* (Baltimore: Gateway, 1985), 205–6; *History of Litchfield County, Connecticut* (Philadelphia: J. W. Lewis, 1881), 264–68; James Savage, *A Genealogical Dictionary of the First Settlers of New England*, 4 vols. (Boston: Little, Brown, 1860), 2: 151.

4. "Warrantee Maps of the Townships in Luzerne County" (copies at Wyoming Valley Historical Society, Wilkes-Barre, Penn.), 20; William H. Egle, "History of Sullivan County," *Notes and Queries: Historical, Biographical and Genealogical*, 4th series, 2 (Oct. 1894): 195; Albert E. Van Deusen, comp., *The Public Records of the State of Connecticut*, 9 vols. (Hartford: Connecticut State Library, 1953), 6: 123–24, 9: 285; Samuel W. Durant, *History of Kalamazoo County, Michigan* (Philadelphia: Everts and Abbott, 1880), 454–55.

5. Durant, *History of Kalamazoo*, 455; George B. Kulp, *Families of the Wyoming Valley*, 3 vols. (Wilkes-Barre, Penn.: George B. Kulp, 1890), 3: 711, 1229–30; H. C. Bradsby, ed., *History of Luzerne County, Pennsylvania* (Chicago: S. B. Nelson, 1893), 586–88, 1074; *Atlas of Luzerne County, Pennsylvania* (Philadelphia: A. Pomeroy, 1873), 85, 93.

6. Copy of Reginald Haines to editor of *London Times*, Nov. 11, 1903, Family files, HF; Christopher Hibbert, *London: The Biography of a City* (London: William Morrow, 1969), 147; William Kent, *An Encyclopedia of London* (London: J. M. Dent, 1937), 518–23, 651–53; John Walter Osbourne, *John Cartwright* (Cambridge, England: Cambridge University Press, 1972), esp. 127–33; copies of John Cartwright to Joseph Haynes, May 1, 1821, Feb. 10, 1823, Family files, HF. In the 1600s the family name was spelled "Haines."

7. Family Bible and Haynes's autobiography notes, HF. Haynes believed that the family business was passed on to his father's older brother, Francis. Francis died at the age of four, however.

8. Haynes's autobiography notes, HF. James S. Haynes described himself as a farmer in the ship passenger list when he departed from England.

9. Bradsby, *History of Luzerne*, 554, 587; Luzerne County Deeds (Luzerne County Courthouse, Wilkes-Barre, Penn.), 51: 419, 61: 56; *History of Luzerne, Lackawanna, and Wyoming Counties, Pennsylvania* (New York: W. W. Munsell, 1880), 253–55; Stewart Pearce, *Annals of Luzerne County*, 2nd ed. (Philadelphia: J. B. Lippincott, 1866), 196.

10. Family Bible, HF; Schuylkill County Deeds (Schuylkill County Courthouse, Pottsville, Penn.), 47: 382–84, 48: 534, 63: 384; Luzerne County

Deeds, 89: 9; *County Atlas of Carbon, Pennsylvania* (New York: F. W. Beers, 1875), 18.

11. Haynes's autobiography notes, HF.

12. Ibid.

13. Ibid. See Chapters 7 and 11 below for Haynes's involvement in temperance and prohibition crusades.

14. Donald L. Miller and Richard E. Sharpless, *The Kingdom of Coal: Work, Enterprise, and Ethnic Communities in the Mine Fields* (Philadelphia: University of Pennsylvania Press, 1985), 1–82; Anthony F. C. Wallace, *St. Clair: A Nineteenth-Century Coal Town's Experience with a Disaster-Prone Industry* (New York: Knopf, 1987), 7–53.

15. Miller and Sharpless, *Kingdom of Coal*, 136–70; Wallace, *St. Clair*, 320–65; James Walter Coleman, *The Molly Maguire Riots* (Richmond: Garrett & Massie, 1936), 40–69; Wayne G. Broehl, Jr., *The Molly Maguires* (Cambridge: Harvard University Press, 1964), 1–101.

16. Haynes's autobiography notes, HF; *Los Angeles Record*, July 13, 1929. Haynes "remembered" the incident at Yorktown but confused many details; his account might have been exaggerated or based on a similar event that occurred much later.

17. *McElroy's Philadelphia City Directory* (Philadelphia: E. C. and J. Biddle, 1864 and 1867); Haynes's autobiography notes, HF; *Maps of the City of Philadelphia*, 6 vols. (Philadelphia: Ernest Hexamer & William Locher, 1859), 6: 76.

18. Haynes's autobiography notes, HF.

19. Ibid.

20. Ibid.

21. Ibid.; W. J. Maxwell, comp., *General Alumni Catalogue: The University of Pennsylvania* (Philadelphia: University of Pennsylvania, 1922), 389, 556; Edward Potts Cheyney, *History of the University of Pennsylvania, 1740–1940* (Philadelphia: University of Pennsylvania Press, 1940), 272–73, 296–97.

22. Haynes's autobiography notes, HF; *Atlas of the City of Philadelphia* (Philadelphia: G. W. Bromley, 1887), vol. 4; Maxwell Whiteman, "Philadelphia's Jewish Neighborhood," in Allen F. Davis and Mark H. Haller, eds., *The Peoples of Philadelphia: A History of Ethnic Groups and Lower-Class Life, 1790–1940* (Philadelphia: Temple University Press, 1973), 231–54; Dennis Clark, *The Irish in Philadelphia: Ten Generations of Urban Experience* (Philadelphia: Temple University Press, 1973), 48; James T. Kloppenberg, *Uncertain Victory: Social Democracy and Progressivism in European and American Thought, 1870–1920* (New York: Oxford University Press, 1986), 208–9.

23. William B. Atkinson, ed., *The Philadelphia Medical Register and Directory* (Philadelphia: Collins, 1875), 118–21; Frederick P. Henry, *Standard History of the Medical Profession of Philadelphia* (Chicago: Goodspeed Bros., 1897), 297–98; Haynes to Governor George C. Pardee, Apr. 6, 1903, box 70, George C. Pardee Correspondence and Papers, Bancroft.

24. U.S. Department of Commerce, Bureau of the Census, *Seventh Census of the United States: Population* (1850), Philadelphia, roll 793, p. 145; idem, *Eighth Census of the United States* (1860), Philadelphia, roll 1089, p. 221; Carbon County Deeds (Carbon County Courthouse, Jim Thorpe, Penn.), 9: 46–48, 10: 30–31; biographical form on Dora Haynes (1915), Los Angeles Public Library files; *Boyd's Wilkes-Barre City Directory* (1873–74, 1880–82). On the

social structure of Wilkes-Barre see Edward J. Davies, II, *The Anthracite Aristocracy: Leadership and Social Change in the Hard Coal Regions of Northeastern Pennsylvania, 1800–1930* (DeKalb: Northern Illinois University Press, 1985), 16–72.

25. *Wellesley Catalogue* (1880–81), and Alumni Biography files, Wellesley College Archives, Wellesley, Mass.; John and Dora Haynes's wedding certificate, HF.

26. Haynes to Franklin M. Henzel, July 1, 1918, box 195, HP; *Gopsill's Philadelphia Directory* (Philadelphia: James Gopsill, 1887).

27. Haynes's autobiography notes, HF.

28. Ibid.; Haynes to William B. Munro, Aug. 23, 1923, box 170, HP; Haynes to Gifford Pinchot, June 7, 1922, HF; Philip S. Benjamin, "Gentlemen Reformers in the Quaker City, 1870–1912," *Political Science Quarterly*, 85 (Mar. 1970): 61–79; George Vickers, *The Fall of Bossism: A History of the Committee of 100 and the Reform Movement in Philadelphia and Pennsylvania* (Philadelphia: A. C. Bryson, 1883); *Report of the Committee of One Hundred* (Philadelphia: Thomas S. Dando, 1884).

29. Haynes's autobiography notes and agreement between Haynes and William B. Scull, Mar. 12, 1887, HF. Los Angeles as a haven for the sick is discussed in John E. Baur, *The Health Seekers of Southern California, 1870–1900* (San Marino, Calif.: Huntington Library, 1959).

CHAPTER TWO

1. *Los Angeles Times*, May 8, 9, 1887. All newspapers cited hereafter were published in Los Angeles unless otherwise noted.

2. Glenn S. Dumke, *The Boom of the Eighties in Southern California* (San Marino, Calif.: Huntington Library, 1944), 3–58; Robert M. Fogelson, *The Fragmented Metropolis: Los Angeles, 1850–1930* (Cambridge, Mass.: Harvard University Press, 1967), 1–134.

3. Haynes to Mrs. Howard F. Withington, Jan. 22, 1932, unidentified clipping, Nov. 4, 1917, and Haynes's autobiography notes, HF; *Corran's Los Angeles City Directory* (1888, 1893).

4. Board of Examiners of the Medical Society of the State of California, *Official Register and Directory of Physicians and Surgeons*, 9th ed. (San Francisco: Office of Registrar and Director of Physicians and Surgeons, Jan. 1897); *Southern California Practitioner*, 2 (July–Oct. 1887): 251, 287–90, 292–94; *Times*, Nov. 14, 1906.

5. *An Illustrated History of Los Angeles County, California* (Chicago: Lewis, 1889), 233–34; Edward E. Harnagel, M.D., "The Life and Times of Walter Lindley, M.D., 1852–1922, and the Founding of the California Hospital," *Southern California Quarterly*, 53 (Dec. 1971): 303–15, esp. 311.

6. *University of Southern California Yearbook, 1888–1889* (Los Angeles: University of Southern California, 1889), 58; George L. Cole, M.D., *Medical Associates of My Early Days in Los Angeles* (Los Angeles: Los Angeles County Medical Association, 1930), 55; various articles in the *Southern California Practitioner* (1887–1901); Haynes to Oscar E. Muellar, Dec. 19, 1936, HF; Harris Newmark, *Sixty Years in Southern California, 1853–1913*, 3rd ed. (Boston:

Houghlin Mifflin, 1930), 649; *Times,* July 8 and Oct. 12, 1892, Mar. 15 and Sept. 2, 1893, Mar. 12, 1898.

7. *Times,* Oct. 19, 21, 1898; *Evening Express,* Oct. 19, 1898; Francis Haynes file, HF; Cole, *Medical Associates,* 53–55.

8. Handwritten notes by Dora Haynes in an account ledger, HF; W. J. Maxwell, comp., *General Alumni Catalogue: The University of Pennsylvania* (Philadelphia: University of Pennsylvania Press, 1922), 607; George H. Kress, *A History of the Medical Profession in Southern California,* 2nd ed. (Los Angeles: Times-Mirror Press, 1910), 132.

9. "Report to Stockholders of California Hospital, December 16, 1902," "Medical 1" Scrapbook, Walter Lindley Collection, Honnold; Raymond G. Taylor, "Recollections of Sixty Years of Medicine in Southern California," 4 vols. (unpublished typescript, Los Angeles County Medical Association Library, 1956), 4:94–95; William R. Molony, M.D., "Medical Practice in Los Angeles in the Early Part of This Century," unpublished typescript (Los Angeles County Medical Association Library, 1966), 28–29.

10. *Evening Express,* Oct. 11, 1899; *Herald,* May 6, 1900; *Times,* Feb. 3, 1901; John R. Haynes, "On the Treatment of Inevitable Abortion" (1891), and idem, "Infusion of Normal Salt Solution in Disease" (1900), HF; idem, "Tuberculosis of the Ovaries," *Southern California Practitioner,* 17 (June 1902): 244–46; idem, "Duty of Railroads in Transportation of Tuberculosis Passengers," *Journal of the American Medical Association,* 48 (Jan. 19, 1907): 210–12; *Los Angeles Academy of Medicine,* pamphlet (1906), UCLA Biomedical Library.

11. *Herald,* Feb. 18, 1905, Jan. 13, 1909; *Monrovia News,* Oct. 7, 1905; *Times,* Oct. 14 and June 5, 27, 1908, Dec. 31, 1909; "Inventory of Safe Deposit Box, June 1899," and Haynes's autobiography notes, HF.

12. "Inventory of Safe Deposit Box" and Haynes's autobiography notes, HF; John E. Baur, *Health Seekers of Southern California, 1870–1900* (San Marino, Calif.: Huntington Library, 1959), 135; Quartette Mining Company, annual reports (1906, 1907, 1909, 1910), box 152, HP; "Pan America Gold Dredging Company," prospectus (c. 1906), and Los Angeles County, Articles of Incorporation files 2811, 2822, 2825, 2906, 3071, 3920, 4404, and 6026, Seaver; *Times,* Nov. 16, 1906.

13. Haynes's account ledger (1892–1901), HF; Haynes to Gaylord Wilshire, Jan. 15, July 27, Oct. 31, 1902, and H. L. Knight to Wilshire, Feb. 5, 8, 10, 1902, box 1, H. Gaylord Wilshire Papers, UCLA.

14. Los Angeles Chamber of Commerce, "Minutes of Meetings of Board of Directors," 3: 251, 5: 189, California Historical Society History Center, Los Angeles; Charles Dwight Willard, *A History of the Chamber of Commerce of Los Angeles, California* (Los Angeles: Kingsley, Barnes & Neuner, 1899), 245; *Times,* July 29, 1893; Chamber of Commerce, *Bulletin,* Nov. 12, 1928; Stephen P. Erie, "City Unlimited: Building the Los Angeles Growth Machine, 1880–1930," paper presented at the annual meeting of the American Political Science Association, San Francisco, Sept. 1990. The membership of the Chamber of Commerce in the late nineteenth century has caused confusion among city historians since there were two John Hayneses in the Chamber before 1900. The other (also born in Pennsylvania) was a lawyer and judge who lived in Los Angeles from about 1887 to 1892, when he moved to San Francisco. He served as a Chamber director from 1889 to 1891. On this confusion see Willard, *History*

of the Chamber of Commerce, 77, and W. W. Robinson, *Lawyers of Los Angeles* (Los Angeles: Los Angeles Bar Association, 1959), 270, 316, 357. On the other John Haynes see "Minutes of the Chamber of Commerce," 2: 33 (Sept. 4, 1890); *Times*, Mar. 18, 1890, Nov. 13, 1894; "Great Register of Los Angeles County" (1890), Seaver; *Los Angeles City Directory* (1887–94).

15. George I. Cochran to H. W. O'Melveny, July 6, 1896, box 4, Jackson A. Graves Papers, Huntington.

16. Marco R. Newmark, "Pioneer Clubs of Los Angeles," *Historical Society of Southern California Quarterly*, 31 (1949): 313; *Society of Colonial Wars in the State of California*, pamphlet (1915), Seaver, 72; *Greater Los Angeles*, 2 (Jan. 1897): 2; various certificates in "Personal 2" and "Personal 3" Scrapbooks, HP; *Times*, Nov. 13, 1903; Scribes brochure (1900), HF.

17. *Evening Express*, Sept. 25, 1897, Oct. 19, 1898; *Times*, June 24, 1894; Boyle Workman, *The City That Grew* (Los Angeles: Southland, 1935), 252; Newmark, "Pioneer Clubs," 304, 307.

18. *Los Angeles Bluebook* (Los Angeles: Los Angeles Bluebook Co., 1894–95); *Times*, Aug. 27, Sept. 2, 1893, July 4, 13, Sept. 29, Dec. 11, 1895, Mar. 11, Apr. 30, 1896, Aug. 21, 1897; *Los Angeles Herald and Express*, Feb. 16, Apr. 15, July 22, 1942; *Southern California Practitioner*, 20 (Feb. 1905): 75; *Journal of the Third Annual Convention*, booklet (Los Angeles Diocese Episcopal Church, 1898), 10.

19. Stephen M. White to Haynes, Dec. 8, 1898, White to Henry White, June 17, 1899, box 16, Haynes/White correspondence, box 26, Stephen Mallory White Papers, Stanford; Leroy E. Mosher, *Stephen M. White: His Life and His Work*, 2 vols. (Los Angeles: Times-Mirror, 1903), 1: 21.

20. H. Gaylord Wilshire, "Dr. John R. Haynes," *Direct Legislation Record*, 8 (Dec. 1902): 75; *California Blue Book, 1893* (Sacramento: N.p., 1893).

21. "Souvenir of Complimentary Dinner to T. E. Gibbon, Esq." (Aug. 3, 1900), Thomas E. Gibbon Papers, Huntington; Frederic Cople Jaher, *The Urban Establishment: Upper Strata in Boston, New York, Charleston, Chicago, and Los Angeles* (Urbana: University of Illinois Press, 1982), 612–54.

22. Deed (945 South Pearl Street), HF; Los Angeles County Assessor's Records, 30: 27 (1900–1910), Los Angeles County Archives; *Times*, May 13, 1893; U.S. Department of Commerce, Bureau of the Census, *Twelfth Census of the United States: Population* (1900), California, 12: 242A.

23. *Evening Express*, Nov. 25, 1891; *Times*, Mar. 2, 1893, Mar. 12, 1899; Haynes's autobiography notes, HF.

24. *Times*, Feb. 8, 1889, May 29–June 3, Oct. 29, 30, Nov. 5, 1890; *Toronto World*, Oct. 9, 20, 30, Nov. 8, 15, 1890. Francis was divorced from his wife, Mary, in 1877; the couple had one son.

25. James M. Guinn, *Historical and Biographical Record of Los Angeles and Vicinity* (Chicago: Chapman, 1901), 452–54; Harnagel, "Walter Lindley," 303–15; *Times*, Jan. 14, 1893, Nov. 14, 1906.

CHAPTER THREE

1. John Whiteclay Chambers II, *The Tyranny of Change: America in the Progressive Era, 1900–1917* (New York: St. Martin's, 1980), 105–14, quotes from

108–10; Richard L. McCormick, "The Discovery That Business Corrupts Politics: A Reappraisal of the Origins of Progressivism," *American Historical Review*, 86 (Apr. 1981): 247–74; John D. Buenker, John C. Burnham, and Robert M. Crunden, *Progressivism* (Cambridge, Mass.: Schenkman, 1977); Robert M. Crunden, *Ministers of Reform: The Progressives' Achievements in American Civilization, 1889–1920* (New York: Basic Books, 1982); Daniel Levine, *Varieties of Reform Thought* (Madison: State Historical Society of Wisconsin, 1964), esp. 109–17. For a historiographical background of progressivism see Daniel T. Rogers, "In Search of Progressivism," in Stanley I. Kutler and Stanley N. Katz, eds., *The Promise of American History: Progress and Prospects* (Baltimore: Johns Hopkins University Press, 1982), 113–32; and Robert H. Wiebe, "The Progressive Years, 1900–1917," in William H. Cartwright and Richard L. Watson, Jr., *The Reinterpretation of American History and Culture* (Washington, D.C.: National Council for the Social Studies, 1973), 425–42.

2. Chambers, *Tyranny of Change*, 105–14, quotes from 106–7.

3. These categories of reformers are based on a variation of interpretations in Russell B. Nye, *Midwestern Progressive Politics: A Historical Study of Its Origins and Development, 1870–1950* (East Lansing: Michigan State College Press, 1951), 193; Albert Howard Clodius, "The Quest for Good Government in Los Angeles, 1890–1910" (Ph.D. diss., Claremont Graduate School, 1953), 482; and Melvin Holli, "Urban Reform in the Progressive Era," in Lewis L. Gould, ed., *The Progressive Era* (Syracuse, N.Y.: Syracuse University Press, 1974), 139–40. For another interpretation see John D. Buenker, "Sovereign Individuals and Organic Networks: Political Culture in Conflict During the Progressive Era," *American Quarterly*, 40 (June 1988): 187–204.

4. *Times*, Aug. 8, Nov. 10, 12, 14, 15, 18, 20, 27, Dec. 2, 1890, Nov. 27, 29, Dec. 3, 7, 13, 1892, Jan. 28, 1893, Apr. 1, 19, 1894; Donald Ray Culton, "Charles Dwight Willard: Los Angeles City Booster and Progressive Reformer, 1888–1914" (Ph.D. diss., University of Southern California, 1971), 109–12.

5. *Evening Express*, Aug. 7, Sept. 22, 1896, Dec. 11, 1897.

6. *Evening Express*, Oct. 22, 29, 1896, Feb. 4, May 19, June 26, Nov. 13, 23, Dec. 12, 1897, July 16, 1898; Charles D. Willard to Samuel Willard, Nov. 13, 1896, box 5, Charles D. Willard Papers, Huntington; Culton, "Willard," 113–21.

7. Charles D. Willard, *The Free Harbor Contest at Los Angeles* (Los Angeles: Kingsley-Barnes and Neuner, 1899), 9–123; Curtis Grassman, "The Los Angeles Free Harbor Controversy and the Creation of a Progressive Coalition," *Southern California Quarterly*, 55 (Winter 1973): 445–69; Stephen M. White Scrapbooks, Seaver.

8. William F. Deverell, "Building an Octopus: Railroads and Society in the Late Nineteenth Century Far West" (Ph.D. diss., Princeton University, 1989), 165–217.

9. Haynes to Stephen M. White correspondence, 1890s, box 26, Stephen M. White Papers; *Evening Express*, Apr. 7, 1896; *Times*, Apr. 9, 1896.

10. Culton, "Willard," 188–94; *Times*, Nov. 8, 1900; invitation to Municipal League meeting, May 24, 1901, "Personal 2" Scrapbook, HP.

11. *Evening Express*, Sept. 6, 1898, Oct. 23, 1899, Nov. 12, 1900; Ralph Edward Shaffer, "A History of the Socialist Party of California" (M.A. thesis, University of California, Los Angeles, 1951), 3–19; Grace H. Stimson, *Rise of*

the Labor Movement in Los Angeles (Berkeley: University of California Press, 1955), 218–23.

12. Howard H. Quint, "Gaylord Wilshire and Socialism's First Congressional Campaign," *Pacific Historical Review*, 26 (Nov. 1957): 327–30; *Times*, Dec. 14, 1894, Jan. 22, Mar. 17, 22, 1895; *Evening Express*, Nov. 9, 1895, Feb. 19, Apr. 6, May 8, Nov. 9, 12–14, 27, 1897.

13. Joan M. Jenson, "After Slavery: Caroline Severance in Los Angeles," *Southern California Quarterly*, 48 (June 1966): 175–86; Quint, "Wilshire," 327–40; Ralph Hancock, *Fabulous Boulevard* (New York: Funk & Wagnalls, 1949, 85–112; Kevin Starr, *Inventing the Dream: California Through the Progressive Era* (New York: Oxford University Press, 1985), 208.

14. *Evening Express*, Jan. 24, May 7, 14, 1900; *Times*, Mar. 11, Apr. 28, June 3, 1895, Sept. 26, 1898.

15. James T. Kloppenberg, *Uncertain Victory: Social Democracy and Progressivism in European and American Thought, 1870–1920* (New York: Oxford University Press, 1986), 239.

16. Starr, *Inventing the Dream*, 211, 218; Charles H. Hopkins, *The Rise of the Social Gospel in American Protestantism, 1865–1915* (New Haven, Conn.: Yale University Press, 1940), 179.

17. *Times*, June 11, 1896; Haynes's autobiography notes, HF.

18. *Evening Express*, Sept. 10, 1898; Haynes's autobiography notes, HF.

19. Richard B. Dressner, "William Dwight Porter Bliss's Christian Socialism," *Church History*, 47 (Mar. 1978): 66–82; Christopher L. Webber, "William Dwight Porter Bliss (1856–1926): Priest and Socialist," *Historical Magazine of the Protestant Episcopal Church*, 28 (Mar. 1959): 11–39; Peter J. Frederick, *Knights of the Golden Rule: The Intellectual as Christian Social Reformer in the 1890s* (Lexington: University Press of Kentucky, 1976), 84–98.

20. Howard H. Quint, *The Forging of American Socialism: Origins of the Modern Movement*, 2nd ed. (New York: Bobbs-Merrill, 1964), 109–26; James Dombrowski, *The Early Days of Christian Socialism in America* (New York: Columbia University Press, 1936), 96–107.

21. *Evening Express*, Sept. 3, 1897; *Social Economist*, 2 (Mar. 5, 1898): 2.

22. *Evening Express*, Jan. 8, 10, 11, 1898.

23. Kathleen D. McCarthy, *Noblesse Oblige: Charity and Cultural Philanthropy in Chicago, 1849–1929* (Chicago: University of Chicago Press, 1982).

24. *Times*, Jan. 21, 1898; Frederick, *Knights of the Golden Rule*, 18–21. Robert Crunden, in *Ministers of Reform*, 16, sees religion as the primary motivation for social-reform activism.

25. *Evening Express*, Jan. 22, 24, 31, Feb. 3, 19, 1898; *Times*, Feb. 3, 7, 10, 1898; *Herald*, Feb. 19, 1898.

26. *Evening Express*, Mar. 14, Sept. 19, 1898; Quint, *Forging of American Socialism*, 259.

27. "Union Reform League Memorial to Board of Freeholders," typescript (1898), box 102, HP; *Capital*, 8 (Dec. 3, 1898): 3; *Evening Express*, Dec. 3, 5, 1898.

28. *Evening Express*, Jan. 2, 1899; Quint, *Forging of American Socialism*, 260; W. D. P. Bliss, "Union Reform League Activities," *Arena*, 2 (July 1899): 111–14.

29. Quint, *Forging of American Socialism*, 261–64; *Evening Express*, July 4,

1899; W. D. P. Bliss, "Unite or Perish," *Arena* 22 (July 1899): 78–89; W. D. P. Bliss, "The Social Reform Union," *Arena*, 22 (Aug. 1899): 272–75.

30. *Bulletin of the Social Reform Union*, 1 (Nov. 1, 1899): 3–5; 1 (Sept. 15, 1899): 1; 1 Nov. 15, 1899): 1, 3.

31. Ibid., 1 (Nov. 30, 1899): 1; Quint, *Forging of American Socialism*, 264–70; John R. Haynes, speech to the Second National Social and Political Conference, 1901, "Public Ownership" Scrapbook, HP; *Direct Legislation Record*, 8 (Sept. 1901): 43–45.

32. *Evening Express*, Oct. 27, Nov. 29, 1899, Jan. 24, Aug. 29, Oct. 2, 31, 1900.

33. Ibid., Feb. 5, 27, 1901; *Herald*, June 9, 1901; Culton, "Willard," 187–88.

34. *Evening Express*, Sept. 26, Oct. 5, 23, 24, 1900, and Sept. 1900 through Apr. 1901; *Times*, Nov. 27, 1900.

35. *Herald*, Jan. 30, 1901; *Evening Express*, Feb. 2, 1901.

36. *Herald*, June 10, 1901.

37. *Evening Express*, Aug. 29, 1900; *Times*, Aug. 30, 1900.

CHAPTER FOUR

1. Eltweed Pomeroy, "Direct Legislation," in W. D. P. Bliss, ed., *New Encyclopedia of Social Reform* (New York: Funk & Wagnalls, 1908), 384–87; William B. Munro, "Initiative and Referendum," *Encyclopedia of the Social Sciences*, 15 vols. (New York: MacMillan, 1932), 8: 50–52; Thomas E. Cronin, *Direct Democracy: The Politics of the Initiative, Referendum, and Recall* (Cambridge, Mass.: Harvard University Press, 1989), 125–58.

2. Margaret A. Schaffner, "The Recall," *Yale Review*, 18 o.s. (Aug. 1909): 206–9; Merrill Jenson, *The Articles of Confederation: An Interpretation of the Social-Constitutional History of the American Revolution, 1774–1781* (Madison: University of Wisconsin Press, 1970), 264; Herbert S. Swan, "The Use of the Recall in the United States," in William Munro, ed., *The Initiative, Referendum and Recall* (New York: D. Appleton, 1916), 298–99; Eltweed Pomeroy, "Needed Political Reforms," *Arena*, 28 (Nov. 1902): 470. For an array of contemporary arguments on the recall see Edith M. Phelps, comp., *Selected Articles on the Recall Including the Recall of Judges and Judicial Decisions* (New York: H. W. Wilson, 1915). John R. Haynes usually considered the three measures as one, so they will be treated the same way here except where noted.

3. Eltweed Pomeroy, "The Direct Legislation Movement," *Arena*, 16 (June 1896): 29–43; Lloyd Sponholtz, "The Initiative and Referendum: Direct Democracy in Perspective," *American Studies*, 14 (Fall 1973): 44–46; David B. Magleby, *Direct Legislation: Voting on Ballot Propositions in the United States* (Baltimore: Johns Hopkins University Press, 1984), 31.

4. Pomeroy, "Direct Legislation," 385–86; Magleby, *Direct Legislation*, 27–30 (Magleby here provides a good synthesis of the arguments concerning direct legislation); Ellis Paxton Oberholtzer, *The Referendum in America Together with Some Chapters on the Initiative and Recall* (New York: Scribner's, 1912); William B. Munro, ed., *The Initiative, Referendum and Recall* (New York: D. Appleton, 1912), 1–297; Edith M. Phelps, comp., *Selected Articles on the Initiative and Referendum* (Minneapolis: H. W. Wilson, 1909); Howard H. Quint, *The*

Forging of American Socialism: Origins of the Modern Movement, 2nd ed. (New York: Bobbs-Merrill, 1964) 329–30.

5. *California Social-Democrat*, Nov. 23, 1912, Oct. 25, 1913; Sponholtz, "Initiative and Referendum," 46–47; Eltweed Pomeroy, "Direct Legislation," in W. D. P. Bliss, ed., *Encyclopedia of Social Reform* (New York: Funk & Wagnalls, 1897), 500.

6. *Times*, Sept. 17, 1898; *Direct Legislation Record*, 5 (Dec. 1898): 75; *Capital*, 8 (Dec. 10, 1898): 4.

7. Articles on direct legislation in *Arena*, 22 (July 1899): 97–100. In a letter to Bliss outlining his reform priorities in June 1898, Haynes did not mention direct legislation. Haynes to Bliss, June 19, 1898, in *Social Messenger* clipping in "Direct Legislation in Los Angeles and How It Works" Scrapbook, HP.

8. *Times*, May 21, June 5, 9, July 4, 28, 1900; *Herald*, May 6, July 31, 1900. This was the last time Haynes received the endorsement of the *Times* for anything.

9. *Evening Express*, Sept. 22, 1900; H. Gaylord Wilshire, *A Business-Like City Charter*, pamphlet (June 4, 1900); John R. Haynes, "The Introduction of the Initiative, Referendum, and Recall to Los Angeles," speech to the University Club, 1909, "Recall" Scrapbook, and Haynes to Thomas H. Reed, June 20, 1911, "Mining" Scrapbook, HP.

10. W. C. Petchner to J. W. Park, Aug. 28, 1912, and W. H. Stuart to Haynes, Aug. 25, 1912, box 41, HP; Frank E. Parsons, *The City for the People* (Philadelphia: C. F. Taylor, 1899), 313, 373, 386.

11. Haynes, "Introduction of the Initiative."

12. *Herald*, Sept. 2, 1900, *Evening Express*, Sept. 29, 1900; *Times*, Oct. 2, 1900.

13. *Times*, Sept. 1, 25, 1900; *Evening Express*, Oct. 2, 5, 9, 16, 22, 1900.

14. *Evening Express*, Feb. 5, 1901; *Herald*, June 9, 1901; Haynes, "Direct Legislation as Applied to Los Angeles," *Saturday Post*, Oct. 13, 1900, 11–12; Haynes, speech to the Second National Social and Political Conference, 1901; *Direct Legislation Record*, 7 (Sept. 1901): 43–45; Haynes to Henry Demarest Lloyd, Apr. 17, 1902, and Lloyd to Haynes, Sept. 7, 1902, box 12, Henry Demarest Lloyd Papers, SHSWA.

15. Janice Jacques, "The Political Reform Movement in Los Angeles, 1900–1909" (M.A. thesis, Claremont Graduate School, 1948), 17–18; Haynes, "Introduction of the Initiative."

16. Haynes, "Introduction of the Initiative."

17. Ibid.; *Times*, Apr. 4, 1902.

18. "Municipal Notes," *Direct Legislation Record*, 8 (Sept. 1902): 46–47; Haynes, "Introduction of the Initiative."

19. Eltweed Pomeroy, "How Los Angeles Got Direct Legislation," *Wilshire's Monthly*, 5 (Apr. 1903): 12–15; Jacques, "Political Reform," 20; *Los Angeles Socialist*, Nov. 22, 29, 1902.

20. C. D. Willard to Haynes, June 9, 1902, "Personal 2" Scrapbook, HP; *Times*, July 10, Sept. 30, Nov. 16, 23, 1902; Haynes's autobiography notes, HF; Jacques, "Political Reform," 21–23. Haynes thought the "nameless attorney" was assistant city attorney Herbert J. Goudge.

21. "Direct Legislation in the Los Angeles City Charter," leaflet (Municipal League of Los Angeles, 1902), box 43, and Haynes, "Introduction of the Initiative," HP.

22. *Direct Legislation Record*, 9 (Mar. 1903): 6–9.

23. *Herald*, Jan. 24, 1903; "The Final Passing of the Los Angeles Charter," *Direct Legislation Record*, 9 (Mar. 1903): 9–10; California, Legislature, Assembly, *Journal of the Assembly*, 35th sess. (Sacramento, 1903), 193, 233; California, Legislature, Senate, *Journal of the Senate During the 35th Session of the Legislature of the State of California* (Sacramento, 1903), 174.

24. *Direct Legislation Record*, 8 (Sept. 1902): 42; H. Gaylord Wilshire, "Dr. John R. Haynes," *Direct Legislation Record*, 8 (Dec. 1902): 74–75; Benjamin O. Flower, *Progressive Men, Women, and Movements of the Past Twenty-five Years* (Boston: The New Arena, 1914), 68–69. This Direct Legislation League was one of several in Los Angeles and the one that existed until Haynes's death, in the 1930s.

25. Haynes to Frederick H. Rindge, Oct. 10, 1902, Haynes to National American Woman Suffrage Association, June 13, 1905, Haynes to California labor unions, Jan. 28, 1905, and to California ministers, Dec. 30, 1904, box 50, HP.

26. Copy of petition for initiative and referendum constitutional amendments, and letters from state office candidates (1902), box 35, HP; *Herald*, Dec. 5, 1902; *Express*, Sept. 3, 1902; Thomas Gibbon to Haynes, Sept. 11, 1902, Thomas E. Gibbon Papers, Huntington.

27. *Express*, Feb. 27, 1903; Haynes correspondence with Guy Lathrop, 1902–3, box 35, P. B. Prebble to Haynes, Feb. 10, 1903, and Haynes to E. W. Camp, n.d. (1903), box 41, HP.

28. Haynes's account ledger (1892–1901), HF.

29. James T. Van Rensselaer to Caroline Severance, Feb. 19, 1904, et al., box 24, Nelson O. Nelson letters to Severance, box 21, Benjamin O. Flower to Severance, May 1, 1905, Bertha Wilkins to Severance, Apr. 18, 1904, box 34, and other letters in the Caroline Severance Papers, Huntington.

30. David A. Shannon, *The Socialist Party of America: A History* (New York: Macmillan, 1955), 57–58; Gustuvus Myers, "Our Millionaire Socialists," *Cosmopolitan*, 41 (Oct. 1906): 596–605; Kevin Starr, *Inventing the Dream: California Through the Progressive Era* (New York: Oxford University Press, 1985), 218.

31. *Graphic*, 20 (July 30, 1904): 2; Nelson O. Nelson to Caroline Severance, October 24, 1904, box 21, Caroline Severance Papers, Huntington; "Kid Glove Socialists," editorial, *Times*, July 6, 1903.

32. John R. Haynes, speech to X Club, 1915, "Articles, Speeches" Scrapbook, HP.

33. Ralph Hancock, *Fabulous Boulevard* (New York: Funk and Wagnalls, 1949), 94–104; Haynes to Gaylord Wilshire, Sept. 27, 1902, box 1, H. Gaylord Wilshire Papers, UCLA; Haynes to Mrs. George L. Cole, Sept. 5, 1935, HF; H. G. Otis to U.S. Consul General in London, June 15, 1899, Autograph Book, HP; biographical note (probably by George L. Cole), "Travel 1" Scrapbook, Walter Lindley Collection, Honnold.

34. Haynes to Margaret Sanger, Oct. 8, 1931, box 8, and card of Hotel Cecil, Autograph Book, HP; Haynes's autobiography notes on 1903 trip to Europe, HF. For a discussion of the larger "transatlantic connection" concept see James T. Kloppenberg, *Uncertain Victory: Social Democracy and Progressivism in European and American Thought, 1870–1920* (New York: Oxford University Press, 1986).

35. Haynes to J. Ramsay MacDonald, July 19, 1929, HF; Haynes to Mrs.

Beatrice Webb, Oct. 12, 1934, box 66, HP; *Herald*, Oct. 7, 1903; *Times*, Oct. 7, 1903.

36. *Los Angeles Socialist*, July 2, 1904; *Common Sense*, Dec. 16, 1905; *Express*, Oct. 22, 1902; Grace H. Stimson, *Rise of the Labor Movement in Los Angeles* (Berkeley: University of California Press, 1955), 223–24, 281–82.

37. File 3976, Los Angeles County Articles of Incorporation, Seaver; *Los Angeles Socialist*, Dec. 6, 1902; James Truslow Adams, ed., *Dictionary of American History*, 2nd rev. ed., 5 vols. (New York: Scribners, 1940), 2: 56; Walter J. Thompson to Haynes, Apr. 25, 1902, "Personal 2" Scrapbook, HP.

38. Wilshire, "John R. Haynes," 74; Walter Lindley to Hervey Lindley, Aug. 23, 1902, box 41, HP; *Capital*, 16 (Sept. 20, 1902): 4, and (Oct. 4, 1902): 4; *Times*, Aug. 30, 1900; *Record*, Feb. 2, 1903.

39. *Saturday Post*, Oct. 13, 1900, clipping in "Personal 2" Scrapbook, HP; *Times*, Apr. 28, 1903; Donald Ray Culton, "Charles Dwight Willard: Los Angeles City Booster and Progressive Reformer, 1888–1914" (Ph.D. diss., University of Southern California, 1971), 194–98, 243–52.

40. *Herald*, Jan. 25, 1903; *Express*, Apr. 11, 1903; M. P. Snyder to Haynes, Dec. 8, 1904, box 53, Collection 100, UCLA.

41. Stimson, *Rise of the Labor Movement*, 282; Charles Dwight Willard, "A Political Experiment," *Outlook*, 78 (Oct. 22, 1904): 472–75; Eltweed Pomeroy, "The First Discharge of a Public Servant," *Independent*, 58 (Jan. 12, 1905): 69–71.

42. *Express*, June 18, 1904; *Daily Journal*, May 5, 1903; Fred W. Viehe, "The First Recall: Los Angeles Urban Reform or Machine Politics?," *Southern California Quarterly*, 70 (Spring 1988): 3–9; Richard Henry Norton, *Reminiscences of an Agitator* (Los Angeles: Glass Book Binding, 1912), 14–38.

43. John R. Haynes, "The Recall of Councilman Davenport," speech, "Recall" Scrapbook, HP; Stimson, *Rise of the Labor Movement*, 282–85; Culton, "Willard," 238–41; Viehe, "First Recall," 16–19; Norton, *Reminiscences*, 29–30; *Times*, July–Sept. 1904.

44. Davenport vs. City of Los Angeles, 146 Cal. 508 (1905); *Times*, Apr. 6, 1905.

45. Stimson, *Rise of the Labor Movement*, 285–86.

46. Haynes's autobiography notes, Haynes to Otis, July 4, 1898, box 147, and Otis to Haynes, Dec. 7, 1901, Autograph Book, HP; *Times*, July 14, 1900, July 6, 1903.

CHAPTER FIVE

1. Frank Parsons, "Municipal Ownership" and "Public Ownership," in W. D. P. Bliss, ed., *New Encyclopedia of Social Reform* (New York: Funk and Wagnalls, 1908), 788–95, 1001–10.

2. *Evening Express*, Feb. 19, May 8, 1897; *Times*, Aug. 19, 1899, May 2, 1900; Robert M. Fogelson, *The Fragmented Metropolis: Los Angeles, 1850–1930* (Cambridge, Mass.: Harvard University Press, 1967), 229–30.

3. Files 547, 5562, box A-7, and City Council Minutes, 67: 302 (Apr. 27, 1903), Los Angeles City Records Center.

4. John R. Haynes, "Plea for Municipal Ownership," *Graphic*, 21 (Dec. 3, 1904): 15; *Express*, Dec. 20, 1904; *Times*, Dec. 6, 1904.

5. *Times*, Mar. 28, 1905, Jan. 27, 1907; *Examiner*, Mar. 19, 1905; George M. Wallace, *Joseph Francis Sartori, 1858–1946* (Los Angeles: Ward Ritchie, 1948), 78–79; City Gas Company brochure (1907), box 173, HP; William W. Clary, *History of the Law Firm of O'Melveny and Myers, 1885–1965*, 2 vols. (Los Angeles: privately printed, 1966), 1: 284–85.

6. Abraham Hoffman, *Vision or Villainy: Origins of the Owens Valley–Los Angeles Water Controversy* (College Station: Texas A & M University Press, 1981), 91–98, 125–28; Haynes's autobiography notes regarding Harrison Gray Otis, box 147, HP.

7. *Examiner*, Sept. 17, 1905; Nelson S. Van Valen, "Power Politics: The Struggle for Municipal Ownership of Electrical Utilities in Los Angeles, 1905–1937" (Ph.D. diss., Claremont Graduate School, 1963), 24–29.

8. *Examiner*, Mar.–July 1905. Examples of the *Times's* editorial abuse of Hearst can be found in almost every issue in this year.

9. *Examiner*, May 21, Nov. 2, Dec. 28, 1905, Mar. 18, Nov. 28, 1906; clippings concerning William Randolph Hearst in box 190, HP. See discussion of streetcar fenders below.

10. Henry E. Huntington to H. G. Otis, May 7, 1904, document HM7849, Henry E. Huntington Papers, Huntington; Grace H. Stimson, *Rise of the Labor Movement in Los Angeles* (Berkeley: University of California Press, 1955), 258–59, 266–69, 299–306; Richard C. Miller, "Otis and His *Times*: The Career of Harrison Gray Otis of Los Angeles" (Ph.D. diss., University of California, Berkeley, 1961), 224–45.

11. Stimson, *Rise of the Labor Movement*, 306–8; *Fresno Evening Democrat*, Feb. 22, 1906, clipping in box 177, HP; *Times*, Feb. 23, 1906; Ralph Edward Shaffer, "A History of the Socialist Party of California" (M.A. thesis, University of California, Los Angeles, 1951), 65–66.

12. Publicity flier (Public Ownership party?, 1906), box 171, HP; *Examiner*, Dec. 3, 1906; John R. Haynes, "'Some Arguments Against Municipal Ownership' Refuted," *Graphic*, 24 (June 23, 1906): 9–10, 12–14.

13. Haynes's autobiography notes, HF; *Common Sense*, July 8, Sept. 30, Dec. 16, 1905, June 30, 1906, Feb. 6, 1909; *Times*, Oct. 13, 1905; *Southern California Practitioner*, 20 (Feb. 1905): 75; *Examiner*, Jan. 9, 1905; J. A. Wayland to Haynes, Oct. 17, 1905, "Personal 2" Scrapbook, HP; *Graphic*, Jan. 14, 1906, clipping in box 516, Jack London Papers, Huntington.

14. *Scientific American* contains descriptions and illustrations of numerous streetcar fenders in issues throughout the 1890s and early 1900s. For more details on the following fender controversy see Tom Sitton, "The Los Angeles Fender Fight in the Early 1900s," *Southern California Quarterly*, 72 (Summer 1990): 139–56.

15. John R. Stilgoe, *Metropolitan Corridor: Railroads and the American Scene* (New Haven, Conn.: Yale University Press, 1983), 167–88; John P. Fox, "The Needless Slaughter by Street-Cars," *Everybody's Magazine*, 16 (Mar. 1907): 344–52.

16. Newspaper clippings, esp. from the *San Francisco Examiner* and *San Francisco Call*, 1897–1900, in vols. 34–40, Huntington Scrapbooks 7/1, Huntington; *Herald*, Sept. 5, 1895; *Evening Express*, June 16, Aug. 21, 28, 1899; *Times*, Feb.

8, 1900; *Statutes of California and Amendments to the Codes* (Sacramento, 1899), 183.

17. *Times*, Mar. 11, 1905; *Herald*, Mar. 10, 1905; report of committee to investigate streetcar operations to Board of Directors of Municipal League of Los Angeles, Mar. 28, 1905, Fenders file, HF.

18. *Times*, Mar. 2, 1905; *Graphic*, Feb. 25, 1905, clipping in "Personal 2" Scrapbook, HP; Haynes to William H. Davis, Mar. 10, 1906, box 44, and completed fender questionnaire, box 67, HP; "The Fender Fight," typescript (1926), Fenders file, HF.

19. Voters' League pamphlets and correspondence in box 220, HP; *Common Sense*, Sept. 23, 1905; John R. Haynes, "The Electric Juggernaut," *Pacific Outlook*, 3 (Sept. 21, 1907): 10; John R. Haynes, "The Actual Workings of the Initiative, Referendum and Recall," *National Municipal Review*, 1 (Oct. 1912): 586–602.

20. *Record*, Aug. 26, Sept. 21, Nov. 1, 1905; *Examiner* articles, esp. May–Sept. 1905, in vol. 3, Huntington Scrapbooks 7/2, Huntington; copy of petition in Fenders file, HF.

21. *Examiner*, Sept. 17, 1905; *Graphic*, 23 (Sept. 25, 1905): 7–9. Haynes gave his University Club speech on September 14.

22. *Examiner*, Jan. 5, 16, 1906; Voters' League petition to city council, Jan. 8, 1906, City Council Minutes, 71: 550, Los Angeles City Records Center.

23. William E. Dunn to Haynes, Jan. 18, 1906, Fenders file, HF; *Times*, Mar. 22, 1906; *Express*, May 8, Sept. 24, 1906.

24. *Times*, June 3, 4, Dec. 3, 1905; *Common Sense*, Dec. 30, 1905, Jan. 13, 1906; *Examiner*, Oct. 30, 1905; "Gothenburg System," pamphlet (c. 1905), "Personal 2" Scrapbook, HP; William Mead to Thomas Gibbon, Jan. 20, 1906, Thomas E. Gibbon Papers, Huntington.

25. *Union Labor News*, Apr. 6, 1906; Frederick L. Bird and Frances M. Ryan, *The Recall of Public Officers: A Study of the Operation of the Recall in California* (New York: Macmillan, 1903), 231–34; *Times*, Aug. 25, Oct. 8, 13, 14, 19, Nov. 10, 1905, Jan. 27, Feb. 2, June 16, 1906; *Common Sense*, Oct. 21, 1905.

26. *Examiner*, Dec. 8, Jan. 25, 1904; letters to Haynes from legislative candidates (1904), boxes 43 and 50, E. S. Chapman to Haynes, Aug. 22, 1904, box 43, letters from Haynes to unions, Jan. 21, 1905, and to ministers, Dec. 30, 1904, box 50, Cornelius W. Pendleton to Haynes, Jan. 11, 1905, "Constitutional Direct Legislation and Direct Legislation in Southern California" Scrapbook, HP.

27. Ex Parte Pfahler, 88 Pac Rep 270 (1906).

28. *Express*, Oct. 15, 1906; *Examiner*, Oct. 14, 1906; Haynes's autobiography notes on the initiative, box 44, HP.

29. *Graphic*, 20 (July 30, 1904): 2; *Los Angeles City Directory* (1904, 1905); *The Sunset Club of Los Angeles* (Los Angeles: Sunset Club, 1916), 2:41, 43, photographs; John R. Haynes, "Direct Legislation for State Purposes," *Transactions of the Commonwealth Club of California*, 1 (Jan. 1905): 29–31.

30. U.S. State Department pass, June 7, 1899, HF; "Great Register of Los Angeles County" (1902), Seaver. Biographical accounts at this time include *Graphic*, 20 (July 30, 1904): 2–3; *Conservative News*, 2 (July 1905): 1; *Examiner*, Nov. 2, 1905; *Herald*, Nov. 26, 1905.

31. "History of Dr. John R. Haynes," typescript (c. Jan. 1908), HF; Haynes to H. D. Lloyd, Apr. 17, 1902, box 12, Henry Demarest Lloyd Papers, SHSWA.

32. Haynes's autobiography notes, "The San Francisco Earthquake," HF; *Examiner*, Apr. 26, 1906.

33. Haynes's autobiography notes, "The San Francisco Earthquake," Haynes to Lord Russell, July 13, 1923, HF.

34. *Express*, Apr. 29, 1906; John Castillo Kennedy, *The Great Earthquake and Fire: San Francisco, 1906* (New York: William Morrow, 1963), 217–18.

35. *Express*, May 12, 1906; *Southern California Practitioner*, 21 (May 1906): 249.

36. Ella Giles Ruddy, ed., *The Mother of Clubs: Caroline M. Seymour Severance* (Los Angeles: Baumgardt, 1906), esp. 180–81; minutes of meetings of the Severance Club (1906–40), box 6, Theodore P. Gerson Papers, UCLA; Harold Story, "Memoirs of Harold Story," 2 vols. (University of California, Los Angeles, Oral History Program, 1967), 1: 495–96.

37. *Evening News*, July 4, 1906; *Examiner*, Oct. 17, 1906.

38. Haynes to Dora Haynes, telegram, Aug. 28, 1906, "Personal 3" Scrapbook, HP; Haynes's autobiography notes, "A Trip to Russia During the Revolution of 1906," HF.

CHAPTER SIX

1. *Times*, July 3, 1906; George Mowry, *The California Progressives* (Berkeley: University of California Press, 1951), 41–42.

2. *Evening News*, July 3, 1906; *Times*, Nov. 17, 1906; Albert Howard Clodius, "The Quest for Good Government in Los Angeles" (Ph.D. diss., Claremont Graduate School, 1953), 125–27; Walton Bean, *Boss Ruef's San Francisco* (Berkeley: University of California Press, 1952), 67–163.

3. George Baker Anderson, "What the Cranks Have Done," *Pacific Outlook*, 2 (May 25, 1907): 8–12; Marshall Stimson, *Fun, Fights, and Fiestas in Old Los Angeles* (Los Angeles: privately printed, 1966), 318; Martin J. Schiesl, "Progressive Reform in Los Angeles Under Mayor Alexander, 1909–1913," *California Historical Quarterly*, 54 (Spring 1975): 42–44; Martin J. Schiesl, *The Politics of Efficiency: Municipal Administration and Reform in America, 1880–1920* (Berkeley: University of California Press, 1977), 88–110.

4. Russ Avery to Edward Dickson, Mar. 15, 1906, box 1, Edward A. Dickson Papers, UCLA; *Graphic*, Sept. 1, 1906, clipping in vol. 2, Scrapbook 235635, Huntington; Clodius, "Quest for Good Government," 125–26. "Federal 'bunch'" refers to the political circle of U.S. Marshall Leo Youngworth.

5. *Graphic*, 25 (Sept. 1, 1906): 3–5; *Times*, July 8, 1912; *Record*, Nov. 8, 1905; *Examiner*, June 14, 1904, Aug. 21, 1906; *Common Sense*, June 3, 1905; Robert J. Burdette, ed., *American Biography and Genealogy, California Edition*, 2 vols. (New York: Lewis, 1915), 2: 1060–62.

6. *Herald*, Nov. 1, 1906; Moses Sherman to Warren Porter, Mar. 16, 1907, et al., Book 3, Moses Sherman Papers, Sherman Library, Corona del Mar, Calif. See Chapter 7 below for more discussion of the Southern Pacific in state politics and in other California cities.

7. *Times*, Mar. 25, 1902, Mar. 23, Oct. 24, 1906; *Express*, Oct. 25, 1905, Nov. 1, 1906; *Examiner*, Feb. 4, 1906.

8. Mowry, *California Progressives*, 1–22. For an interpretation of reformers as a component of the machine, see Frederick W. Viehe III, "The Los Angeles Progressives: The Influence of the Southern Pacific Machine on Urban Politics, 1872–1913" (Ph.D. diss., University of California, Santa Barbara, 1983).

9. C. D. Willard to Haynes, July 23, 1906, HF; Haynes to William H. Davis, Mar. 10, 1906, box 44, HP.

10. *Record*, Aug. 4, 1906; *Herald*, Nov. 18, 1906; *Express*, Nov. 1, 1906; *Examiner*, Oct. 19, 1906; Clodius, "Quest for Good Government," 130–34.

11. *Union Labor News*, Jan. 26, 1906; *Examiner*, Sept. 29, Nov. 3, 1906; *Times*, Sept. 29, 1906; *Graphic*, Feb. 3, 1906, clipping in "Personal 2" Scrapbook, HP; *Herald*, Oct. 28, 1906; *Common Sense*, Sept. 15, Nov. 24, 1906; Clodius, "Quest for Good Government," 133–34.

12. *Graphic*, 25 (Nov. 29, 1906): 10, 12–13; *Times*, Feb. 2, 1906, et al.; *Express*, Sept. 19, 1908; *Herald*, Oct. 20, 1906; *Union Labor News*, Sept. 28, Nov. 9, 1906; Clodius, "Quest for Good Government," 144–49.

13. *Times*, Nov. 30, 1906; *Record*, Oct. 27, 1906; *Express*, Nov. 29, 1906; Alexander MacKeigan to Major Truman Cole, Dec. 6, 1906, "Political 6" Scrapbook, Walter Lindley Collection, Honnold; interview with Francis Haynes Lindley, Oct. 1, 1986, Los Angeles, Calif.

14. *Times*, Oct. 24, Dec. 3–5, 1906; *Examiner*, Dec. 16, 1906; Clodius, "Quest for Good Government," 140–53; Harry Chandler to Henry E. Huntington, Dec. 22, 1906, document HM11574, Henry E. Huntington Papers, Huntington.

15. *Southern California Practitioner*, 21 (Jan. 1906): 48, 22 (Feb. 1907): 64, 22 (Apr. 1907): 236, 23 (Feb. 1908): 65, 24 (Mar. 1909): 146, 26 (Aug. 1911): 413; Helen Eastman Martin, M.D., *The History of the Los Angeles County Hospital (1878–1968) and the Los Angeles County–University of Southern California Medical Center (1968–1978)* (Los Angeles: University of Southern California Press, 1979), 280.

16. *Evening News*, Dec. 27, 1907; *Express*, Dec. 30, 1907, Jan. 21, 1908; Clarence Darrow, *The Story of My Life* (New York: Scribner's, 1932), 164–71. Haynes again loaned money to Darrow while the latter defended the McNamara brothers in Los Angeles in 1911. The lawyer did not repay the loan until a decade later. Darrow to Haynes, Nov. 19, 1924, HF.

17. Haynes's autobiography notes, Haynes to Maysie Miller, Oct. 24, 1934, and Haynes to T. M. Althausen, June 25, 1930, HF.

18. *Express*, Oct. 4, 1906; *Record*, Oct. 5, 1906; *Times*, Dec. 16, 1906, Apr. 18, 1907; *Examiner*, Feb. 2, Apr. 10, 17, May 2, 1907.

19. Copy of J. W. Range's statement, June 15, 1907, box 68, HP; *Examiner*, May 25, June 7, 16, 1907; *Times*, June 4, 1907.

20. *Evening News*, July 16, 1907; *Examiner*, July 14, 1907; *Record*, Aug. 21, 1907; *Times*, Aug. 22, 1907. Police courts have since been consolidated into municipal courts in Los Angeles County.

21. *Times*, Sept. 1, 1907; *Examiner*, Sept. 15, 1907; John R. Haynes, "The Electric Juggernaut," *Pacific Outlook*, 3 (Sept. 21, 1907): 10–11.

22. *Examiner*, Sept. 15, 1907.

23. *Times*, Nov. 14, 15, 1907; *Examiner*, Nov. 17, 1907; *Record*, Nov. 15, 1907; Haynes to Dr. Norman Bridge, Jan. 22, 1906, HF.

24. W. H. Douglas to Haynes, Dec. 12, 1907, Fenders file, HF; *Examiner*, Dec. 4, 1907; *Times*, Dec. 11, 1907.

25. *Express*, Jan. 4, 1908; *Examiner*, Jan. 20, 1908; *Herald*, July 17, 1908; *Times*, Sept. 8, 1908; Joseph McMillan to Haynes, June 24, 1908, "Personal 2" Scrapbook, HP; "The Fender Fight," typescript (1926), Fenders file, HF.

26. *Express*, Dec. 21, 1906; *Times*, January 6, 1907; John R. Haynes, "The Public Is Sophisticated," *Pacific Outlook*, 1 (Dec. 29, 1906): 8–9.

27. *Express*, Aug. 28, 1907; clippings in box 18, HP; John R. Haynes, "The Actual Workings of the Initiative, Referendum and Recall," *National Municipal Review*, 1 (Oct. 1912): 586–94.

28. Gaylord Wilshire to Keir Hardie, June 19, 1906, and Faith Chevallier to Haynes, Aug. 18, 1908, HF; Eugene V. Debs to Haynes, Aug. 3, 1908, box 190, and unsigned letters to Haynes, Mar. 16, 1909, box 188, HP; *Common Sense*, Nov. 10, 1906 (supplement), Feb. 6, 1909.

29. *Times*, Jan. 9, 27, Feb. 17, Mar. 30, 1907, Jan. 18, Mar. 3, 17, Apr. 12, 1908, Jan. 31, 1909; *Express*, Jan. 26, 1907; *Record*, Apr. 2, 1907; *San Francisco Chronicle*, Apr. 2, 1907.

30. Haynes to Francis Heney, July 3, 1907, "Pointers" statement, box 147, and Haynes to Lincoln Steffens, July 10, 1907, box 193, HP; *Times*, July 2, 1907.

31. Caroline Severance to Haynes, Dec. 4, 1907, Autograph Book, HP; *Times*, Nov. 14, 1907.

32. *Graphic*, Mar. 7, 1908, clipping in "Personal 2" Scrapbook, HP; *Times*, Mar. 3, 17, 27, 1908.

33. *Times*, Apr. 12, 1906; *Express*, Mar. 29, 1908; Senator Frank P. Flint to Haynes, Mar. 20, 1908, Senator George C. Perkins to Haynes, Mar. 20, 1908, et al., box 53, Collection 100, UCLA.

34. *Record*, Oct. 18, 1906; *Times*, Dec. 8, 1907; affidavit of Charles Kiener, Sept. 11, 1907, and H. L. Adams to Haynes, Feb. 17, 1908, HF.

35. *Times*, Feb. 12, 19, 23, 1908; *Herald*, *Examiner*, and *Evening News*, Feb. 19, 1908; *Express*, Feb. 12, 19, 1908; *Graphic*, Feb. 27, 1908, and *Pacific Outlook*, Feb. 22, 1908, clippings in "Personal 2" Scrapbook, HP.

36. *Democracy—Civil Service News*, May 9, 1908, clipping in box 27, HP; *Times*, Feb. 17, Dec. 16, 1909; *Express*, Feb. 24, 1909; *Herald*, Feb. 17, 1909.

37. John R. Haynes, "Speech at Elysian Park," typescript, May 1908, box 132, HP.

38. C. D. Willard to Mary Frances Willard, Dec. 13, 1906, box 11, Charles D. Willard Papers, Huntington.

39. *Express*, Jan. 24, 26, 1907; Lincoln Steffens, *The Autobiography of Lincoln Steffens* (New York: Literary Guild, 1931), 570–74.

40. City Club brochures, boxes 26 and 110, HP; Stimson, *Fun, Fights, and Fiestas*, 168.

41. *Herald*, Sept. 30, 1907; *Examiner*, Aug. 17, 1907, Feb. 26, 1908; Robert M. Fogelson, *The Fragmented Metropolis: Los Angeles, 1850–1930* (Cambridge, Mass.: Harvard University Press, 1967), 213.

42. *Saturday Post*, Oct. 13, 1900; *Herald*, Mar. 8, 1908; *Examiner*, Mar 11,

1908; Grace H. Stimson, *Rise of the Labor Movement in Los Angeles* (Berkeley: University of California Press, 1955), 323.

43. *Express*, July 14, 1908; *Times*, Feb. 4, 1909; *Examiner*, Jan. 30, 1909; *Herald*, Jan. 1, 1909; petition with proposed charter changes, Aug. 14, 1908, box 102, HP; Clodius, "Quest for Good Government," 394–99.

44. *Times*, Dec. 5, 1906, Aug. 30, 1908, Feb. 11, 1909, Nov. 20, 1917; *Express*, Oct. 7, 1908; *Examiner*, Oct. 7, 1908; clippings in "Direct Legislation in Los Angeles and How It Works" Scrapbook, HP.

45. C. D. Willard, "The Recall in Los Angeles," *La Follette's*, 31 (Aug. 7, 1909), 7–9, 15.

46. *Herald*, Jan. 7–Mar. 5, 27, 1909; Clodius, "Quest for Good Government," 158–67.

47. Meyer Lissner to Edward A. Dickson, Jan. 7, 1909, box 2, Meyer Lissner Papers, Stanford; *Times*, Jan. 8, 18, 1909; *Herald*, Jan. 21, 1909; Willard, "Recall in Los Angeles," 7–9.

48. *Times*, Feb. 6, 1909; *Herald*, Mar. 27, 1909.

49. *Times*, Jan. 31, Feb. 13, Mar. 7, 1909; *Record*, Feb. 18, Mar. 20, 1909; *Examiner*, Mar. 12, 1909; Stimson, *Rise of the Labor Movement*, 325; Joseph Gerald Woods, "The Progressives and the Police: Urban Reform and the Professionalization of the Los Angeles Police" (Ph.D. diss., University of California, Los Angeles, 1973), 34. The dilemma of reformers afraid to make a mistake by working with labor as they had in the 1904 Davenport recall is pointed out in Fred W. Viehe, "The First Recall: Los Angeles Urban Reform or Machine Politics?," *Southern California Quarterly*, 70 (Spring 1988): 21–22.

50. *Examiner*, Mar. 12, 15, 1909; E. T. Earl to Francis Heney, Mar. 25, 1909, box 1, Francis Heney Papers, Bancroft; Reynold Blight, "The Recall of the Mayor of Los Angeles," *Independent*, 66 (Apr. 22, 1909): 861–63. The *Record* also claimed credit for Harper's resignation in its story of March 12, 1909.

51. *Record*, Mar. 25, 1909; *Herald*, Mar. 25, 1909; *Times*, Mar. 27, 1909; *Common Sense*, Mar. 13, 27, 1909.

52. Draft of Haynes to George Baker Anderson, 1908 (not sent), HF.

CHAPTER SEVEN

1. George Mowry, *The California Progressives* (Berkeley: University of California Press, 1951), 9–12, 17–18; W. H. Hutchinson, "Southern Pacific: Myth and Reality," *California Historical Society Quarterly*, 48 (Dec. 1969): 325–34.

2. Mowry, *California Progressives*, 12–17; Stuart Daggett, *Chapters on the History of the Southern Pacific*, 2nd ed. (New York: Augustus M. Kelley, 1966), 154–68, 199–221, 395–424; William F. Deverell, "Building an Octopus: Railroads and Society in the Late Nineteenth Century Far West" (Ph.D. diss., Princeton University, 1989), 266–308; Ward McAfee, *California's Railroad Era, 1850–1911* (San Marino, Calif.: Golden West Books, 1973) 133–79, 211–25.

3. Hutchinson, "Southern Pacific," 325–34; Royce D. Delmatier, Clarence F. McIntosh, and Earl G. Waters, eds., *The Rumble of California Politics, 1848–1970* (New York: John Wiley, 1970), 125–64; letters and telegrams from Parker to Governor George Pardee, 1903–5, box 93, George C. Pardee Correspondence and Papers, Bancroft.

4. *Times*, Jan. 10, 1905, Jan. 8, Mar. 15, 1907; Mowry, *California Progressives*, 57–65; telegrams from Parker to Philip Stanton, 1907–9, box 1, Philip A. Stanton Papers, Huntington; newspaper clippings on 1906 election in box 55, HP.

5. Spencer C. Olin, Jr., *California's Prodigal Sons: Hiram Johnson and the Progressives, 1911–1917* (Berkeley: University of California Press, 1968), 2–3; Mowry, *California Progressives*, 89.

6. John R. Haynes, "Birth of Democracy in California," typescript, box 34, J. A. Muir to W. F. Parker, Aug. 24, 1902, box 41, and Haynes to Frank P. Flint, Apr. 29, 1910, box 152, HP.

7. Haynes to William H. Davis, Mar. 10, 1906, box 44, HP.

8. Haynes to E. W. Camp, n.d., box 41, HP; Allan A. MacRae, "The Rise of the Progressive Movement in the State of California" (M.A. thesis, Occidental College, 1923), 15–16.

9. MacRae, "Rise of the Progressive Movement," 16–18 (quote based on Haynes interview in 1922); Haynes to Davis, Mar. 10, 1906, box 44, HP.

10. MacRae, "Rise of the Progressive Movement," 18–20.

11. Haynes to George C. Pardee, Oct. 15, 1906, box 70, George C. Pardee Correspondence and Papers, Bancroft.

12. For an example of the anti-SP protest see W. H. Hutchinson, "Prologue to Reform: The California Anti-Railroad Republicans, 1899–1905," *Southern California Historical Quarterly*, 44 (Sept. 1962): 175–83. On the 1906 Santa Cruz convention see, among others, Delmatier, McIntosh and Waters, *Rumble of California Politics*, 146–49.

13. J. Gregg Lane, "The Lincoln-Roosevelt League: Its Origin and Accomplishments," *Quarterly of the Historical Society of Southern California*, 25 (Sept. 1943): 79–91; Mowry, *California Progressives*, 57–72.

14. Lane, "Lincoln-Roosevelt League," 87–89; Alice Rose, "Rise of the California Insurgency" (Ph.D. diss., Stanford University, 1942), 399–400.

15. Haynes to Meyer Lissner, Feb. 8, 1908, box 17, and Lissner to Haynes, Feb. 3, 1908, box 1, Meyer Lissner Papers, Stanford. Lane, "Lincoln-Roosevelt League," 89, believes Haynes attended the August 1 meeting, but Haynes was not listed in newspaper reports of the *Express, Sacramento Bee, Sacramento Union,* or *Stockton Record*, all reform papers with major stories on this event. See also Marshall Stimson, *Fun, Fights, and Fiestas in Old Los Angeles* (Los Angeles: privately printed, 1966), 163.

16. Haynes to Lissner, Dec. 21, 1908, box 17, and Lissner to Haynes, Dec. 21, 28, 1908, box 1, Meyer Lissner Papers, Stanford; Mowry, *California Progressives*, 73–80.

17. Haynes to Milton T. U'Ren, Dec. 23, 1908, U'Ren to Haynes, Feb. 18, Mar. 18, 1909, and Isadore Jacobs to Haynes, Dec. 9, 1908, box 42, HP.

18. Direct Legislation file, box 36, Meyer Lissner Papers, Stanford; Mowry, *California Progressives*, 80–83; typescript of interview with George Baker Anderson, Sept. 8, 1938, box 38, Alice M. Rose Papers, Stanford; Franklin Hichborn, *Story of the Session of the California Legislature of 1909* (San Francisco: James H. Barry, 1909), esp. 68–112; Eric Falk Petersen, "The Adoption of the Direct Primary," *Southern California Quarterly*, 54 (Winter 1972): 363–78.

19. Mowry, *California Progressives*, 105–34; M. Stimson, *Fun, Fights, and Fiestas*, 176–77.

20. Haynes to Hiram Johnson, Mar. 31, May 4, 1910, box 7, and Johnson to Haynes, Apr. 21, 1910, Part 1, box 1, Hiram W. Johnson Papers, Bancroft; John R. Haynes, "Social Conditions in Europe," *Pacific Outlook*, 9 (Nov. 26, 1910): 5.

21. Olin, *California's Prodigal Sons*, 36–55; Mowry, *California Progressives*, 135–47; Franklin Hichborn, *Story of the Session of the California Legislature of 1911* (San Francisco: James H. Barry, 1911), 11–344.

22. Miscellaneous documents in box 2, Alice M. Rose Papers, Stanford; Haynes's autobiography notes, box 44, drafts of direct-legislation proposals, box 36, HP; *Sacramento Bee*, Aug. 14, 1941.

23. Milton U'Ren to Haynes, Sept. 18, 19, 1911, et al., box 42, and Haynes to Hiram Johnson, Aug. 18, 1911, box 41, newspaper clippings in box 36 and in "Constitutional Direct Legislation" Scrapbook and "Direct Legislation in Southern California" Scrapbook, HP; V. O. Key and Winston W. Crouch, *The Initiative and Referendum in California* (Berkeley: University of California Press, 1939), 434–44; *Times*, Aug. 27, 1911; *California Outlook*, 11 (Sept. 9, 1911): 1; *San Bernardino News*, Oct. 6, 1911.

24. *Tribune*, July 9, 1911; Haynes to William P. Owens (1911), box 41, HP.

25. Mowry, *California Progressives*, 149; George Creel, "What About Hiram Johnson," *Everybody's Magazine*, 31 (Oct. 1914): 459.

26. Haynes to National American Woman Suffrage Association, June 13, 1905, box 50, HP; *Capital*, 12 (Dec. 15, 1900): 7; *Herald*, Apr. 4, 1909.

27. Mary M. Keith to Hiram Johnson, May 29, 1911, Part 2, box 42, Hiram W. Johnson Papers, Bancroft; Ida Husted Harper, ed., *History of Woman Suffrage*, 6 vols., reprint of 1922 edition (New York: Source Book Press, 1970), 6: 27–41; John Hyde Braly, *Memory Pictures: An Autobiography* (Los Angeles: Neuner, 1912), 223–36; *Herald*, Apr. 6, 1910.

28. Braly, *Memory Pictures*, 252; Harper, *History of Woman Suffrage*, 6: 41–42.

29. *Herald*, Oct. 11, 1910, Dec. 28, 1911; *Tribune*, Sept. 8, 1911; *Express*, Sept. 14, 1911; M. Stimson, *Fun, Fights, and Fiestas*, 186; Harper, *History of Woman Suffrage*, 6: 42–51. The campaign can be followed through clippings in "Woman Suffrage" Scrapbook, HP. See also Jane Apostol, "Why Women Should Not Have the Vote: Anti-Suffrage Views in the Southland in 1911," *Southern California Quarterly*, 70 (Spring 1988): 29–42.

30. Olin, *California's Prodigal Sons*, 46–49.

31. Paul Scharrenberg, "Reminiscences . . ." (University of California, Berkeley, Regional Oral History Project, 1954), 60–61; telegram from Katherine P. Edson to Haynes, Mar. 16, 1913, box 18, and announcement for Socialist Open Forum (1915), "Personal 2½" Scrapbook, HP; *Express*, Feb. 24, 1912; *San Francisco Star*, Mar. 30, 1912. On the crusade for mining safety see Chapter 9 below.

32. *Tribune*, Jan. 7, Dec. 20, 1912; *California Social-Democrat*, Sept. 6, 1912, Feb. 22, June 28, 1913; Haynes's autobiography notes, HF.

33. John R. Haynes, "The Strike in Colorado," address, Aug. 24, 1914, box 194, and receipt of Hoppickers Defense Committee, Jan. 9, 1914, "Personal 2" Scrapbook, HP.

34. *Evening Express*, June 27, 1900; Gilman O. Ostrander, *The Prohibition Movement in California, 1848–1933* (Berkeley: University of California Press, 1957), 85–116. On the position of the Socialists see *Los Angeles Socialist*, Aug.

8, 1903, and *California Social-Democrat*, Feb. 26, 1916. The Socialists believed the correct solution was a major change in the socioeconomic system: with socialism there would be no more reason for citizens to drink their troubles away. *Common Sense*, June 10, 1905, Jan. 19, 1907.

35. Kevin Starr, *Inventing the Dream: California Through the Progressive Era* (New York: Oxford University Press, 1985), 244–45; Hichborn, *California Legislature of 1911*, 190–225. General histories of the Prohibition movement and its relationship to progressives include James H. Timberlake, *Prohibition and the Progressive Movement, 1900–1920*, rev. ed. (New York: Atheneum, 1970); Norman H. Clark, *Deliver Us from Evil: An Interpretation of American Prohibition* (New York: Norton, 1976); and Jack S. Blocker, Jr., *Retreat from Reform: The Prohibition Movement in the United States, 1890–1913* (Westport, Conn.: Greenwood, 1976).

36. Haynes to Ralph Reed, Mar. 2, 1915, Haynes's autobiography notes, and "Medical Articles" Scrapbook, HF; Haynes to Frank Wiggins, May 11, 1916, box 168, HP.

37. *Graphic*, 20 (July 30, 1904): 3; "Inventory of House Contents, 2324 S. Figueroa" (c. 1919), HF; resolutions of Women's Christian Temperance Union, box 228, HP: *Times*, July 11, 1912.

38. Haynes to [unidentified], Sept. 30, 1905, box 73, HP; *Times*, Dec. 17, 1907; Haynes to John D. Works, July 22, 1922, box 3, John D. Works Papers, Stanford; *Express*, Nov. 25, 1905, Sept. 7, 1909; *Western Graphic*, 7 (Oct. 21, 1899): 17; Haynes to George Kress, Nov. 7, 1928, HF; *Herald and Express*, June 13, 1933.

39. Olin, *California's Prodigal Sons*, 57–58; Mowry, *California Progressives*, 158–64; La Follette circular (Nov. 1911), box 93, Franklin Hichborn Papers, UCLA.

40. John R. Haynes, typescript speech to Women's Progressive League, May 4, 1912, box 228, HP; E. T. Earl to Meyer Lissner, June 6, 1912, box 15, Meyer Lissner Papers, Stanford; Mowry, *California Progressives*, 165–86; Olin, *California's Prodigal Sons*, 60–63; John Allen Gable, *The Bull Moose Years: Theodore Roosevelt and the Progressive Party* (Port Washington, N.Y.: Kennikat, 1978), 3–156. At the 1912 Republican convention Haynes replaced William Stephens, an elected alternate who could not attend.

41. Ralph Edward Shaffer, "A History of the Socialist Party of California" (M.A. thesis, University of California, Los Angeles, 1951), 45, 153–54; Delmatier, McIntosh, and Waters, *Rumble of California Politics*, 179–80; Mowry, *California Progressives*, 100; Thomas R. Clark, "Labor and Progressivism 'South of the Slot': The Voting Behavior of the San Francisco Working Class, 1912–1916," *California History*, 66 (Sept. 1987): 201.

42. *Examiner*, June 14, 1937.

43. *California Social-Democrat*, Jan. 18, 1913; John R. Haynes, "Fundamental Democracy—Socialism," typescript speech, May 1912, box 190, and John R. Haynes, address to Women's Progressive League, May 4, 1912, box 228, HP.

44. Haynes to Carl Thompson, Apr. 17, 1930, box 177, and C. D. Willard to Haynes, May 17, 1913, "Personal 2" Scrapbook, HP; Haynes to Gaylord Wilshire, Oct. 16, 1913, box 2, H. Gaylord Wilshire Papers, UCLA.

45. Haynes to Hiram Johnson, May 19, 1915, box 87, and Johnson to Haynes, Sept. 11, 1911, box 41, HP; copies of Haynes to Meyer Lissner, Jan. 1, 1915,

May 11, 1916, Part 2, box 16, Hiram W. Johnson Papers, Bancroft; Edward A Dickson to Johnson, July 22, 1914, box 9, Edward A. Dickson Papers, UCLA.

46. Hiram Johnson to Haynes, July 10, 1916, "Personal 2½" Scrapbook, and Jan. 23, 1917, box 36, telegram from Haynes to editor of *Everybody's Magazine,* Sept. 30, 1914, and Haynes to Johnson, Apr. 11, 12, 17, 1916, box 87, HP.

47. Johnson to Lissner, Jan. 8, Dec. 12, 1912, box 18, Meyer Lissner Papers, Stanford; Lissner to Johnson, Oct. 30, 1911, Part 2, box 20, and Apr. 1, 1912, Part 2, box 21, Hiram W. Johnson Papers, Bancroft.

48. Brochure of National Committee on Prison Reform (1913), box 12, "Report on Visit to San Quentin," typescript (December 6, 1915), box 165, "Report on the Care of the Insane and the Care of Adult Offenders" (October 1918), box 16, John R. Haynes, "The Passing of the City and County Jails," typescript of speech, December 16, 1920, box 133, and various reports in boxes 16 and 22, HP.

49. John R. Haynes, "The State Institutions of California," typescript speech, June 10, 1918, and "Problems of Sanitation in California Infirmaries," typescript speech, box 72, HP; John R. Haynes, "Sterilization of the Unfit," *Pacific Coast Journal of Nursing,* 18 (Sept. 1922): 548–53, (Oct. 1922): 608–12. See Chapter 11 below for an examination of Haynes's view on sterilization of the unfit.

50. Haynes letters to California legislators, 1917, box 36, Haynes to Hiram Johnson, May 28, 1915, box 87, HP; *Tribune,* May 24, 1915; Johnson to Katherine P. Edson, May 28, 1915, box 2, and Edson to Johnson, June 3, 1915, box 1, Katherine P. Edson Papers, UCLA; *Times,* June 13, 1915.

51. Johnson to Haynes, Nov. 16, 1914, "Personal 2" Scrapbook, HP; John R. Haynes, "Abuses of the Initiative, Referendum and Recall and the Remedies," *California Outlook,* 17 (Dec. 5, 1914): 13–14; Franklin Hichborn, *Story of the Session of the California Legislature of 1915* (San Francisco: James H. Barry, 1916), 101–8.

52. Haynes to California state senators, Mar. 29, 1915, box 36, HP; Haynes to Edward A. Dickson, Mar. 9, Apr. 7, 1915, box 3, Edward A. Dickson Papers, UCLA; Hichborn, *California Legislature of 1915,* 66–100.

53. Olin, *California's Prodigal Sons,* 70–90; Franklin Hichborn, *Story of the Session of the California Legislature of 1913* (San Francisco: James H. Barry, 1913), 213–47, 296–353.

54. Haynes to "Fellow Progressives," Jan. 16, 1914, box 17, Meyer Lissner Papers, Stanford; Katherine Edson to Hiram Johnson, Apr. 18, 1914, box 1, Katherine P. Edson Papers, UCLA; Hichborn, *California Legislature of 1915,* esp. 242; Mary Ann Mason Burki, "The California Progressives: Labor's Point of View," *Labor History,* 17 (Winter 1976): 24–37; Clark, "Labor and Progressivism," 197–207.

55. Haynes to Woodrow Wilson, June 23, 1913, Ser. 4, file 609, microfilm reel 288, and Feb. 9, 5, 11, 1916, Ser. 4, file 3156, microfilm reel 345, Woodrow Wilson Papers, LC; John R. Haynes, "Why I Favor the Re-election of President Wilson," typescript speech, 1916, and Haynes to Wilson, July 11, 1913, HF; newspaper clippings in box 58, HP; Robert E. Hennings, *James D. Phelan and the Wilson Progressives of California* (New York: Garland, 1985), 131–39.

56. Mowry, *California Progressives,* 273–77. For the Hughes campaign see Olin, *California's Prodigal Sons,* 136–60.

57. Lissner to Edson, July 13, 1916, box 2, Katherine P. Edson Papers, UCLA;

1916 campaign flier, Part 2, box 12, Hiram W. Johnson Papers, Bancroft; Johnson to Haynes, July 10, 1916, "Personal 2½" Scrapbook, HP.

58. Haynes to Johnson, Dec. 17, 1916, box 87, HP.

59. Ibid.

60. Mowry, *California Progressives*, 274–81; Olin, *California's Prodigal Sons*, 169–70; Kemper Campbell, "Reminiscences of Kemper Campbell" (University of California, Berkeley, Regional Cultural History Project, 1954), 24–25, 34–35.

61. Spencer C. Olin, Jr., *California Politics, 1846–1920: The Emerging Corporate State* (San Francisco: Boyd and Fraser, 1981), 70.

CHAPTER EIGHT

1. Albert Howard Clodius, "The Quest for Good Government in Los Angeles, 1890–1910" (Ph.D. diss., Claremont Graduate School, 1953), 214–392; Martin J. Schiesl, "Progressive Reform in Los Angeles Under Mayor Alexander, 1909–1913," *California Historical Quarterly*, 54 (Spring 1975): 41–42.

2. Good Government Organization circular, July 17, 1909, box 16, Meyer Lissner Papers, Stanford; Martin J. Schiesl, "Politicians in Disguise: The Changing Role of Public Administrators in Los Angeles, 1900–1920," in Michael H. Ebner and Eugene M. Tobin, eds., *The Age of Urban Reform: New Perspectives on the Progressive Era* (Port Washington, N.Y.: Kennikat, 1977), 107; Clodius, "Quest for Good Government," 404–5.

3. *Graphic*, Oct. 23, 1909, clipping in "Personal 3" Scrapbook, Walter Lindley Collection, Honnold; C. D. Willard to Samuel Willard, Nov. 25, 1909, box 6, Charles D. Willard Papers, Huntington.

4. *Times*, Dec. 8, 1909; *Pacific Outlook*, 7 (Dec. 4, 1909): 1; Municipal League election letter, Nov. 2, 1909, box 110, HP.

5. George Alexander to Haynes, Nov. 12, 1909, HF; Charles O. Morgan to Haynes, Nov. 12, 1909, box 41, HP; John R. Haynes, "Significance of the Election," *Pacific Outlook*, 7 (Dec. 11, 1909): 5.

6. Schiesl, "Progressive Reform," 42–45; Schiesl, "Politicians in Disguise," 192.

7. Schiesl, "Progressive Reform," 43–45; John R. Haynes, address before the Sunset Club, Mar. 29, 1912, HF.

8. *Pacific Outlook*, 7 (Dec. 18, 1909): 2–3.

9. Ibid., 7 (July 17, 1909): 7; 8 (Feb. 5, 1910): 6–7; 8 (Feb. 9, 1910): 6; *Express*, July 3, 1909; Haynes's account ledger (1893–1911), HF; Martin Bekins to Hiram Johnson, Apr. 27, 1911, Part 2, box 10, Hiram W. Johnson Papers, Bancroft.

10. Mary A. Veeder, "The Working of a Housing Commission," *California Outlook*, 13 (Sept. 14, 1912): 12–13; Municipal Housing Association file, box 154, HP; *Tribune*, Dec. 7, 1912; Gibbon to Haynes, Dec. 23, 1912, Aug. 4, 1913, Thomas E. Gibbon Papers, Huntington; *Examiner*, Mar. 2, July 11, 1912; Reynold Blight to Haynes, Mar. 19, 1912, HF.

11. Haynes to City Council, Apr. 22, 1915, HF.

12. Copy of Haynes to Lissner, May 11, 1916, Part 2, box 16, Hiram W. Johnson Papers, Bancroft; *Times*, Mar. 4, 1913, Nov. 13, Jan. 18, 1914; Haynes to City Council, July 27, 1918, and other civil service material in box 110, and

George T. Keys to Haynes, Dec. 18, 1916, Haynes to J. G. Burke, Aug. 23, 1915, box 27, HP.

13. Schiesl, "Progressive Reform," 45.

14. David A. Shannon, *The Socialist Party of America: A History* (New York: Macmillan, 1955), 40–42; "Municipal Platform Socialist Party of Los Angeles" (1911), box 57, HP. On Job Harriman see Knox Mellon, Jr., "Job Harriman: The Early and Middle Years, 1861–1912" (Ph.D. diss., Claremont Graduate School, 1972).

15. Grace H. Stimson, *Rise of the Labor Movement in Los Angeles* (Berkeley: University of California Press, 1955), 366–406.

16. *Times*, Dec. 7, 1910, Jan. 8, 1911; *Examiner*, Oct. 31, 1911.

17. *Times*, Nov. 2, 1911; *San Pedro News*, June 7, 1911; *California Social-Democrat*, Sept. 23, 1911.

18. Mellon, "Job Harriman," 157–72; *California Social-Democrat*, Aug. 19, 1911.

19. Marshall Stimson, *Fun, Fights, and Fiestas in Old Los Angeles* (Los Angeles: privately printed, 1966), 215; Meyer Lissner to C. D. Willard, Dec. 7, 1911, and Lissner to F. D. Hogoboom, Nov. 7, 1911, box 3, Meyer Lissner Papers, Stanford; Edward A. Dickson to Hiram Johnson, n.d., Part 2, box 12, and Willard to Johnson, n.d., Part 2, box 36, Hiram W. Johnson Papers, Bancroft.

20. Mellon, "Job Harriman," 174–83; James P. Kraft, "The Fall of Job Harriman's Socialist Party: Violence, Gender and Politics in Los Angeles, 1911," *Southern California Quarterly*, 70 (Spring 1988): 43–68; Herbert Shapiro, "The McNamara Case: A Window on Class Antagonism in the Progressive Era," *Southern California Quarterly*, 70 (Spring 1988): 69–94.

21. *Herald*, Feb. 16, 1910, Mar. 4, 7, 1911; *Times*, Mar. 5, 1911.

22. *Herald*, Mar. 29, 1911; *Express*, Feb. 2, Mar. 14, 1912; *Examiner*, Feb. 28, 1912; *Tribune*, Mar. 28, 1912.

23. Clinton Woodruff to Meyer Lissner, Apr. 16, May 27, June 5, 1912, box 26, and telegram from Lissner to Woodruff, June 1, 1912, box 16, Meyer Lissner Papers, Stanford.

24. "The National Municipal League," *California Outlook*, 13 (July 6, 1912): 9; "Program for Eighteenth Annual Meeting of the National Municipal League . . . 1912," box 157, HP; *Herald*, July 12, 1912; *Times*, July 11, 1912.

25. *Times*, Apr. 26, Oct. 1, 1912; *Tribune*, June 8, 1912; *Record*, Nov. 30, 1912; Robert M. Fogelson, *The Fragmented Metropolis: Los Angeles, 1850–1930* (Cambridge, Mass.: Harvard University Press, 1967), 215–16. Haynes and freeholder secretary John J. Hamilton sent questionnaires concerning the commission form of government to cities throughout the U.S. For comments of officials in commission cities see files in boxes 103, 104, HP.

26. *Express*, Oct. 4, 1912; *Citizen*, Nov. 29, 1912; *Herald*, Oct. 18, Nov. 26, 1912; *Examiner*, Dec. 2, 1912; typescripts of Haynes's speeches in box 104, HP.

27. *Express*, Dec. 3, 1912; *Times*, Nov. 19, Dec. 3, 4, 1912.

28. *Examiner*, Nov. 26, 27, 1912; *Times*, Nov. 27, 1912; *Herald*, Dec. 4, 1912.

29. *Herald*, Dec. 4, 1912; *Times*, Dec. 4, 1912; memorandum from John J. Hamilton to Haynes, Dec. 4, 1912, box 103, HP.

30. *Times*, Dec. 13, 1912.

31. Dora Haynes to Caroline Severance, Dec. 24, 1912, box 18, Caroline Severance Papers, Huntington.

32. "Proportional Representation, Leaflet #2" (Social Reform Union, 1899), box 168, HP; Clarence Gilbert Hoag and George H. Hallett, Jr., *Proportional Representation* (New York: Macmillan, 1926), 11–195; George H. Dunlop, "Proportional Representation at Los Angeles," *National Municipal Review*, 3 (Jan. 1914): 92–95.

33. Municipal League flier for 1913 election, box 104, Progressive Party County Central Committee bulletin, Mar. 17, 1913, box 18, and Haynes to Meyer Lissner, Feb. 24, 1913, box 168, HP; *Express*, June 29, 1912; Proportional Representation League flier (1913), box 44, Meyer Lissner Papers, Stanford.

34. *Express*, Mar. 8, 1913; *Tribune*, Mar. 19, 1913; E. T. Earl to Lissner, Mar. 8, 1913, box 15, and John J. Hamilton to Lissner, Sept. 27, Oct. 8, 1912, box 17, Meyer Lissner Papers, Stanford.

35. *Times*, Dec. 13, 1912; *Examiner*, Dec. 7, 1912.

36. *California Social-Democrat*, Mar. 23, 1913; *Tribune*, Mar. 19, 1913; *Times*, Mar. 23, 1913; *Examiner*, Mar. 23, 1913; *California Outlook*, 14 (Mar. 22, 1913): 6.

37. *Tribune*, Dec. 12, 13, 1914; *Examiner*, Nov. 23, Dec. 25, 1914; Town Hall, *A Study of the Los Angeles City Charter* (Los Angeles: Town Hall, 1963), 47; clippings in box 105, HP.

38. Clippings in "George Dunlop" Scrapbook, HP; *Tribune*, Apr. 16, 29, 1916; *Times*, Mar. 26, June 4, 8, 1916.

39. Martin J. Schiesl, *The Politics of Efficiency: Municipal Administration and Reform in America, 1880–1920* (Berkeley: University of California Press, 1977), 157–58; Schiesl, "Progressive Reform," 47–50; E. Allen Phillips to Haynes, Jan. 19, 1914, HF; *Municipal News*, Apr. 9, 1913; Abraham Hoffman, "The Los Angeles Aqueduct Investigation Board of 1912: A Reappraisal," *Southern California Quarterly*, 62 (Winter 1980): 329–60.

40. *Times*, Mar. 29, May 4, 1913; Marshall Stimson, "Why We Went to the Municipal Conference of 1913," *California Outlook*, 14 (Apr. 5, 1913): 5.

41. E. T. Earl to Hiram Johnson, Mar. 29, 1913, and Kemper Campbell to Johnson, Oct. 14, 1914, Part 2, box 10, Hiram W. Johnson Papers, Bancroft; *Express*, Apr. 11, 1913; Earl to Chester Rowell, Apr. 9, 1913, box 13, Chester Rowell Papers, Bancroft.

42. *Times*, Apr. 30–May 4, 8, 1913; *Express*, Apr. 22, 1913; *California Social-Democrat*, Apr. 5, 1913; H. H. Rose circular, May 21, 1913, box 23, Meyer Lissner Papers, Stanford.

43. *Times*, May 29, June 4, 1913; *Examiner*, June 5, 1913; Dell Schweitzer to John W. Shenk, May 14, 1913, box 22, Meyer Lissner Papers, Stanford; Fogelson, *Fragmented Metropolis*, 217–20.

44. *Examiner*, Dec. 2, 1913. On the demise of progressivism in Los Angeles in 1913 see Clodius, "Quest for Good Government," 540–42, and Fogelson, *Fragmented Metropolis*, 217.

45. Schiesl, "Politicians in Disguise," 111; "Los Angeles Mayoralty and Other Municipal Affairs," *National Municipal Review*, 5 (July 1916): 485–86; Ernest S. Griffith, *A History of American City Government: The Progressive Years and*

Their Aftermath, 1900–1920, 2nd ed. (New York: National Municipal League, 1983), 135.

46. Nelson S. Van Valen, "Power Politics: The Struggle for Municipal Ownership of Electrical Utilities in Los Angeles, 1905–1937" (Ph.D. diss., Claremont Graduate School, 1963), 46–62.

47. Ibid., 66–83; *Express*, Apr. 30, 1913.

48. Van Valen, "Power Politics," 83–88; *Express*, Apr. 30, 1913; *Tribune*, Apr. 15, 1913; *Times*, Apr. 5, 1913; *Examiner*, Apr. 13, 1913; fliers of Municipal Conference and Voters Educational Association, and pamphlets in box 136, HP.

49. *Times*, Oct. 21, 1913; Van Valen, "Power Politics," 88–92.

50. *Times*, Apr. 14, 1914; *Municipal Ownership Bulletin*, May 1, 1914, in Scrapbook 235635, Huntington.

51. H. S. Ryerson to E. L. Lewis, May 1, 1914, box 136, W. E. Dunn memo, n.d., box 137, Meyer Lissner to executive board members, May 4, 1914, and minutes of PPBC meetings, Apr.–May 1914, box 140, HP; Van Valen, "Power Politics," 100–108; *California Social-Democrat*, May 2, 1914.

52. *Examiner*, May 12, 1914; John W. Kemp to Haynes, Oct. 20, 1916, Ezra Scattergood to Haynes, Feb. 10, 1917, and John B. Miller to Haynes, Feb. 10, 1917, box 135, HP; Van Valen, "Power Politics," 127–33.

53. *Herald*, Jan. 5, 1917; *Record*, Jan. 27, 1917, PPBC files in boxes 137 and 140, HP; *Times*, Mar. 19, Apr. 9, 17, 28, 1916, Jan. 1, 11, 1917; Van Valen, "Power Politics," 133–55.

54. Ralph Hancock, *Fabulous Boulevard* (New York: Funk and Wagnalls, 1949), 114–17; George Mowry, *The California Progressives* (Berkeley: University of California Press, 1951), 124. Otis and Earl were members of the land syndicate that purchased property in the San Fernando Valley before the announcement of the Owens Valley aqueduct project in 1905.

55. Earl to Harley Brundige and Edward Dickson, July 8, 1907, box 1, Edward A. Dickson Papers, UCLA; Lissner to Theodore Roosevelt, July 12, 1912, box 23, Meyer Lissner Papers, Stanford.

56. *Times*, Nov. 3, 7, 14, 21, 1917; Earl to Lissner, July 15, 1912, box 15, Meyer Lissner Papers, Stanford; John Neylan, "Politics, Law, and the University of California" (University of California, Berkeley, Regional Cultural History Project, 1961), 22–27.

57. Haynes to Earl, Jan. 29, Apr. 16, 1915, HF; *Times*, Nov. 6, 15, 1917; *Express*, Nov. 7, 1914.

58. Joseph Gerald Woods, "The Progressives and the Police: Urban Reform and the Professionalization of the Los Angeles Police" (Ph.D. diss., University of California, Los Angeles, 1973), 46–47; "Frederick J. Whiffen for Mayor" flier, and sample ballots, box 58, HP; "The Los Angeles Primary," *Sunset Magazine*, 34 (June 1915): 1078–79; *California Social-Democrat*, May 1, 1915.

59. *Times*, Sept. 1, 2, 1916, Nov. 6, 1917; *Record*, Aug. 29, 1916, and clippings in Scrapbooks 7 and 8, Thomas E. Woolwine Papers, Huntington; James H. Richardson, *For the Life of Me: Memoirs of a City Editor* (New York: Putnam's, 1954), 79–81.

60. Schiesl, "Politicians in Disguise," 112–13; Haynes to Frederick T. Woodman, Jan. 11, 1917, and Woodman reelection flier, "Personal 2½" Scrapbook, HP; *Times*, Jan. 11, 1917.

61. *Times*, Oct. 14, 1914, Nov. 8, 9, 15, 1917; *Tribune*, Apr. 3, 1914, Oct. 28, 1916; clippings in Scrapbooks 8 and 9, Thomas E. Woolwine Papers, Huntington.

62. *Tribune*, Apr. 14, 1915; copy of Los Angeles County ordinance 380 N.S., and Haynes to Board of Supervisors, July 7, 1920, box 141, HP.

63. Richard C. Miller, "Otis and His *Times*: The Career of Harrison Gray Otis of Los Angeles" (Ph.D. diss., University of California, Berkeley, 1961), 197–98; Haynes to Earl, Dec. 4, 1916, box 76, HP; *Tribune*, Nov. 28, 1916.

64. *Times*, Dec. 7, 1910, Oct. 26, Nov. 19, 1912, Mar. 26, 1913, Jan. 14, 1915.

65. Ibid., Dec. 7, 1910; Marshall Taylor to Haynes, Dec. 6, 1910, "Personal 2" Scrapbook, HP.

66. Haynes to Harry Chandler, Dec. 14, 1916, box 36, HP; Haynes to William Stephens, Sept. 6, 1917, HF; Haynes to Chandler (1920), as quoted in Robert Gottlieb and Irene Wolt, *Thinking Big: The Story of the "Los Angeles Times," Its Publishers, and Their Influence on Southern California* (New York: Putnam's, 1977), 196.

67. *Times*, Oct. 12, Nov. 1–Dec. 1, 1917; "Trials of Los Angeles County Supervisors," *National Municipal Review*, 7 (Jan. 1918): 95.

68. *Tribune*, Oct. 10, 1911, June 1, 1913; Dora Haynes to Caroline Severance, Dec. 29, 1913, box 18, Caroline Severance Papers, Huntington.

69. Dora Haynes to Caroline Severance, Dec. 24, 1912, box 18, Caroline Severance Papers, Huntington; handwritten speech on women's suffrage (1911), box 227, HP.

70. *Examiner*, Sept. 13, 1913; clippings (1912–20) in "Woman Suffrage" Scrapbook, and notes on Southern California Civic League, box 271, HP; *Tribune*, Nov. 9, 1913; U.S. Senate, "Woman Suffrage," doc. 488, 63rd Cong., 2nd sess., 1914; Haynes to J. P. Tumulty, Nov. 13, 1917, microfilm reel 210, Ser. 4, folder 89, Woodrow Wilson Papers, LC. For background on the Alice Paul incident see Sally Hunter Graham, "Woodrow Wilson, Alice Paul, and the Woman Suffrage Movement," *Political Science Quarterly*, 98 (Winter 1983–84): 665–79.

71. Michael Regan, *Mansions of Los Angeles* (Los Angeles: Regan, 1965), 8–45; *Baist's Real Estate Atlas of Surveys of Los Angeles* (Philadelphia: G. William Baist, 1910, 1921).

72. *Times*, Nov. 3, 1912; Herbert Crowly, "The Country House in California," *Architectural Record*, 34 (Dec. 1913): 507, 508, 512; Una Nixon Hopkins, "Some Phases of Domestic Architecture in the Southwest," *International Studio*, 53 (Sept. 1914): 49–50; Frank Calvert, *Homes and Gardens of the Pacific Coast: Volume 2, Los Angeles* (Los Angeles: Beaux Arts Society, c. 1926), n.p.

73. *Los Angeles City Directory* (1914); *Examiner*, June 13, 1912; Anne M. Mumford to U.S. Immigration and Naturalization Service, Mar. 27, 1940, HF.

74. J. W. Park to Judson King, Apr. 17, 1917, box 158, HP; Park to Haynes, Nov. 10, 1916, HF; "Woodrow Wilson and Jos. W. Park Letters," *California Outlook*, 13 (Oct. 26, 1912): 7–8.

75. Letters of introduction, 1911, and photos in Photograph Album, HF; *Southern California Practitioner*, 28 (Sept. 1913): 309.

76. *The Sunset Club of Los Angeles* (Los Angeles: Sunset Club, 1916), 2: 45, 48–49, 81, photographs; Haynes, address before the Sunset Club, Mar. 29,

1912, HF; report of Mrs. Henrietta Housh to Fine Arts League, June 10, 1913, Fine Arts League Collection, Seaver; *The X Club* (Los Angeles: X Club, 1928), 17–18, 38, 40–41.

77. Index to deeds, 1909–17, Los Angeles County Registrar-Recorder's Office; William W. Clary, *History of the Law Firm of O'Melveny and Myers, 1885–1965* (Los Angeles: privately printed, 1966), 1: 247–60; Articles of Incorporation, 6026, 8448, 10330, Seaver.

78. Gaylord Wilshire to Haynes, Mar. 27, 1910, and Mary Wilshire to Dora Haynes, Dec. 21, 1910, box 226, HP.

79. Wilshire to Haynes, July 20, 1913, "Mining" Scrapbook and file on Wilshire, box 226, HP; Wilshire to Henry Hyndman, July 20, 1918, box 2, H. Gaylord Wilshire Papers, UCLA.

CHAPTER NINE

1. *Express*, Nov. 19, 1910; John R. Haynes, "Democracy and Social Progress," in William M. Bell, ed., *Addresses, World's Social Progress Congress* (Dayton, Ohio: Otterbein, 1915), 336. David M. Kennedy, *Over Here: The First World War and American Society* (New York: Oxford University Press, 1980), provides background on the U.S. during the war.

2. John R. Haynes, speech to workers of Red Cross Membership Drive, 1917, box 73, and Haynes to W. L. Hathaway, Jan. 12, 1918, and clippings in box 65, HP.

3. Telegram from Governor Stephens to Haynes, Apr. 5, 1917, box 23, HP; California State Council of Defense, *Report*, Apr. 6, 1917–Jan. 1, 1918 (Sacramento, 1918), 3–8.

4. Haynes's statements on daylight savings time and "Report of Committee on Relief," Apr. 7, 1917, and files in boxes 22 and 23, and John R. Haynes, "Centralization in Relief," typescript speech, 1917, box 73, HP.

5. Haynes to A. H. Naftzger, Apr. 9, 1917, and Naftzger to Haynes, May 16, 1917, box 23, HP.

6. John R. Haynes, "The General Program of Defense," *The Clubwoman*, 9 (May 1917): 8–11; *Times*, May 3, 1917.

7. Haynes, "General Program of Defense," 8–11; Haynes to Naftzger, Apr. 9, 12, 1917, box 23, HP.

8. Haynes to Naftzger, June 14, 1917, box 23, HP; *Examiner*, Sept. 3, 1917.

9. Haynes to Stephens, Sept. 20, 1917, box 23, HP.

10. Haynes to Stephens, Apr. 9, 1917, box 23, HP; John R. Haynes, "Individual Savings and the Public Welfare," in California State Council of Defense, *California in the War* (Sacramento, 1918), 57–60; California State Council of Defense, *Report* (1918), 49–53; telegram from Haynes to Woodrow Wilson, June 25, 1917, Series 4, file 4010, microfilm reel 360, Woodrow Wilson Papers, LC.

11. Files on strikes and mining in boxes 152, 194, and 195, and "Mining" Scrapbook, HP.

12. Haynes to Senator Frank Flint, Apr. 29, 1910, box 152, and John R. Haynes, "A Federal Mining Commission," Senate doc. 205, 62nd Cong., 2nd sess., 1912, box 72, HP. William Graebner, *Coal-Mining Safety in the Progressive*

Period: The Political Economy of Reform (Lexington: University Press of Kentucky, 1976), examines the subject in a national context.

13. William Randolph Hearst to Haynes, Nov. 4, 1911, and John B. Andrews to Haynes, Oct. 28, 1911, "Mining" Scrapbook, Haynes to Andrews, Oct. 21, 1911, box 1, and Haynes to John White, Oct. 20, 1911, box 152, HP; *Examiner*, Dec. 17, 1911.

14. Haynes to Senator John Works, Feb. 29, 1912, Works to Haynes, Mar. 5, 1912, James McLachlan to Haynes, Mar. 6, 1912, and Haynes to Andrews, Jan. 29, 1916, June 12, 1918, box 1, HP; Haynes to Col. S. S. McClure, Jan. 30, 1912, S. S. McClure Papers, Lilly; John R. Haynes, "A Federal Mining Commission," *American Labor Legislation Review*, 2 (Feb. 1912): 140–52; John R. Haynes, "The Terrible Mining Game," *Western Comrade*, 6 (Sept. 1913): 188–90.

15. *Express*, July 3, 1918; *Times*, July 13, 1918; telegram from Haynes to Governor Stephens, July 3, 1918, box 203, and Franklin Henzel to Haynes, July 8, 16, 20, Aug. 2, 1918, box 194, HP; Louis B. Perry and Richard S. Perry, *A History of the Los Angeles Labor Movement, 1911–1941* (Berkeley: University of California Press, 1963), 80–85.

16. *Times*, Dec. 20, 21, 1917; Perry and Perry, *Los Angeles Labor Movement*, 154.

17. N. A. Smythe to Haynes, Nov. 23, 1918, Feb. 15, 1919, Haynes to Smythe, Oct. 7, Dec. 10, 1918, box 221, HP.

18. Haynes to Thomas Everitt, Nov. 14, 1918, box 158, HP.

19. Haynes to Miles Poindexter, Mar. 31, 1916, Haynes to George W. Norris, Apr. 1, 1916, and Haynes to Hiram Johnson, June 12, 1917, box 83, HP; Haynes to William G. McAdoo, Dec. 14, 1917, HF.

20. Haynes to B. R. Baumgardt, July 16, 1928, box 6, HP.

21. John R. Haynes, statement on Morals Efficiency Association, Oct. 8, 1917, box 73, HP; *Herald*, July 29, 1917.

22. Haynes to Dr. A. S. Shiels, Dec. 24, 1917, box 53, Haynes to U.S. Intelligence Department, Oct. 15, 1917, and Haynes to Secretary, Sons of the Revolution, Aug. 24, Sept. 16, 1918, box 65, HP. Keeping in mind Dr. Haynes's view of Germans at the time, it seems probable that Dora Haynes refrained from telling him that, according to her father, her own nephew "thinks the Germans are the best people on earth and wants them to win." Alfred W. Fellows to Dora Haynes, Feb. 19, 1917, box 270, HP.

23. Haynes to Right Reverend Joseph H. Johnson, Aug. 2, 1923, and Haynes to Joseph Tumulty, July 23, 1919, HF; Statement of John R. Haynes, Mrs. Walter Lindley, and Robert P. Fite, Sept. 18, 1919, box 65, HP; Kennedy, *Over Here*, 73–75; H. C. Peterson and Gilbert C. Fite, *Opponents of War, 1917–1918* (Madison: University of Wisconsin Press, 1957), 3–263; John A. Thompson, *Reformers and War: American Progressive Publicists and the First World War* (Cambridge, Eng.: Cambridge University Press, 1987), 220–30.

24. *California Social-Democrat*, Jan. 18, 1913; John R. Haynes, "Fundamental Democracy—Socialism," typescript speech, May 12, box 190, HP; Haynes, "Democracy and Social Progress," 336–50.

25. Haynes to Wilshire, Oct. 16, 1913, box 2, and Wilshire to Haynes, Nov. 3, 1913, box 10, H. Gaylord Wilshire Papers, UCLA.

26. John R. Haynes, "Labor Day Address," typescript, 1930, and Haynes's autobiography notes, HF.

27. John R. Haynes, "What I Believe and Why," typescript speech to X Club, 1915, HF; Haynes to Mary Sanford, Mar. 13, 1917, box 86, HP.

28. Haynes to Board of Trustees of University of Pennsylvania, July 22, 1915, and H. M. Lippincott to Haynes, Oct. 15, 1915, box 27, HP; Haynes to H. M. Lippincott, Oct. 6, 1915, box 53, Collection 100, UCLA; Lightner Witmer, *The Nearing Case* (New York: B. W. Huebsch, 1915).

29. Haynes to Mary Sanford, Nov. 28, 1917, box 86, HP.

30. Harry W. Laidler to Haynes, Dec. 10, 1917, box 86, HP.

31. Haynes, "General Program of Defense," 8; Gustuvus Myers, "Why Idealists Quit the Socialist Party," *Nation*, Feb. 15, 1917, 181–82; David A. Shannon, *The Socialist Party of America: A History* (New York: Macmillan, 1955), 99–103.

32. Shannon, *Socialist Party*, 103; "Another 'After the War' Program," *Survey*, 40 (Sept. 14, 1918): 673–74; James Weinstein, *The Corporate Ideal in the Liberal State, 1900–1918* (Boston: Beacon, 1968), 244–46; John Spargo to Haynes, June 26, 1917, and W. E. Walling to Haynes, July 13, 1918, box 189, HP.

33. Haynes to William E. Rappard, May 6, 1912, Haynes to Henry F. Forster, Sept. 7, 1916, et al., "Recall" Scrapbook and box 41, HP. Entire issues of the *Annals of the American Association of Political and Social Science* were devoted to direct legislation in 1912 and 1923.

34. Robert Owen to Haynes, Jan. 14, 1914, Aug. 18, 1915, and Judson King to Haynes, June 6, 1914, Mar. 7, 1917, box 158, HP; King to Haynes, Nov. 22, 1913, HF; John R. Haynes, "Direct Government in California," Senate doc. 738, 64th Cong., 2nd sess., 1917.

35. Haynes to Thomas H. Everitt, Nov. 14, 1918, box 158, HP; Thompson, *Reformers and War*, 217–20.

36. Haynes to Joseph Tumulty, July 23, 1919, HF; Haynes to Hiram Johnson, Feb. 19, 1918, box 87, HP.

37. Upton Sinclair to Haynes, Nov. 18, 1905, Autograph Book, Sinclair to Haynes, Aug. 2, 1906, and *Graphic* clipping, June 9, 1906, "Personal 2" Scrapbook, HP.

38. Sinclair to Haynes, Apr. 4, Nov. 5, Dec. 9, 1917, "Personal 2½" Scrapbook, HP; Haynes to Sinclair, Mar. 13, 1917, Aug. 13, 1919, Upton Sinclair Papers, Lilly; Sinclair to Haynes, June 17, 1917, and Haynes to William Ghent, Dec. 20, 1921, HF.

39. Sinclair to Haynes, Dec. 22, 1916, Mar. 19, 1917, "Personal 2½" Scrapbook, HP; Haynes to Sinclair, Mar. 13, 1917, Feb. 2, 1921, Upton Sinclair Papers, Lilly.

40. Upton Sinclair, ed. *The Cry for Justice: An Anthology of the Literature of Social Protest*, 2nd ed. (Los Angeles: Upton Sinclair, 1921), 2; Haynes to Sinclair, Apr. 12, 1921, Sinclair to Haynes, Feb. 3, 1922, Upton Sinclair Papers, Lilly; file on *Cry for Justice*, HF.

41. John R. Haynes, "Higher Education and Child Labor," *The Western Collegian*, May 3, 9, 13, 1914, clipping in "Personal 2½" Scrapbook, miscellaneous clippings and other material in boxes 25, 26, 156, HP.

42. Haynes to Everett Wheeler, Dec. 5, 1924, Haynes to Elbert Wing, Feb. 11, 1915, Julia C. Lathrop to Haynes, Feb. 26, 1915, and Haynes to E. P. Ryland, June 7, 1916, box 26, HP.

43. Haynes to Hiram Johnson, June 26, 1918, box 87, Haynes to National Child Labor Committee, Aug. 5, 1918, box 26, and John R. Haynes, "The Supreme Court," speech, n.d., box 73, HP.

44. Haynes to Woodrow Wilson, Feb. 9, Apr. 10, May 11, 1916, Ser. 4, file 3156, microfilm reel 345, and Haynes to James Phelan, Apr. 10, 1916, Ser. 4, file 76A, microfilm reel 199, Woodrow Wilson Papers, LC.

45. For the Red Scare era see Robert K. Murray, *Red Scare: A Study in National Hysteria, 1919–1920* (Minneapolis: University of Minnesota Press, 1955).

46. *Times*, Nov. 26, 29, Dec. 2, 1919; Robert Gottlieb and Irene Wolt, *Thinking Big: The Story of the "Los Angeles Times," Its Publishers, and Their Influence on Southern California* (New York: Putnam's, 1977), 185–89.

47. Harold Story, "Memoirs of Harold Story," 2 vols. (University of California, Los Angeles, Oral History Program, 1967), 1: 161–62, 495–96; Kevin Starr, *Inventing the Dream: California Through the Progressive Era* (New York: Oxford University Press, 1985), 218.

48. Copy of Kate Crane Gartz to Milbank Johnson, Oct. 12, 1920, box 6, HP; Kate Crane Gartz, *The Parlor Provocateur: Or, From Salon to Soap-box* (Pasadena, Calif.: Mary Craig Sinclair, 1923), esp. 28–32, 112. See also Kate Crane Gartz's *Letters of Protest* and *More Letters* (1926), *Still More Letters* (1931), and *Prophetic Letters* (1937), all published with the help of Mary Craig Sinclair.

49. *Record*, Mar. 13, 1913, Nov. 25, 1919.

50. Copy of Haynes to Thomas L. Woolwine, Nov. 25, 1919, "Personal 5" Scrapbook, Walter Lindley Collection, Honnold; Upton Sinclair, "The White Terror," *Appeal to Reason* (Nov. 1919), clipping in "Personal 2½" Scrapbook, HP.

51. *Times*, Nov. 29, 1919; quote cited in Gottlieb and Wolt, *Thinking Big*, 186.

52. *Times*, Nov. 3, 1921; Harry W. Laidler to Haynes, Oct. 6, 1921, and Haynes to Lord John Russell, Oct. 4, 1923, HF.

53. Max Eastman to Haynes, July 15, Sept. 16, 1916, "Personal 2½" Scrapbook, HP; Shannon, *Socialist Party*, 57.

54. Haynes to Johnson, May 9, 1919, box 88, and Johnson to Haynes, May 15, 1919, box 87, HP; George Mowry, *The California Progressives* (Berkeley: University of California Press, 1951), 281–82.

55. Haynes to William H. Taft, Aug. 9, 1919, Series 3, file 1, microfilm reel 211, William H. Taft Papers, LC; Meyer Lissner to Johnson, Aug. 31, 1921, Part 3, box 18, Hiram W. Johnson Papers, Bancroft; Haynes to May A. Higgins, Apr. 20, 1923, box 106, and Eleanor Banning McFarland to Haynes, May 15, 1928, box 93, HP.

56. Franklin Hichborn to Haynes, May 28, 1920, box 160, Franklin Hichborn Papers, UCLA; *San Francisco Examiner*, Mar. 23, 1920; *Times*, Jan. 24, Feb. 17, 1920.

57. Haynes to Meyer Lissner, May 29, July 26, 1920, box 17, Meyer Lissner Papers, Stanford; Haynes to Rudolph Spreckels, Apr. 1, 1920, box 37, and Hiram Johnson to Haynes, Sept. 2, 1920, box 88, HP; copy of Meyer Lissner to C. K. McClatchey, Feb. 16, 1920, Part 3, box 18, Hiram W. Johnson Papers, Bancroft; Mowry, *California Progressives*, 282–84.

CHAPTER TEN

1. The view that World War I marked the demise of the Progressive Era is presented in many sources, including Richard Hofstadter, *The Age of Reform: From Bryan to FDR* (New York: Vintage Books, 1955), 272–75, and Ernest S. Griffith, *A History of American City Government: The Progressive Years and Their Aftermath, 1900-1920*, 2nd ed. (New York: National Municipal League, 1983), 134, 266–67. For a revision of this view see Eugene M. Tobin, *Organize or Perish: America's Independent Progressives, 1913–1933* (Westport, Conn.: Greenwood, 1986), esp. 3–11; Burl Noggle, "Configuration of the Twenties," in William H. Cartwright and Richard L. Watson, Jr., eds., *The Reinterpretation of American History and Culture* (Washington, D.C.: National Council for the Social Studies, 1973), 469–71, 483–84; Daniel T. Rogers, "In Search of Progressivism," in Stanley I. Kutler and Stanley N. Katz, eds., *The Promise of American History: Progress and Prospects* (Baltimore: Johns Hopkins University Press, 1982), 113–32; Ellis W. Hawley, *The Great War and the Search for a Modern Order: A History of the American People and Their Institutions, 1917–1933* (New York: St. Martin's, 1979), 3–150.

2. Jackson K. Putnam, "The Persistence of Progressivism in the 1920s: The Case of California," *Pacific Historical Review*, 35 (Nov. 1966): 395–411.

3. George Mowry, *The California Progressives* (Berkeley: University of California Press, 1951), 275–80; H. Brett Melendy and Benjamin F. Gilbert, *The Governors of California: From Peter H. Burnett to Edmund G. Brown* (Georgetown, Calif.: Talisman, 1965), 322–34.

4. Haynes to Governor William D. Stephens, Mar. 17, Apr. 28, 1919, Stephens to Haynes, May 13, 1921, Franklin Hichborn to Haynes, Jan. 28, 1921, box 19, Haynes to Stephens, Oct. 22, 1921, box 6, HP; Haynes to Stephens, May 18, 1917, et al., HF.

5. Haynes to Stephens, May 23, 1918, HF; 1918 Election file, box 58, HP; H. Brett Melendy, "California's Cross-Filing Nightmare: The 1918 Gubernatorial Election," *Pacific Historical Review*, 33 (Aug. 1964): 317–30. "Cross-filing" in state primaries allowed candidates to compete for the nomination of any party, regardless of their own affiliation and without party label. Established in 1913 by the progressives to combat partisan political power, cross-filing was finally eliminated in 1959.

6. Jackson K. Putnam, *Modern California Politics*, 2nd ed. (San Francisco: Boyd and Fraser, 1984), 4–8; *San Francisco Call*, June 1, 1922.

7. Stephens to Haynes, Nov. 25, 1918, Haynes to Senator A. E. Boynton, Dec. 16, 1918, and Efficiency and Economy Committee file in box 13, HP; California Committee on Efficiency and Economy, *Report* (Sacramento, 1919); Putnam, *Modern California Politics*, 6–7.

8. Final Report, Stephens for Governor Club" (Nov. 8, 1922), box 193, HP; Putnam, *Modern California Politics*, 5–9.

9. Haynes to Stephens, Jan. 2, 1923, box 217, HP; *Express*, Jan. 11, 1923.

10. Haynes's autobiography notes, HF; *Herald*, Oct. 19, 1902; Haynes to Chester Rowell, July 23, 1919, box 15, Chester Rowell Papers, Bancroft; Haynes to Sayre MacNeil (and other regents), Apr. 18, 1919, box 216, Better America

Federation file, box 6, brochure on Smith-Towner bill (1921) and Haynes's letters to congressmen, box 54, HP.

11. Putnam, *Modern California Politics*, 8–9.

12. Haynes to Hichborn, June 22, 1922, and William Kent to Haynes, July 24, 1922, box 59, HP; Harry Chandler to H. E. Huntington, Aug. 9, 1922, telegram, HM11574, Henry E. Huntington Papers, Huntington; Paul Doherty to Hiram Johnson, Feb. 17, 1921, Part 3, box 33, Hiram W. Johnson Papers, Bancroft; Mowry, *California Progressives*, 275–85.

13. Haynes to Johnson, Sept. 23, 1922, box 42, Haynes to Johnson, June 29, 1921, and Johnson to Haynes, July 5, 1921, box 88, HP; Haynes to Chester Rowell, Sept. 16, 1920, box 1, Chester Rowell Papers, Bancroft; Burl Noggle, *Into the Twenties: The United States from Armistice to Normalcy* (Urbana: University of Illinois Press, 1974), 183–99.

14. Edwin Layton, "The Better America Federation: A Case Study of Superpatriotism," *Pacific Historical Review*, 30 (May 1961): 137–47; *Times*, May 25, 1920, May 19, 1922; Wilda Smith to Frank P. Merriam, Sept. 16, 1920, box 3, Frank P. Merriam Papers, Bancroft; Edson to Mrs. Medill McCormick, Aug. 19, 1920, box 1, Katherine P. Edson Papers, UCLA.

15. Will C. Wood to Haynes, July 23, 1920, and other material in boxes 5 and 6, HP; *Times*, Aug. 15, 1920, Jan. 8, 1930; *Examiner*, July 29, 1922; *San Jose Union*, Dec. 11, 1920; *Sacramento Union*, Aug. 19, 1920.

16. Haynes to B. R. Baumgardt, July 16, 1928, and Haynes to Dr. Henry Harrower, Apr. 13, 1921, box 6, HP; Haynes to Benjamin F. Bledsoe, Jan. 15, 1921, HF; *San Francisco Call*, Aug. 18, 1920.

17. *San Francisco Call*, Aug. 13, 18, 1920; *Boyle Heights News*, Apr. 21, 1921; copy of Hichborn to Rudolph Spreckels, Aug. 11, 1920, and Better America Federation files, boxes 5 and 6, HP.

18. Haynes to Hichborn, Jan. 12, 1921, box 19, and files on California Legislature in box 19, HP; *Examiner*, June 16, 1923; *San Francisco Examiner*, June 21, 1923; Franklin Hichborn, *Story of the Session of the California Legislature of 1921* (San Francisco: James H. Barry, 1922), esp. 78, 201–7, 211.

19. Haynes to Frank Wiggins, Feb. 3, 1923, Haynes to John F. Neylan, Mar. 1, 1923, and files in box 68, Haynes to Monsignor Charles A. Raman, Feb. 7, 1923, box 12, and Haynes to Simon Lubin, Feb. 8, 1923, Haynes to Will C. Wood, Feb. 8, Mar. 1, 1923, box 16, HP.

20. *Times*, May 18, 1923.

21. Ibid., Jan. 6, 8, 1923; letters from Franklin Hichborn to Haynes, May 1923 and Hichborn to editor of the *Express*, May 21, 1923, box 217, HP.

22. Telegram from Haynes to R. G. Sproul, May 17, 1923, Haynes to George I. Cochran (and other regents), June 1, 1923, box 217, minutes of UC Board of Regents meeting, June 12, 1923, box 216, HP; copy of Garret McEnerney to Haynes, May 18, 1923, box 19, Edward A. Dickson Papers, UCLA; Haynes to Senator Herbert C. Jones, Mar. 9, 1925, box 29, Herbert C. Jones Papers, Stanford.

23. Russell M. Posner, "The Progressive Voters League, 1923–26," *California Historical Society Quarterly*, 36 (Sept. 1957): 251–56; copy of Haynes to J. M. Inman, Oct. 29, 1923, Jones to Haynes, Nov. 7, 19, 1923, Jan. 2, 1924, Haynes to Jones, Aug. 11, 1924, and Progressive Voters League file, box 166, HP.

24. Copy of Rudolph Spreckels to Haynes, Aug. 1, 1924, box 39, Herbert C.

Jones Papers, Stanford; Franklin Hichborn, "California Politics, 1891–1939," 5 vols., typescript (1939), 4: 2176–2208; John L. Shover, "The California Progressives and the 1924 Election," *California Historical Quarterly,* 51 (Spring 1972): 59–74; Russell M. Posner, "A Progressive Runs for President: The La Follette Campaign in California," *The Californians,* 2 (Jan./Feb. 1984): 17–21.

25. Haynes to William G. McAdoo, Jan. 30, 1924, box 8, HP; Haynes to William H. Workman, Aug. 28, 1924, Haynes to Hichborn, July 26, Aug. 11, 24, 1924, and John R. Haynes, "How I Shall Vote on Nov. 4, 1924, and Why," typescript speech, HF.

26. Hiram Johnson to Haynes, Jan. 23, 1917, and 1919 Legislature file, box 36, HP; Hichborn, *California Legislature of 1921,* 188–90.

27. Haynes to Seward Simons, Oct. 16, 1917, Haynes to Henry Van Arsdale, Sept. 7, 1918, Haynes to Eugene T. Lies, May 8, 1918, and other material on Proposition 20, box 84, HP; *Tribune,* June 3, 1918. Haynes's view of physicians as interested primarily in the advancement of their profession, not social reform, is echoed in James G. Burrow, *Organized Medicine in the Progressive Era: The Move Toward Monopoly* (Baltimore: Johns Hopkins University Press, 1977), and Alan I. Marcus, "Professional Revolution and Reform in the Progressive Era: Cincinnati Physicians and the City Elections of 1897 and 1900," *Journal of Urban History,* 5 (Feb. 1979): 183–207. Lloyd C. Taylor, Jr., in *The Medical Profession and Social Reform, 1885-1945* (New York: St. Martin's, 1974), presents the opposite view.

28. *Express,* Apr. 6, 1897; *Times,* Dec. 11, 1894, Mar. 17, 1895; Single Tax file, box 187, HP; *California Social-Democrat,* May 6, 13, June 2, 24, July 1, 1916; Arthur Nichols Young, *The Single Tax Movement in the United States* (Princeton, N.J.: Princeton University Press, 1916), 290, 310.

29. Brochures and other material in Single Tax file, box 186, and Great Adventure, box 34, HP.

30. Phillip D. Wilson to Haynes, Nov. 7, 1917, box 36, HP; John R. Haynes, "California Sticks to the Initiative and Referendum," *National Municipal Review,* 12 (Mar. 1923): 116–17.

31. Haynes to Paul Scharrenberg, May 12, 1919, Haynes to Governor William Stephens, Apr. 9, 1919, and Haynes to members of the Direct Legislation League, Nov. 14, 1917, box 36, HP; *Times,* Mar. 8, 1919; Hichborn, *California Legislature of 1921,* 191–99.

32. Haynes, "California Sticks to the Initiative and Referendum," 117.

33. John R. Haynes, address before the Sunset Club, Mar. 29, 1912, "Articles, Speeches" Scrapbook, HP; John R. Haynes, "Needed Reform in Taxation," *California Social-Democrat,* July 29, 1916.

34. Haynes to Governor Stephens, Apr. 9, 1919, Haynes to state senators, Dec. 31, 1918, box 36, HP; Haynes to Paul Scharrenberg, Feb. 19, 1921, box 159, Franklin Hichborn Papers, UCLA.

35. Haynes to Franklin Hichborn, Feb. 3, Oct. 25, 1920, Hichborn to Haynes, Feb. 12, 1920, and League to Protect the Initiative file, boxes 93, 94, HP.

36. Haynes to Harry M. McKee, Aug. 13, 1920, and Haynes to Francis Heney, Oct. 18, 1920, box 37, Haynes to Hichborn, Sept. 2, 1920, and Bertha Cable to Hichborn, Mar. 10, 1920, box 94, HP; Haynes to James Phelan, Sept. 1, 1920, box 59, James Phelan Papers, Bancroft; Haynes to Chester Rowell, Sept. 11,

1920, box 1, Chester Rowell Papers, Bancroft; John R. Haynes, address to the City Club, Aug. 21, 1920, HF.

37. Haynes to Hichborn, Nov. 6, 1920, box 93, HP.

38. Haynes to C. C. Young, et al., Apr. 15, 1921, box 38, HP; Hichborn, *California Legislature of 1921*, 204–16.

39. Haynes, "California Sticks to the Initiative and Referendum," 117; Haynes to Upton Sinclair, Sept. 29, 1922, Haynes to J. Stitt Wilson, Oct. 3, 1922, and Haynes to Hiram Johnson, Aug. 17, 1922, box 94, William Jennings Bryan to Haynes, Sept. 21, 1922, and League to Protect the Initiative file, box 93, and "Initiative Campaign 1922" Scrapbook, HP.

40. Haynes, "California Sticks to the Initiative and Referendum," 118; Legislature files in box 19, HP; Franklin Hichborn, "Sources of Opposition to Direct Legislation in California," *Transactions of the Commonwealth Club of California*, 35 (Mar. 3, 1931): 535–36.

41. [Great Adventure], *The Henry George Standard*, Nov. 1922, literature in Single Tax file, and Haynes to Staughton Cooley, Jan. 4, 1922, box 186, and People's Anti–Single Tax League circular (June 17, 1924), box 38, HP.

42. Hichborn, *California Legislature of 1921*, 168–69; Arthur M. Schlesinger, Jr., *The Crisis of the Old Order, 1919–1933*, vol. 1 of his *The Age of Roosevelt*, 3 vols. (Boston: Houghton Mifflin, 1957), 124.

43. Haynes to Spreckels, July 28, 1921, et al., Haynes to Hichborn, June 23, 1922, et al., box 159, Franklin Hichborn Papers, UCLA; Hichborn, "California Politics," 3: 1958–2019.

44. Haynes to C. C. Young, Jan. 13, 1923, Haynes to William Kehoe, Jan. 29, 1923, and other material in Jones Committee file, box 178, HP; Hichborn, "California Politics," 3: 2021–53; *San Francisco Call*, Feb. 23, 1923.

45. Haynes's account ledger (1921–27) HF; Hichborn, "California Politics," 4: 2218–64, 2371–80.

46. Haynes to City Council, Dec. 2, 1918, box 110, HP; *Examiner*, Jan. 22, 1919; file on 1919 medical survey, HF.

47. Haynes to Ralph Criswell, Sept. 5, 1918, Neal P. Olsen to Haynes, Sept. 11, 1918, and Woodman to Haynes, Sept. 19, 1918, box 133, and Haynes to John B. Elliott, June 19, 1919, box 270, HP.

48. 1919 Election files in boxes 135, 137, and 138, HP.

49. Haynes to F. W. Blanshard, Apr. 28, 1919, box 58, and John R. Haynes, "Public Ownership," autobiography typescript, box 170, HP; *Examiner*, June 2, 1919; Joseph Gerald Woods, "The Progressives and the Police: Urban Reform and the Professionalization of the Los Angeles Police" (Ph.D. diss., University of California, Los Angeles, 1973), 47–48.

50. Haynes to William Randolph Hearst, Aug. 31, 1923, HF; Haynes to M. Eldridge, Apr. 16, 1921, box 38, and Haynes to Max Ihmsen, July 22, 1918, box 147, HP; *Times*, May 20, 1921.

51. *Examiner*, Sept. 28, 1923; "A Friend" to Hearst, Nov. 17, 1925, box 147, HP. Chandler was also attacked constantly by other Los Angeles newspapers, especially the *Record*; see files on Harry Chandler in boxes 147 and 148, HP.

52. Marion C. Mohen to Haynes, Dec. 18, 1920, and Haynes to Mohen, Dec. 20, 1920, "Personal 1" Scrapbook, and Haynes to J. B. Elliott, June 19, 1919, box 270, HP.

53. *Times*, Aug. 4, 1921, Jan. 25, 1922; Department of Water and Power files in box 113, HP; Department of Water and Power employment file, HF.

54. Nelson S. Van Valen, "Power Politics: The Struggle for Municipal Ownership of Electrical Utilities in Los Angeles, 1905–1937" (Ph.D. diss., Claremont Graduate School, 1963), 187–92.

55. *Times*, Aug. 3, 6, Sept. 3, 4, 1921; *Express*, Aug. 15, 1921; *Examiner*, Oct. 1, 1921; Van Valen, "Power Politics," 192–210, quote on 197.

56. *Examiner*, Jan. 15, Feb. 27, 1922; *Herald*, Jan. 26, 1922; clippings in "Sale of Power Bonds 1921" Scrapbook, HP.

57. Haynes to Rudolph Spreckels, May 7, 1923, box 159, Franklin Hichborn Papers, UCLA; *Times*, Sept. 9, 1921; John J. Hamilton to Haynes, Sept. 15, 1923, and Hamilton to John J. Kemp, et al., Dec. 29, 1924, box 177, HP; John R. Haynes, "Public Power League," *Los Angeles School Journal*, 5 (Sept. 12, 1921): 19.

58. Hamilton to R. W. Borough, Sept. 15, 1923, and other material in box 177, Haynes to Mr. and Mrs. Durfee, Apr. 24, 1924, S. K. Decker to Haynes, Apr. 17, 1924, and 1924 Bond Election files in boxes 135, 139, 140, HP; Van Valen, "Power Politics," 211–20, 230–54.

59. Abraham Hoffman, *Vision or Villainy: Origins of the Owens Valley–Los Angeles Water Controversy* (College Station: Texas A & M University Press, 1981), 74–184; William H. Kahrl, *Water and Power: The Conflict Over Los Angeles' Water Supply in the Owens Valley* (Berkeley: University of California Press, 1982), 1–317; "The 'Owens Valley Revolt,' " *Municipal League Bulletin*, July 15, 1924, 1–5.

60. Hoffman, *Vision or Villainy*, 184–203, 234–43; files on Mayor's Conciliation Committee, box 11, Jackson A. Graves Papers, Huntington; John Walton, "Picnic at Alabama Gates," *California History*, 65 (Sept. 1986): 193–206; Los Angeles Department of Public Service, "The Dynamite Holdup" (pamphlet), and other material in box 122, HP; Gordon R. Miller, "Los Angeles and the Owens River Aqueduct" (Ph.D. diss., Claremont Graduate School, 1977), 223–60.

61. Metropolitan Water District of Southern California, *History and First Annual Report* (Los Angeles: Metropolitan Water District, 1939), 26–37; California Colorado River Commission, *Colorado River and Boulder Canyon Project* (Sacramento, 1931); Paul L. Kleinsorge, *The Boulder Canyon Project: Historical and Economic Aspects* (Stanford, Calif.: Stanford University Press, 1941), 1–184; Norris Hundley, Jr., *Water and the West: The Colorado River Compact and the Politics of Water in the American West* (Berkeley: University of California Press, 1975).

62. *Times*, Dec. 10, 1921.

63. Ibid., Dec. 11, 1921; *Record*, Dec. 16, 1921; Louis Bartlett, "Memoirs" (University of California, Berkeley, Regional Cultural History Project, 1957), 152–53.

64. John R. Haynes, "A Canyon and a City," *Survey Graphic*, 52 (June 1924): 279–83; *Times*, May 27, 1923; *Examiner*, June 4, 1923; Haynes to Franklin Hichborn, Mar. 27, 1925, box 19, HP; Remi Nadeau, *The Water Seekers* (Garden City, N.Y.: Doubleday, 1950): 196–97.

65. Tom Sitton, "The 'Boss' Without a Machine: Kent K. Parrot and Los Angeles in the 1920s," *Southern California Quarterly*, 67 (Winter 1985): 367–68.

66. Ibid., 368–69.

67. Haynes to Governor Stephens, Jan. 23, 1922, and Parrot to Haynes, Aug. 25, 1922, box 59, Haynes to Parrot, May 14, 19, 1923, box 106, and Haynes to Mayor Cryer, July 26, 1924, et al., box 131, HP.

68. Sitton, "Boss Without a Machine," 369–74.

69. Haynes to George G. Young, Apr. 20, 1923, and Haynes to Parrot, Apr. 26, 1923, box 59, HP; *Examiner*, Apr. 27, 30, 1923; *Record*, Apr. 21, 1923; *Times*, Apr. 25—May 1, 1923; clippings in Scrapbook 17A, Edward A. Dickson Papers, UCLA; Louis B. Perry and Richard S. Perry, *A History of the Los Angeles Labor Movement, 1911–1941* (Berkeley: University of California Press, 1963), 182–89.

70. *Record*, Apr. 26, 1923; typescript memo on 1923 election, Haynes to Parrot, May 14, 19, 1923, Haynes to George G. Young, Apr. 23, 1923, and files in box 106, HP. Mayor Cryer had asked for a new charter in his 1922 annual message.

71. *Citizen*, Apr. 27, 1923; *Times*, June 16, July 3, 1918; O. C. Bay to Haynes, Jan. 3, 1923, "Personal 1" Scrapbook, HP; Perry and Perry, *Los Angeles Labor Movement*, 83, 101, 112; Richard Norman Baisden, "Labor Unions in Los Angeles Politics" (Ph.D. diss., University of Chicago, 1958), 36–39, 51.

72. Haynes to Robert M. Clarke, June 23, 1923, Statement of the Citizens Committee of 10,000, Feb. 13, 1924, and other material in charter files in boxes 105 and 106, and clippings in "Personal 2½" Scrapbook, HP; *Citizen*, Nov. 2, 1923.

73. C. A. Dykstra, "Los Angeles Returns to the Ward System," *National Municipal Review*, 14 (Apr. 14, 1925): 210–12.

74. *Examiner*, Nov. 18, 21, 1919; Haynes to Board of Supervisors, July 3, 1920, and material in Charities file, box 141, and miscellaneous files in box 145, HP.

75. *Times*, Mar. 28, 1920; Haynes's circular letter, Mar. 30, 1920, and Haynes to Mayor and City Council, Mar. 21, 1920, box 68, HP.

76. *Examiner*, July 19, Oct. 11, 1921; Haynes to Mayor Cryer, July 22, 1921, Haynes to August Vollmer, Aug. 4, 1923, box 133, and 1921 Election files, box 58, HP; Woods, "Progressives and Police," 222–23, 228–31.

77. *Times*, July 29, Aug. 1–3, 16, 18, 1923; *Record*, Nov. 23, 1923, Mar. 3, 1924.

78. *Times*, Apr. 12, 1925; *Record*, Apr. 13, 1925.

79. *Record*, Mar. 28, Apr. 30, 1925; *Examiner*, Apr. 16, May 3, 1925; newspaper clippings on 1925 election in boxes 59 and 60, HP; Woods, "Progressives and Police," 226–28.

80. Robert M. Fogelson, *The Fragmented Metropolis: Los Angeles, 1850–1930* (Cambridge, Mass.: Harvard University Press, 1967), 220.

81. Haynes to Parrot, Mar. 10, 1925, box 59, HP; *Times* Apr. 12, May 1, 1925.

82. Haynes to Harlan Palmer, Apr. 24, 1925, et al., box 59, Bledsoe file, box 8, and 1925 Election files, box 60, HP; Anne M. Mumford to Franklin Hichborn, Mar. 9, 1925, et al., box 159, Franklin Hichborn Papers, UCLA.

83. Ralph Arnold to Herbert Hoover, Apr. 30, 1926, box 226, Ralph Arnold Papers, Huntington; Henry E. Huntington to William M. Garland, Apr. 23, 1925, HM12528, Henry E. Huntington Papers, Huntington.

84. Robert W. Kenny, "My First Forty Years in California Politics, 1922–1962" (University of California, Los Angeles, Oral History Program, 1964), 36.

85. Winston Wutkee (interviewer), "Godfather of UCLA: Regent Edward A. Dickson," 2 vols. (University of California, Los Angeles, Oral History Program, 1983), 2: 398; clippings in "Woman Suffrage" Scrapbook, HP; Katherine P. Edson to Hiram Johnson, Oct. 24, 1924, box 1, Katherine P. Edson Papers, UCLA.

86. League of Women Voters of Los Angeles, typescript, box 1, League of Women Voters of Los Angeles Collection, Urban Archives, California State University, Northridge; Jean Loewy, "Katherine Philips Edson and the California Suffrage Movement, 1919–1920" *California Historical Society Quarterly*, 47 (Dec. 1968): 344–47.

87. Mrs. Edmond M. Lazard to Haynes, Jan. 15, 1935, and Mrs. George B. Mangold to Trustees of the Haynes Foundation, Feb. 11, 1938, box 93, HP; program of "Thanksgiving Celebration" (1920), box 9, Frances Noel Papers, UCLA.

88. Pamphlets and other material in boxes 1, 26, 318, League of Women Voters Papers, LC; *Herald*, Oct. 23, 1920; clippings on "Women's Party Amendment" (1924–25) in box 227, HP; Dora Haynes to Mr. P. D. Noel, May 9, 1922, box 10, Frances Noel Papers, UCLA.

89. Maysie Miller to Dora Haynes, Feb. 10, Nov. 30, 1921, et al., box 271, HP; *Times*, May 24, 1919, Apr. 11, 1919, May 6, 1925.

90. *Record*, Apr. 26, 1923; Edwin O. Palmer, *History of Hollywood*, rev. ed. (Hollywood, Calif.: Edwin O. Palmer, 1938), 211.

91. *Annals of the Sunset Club*, 3: 96–110.

92. *Who's Who on the Pacific Coast* (Chicago: A. N. Marquis, 1951), 466.

CHAPTER ELEVEN

1. Haynes to Mrs. John Randolph Haynes, Mar. 1, 1922, box 270, HP.

2. Ibid.

3. Louis Bartlett to Haynes, Nov. 28, 1923, HF.

4. Merle Curti, "Subsidizing Radicalism: The American Fund for Public Service, 1921–41," *Social Service Review*, 33 (Sept. 1959): 274–95; Waldemar A. Nielsen, *The Big Foundations* (New York: Columbia University Press, 1972), 21–46, 170–90, 250–56.

5. Haynes to J. Wiseman Macdonald, Aug. 25, 1927, HF; Haynes to Andrew Mellon, Feb. 18, 1924, box 78, HP.

6. Haynes to Rudolph Spreckels, Aug. 14, 1924, Hichborn to Haynes, Sept. 20, 1926, and "The John Randolph Haynes and Dora Haynes Foundation Declaration of Trust, September 22, 1926," HF.

7. "Haynes Foundation Declaration of Trust," HF; *Times*, Mar. 28, 1928.

8. Haynes's autobiography notes, HF.

9. Interview with Francis Haynes Lindley, Sept. 19, 1986; Lindley to Haynes, July 21, 1925, box 177, Haynes to Governor C. C. Young, Dec. 30, 1926, box 229, HP; *Who's Who in California, 1979–1980* (San Clemente, Calif.: Who's Who Historical Society, 1979), 193.

10. Hichborn/Haynes correspondence, 1923–27, HF.

11. Haynes to K. C. Smith et al., Oct. 23, 1930, HF.

12. *Examiner*, Dec. 10, 1931.

13. Trustee and Correspondence files, HF.

14. *Dictionary of American Biography*, supp. 4, 246–48.

15. "Minutes of Meetings of the Board of Trustees, Haynes Foundation," 1: 20–21 (June 6, 1928), and Haynes's account ledgers (1921–27, 1928–37), HF.

16. Richard T. Ely to Haynes, Apr. 6, 1921, box 73, Nov. 11, 1921, box 76, Dec. 11, 1923, box 85, Jan. 12, 1925, box 90, Haynes to Ely, June 22, 1923, box 84, Mar. 10, 1925, box 91, Richard T. Ely Papers, SHSWA; Frederick L. Bird and Frances M. Ryan, *Public Ownership on Trial: A Study of Municipal Light and Power in California* (New York: New Republic, 1930); Haynes survey files in *Public Ownership on Trial* file, box 174, and Haynes to Gifford Pinchot, Mar. 29, 1917, Pinchot to Haynes, Apr. 9, 1917, and other material in box 158, HP; Haynes / F. L. Bird correspondence, 1930, HF.

17. Carl Thompson to Haynes, Oct. 9, 1917, box 176, Haynes to Thompson, Jan. 8, Dec. 28, 1929, May 3, 1930, box 177, HP; Haynes's account ledger (1928–37), HF.

18. Frederick L. Bird and Frances M. Ryan, *The Recall of Public Officers: A Study of the Operation of the Recall in California* (New York: Macmillan, 1930), esp. 242–43, 342; quote on 342.

19. Judson King to Haynes, May 28, 1921, Haynes to King, Dec. 28, 1925, et al., HF; Haynes to Thomas H. Everitt, Nov. 14, 1918, box 158, and King/ Haynes correspondence in boxes 158, 170, 171, 221, HP.

20. Haynes to Will H. Anderson, Jan. 4, 1934, HF; Haynes to Dora Haynes, Oct. 13, 1923, box 51, HP; John R. Haynes, "The Direct Primary," *California League of Women Voters Bulletin*, Mar. 1927, 4–5.

21. John R. Haynes, "The Widening Sphere of Municipal Activities," type-script speech for USC economics classes, Nov. 24, 1915, and other speeches, box 153, HP; memorandum from Haynes to trustees of the Haynes Foundation (c. 1933), HF.

22. Haynes's autobiography notes, HF.

23. Haynes to Hiram Johnson, Feb. 2, 1923, Haynes to Owen Lovejoy, Dec. 18, 1925, Haynes to Everett P. Wheeler, Dec. 5, 1924, box 26, HP; *Examiner*, Feb. 11, 1935; Haynes to Robert A. Millikan, Jan. 23, 1937, HF.

24. *Saturday Night*, Feb. 6, 1926, 1–2; Haynes to John B. Andrews, Feb. 4, 1924, Dec. 7, 1932, et al., box 1, and Mining file, box 152, HP; "Minutes of Meetings of the Board of Trustees, Haynes Foundation," 1: 20–21 (June 6, 1928), and Haynes's account ledger (1928–37), HF.

25. Emily Sims Marconnier to Haynes, June 1, 1935, box 156, HP; William L. O'Neill, *Everyone Was Brave: The Rise and Fall of Feminism in America* (Chicago: Quadrangle Books, 1969), 95–98, 152–53, 232–40; Haynes to Meyer Lissner, May 21, 1919, box 17, Meyer Lissner Papers, Stanford; Katherine Dennis to Haynes, Dec. 31, 1925, Haynes to Paul Kellogg, Dec. 1, 1925, et al., HF; *Survey* file, box 197, HP. On Kellogg see Clarke A. Chambers, *Paul U. Kellogg and the "Survey": Voices for Social Welfare and Social Justice* (Minneapolis: University of Minnesota Press, 1971).

26. Remson Bird's statement (1944), typescript, and Gordon S. Watkins, "John Randolph Haynes and Dora Haynes and Their Sound Ideals," typescript speech, Nov. 29, 1944, HF.

27. Haynes's account ledger, (1928–37), HF.

28. Donald K. Pickins, *Eugenics and the Progressives* (Nashville, Tenn.: Vanderbilt University Press, 1968), 3–130; Daniel J. Kevles, *In the Name of Eugenics: Genetics and the Uses of Human Heredity* (New York: Knopf, 1985), esp. 59–94; David B. Danbom, *"The World of Hope": Progressives and the Struggle for an Ethical Public Life* (Philadelphia: Temple University Press, 1987), 181.

29. Haynes's autobiography notes, HF.

30. Haynes to Estelle Lawton Lindsey, Feb. 2, 1917, and Birth Control file, box 8, and Haynes's questionnaires to institutions and replies, 1916, box 193, HP; Haynes to Mrs. Carrie P. Bryant, Oct. 3, 1914, HF.

31. *Social Messenger* clipping (1898), in "Direct Legislation in Los Angeles and How It Works" Scrapbook, and John R. Haynes, "The State Institutions of California," typescript speech, June 10, 1918, box 72, HP.

32. John R. Haynes, "Sterilization of the Unfit," *Pacific Coast Journal of Nursing*, 18 (Sept. 1922): 548–53, (Oct. 1922): 608–12.

33. Haynes to William Blumenthal, July 3, 1922, and Sterilization file, box 193, and Eugenics files, box 65, HP.

34. Haynes to C. C. Young, Jan. 15, 1930, Haynes to Ransome Sutton, Aug. 17, 1933, Haynes to Rockwell C. Hunt, Feb. 4, 1935, and Haynes's account ledger (1928–37), HF; *Palm Springs Limelight*, Jan. 28, 1934.

35. Haynes to Estelle L. Lindsey, Feb. 2, 1917, and Margaret Sanger to Haynes, Dec. 20, 1934, HF; Haynes to Sanger, Dec. 16, 1925, Feb. 20, 1930, Sanger to Haynes, Jan. 22, 1930, Haynes to Joe Crail, Jan. 16, 1930, and Birth Control files in boxes 7 and 8, HP; *Times*, July 2, 1937.

36. Fourth Report of the Committee on Selective Immigration of the American Eugenics Society, Inc." (June 30, 1928), box 78, HP; Mark H. Haller, *Eugenics: Hereditarian Attitudes in American Thought*, rev. ed. (New Brunswick, N.J.: Rutgers University Press, 1984), 144–59; various articles in *Eugenics Review*, 1928–30.

37. A. P. Watts to Haynes, Jan. 26, 1931, and Haynes's autobiography notes, HF; *Examiner*, May 18, 1923; California League questionnaire, signed Apr. 20, 1923, box 106, and *Pacific Defender*, Dec. 19, 1929, clipping in box 73, HP.

38. Haynes to A. H. Briggs, Aug. 16, 1933, Haynes to S. T. Montgomery, Feb. 28, 1925, Oct. 4, 1926, box 4, and Election files, box 61, HP; Franklin Hichborn to Haynes, July 2, 1921, box 160, and Haynes to Hichborn, Aug. 1, 1921, box 159, Franklin Hichborn Papers, UCLA; Wendell E. Harmon, "A History of the Prohibition Movement in California" (Ph.D. diss., University of California, Los Angeles, 1955), 245–76.

39. John R. Haynes, "Prohibition," speech, June 25, 1926, and other typescript speeches, box 168, and Haynes's statement in *National Liberator*, 4 (Sept. 1933): 4, clipping in box 72, HP.

40. "Sequoya League–Los Angeles Council," pamphlet (1906), box 79, HP; Francis E. Watkins, "Charles F. Lummis and the Sequoya League," *Quarterly of the Historical Society of Southern California*, 26 (June–Sept. 1944): 99–114; John Collier, *From Every Zenith: A Memoir and Some Essays on Life and Thought* (Denver: Sage Books, 1963), 115–16.

41. Robert Ingersoll Brown to Haynes, March 19, 1923, "Personal 2½" Scrapbook, and AIDA files, box 211, HP; Kenneth R. Philp, *John Collier's Crusade for Indian Reform, 1920–1954* (Tucson: University of Arizona Press, 1977), 46–47.

42. Alida C. Bowler to Anne Mumford, Sept. 21, 1926, Haynes to John Collier, Aug. 9, 1927, Jan. 7, 1928, and Collier to Haynes, Oct. 6, 1925, box 2, HP; Haynes/Collier correspondence, 1921–37, HF; Collier, *From Every Zenith*, 115–35, quote on 116.

43. Haynes to Hiram Johnson, Dec. 31, 1932, box 79, Haynes correspondence in box 2, and Office of Indian Affairs files, boxes 211 and 212, HP; Collier, *From Every Zenith*, 148–56; Lawrence C. Kelly, "Choosing the New Deal Indian Commissioner: Ickes vs. Collier," *New Mexico Historical Review*, 49 (Oct. 1974): 269–87.

44. Haynes correspondence in boxes 2, 78–81, and 211–12, HP, and in files of HF; Owens Valley Indians file, box 123, HP; *Record*, July 11, 1929; Los Angeles Chamber of Commerce *Bulletin*, Nov. 7, 1937, 2.

45. Roger Baldwin to Haynes, Apr. 1, 1922, Dec. 12, 1922, box 27, and NPGL file, box 158, HP; Haynes to Rand School of Social Service, June 23, 1921, HF.

46. Martin Zanger, "Politics of Confrontation: Upton Sinclair and the Launching of the ACLU in Southern California," *Pacific Historical Review*, 38 (Nov. 1969): 383–94; Upton Sinclair, *The Autobiography of Upton Sinclair* (New York: Harcourt, Brace and World, 1962), 228–32.

47. Sinclair to Haynes, May 29, 1923, Upton Sinclair Papers, Lilly; Zanger, "Politics of Confrontation," 395–403; Financial files, HF; Mary Craig Sinclair, *Southern Belle* (New York: Crown, 1957), 281–86.

48. Clinton J. Taft to Haynes, Sept. 27, 1934, and E. P. Ryland to Haynes, July 23, 1937, box 27, HP; Haynes to Roger Baldwin, July 9, 1926, HF; Upton Sinclair to Haynes, Sept. 22, 1927, June 4, 1928, Upton Sinclair Papers, Lilly.

49. John R. Haynes, "What I Believe and Why," typescript speech to X Club, 1915, "Articles, Speeches" Scrapbook, and Paul Blanshard to Haynes, Sept. 21, Oct. 15, 1928, box 92, HP.

50. Robert Morss Lovett to Haynes, Mar. 4, 1926, Harry Laidler to Haynes, May 31, 1927, box 93, Laidler to Anne Mumford, Mar. 15, 1927, box 92, and responses from colleges to Haynes (1927), boxes 92, 271, HP; Haynes to Louis Bartlett, Feb. 3, 1936, HF.

51. Laidler to Haynes Foundation, Nov. 29, 1937, Norman Thomas to Mumford, Dec. 4, 1926, box 92, Mumford to Laidler, May 29, 1930, and LID files in boxes 92, 93 HP; Haynes to Dr. Cloyd H. Marvin, Oct. 11, 1929, and Haynes/Laidler correspondence, HF.

52. Haynes to Mrs. Haynes, Mar. 1, 1922, box 270, Haynes to Rev. Joseph Johnson, Jan. 11, 1926, Haynes to William B. Mathews, May 15, 1925, box 71, HP; *Saturday Night*, Apr. 9, 1927, 2; *Record*, July 11, 1929; Good Hope Hospital Correspondence file, HF; Thomas C. Marshall, *Into the Streets and Lanes: The Beginnings and Growth of the Social Work of the Episcopal Church in the Diocese of Los Angeles* (Claremont, Calif.: Saunders Press, 1948), 31.

53. Wilshire to Haynes, Oct. 30, 1924, box 10, H. Gaylord Wilshire Papers, UCLA; Haynes to Wilshire, Nov. 20, 1925, HF; Donald G. Davis, Jr., "The Ionaco of Gaylord Wilshire," *Southern California Quarterly*, 49 (Dec. 1967): 425–53.

54. Haynes's autobiography notes, HF; Collier, *From Every Zenith*, 116.

55. Haynes's autobiography notes and account ledgers, HF; Haynes to A. M. Wilkinson, May 16, 1936, box 67, Haynes to John Eby, June 1, 1932, et al.,

box 109, and W. E. McCulloch to Haynes, July 1, 1926, "Personal 3" Scrapbook, HP.

56. John R. Haynes, statement on Sermon on the Mount and "Social Injustice," typescript speech, c. 1922, HF; Peter J. Frederick, *Knights of the Golden Rule: The Intellectual as Christian Social Reformer in the 1890s* (Lexington: University Press of Kentucky, 1976), 24–25.

57. Haynes, "Social Injustice"; David A. Shannon, *The Socialist Party of America: A History* (New York: Macmillan, 1955), 59.

58. Collier vs. Lindley, 203 Cal Rep 641 (1928); *Times*, Mar. 28, 1928; "Minutes of Meetings of the Board of Trustees, Haynes Foundation," 1: 1–18 (June 9, 1927; Sept. 7, 1927), and Haynes to J. Wiseman Macdonald, Aug. 25, 1927, HF.

59. Haynes to foundation trustees, Aug. 27, 1928, and Haynes, undated memorandums, HF.

60. J. Stitt Wilson to trustees, May 30, 1928, HF; Wilson to Haynes, Oct. 23, 1928, Feb. 2, 1929, Mar. 30, 1930, box 227, HP.

61. Haynes to Upton Sinclair, Sept. 28, 1929, Katie Mae Wilson to Haynes, Dec. 3, 1929, and Grants Denied files, HF.

62. "Minutes of Meetings of the Board of Trustees, Haynes Foundation," 1: 61–79 (Sept. 22, 1930–Feb. 19, 1934), HF; *Who's Who in America, 1946–1947* (Chicago: A. N. Marquis, 1946), 1227.

63. Haynes to Hichborn, Apr. 20, 1931, HF; *Condon's Blue Book of Wealth* (Los Angeles: James Edward Condon, 1931), 143.

CHAPTER TWELVE

1. *Times*, July 6, 1927.

2. Haynes to Franklin Hichborn, July 12, 1925, box 60, Hichborn to Haynes, Sept. 28, 1925, Haynes to Robert M. Clarke, Oct. 8, 1925, Haynes to R. H. Young, Oct. 9, 1925, Haynes to Hichborn, Oct. 8, 12, 1925, box 59, HP; Russell M. Posner, "The Progressive Voters League, 1923–26," *California Historical Society Quarterly*, 36 (Sept. 1957): 256–58.

3. Harry Chandler to Jackson A. Graves, Oct. 2, 1926, box 11, Jackson A. Graves Papers, Huntington; Jackson K. Putnam, *Modern California Politics*, 2nd ed. (San Francisco: Boyd and Fraser, 1984), 10–11.

4. Anne M. Mumford to Progressive Voters League, June 2, 1926, HF; 1926 Election files, box 60, HP. Success brought Giannini the appointment of career educator Will C. Wood as bank commissioner. Wood later joined Giannini's firm. Marquis James and Bessie Rowland James, *Biography of a Bank: The Story of Bank of America* (New York: Harper and Brothers, 1954), 180–84; Royce D. Delmatier, Clarence F. McIntosh, and Earl G. Waters, eds., *The Rumble of California Politics, 1848–1970* (New York: John Wiley, 1970), 213–14.

5. Hichborn to Haynes, Feb. 17, 1926, Haynes to Rudolph Spreckels, Aug. 2, 1926, Spreckels to Haynes, Aug. 4, 1926, and 1926 Election files, box 60, HP; *Times*, Jan. 10, 1926; Posner, "Progressive Voters League," 258–60.

6. Putnam, *Modern California Politics*, 11–12; H. Brett Melendy and Benjamin F. Gilbert, *The Governors of California: From Peter H. Burnett to Edmund G. Brown* (Georgetown, Calif.: Talisman, 1965), 349–60.

7. Haynes to Young, Dec. 30, 1926, Haynes to Mrs. C. C. Young, Jan. 15, 1927, box 229, Haynes to Young, Nov. 30, Dec. 14, 1928, box 43, Haynes to Young, Mar. 30, Apr. 16, 1927, box 228, HP; Haynes/Young correspondence, 1926–30, HF.

8. Haynes to Hichborn, Jan. 25, 1927, Hichborn to Haynes, Jan. 28, 1927, box 229, HP; *Times*, Mar. 17, 1930; Frank Doherty to Hiram Johnson, Mar. 6, 1929, Apr. 22, 1930, Part 3, box 34, Hiram W. Johnson Papers, Bancroft.

9. Haynes to Tom Mooney, May 7, 12, Oct. 15, 1928, June 11, 1929, Haynes to Fremont Older, Dec. 13, 1928, Jan. 4, 1929, Jan. 30, 1930, box 8, Thomas J. Mooney Papers, Bancroft. For Mooney's dilemma see Robert H. Frost, *The Mooney Case* (Stanford, Calif.: Stanford University Press, 1968).

10. Haynes to Young, Aug. 8, 1927, HF; Haynes to Young, Mar. 2, May 17, 1927, box 198, Haynes to Staughton Cooley, Dec. 31, 1927, Haynes to C. K. McClatchy, Oct. 15, 1927, Haynes to Edgar C. Levey, Oct. 8, 1929, box 199, Banking files in box 5, HP; Haynes to Will C. Wood, Mar. 5, 1928, Wood to Haynes, Mar. 10, 1928, box 365, Will C. Wood Papers, California State Library, Sacramento.

11. California Tax Commission, *Final Report, May 5, 1929* (Sacramento, 1929); Edward F. Treadwell, "Tinkering with the Tax Laws," *California Law Review*, 18 (July 1930): 497–510; Norman Loyall McLaren and Vincent K. Butler, Jr., *California Tax Laws of 1929* (San Francisco: Walker's Manual, 1929).

12. *Times*, Feb. 5, March 1, 1930; minutes of the California Constitutional Commission meetings, and Haynes to Hichborn, Feb. 16, 1930, box 15, Haynes to George Dunlop, Apr. 24, 1930, Haynes to Will J. French, Aug. 22, 1930, box 14, HP.

13. California Constitutional Commission, *Report, December 29, 1930* (Sacramento, 1929).

14. California State Unemployment Board, "A County Municipal Program for Combatting Unemployment" (Sacramento, 1931); undated newspaper clipping and Unemployment files, box 205, HP.

15. Edward A. Dickson correspondence with Haynes and others, boxes 18 and 19, Edward A. Dickson Papers, UCLA; Winston Wutkee (interviewer), "Godfather of UCLA: Regent Edward A. Dickson," 2 vols. (University of California, Los Angeles, Oral History Program, 1983), vol. 2; James R. Martin, *The University of California (in Los Angeles): A Resume of the Selection and Acquisition of the Westwood Site* (Los Angeles: James R. Martin, 1925), 29–180.

16. Martin, *University of California*, 47–48; *Herald*, Apr. 10, 1926; Ernest C. Moore to Haynes, Mar. 16, 1926, Anne Mumford to Charles Grove Haines, June 16, 1927, Haynes to D. G. Maelise, Sept. 14, 1931, box 219, HP.

17. Haynes to Young, Feb. 20, 1929, J. W. Buzzell to Haynes, July 13, 1933, box 216, Haynes to Edward Walther, Aug. 5, 1931, box 218, Haynes to Robert Sproul, Dec. 15, 1926, Haynes to Guy Earl, Dec. 15, 1926, box 219, HP.

18. UC Medical School file, box 218, minutes of meetings of the UC Board of Regents, 1930, box 219, Haynes to Frank J. Waters, May 7, 1935, box 20, HP; Haynes to Neylan, Aug. 3, 1937, box 85, John F. Neylan Papers, Bancroft.

19. Civil Service files, box 28, Legislative Session files (1926–33), boxes 19, 20, Haynes to Hichborn, Feb. 16, 1931, box 20, HP; memorandum from Haynes to trustees, n.d., and Haynes/Hichborn correspondence, HF.

20. Frank S. Boggs to Haynes, Jan. 10, 1929, box 39, Haynes to Young, Nov. 23, Dec. 14, 1928, box 43, and Legislature files, boxes 19, 20, 39, HP.

21. Haynes to E. A. Walcott, June 9, 1924, box 28, Haynes to R. S. Huntington, Sept. 20, Dec. 21, 1928, box 42, and May 8, 1928, box 43, HP.

22. Haynes to Orrin K. Murray, Nov. 8, 1929, minutes of the meeting of the Direct Legislation Section of the Commonwealth Club, May 16, 1929, box 42, HP.

23. *Transactions of the Commonwealth Club of California*, 25 (Mar. 3, 1931): 409–590, esp. 559–63.

24. Haynes to Herbert C. Jones, Oct. 20, Dec. 8, 1932, Jones to Haynes, Dec. 23, 1932, Haynes to William H. Waste, Oct. 22, 1932, box 72, Herbert C. Jones Papers, Stanford.

25. Haynes to Editor, *Los Angeles Times*, Nov. 4, 1932, box 39, HP.

26. Haynes to Governor Stephens, Mar. 30, 1921, box 19, Haynes to Hichborn, Jan. 10, 1928, box 60, HP.

27. Haynes to Dr. Irving Fisher, Aug. 1, 1928, box 164, Judson King to Haynes, Sept. 28, 1928, box 221, Public Ownership League of America files, box 157, Hichborn to Haynes, Oct. 31, 1928, Haynes to Hichborn, Nov. 3, 1928, copy of Hichborn to Carl Thompson, Sept. 28, 1928, box 60, HP; Delmatier, McIntosh, and Waters, *Rumble of California Politics*, 209–10; *The Campaign Book of the Democratic Party: Candidates and Issues in 1928* (New York: Democratic National Committee, 1928), 141–48.

28. Paul Scharrenberg, "Reminiscences . . ." (University of California, Berkeley, Regional Oral History Project, 1954), 98; Haynes to Dr. Arthur Briggs, June 17, 1930, and other correspondence in box 61, HP; Haynes's correspondence regarding Anti-Saloon League, 1930, HF; *Times*, Aug. 3, 1930; Delmatier, McIntosh, and Waters, *Rumble of California Politics*, 217–18.

29. Sample ballot, 1930 California General Election, box 106, HP.

30. Melendy and Gilbert, *Governors of California*, 363–78; Putnam, *Modern California Politics*, 13–16.

31. Ralph Arnold to Herbert Hoover, Apr. 30, 1926, box 226, Ralph Arnold Papers, Huntington; Tom Sitton, "The 'Boss' Without a Machine: Kent K. Parrot and Los Angeles in the 1920s," *Southern California Quarterly*, 67 (Winter 1985): 377–79.

32. Haynes to Kent Parrot, June 29, 1925, box 178, HP; *Times*, Nov. 11, 12, 1925.

33. Haynes to George Cryer, June 1, Aug. 5, 1927, June 5, 1928, et al., box 131, HP; Haynes to Upton Sinclair, Feb. 12, 1929, HF; Arthur E. Briggs, "Southern California Renaissance Man," 2 vols. (University of California, Los Angeles, Oral History Program, 1970), 1: 409.

34. Haynes to Carl Thompson, Apr. 13, Oct. 2, 1930, box 177, Haynes to Harold Jones, Mar. 18, 1926, Haynes to C. W. Kinney, Oct. 11, 1917, box 171, Haynes to mayor and city council of Banning, California, Aug. 24, 1931, box 172, HP; *Times*, Nov. 29, 1925.

35. *Grist*, Aug. 21, 1931, box 71, Haynes to W. Clifford Smith, Sept. 23, 1930, Carl Thompson to Haynes, Nov. 4, 1931, copy of Thompson to W. Clifford Smith, Feb. 1, 1932, and Public Ownership League of America files, box 177, HP.

36. Haynes to Joseph Sartori, May 3, 1929, et al., box 118, Department of

Water and Power files, boxes 113–15, and Haynes to Mrs. Eugene O. Mc-
Laughlin, Jan. 16, 1930, "Personal 3" Scrapbook, HP.

37. *Record*, Apr. 13, 14, 1928; Charles F. Outland, *Man-Made Disaster: The
Story of the St. Francis Dam* (Glendale, Calif.: Arthur A. Clark, 1963), 19–230.

38. Los Angeles Water and Power Protective League files, box 140, 1927 Bond
Election file, box 138, HP; *Times*, Nov. 3, 1927; Nelson S. Van Valen, "Power
Politics: The Struggle for Municipal Ownership of Electrical Utilities in Los An-
geles, 1905–1937" (Ph.D. diss., Claremont Graduate School, 1963), 260–70.

39. Haynes to Hiram Johnson, July 3, 1926, Mar. 17, 18, 1930, Part 3, box
43, Hiram W. Johnson Papers, Bancroft; Haynes to Judson King, Oct. 30, 1930,
Hichborn to Haynes, Aug. 13, 1928, and other material in Boulder Canyon files,
boxes 8–12, HP; *Times*, Apr. 27, 1930.

40. Metropolitan Water District of Southern California, *History and First Annual Report* (Los Angeles: Metropolitan Water District, 1939), 37–48; Metropolitan Water District files, boxes 149–51, HP.

41. *Record*, Dec. 16, 1921; Haynes to Clyde Seavey, Oct. 25, 1923, and min-
utes of Telephone Committee meetings, box 202, Southern California Telephone
Company file, box 192, William Mathews to Haynes, Oct. 1, 1925, box 133,
HP; Robert C. Post, "The Fair Fare Fight: An Episode in Los Angeles History,"
Southern California Quarterly, 52 (Sept. 1970): 275–99; Robert M. Fogelson,
The Fragmented Metropolis: Los Angeles, 1850–1930 (Cambridge, Mass.: Har-
vard University Press, 1967), 237–38.

42. *Los Angeles City Employee*, July 1937, 13, 18; Haynes to Cryer, Oct. 10,
1924, May 29, 1928, box 131, HP; *Record*, Jan. 7, 1931; *Express*, May 29,
1931.

43. Michael Creamer to Cryer, Jan. 14, 1927, Rupert Blue to Haynes, Mar. 4,
1926, and Public Health files, box 130, Haynes to Dr. J. L. Pomeroy, Apr. 26,
1927, Haynes to Cryer, July 18, 1928, box 145, HP.

44. Sitton, "Boss Without a Machine," 379–80.

45. *Times*, Apr. 3, 16–May 5, June 6, 1927; *Record*, May 27, 1927; Los Angeles Water and Power Protective League files, box 140, HP; Haynes to Hichborn, June 10, 1927, HF.

46. *Times*, July 1, 1927; Haynes to Jackson A. Graves, July 1, 1927, Graves to
Haynes, July 1, 1927, HF.

47. Haynes to Parrot, Aug. 26, 1927, et al., HF; L. M. Story to Haynes, May
4, 1928, box 140, HP.

48. Haynes to Parrot, Jan. 30, 1936, HF; Sitton, "Boss Without a Machine,"
383–84.

49. Frank Doherty to Hiram Johnson, Jan. 29, 1929, Part 3, box 34, Hiram
W. Johnson Papers, Bancroft; *Examiner*, May 7, 1929; *Times*, Mar. 1, 1929.

50. Haynes to Harlan Palmer, Apr. 8, 1929, box 116, Lew Head to Haynes,
Oct. 5, 1929, box 135, HP; *Municipal League Bulletin*, June 1, 1929, 1; *Times*,
Nov. 24, 1970.

51. *Times*, Mar. 29, Apr. 7, 1929; Haynes to Harlan Palmer, Apr. 8, 1929,
box 116, HP; John Robertson Quinn, "Memoirs of John Robertson Quinn"
(University of California, Los Angeles, Oral History Program, 1966), 84; William Avery to Will C. Wood, May 8, 1929, box 365, Will C. Wood Papers,
California State Library, Sacramento.

52. Bob Shuler to Haynes, Dec. 30, 1924, HF; *Bob Shuler's Magazine*, July

1924, Apr. 1930, et al.; William D. Edmondson, "Fundamentalist Sects of Los Angeles, 1900–1930" (Ph.D. diss., Claremont Graduate School, 1969), 389–424; Duncan Aikman, "Savonarola in Los Angeles," *American Mercury*, Dec. 1930, 426–429; Edmund Wilson, *The American Earthquake: A Documentary of the Twenties and Thirties* (New York: Octagon Books, 1975), 382–89; *Times*, Jan. 3, 1928.

53. *Record*, May 31, 1929; *Times*, May 31, June 1, 1929; *Illustrated Daily News*, May 30, 1929; Joseph Gerald Woods, "The Progressives and the Police: Urban Reform and the Professionalization of the Los Angeles Police" (Ph.D. diss., University of California, Los Angeles, 1973), 264.

54. Doherty to Johnson, June 5, 1929, Part 3, box 34, Hiram W. Johnson Papers, Bancroft; *Times*, July 8, Sept. 25, 1932; *Herald*, Aug. 12, 1931; *Examiner*, May 24, 1931; Leonard Joseph Leader, "Los Angeles and the Great Depression" (Ph.D. diss., University of California, Los Angeles, 1972), 25; Woods, "Progressives and Police," 270–79.

55. *Evening Express*, Oct. 5, 1931; *Record*, July 23, 25, Aug. 20, 1931; Woods, "Progressives and Police," 45–47, 50–52, 67, 286–97; Ernest Jerome Hopkins, *Our Lawless Police: A Study of the Unlawful Enforcement of the Law* (New York: Viking, 1931), esp. 152–59; Clinton J. Taft, *Fifteen Years on Freedom's Front* (Los Angeles: American Civil Liberties Union, 1939), 23–30, quote on 28.

56. Haynes to John C. Porter, June 22, Sept. 16, 1929, box 131, Haynes to Harlan Palmer, July 29, 1929, box 115, HP; *Times*, Dec. 13, 1929; "Bureaus Re-established," *Intake*, Jan. 1930, 3; Van Valen, "Power Politics," 294–99.

57. *Times*, Dec. 12, 1929, Jan. 21, 23, Feb. 2, 1930; *Examiner*, Jan. 21, 1930; "Changes Made in Two Boards," *Intake*, Mar. 1930, 8; Van Valen, "Power Politics," 299–300.

58. Haynes to O. T. Johnson, Jr., June 12, 1930, and other DWP material in box 114, HP; *Times*, Sept. 5, 1930; Van Valen, "Power Politics," 300–305, 320–21.

59. David Woodhead to Haynes, Oct. 8, 1930, box 139, and 1930 Bond Election file, box 138, HP; *Record*, Dec. 5, 1930; "Power Bond Campaign Opens," *Intake*, Oct. 1930, 3.

60. *Gridiron*, Feb. 10, 1931, 8, Mar. 10, 1931, 8, Mar. 24, 1931, 4, June 2, 1931, 8, box 112, and Andrae Nordskog file, box 159, HP; *Times*, Jan. 15, 1931; Abraham Hoffman, *Vision or Villainy: Origins of the Owens Valley–Los Angeles Water Controversy* (College Station: Texas A & M University Press, 1981), 208–43; Van Valen, "Power Politics," 305–7.

61. *Evening Express*, Dec. 11, 1930; *Times*, Apr. 14, 18, 1931; Municipal Light and Power Defense League file, box 155, HP; W. Worth Bernard, "A Critical Study of the Municipal Light and Power Defense League as a Lobbying Organization in Los Angeles" (Independent Study Report, University of Southern California, 1935), 45–56.

62. *Times*, Apr. 8, 1931; *Illustrated Daily News*, May 4, 1931. According to Haynes and others, Boddy began to oppose the city's power program after requesting and receiving a $100,000 loan from O. T. Johnson, Jr.; Haynes had turned down the same request. Haynes to S. C. Simons, Jan. 7, 1931, Simons to Haynes, Jan. 7, 1931, box 155, Haynes to W. R. Hearst, July 6, 1931, box 20, HP.

63. Haynes to Palmer, Sept. 23, 1931, and City Council Investigation file, box 120, HP; *Grist*, Sept. 5, 1931, 3; Haynes to Thomas J. Ford, July 22, 25, 1931, HF; Van Valen, "Power Politics," 309–20.

64. *Los Angeles Chronicle*, July 31, 1931, 7; Haynes to Young Men's Republican Club, Aug. 14, 1931, box 118, HP; Haynes to William Thum, July 16, 1931, HF; John R. Haynes, "A Pointed Statement of Fact About the Municipal Bureau of Power and Light," pamphlet (1931), box 9, Frances Noel Papers, UCLA.

65. Haynes to Martin Luther Thomas, Dec. 31, 1931, copy of Thomas to John A. Eby, May 31, 1932, Haynes to E. A. Cabrera, May 21, 1931, HF; Eby to Haynes, May 27, 1932, box 109, HP.

66. *Herald*, Aug. 12, 1931, and newspaper clippings in Porter file, box 131, HP.

67. Haynes to Hichborn, Aug. 13, 1931, Hichborn to Haynes, Aug. 15, 1931, Haynes to Parrish, Oct. 28, 1931, Haynes to William Thum, Nov. 12, 1931, HF; *Times*, Nov. 3, 1931, Mar. 12, 1932; *Citizen*, Jan. 29, 1932; Haynes to Parrish, Oct. 29, 1931, box 48, HP. The recall was mentioned as early as July 1931, in the *Los Angeles Chronicle*, Feb. 29, 1932, 1–2.

68. *Municipal League Bulletin*, Apr. 20, 1932, 1; *Los Angeles Chronicle*, Apr. 28, 1932; *Power*, Apr. 28, 1932; *Bob Shuler's Magazine*, Mar. 1932, 317, May 1932, 370–71; Woods, "Progressives and Police," 286, 301; Stanley Rogers, "The Attempted Recall of the Mayor of Los Angeles," *National Municipal Review*, 21 (July 1932): 416–19, quote on 417.

69. Department of Water and Power files, box 125, HP; *Examiner*, May 7, 10, 1932; *Times*, May 18, 1932; Van Valen, "Power Politics," 326–30.

70. *Times*, Aug. 13, 23, 1932; *Examiner*, Aug. 15, 1932; Van Valen, "Power Politics," 330–40, quote on 339–40.

71. Bond Election of 1932 file, box 106, HP.

72. Anne Mumford to Franklin Hichborn, Mar. 22, 1924, box 159, Franklin Hichborn Papers, UCLA; Mumford to John Collier, Nov. 9, 1927, box 2, HP; Haynes to Upton Sinclair, Nov. 28, 1927, Mumford to Louis Bartlett, Jan. 11, 1929, HF; *Herald*, Nov. 4, 1927; *Examiner*, Oct. 24, 1933; John Anson Ford, *Thirty Explosive Years in Los Angeles County* (San Marino, Calif.: Huntington Library, 1961), 90–91.

73. Haynes to T. M. Althausen, June 25, 1930, HF.

74. Mumford to Hichborn, Nov. 2, 1927, Jan. 4, 1928, HF; Dora Haynes to Mumford, Feb. 29, 1928, box 227, Mrs. George B. Mangold to Haynes Foundation trustees, Feb. 11, 1938, box 93, HP; files in boxes 126 and 318, League of Women Voters Papers, LC; Dora Haynes to Clara Burdette, May 2, 1933, box 153, Clara Burdette Papers, Huntington.

75. Haynes to John S. Mitchell, Apr. 27, 1926, Haynes to John Henderson, Dec. 21, 1926, Haynes to City Club, June 1, 1928, "Personal 3" Scrapbook, HP; Annandale Golf Club file, HF; *Times*, Dec. 14, 1931, July 2, 1935; *Examiner*, Nov. 29, 1934.

76. *Record*, July 12, 1929; *Examiner*, Jan. 31, 1926; *Annals of the Sunset Club*, 3: 109–10.

77. *Times*, Feb. 26, 1914; A. G. Arnoll to Haynes, Feb. 8, 1926, "Personal 3" Scrapbook, HP; Los Angeles Chamber of Commerce *Bulletin*, Oct. 8, 1934; Leslie R. Saunders to Haynes, Oct. 6, 1926, HF.

78. Haynes to William Kent, July 5, 1927, Haynes to Judson King, Sept. 16, 1927, and Haynes's autobiography notes, HF.

79. Haynes to Edgerton Shore, Jan. 14, 1925, box 202, HP; *Record*, July 10–13, 15–17, 1929.

80. *Record*, July 12, 1929. Other biographical treatments of Haynes at this time include *Who's Who in Los Angeles County* (Los Angeles: Charles J. Lang, 1926), 188; Rockwell Hunt, ed., *California and Californians*, 5 vols. (Chicago: Lewis, 1926), 5: 4–7; Wellington C. Wolfe, *Men of California* (San Francisco: Wellington C. Wolfe, 1926), 122; *Saturday Night*, Feb. 6, 1926, 1–2; Sam T. Clover, *Constructive Californians* (Los Angeles: Saturday Night, 1926), 143–47; Max Stern, "Doctor of Sick Politics," *San Francisco News*, 1929, clipping in box 8, Thomas J. Mooney Papers, Bancroft (reprinted in *Record*, Nov. 4, 1929); Justice B. Detwiler, ed., *Who's Who in California, 1928–29* (San Francisco: Who's Who, 1929), 422; William A. Spalding, *History and Reminiscences, Los Angeles City and County, California*, 3 vols. (Los Angeles: J. R. Finnell, 1931), 2: 86–89; *Record* articles cited above.

CHAPTER THIRTEEN

1. Arthur M. Schlesinger, Jr., *The Crisis of the Old Order, 1919–1933*, vol. 1 of his *The Age of Roosevelt*, 3 vols. (Boston: Houghton Mifflin, 1957), 155–269.

2. Leonard Joseph Leader, "Los Angeles and the Great Depression" (Ph.D. diss., University of California, Los Angeles, 1972), esp. 1–18; Louis B. Perry and Richard S. Perry, *A History of the Los Angeles Labor Movement, 1911–1941* (Berkeley: University of California Press, 1963), 235–37.

3. William E. Leuchtenburg, *Franklin D. Roosevelt and the New Deal, 1932–1940* (New York: Harper and Row, 1963), 4–17; Paul A. Conkin, *The New Deal*, 2nd ed. (Arlington Heights, Ill.: AHM, 1975), 1–19.

4. Judson King to Haynes, Sept. 30, 1932, copy of Franklin D. Roosevelt to King, Oct. 18, 1932, box 158, National Popular Government League files, box 157, 1932 Election file, box 61, HP.

5. Haynes to James Irvine, Oct. 6, 1932, Haynes to Judson King, Sept. 26, 1932, HF; Public Ownership files, box 170, HP.

6. On the New Deal see Barton J. Bernstein, "The New Deal: The Conservative Achievements of Liberal Reform," in Bernstein, *Towards a New Past: Dissenting Essays in American History* (New York: Random House, 1967), 263–88; Conkin, *The New Deal*; Bradford A. Lee, "The New Deal Reconsidered," *Wilson Quarterly*, 6 (Spring 1982):62–76, quote on 62. Older studies include Arthur M. Schlesinger, Jr.'s *Age of Roosevelt* series, consisting of *The Crisis of the Old Order, 1919–1933* (1957), *The Coming of the New Deal* (1959), and *The Politics of Upheaval* (1960) (Boston: Houghton Mifflin); Leuchtenberg, *Roosevelt and the New Deal*. Also see John M. Allswang, *The New Deal and American Politics: A Study in Political Change* (New York: John Wiley, 1978); Gerald D. Nash, *The Great Depression and World War II: Organizing America, 1933–1945* (New York: St. Martin's, 1979).

7. Telegram from Haynes to Roosevelt, Jan. 25, 1934, Louis Bartlett to Haynes, Jan. 26, 1934, Leighton H. Prebles to Haynes, Jan. 29, 1934, box 211, HP.

8. Haynes correspondence with Representatives Thomas Ford, Byron M. Scott, John M. Costello, et al., Haynes to Roosevelt, Oct. 23, 1933, Haynes to Cordell Hull, Mar. 18, 1937, Haynes to Rockwell Hunt, Feb. 4, 1935, HF.

9. James Irvine to Haynes, Sept. 30, 1935, HF; Haynes to Thomas Amlie, Aug. 26, 1935, box 3, Thomas Amlie file, box 4, *Palm Springs Limelight*, Jan. 21, 1934, clipping in "Personal 3" Scrapbook, HP.

10. Haynes to Gifford Pinchot, Nov. 7, 1936, Haynes to John Anson Ford, July 7, 1936, HF; Haynes to Norman Thomas, June 23, 1936, box 63, HP. On the Socialist party and the New Deal, see David A. Shannon, *The Socialist Party of America: A History* (New York: Macmillan, 1955), 227–48.

11. Roy Malcolm to Haynes, May 31, 1937, Haynes to Marvin H. McIntyre, May 31, 1935, Haynes to Senator George W. Norris, June 18, 1935, HF.

12. Haynes to Ford M. Jack, Feb. 9, 1937, Haynes to Cordell Hull, Mar. 18, 1937, HF. For contemporary views of the "court-packing" controversy, see Julia E. Johnson, comp., *Reorganization of the Supreme Court*, The Reference Shelf series, vol. 2, no. 4 (New York: H. W. Wilson, 1937).

13. Otis L. Graham, Jr., *An Encore for Reform: The Old Progressives and the New Deal* (New York: Oxford University Press, 1967), 129–50.

14. Haynes to Louis Bartlett, Sept. 19, 1934, Haynes to Maysie Miller, Oct.24, 1934, Dora Haynes's Will files, HF; *Herald*, Nov. 24, 1934; *Times*, Nov. 24, 1934; *Examiner*, Nov. 26, 1934.

15. Belle Cooper, "A Tribute to Mrs. John R. Haynes," *Saturday Night*, Dec. 8, 1934, 7; Mrs. George B. Mangold to Haynes Foundation trustees, Feb. 11, 1938, box 93, HP; Dora Haynes to Katherine Philips Edson, Apr. 20, 1922, June 27, 1933, box 3, Katherine P. Edson Papers, UCLA.

16. *Hollywood Citizen-News*, Mar. 23, 1935; *Alhambra Post-Advocate*, Feb. 17, 1949; *Examiner*, Mar. 17, 19, 1935.

17. Dora Haynes's Will files, Haynes to Hichborn, July 2, 1935, HF.

18. "Minutes of Meetings of the Board of Trustees, Haynes Foundation," 1: 61–79 (Sept. 22, 1930–Feb. 19, 1934), HF.

19. Ibid., Dec. 5, 1935, copy of John Collier to Harold Von Schmidt, Jan. 3, 1936, Remson Bird, typescript statement (1944), HF; Russell Holmes Fletcher, ed., *Who's Who in California, 1942–43* (Los Angeles: Who's Who, 1941), 78.

20. Haynes to Louis Bartlett et al., Nov. 2, 1933, Hichborn to Haynes, Jan. 4, 1934, Herbert C. Jones to Haynes, Nov. 15, 1933, "The John Randolph Haynes and Dora Haynes Foundation Declaration of Trust, Amended February 19, 1934," HF.

21. President's Reports, 1927–1970 file, Robert Sproul to Haynes, May 11, 1935, HF.

22. Haynes to Rudolph Spreckels, Feb. 21, 1930, Haynes to Upton Sinclair, Apr. 2, 1930, Gross B. Alexander file, HF.

23. John Beardsley to Haynes, Mar. 19, 1934, box 96, HP; Ordean Rockey to Theodore P. Gerson, Mar. 10, 1935, box 2, Anne Mumford to Gerson, box 3, Theodore P. Gerson Papers, UCLA.

24. Hichborn to Haynes, Jan. 10, 1936, Haynes to Dewey Anderson, June 9, 1936, HF; Robert E. Burke, *Olson's New Deal for California* (Berkeley: University of California Press, 1953), 31, 38.

25. Haynes to Hichborn, Jan. 4, 1937, HF.

26. Haynes to Anderson, Mar. 16, Apr. 7, 1937, Haynes to Jones and Hichborn, Apr. 19, 1937, Jones to Haynes, Apr. 12, 1937, HF.

27. "Minutes of Meetings of the Board of Trustees, Haynes Foundation," 1: 127–28 (Dec. 21, 1936–Dec. 6, 1937), HF.

28. Haynes/Rolph correspondence, 1931–34, HF. Haynes was well aware of his standing with Rolph. As the doctor cautioned an officeseeker requesting a written endorsement: "I am of the opinion that such a letter would do you more harm than good." Haynes to Joseph Phillis, July 6, 1931, HF.

29. H. Brett Melendy and Benjamin F. Gilbert, *The Governors of California: From Peter H. Burnett to Edmund G. Brown* (Georgetown, Calif.: Talisman, 1965), 381–84; Wilda Smith to Merriam, Sept. 16, 1920, box 3, Haynes to Merriam, Mar. 30, 1925, May 8, 1933, box 12, Frank P. Merriam Papers, Bancroft; Merriam to Haynes, June 8, 1934, HF; Earl Lee Kelly to Haynes, Feb. 6, 1935, box 2, HP.

30. Haynes to William M. Garland, Oct. 31, 1934, Haynes to Hichborn, Apr. 18, 1934, box 62, Hichborn to Haynes, May 18, 1937, box 40, HP; Haynes to Herbert C. Jones, Mar. 7, 1934, Jones to Haynes, June 18, 1934, copy of Louis Bartlett to Jones, Feb. 20, 1934, box 27, Herbert C. Jones Papers, Stanford.

31. Haynes to Jones, Mar. 7, 1934, copy of Raymond Haight to Hichborn, Aug. 3, 1934, box 93, Haynes to Hichborn, July 17, 1934, box 62, HP; Royce D. Delmatier, Clarence F. McIntosh, and Earl G. Waters, eds., *The Rumble of California Politics, 1848–1970* (New York: John Wiley, 1970), 267.

32. Upton Sinclair to Haynes, Sept. 24, 1929, box 186, HP; Sinclair to Haynes, Feb. 7, Mar. 19, Sept. 13, 1929, June 10, 1930, Feb. 17, Oct. 10, 1931, Upton Sinclair Papers, Lilly; Haynes to R. W. Anderson, Dec. 8, 1928, HF; Martin Zanger, "Upton Sinclair as California's Socialist Candidate for Congress, 1920," *Southern California Quarterly*, 56 (Winter 1974):359–73; Delmatier, McIntosh, and Waters, *Rumble of California Politics*, 272–73.

33. Upton Sinclair, *I, Governor of California, and How I Ended Poverty: A True Story of the Future* (Los Angeles: Upton Sinclair, 1934); Clarence Frederic McIntosh, "Upton Sinclair and the EPIC Movement, 1933–1936" (Ph.D. diss., Stanford University, 1955); Jackson K. Putnam, *Old-Age Politics in California: From Richardson to Reagan* (Stanford, Calif.: Stanford University Press, 1970), 32–48.

34. *Times*, Sept. 1–Nov. 5, 1934; McIntosh, "EPIC Movement," 163–325; Charles E. Larsen, "The EPIC Campaign of 1934," *Pacific Historical Review*, 27 (May 1958): 127–47; Russel M. Posner, "A. P. Giannini and the 1934 Campaign in California," *Southern California Quarterly*, 39 (June 1957): 190–201; Upton Sinclair, *The Autobiography of Upton Sinclair* (New York: Harcourt, Brace, and World, 1962), 268–78.

35. Haynes to Hichborn, June 30, 1934, box 62, John J. Hamilton to editor, *Pasadena Star-News*, clipping in box 186, HP; Hichborn files in box 96, Herbert C. Jones Papers, Stanford.

36. Ed Roberts to "Olbert," Mar. 5, 1934, HF; 1934 General Election sample ballot, box 39, HP; Delmatier, McIntosh, and Waters, *Rumble of California Politics*, 280–81; Michael P. Rogin and John L. Shover, *Political Change in California: Critical Elections and Social Movements, 1890–1966* (Westport, Conn.: Greenwood, 1970), 130–34.

37. Haynes to Hiram Johnson, July 7, 1934, box 62, HP; Delmatier, McIntosh, and Waters, *Rumble of California Politics*, 268.

38. Haynes to Hichborn, Feb. 12, 1937, Frank Waters to Haynes, June 3, 1935, Haynes's correspondence with Waters, Culbert Olson, and Dewey Anderson, boxes 20 and 40, HP.

39. Haynes to Hichborn, Feb. 12, 1935, Haynes to Merriam, Jan. 22, 1935, Haynes to Olson, Feb. 21, 1935, Haynes to Anderson, Feb. 2, 1935, box 40, Waters to Haynes, May 27, 1935, box 20, Haynes to Chris Jesperson, Jan. 10, 1935, box 50, HP.

40. Haynes to Hiram Johnson, Mar. 18, 1932, box 184, HP.

41. Single Tax files, box 186, Haynes to Hichborn, Aug. 4, 1936, box 40, Haynes to Russell N. Lockwood, Apr. 30, 1936, box 186, HP; Jackson H. Ralston, *Confronting the Land Question* (Bayside, N.Y.: American Association for Scientific Taxation, 1945), xiii.

42. Clark vs. Jordan, 7 Cal 2nd 248 (1936); Haynes to Hichborn, Aug. 4, Sept. 1, 1936, box 40, HP; *Times*, Aug. 28, 1936, Sept. 30, 1938.

43. Haynes to Judson King, Mar. 2, 1933, box 158, HP; Haynes to Herbert C. Jones, Jan. 3, 1933, HF.

44. Haynes to Frank Shaw, Jan. 13, 1933, box 131, HP; *Herald*, Apr. 29, 1931; Joseph Gerald Woods, "The Progressives and the Police: Urban Reform and the Professionalization of the Los Angeles Police" (Ph.D. diss., University of California, Los Angeles, 1973), 327; Thomas J. Sitton, "Urban Politics and Reform in New Deal Los Angeles: The Recall of Mayor Frank L. Shaw" (Ph.D. diss., University of California, Riverside, 1983), 35–41.

45. Haynes to Howard Davis, July 3, 1933, and Haynes to James Hyde, July 13, 1933, HF; 1933 Election file, box 62, HP; Sitton, "Urban Politics and Reform," 41–50.

46. Sitton, "Urban Politics and Reform," 56–244.

47. Haynes to Frank Shaw, Aug. 14, 1933, box 131, HP.

48. Haynes to Shaw, June 21, 23, 24, July 6, Oct. 17, 1933, Dec. 17, 1934, Mar. 16, Apr. 30, 1935, Shaw to Haynes, Nov. 4, 1935, box 131, HP; George Grimmer to Haynes, June 18, 1935, Will Anderson to Haynes, Aug. 19, 1935, James Irvine to Haynes, July 4, 1933, HF.

49. *Times*, July 12, 1933.

50. Ibid., June 13, 14, 1933; *Intake*, July 1933, 3, 6.

51. Charter Election of 1935 file, box 106, HP; John R. Haynes, "$1,600,000.00 a Year for Your Pocketbook, Mr. and Mrs. L. A. Citizen," *Los Angeles Chronicle*, Sept. 1935, 9; Nelson S. Van Valen, "Power Politics: The Struggle for Municipal Ownership of Electrical Utilities in Los Angeles, 1905–1937" (Ph.D. diss., Claremont Graduate School, 1963), 363–67.

52. Beverly Bowen Miller, *Phil Swing and Boulder Dam* (Berkeley: University of California Press, 1971), quote on xiii; *Herald and Express*, Oct. 9, 1936; *Examiner*, Sept. 9, 1936; *Intake*, Oct. 1936, 12–13. On construction of the dam see Joseph E. Stevens, *Hoover Dam: An American Adventure* (Norman: University of Oklahoma Press, 1988).

53. Haynes to Los Angeles Gas and Electric Company, Mar. 6, 1922, Al King to Haynes, Mar. 31, 1922, box 147, HP; Van Valen, "Power Politics," 346–55.

54. Charter Election of 1934 files, box 106, Los Angeles Gas and Electric Com-

pany files, box 147, HP; "Three Letters to Employees," *Intake*, Oct. 1934, 12; Van Valen, "Power Politics," 356–60.

55. *Power*, Mar. 30, 1935; *Municipal League Bulletin*, Jan. 17, 1935, 1; Haynes to Frank Shaw, Mar. 16, 1935, box 131, HP; *Herald and Express*, Apr. 1, 1935; *Times*, Mar. 28, 1935; Van Valen, "Power Politics," 360–63.

56. *Times*, Feb. 1, Apr. 13, 1937; *Examiner*, Apr. 7, 1935; Van Valen, "Power Politics," 367–72.

57. Haynes to Murray Seasongood, Sept. 7, 1932, box 157, Haynes to Carl I. Wheat, Sept. 22, 1934, box 106, Haynes to Lester Ready, Nov. 21, 1935, Anthony Pratt to Board of Water and Power commissioners, Mar. 27, 1936, box 147, HP.

58. Vincent Ostrom, *Water and Politics: A Study of Water Policies and Administration in the Development of Los Angeles* (Los Angeles: Haynes Foundation, 1953), 78–85; Franklin P. Buyer to Haynes, Sept. 25, 1934, HF; *Times*, May 10, 1935.

59. Haynes to Ford M. Jack, Mar. 16, 1935, Haynes to E. P. Ryland, Mar. 23, 1936, Haynes to John Anson Ford, July 7, 1936, HF.

60. Legislature files, box 20, National Recovery Act files, box 211, Haynes to John A. Gray, Oct. 7, 1933, box 155, HP; John R. Haynes, "A Great Institution," *Power*, Nov. 1935, 1; John R. Haynes, "Lowest Electric Lighting Rates in United States," *Los Angeles Chronicle*, May 1933, 15; *Examiner*, Aug. 27, 1935.

61. *Intake*, Nov. 1933, 5, June 1936, 12.

62. Haynes to Shaw, Oct. 12, 1937, box 131, HP.

63. Haynes to Shaw, Nov. 16, 1934, box 131, Public Ownership League of America file, box 177, HP.

64. H. Gale Atwater to Haynes, May 16, 1935, Nov. 6, 1936, Jan. 28, 1937, box 153, 1935 Charter Election file, box 107, Anthony Pratt to Board of Water and Power Commissioners, May 11, 1935, box 154, HP; *United Progressive News*, May 5, 1935; Sitton, "Urban Politics and Reform," 103–6.

65. Harry Chandler to Haynes, Aug. 28, 1934, HF; 1934 Charter Election file, box 106, HP; David Halberstam, *The Powers That Be* (New York: Knopf, 1979), 112–14.

66. Shaw to Haynes, April 5, 1937, box 131, D. A. Russell to Haynes, Apr. 15, 1937, box 114, 1937 Municipal Election sample ballot, box 107, HP.

67. John Anson Ford to Haynes, Mar. 5, 1932, Dec. 20, 1933, Mar. 5, 1934, Haynes to Ford, June 9, 1933, HF.

68. Haynes to Ford, May 11, 1937, HF; Sitton, "Urban Reform and Politics," 151–64; Tom Sitton, "Another Generation of Urban Reformers: Los Angeles in the 1930s," *Western Historical Quarterly*, 18 (July 1987): 315–32.

69. Anne Mumford to John Collier, Oct. 28, 1936, HF; Mumford to H. Gale Atwater, Nov. 10, 1936, box 153, HP.

70. Jim Walker, ed., *The Yellow Cars of Los Angeles, Interurbans Special No. 43* (Glendale, Calif.: Interurbans, 1977), 210–13.

71. Haynes to John Baumgartner, Sept. 1936, box 67, HP; Albert Howard Clodius, "The Quest for Good Government in Los Angeles, 1890–1910" (Ph.D. diss., Claremont Graduate School, 1953), 111.

72. Haynes to Lucius Storrs, Feb. 26, 1937, Storrs to Haynes, Mar. 6, May 24, 1937, Haynes to Edgar Hughes, July 12, 1937, box 134, HP; *Examiner*, July 6, 1937.

73. Haynes to Anthony Pratt, July 22, 1937, Haynes letters to five city councilmen, July 22, 1937, Haynes to E. A. Kline, July 30, 1937, box 134, HP. The Pacific Electric removed Eclipse fenders from its cars during World War II.

74. Mumford to Louis Bartlett, Oct. 2, 21, 1937, HF; *Hollywood Citizen-News*, Oct. 22, 30, 1937; *Examiner*, Oct. 24, 1937; *Intake*, Nov. 1933, 3.

CHAPTER FOURTEEN

1. *Hollywood Citizen-News*, Oct. 30, 1937; *Examiner*, Oct. 31, Nov. 2, 1937.

2. *Herald and Express*, Nov. 5, 1937; copy of "Petition for Probate of Will and Codicils," no. 171903, HF.

3. Vincent Ostrom, *Water and Politics: A Study of Water Policies and Administration in the Development of Los Angeles* (Los Angeles: Haynes Foundation, 1953), 73–78.

4. "Passing of Dr. Haynes Mourned by Department," *Intake*, Nov. 1937, 3, 6, and "Haynes Steam Plant Open House," *Intake*, Oct. 1963, 4–5, 21; *Hollywood Citizen-News*, Mar. 6, 1939.

5. *Times*, Nov. 10, 1986; V. O. Key and Winston W. Crouch, *The Initiative and Referendum in California* (Berkeley: University of California Press, 1939), 424–41, 555–63; Laura Tillian, *Direct Democracy: An Historical Analysis of the Initiative, Referendum and Recall Process* (Los Angeles: People's Lobby, 1977), 9–41; Winston W. Crouch, "John Randolph Haynes and His Work for Direct Government," *National Municipal Review*, 27 (Sept. 1938): 434–40, 453; Thomas E. Cronin, *Direct Democracy: The Politics of the Initiative, Referendum, and Recall* (Cambridge, Mass.: Harvard University Press, 1989), 50, 128–33; David D. Schmidt, *Citizen Lawmakers: The Ballot Initiative Revolution* (Philadelphia: Temple University Press, 1989), 222–25.

6. For some recent examples see *Times*, Mar. 26, 1982, Sept. 4, 1983, Sept. 9, Nov. 15, 25, 1984, Mar. 27, Nov. 4, 1990.

7. Interview with Winston W. Crouch, Oct. 5, 1988, Los Angeles; *Herald-Examiner*, Feb. 28, 1988; *Times*, May 31, 1988, Nov. 12, 1990; Charles G. Bell and Charles M. Price, *California Government Today: Politics of Reform* (Homewood, Ill.: Dorsey, 1980), 108–30. Also see Cronin, *Direct Democracy*, x, and David B. Magleby, *Direct Legislation: Voting on Ballot Propositions in the United States* (Baltimore: Johns Hopkins University Press, 1984).

8. Herbert C. Jones to "My Fellow Trustees," Dec. 1, 1937, HF.

9. Anne Mumford to Franklin Hichborn, Jan. 9, 1939, Remson Bird, typescript statement (1944), HF.

10. *The Hichborn Papers*, pamphlet (Haynes Foundation, 1950). For a list of Haynes Foundation publications to 1955 see frontispiece of Edwin A. Cottrell and Helen L. Jones, *The Metropolis: Is Integration Possible?*, vol. 16 of *Metropolitan Los Angeles: A Study in Integration*, 16 vols. (Los Angeles: Haynes Foundation, 1955).

11. Marco R. Newmark, "Medical Profession in the Early Days of Los Angeles," part 2, *Historical Society of Southern California Quarterly*, 34 (June 1952): 166; brochure of Pacific Southwest Academy, and Trustees files, HF. Scholarly publications financed by the Haynes Foundation at that time included Arthur M.

Schlesinger's *The American as Reformer* (Cambridge, Mass.: Harvard University Press, 1950).

12. "Minutes of Meetings of the Board of Trustees, Haynes Foundation," 6: 1296–1300 (Oct. 15, 1952), HF; *Times*, Nov. 17, 1952.

13. Interview with Phyllis Poinsot, Feb. 8, 1988, Los Angeles; Grants files, HF; *Times*, Aug. 2, 1979, Oct. 15, 1988, Mar. 5, 1989; William W. Clary, *History of the Law Firm of O'Melveny and Myers, 1885–1965*, 2 vols. (Los Angeles: privately printed, 1966), 2: 306–9, 395–98.

14. Haynes to Haynes Foundation trustees, Aug. 27, 1928, HF.

Bibliographic Notes

The massive collection of personal correspondence, newspaper clippings, government reports, scrapbooks, reference books, emphemera, serials, and other material in the John Randolph Haynes Papers at UCLA formed the basis for this study. Assembled by Haynes, his friends and associates, Haynes Foundation trustees and librarians, and others, the Haynes collection has been a treasure trove of information on a variety of topics for scholars and others who have used it in the foundation office and, after 1952, at UCLA. This collection is now being supplemented by the large amount of Haynes's personal correspondence and family material formerly located in the Haynes Foundation office in downtown Los Angeles.

Several important manuscript collections contain significant amounts of Haynes correspondence not found in the Haynes Papers, as well as the personal thoughts of some of his associates concerning him and his ideas. The most important are the papers of Hiram W. Johnson, George C. Pardee, John F. Neylan, and Chester Rowell in the Bancroft Library; Meyer Lissner and Herbert C. Jones at Stanford; Caroline Severance at the Huntington Library; Franklin Hichborn, Edward A. Dickson, H. Gaylord Wilshire, and Katherine P. Edson at UCLA; and Upton Sinclair at the Lilly Library.

Many of the sources included in my notes were helpful in areas besides those in which they were cited. In addition, there are a number of works important to my understanding of the subject that were not cited, especially those relating to the 1920s and 1930s. These include:

Borough, Reuben. Papers. UCLA.
Bottles, Scott L. *Los Angeles and the Automobile: The Making of the Modern City*. Berkeley: University of California Press, 1987.

California Progressive Campaign Book for 1914: Three Years of Progressive Administration in California Under Governor Hiram W. Johnson. San Francisco: N.p., 1914.

Carney, Francis M. "The Decentralized Politics of Los Angeles." *Annals of the American Academy of Political and Social Science,* 353 (May 1964): 107–21.

Cleland, Robert G. *California in Our Time, 1900–1940.* New York: Knopf, 1947.

Crouch, Winston W. "Direct Legislation Laboratory." *National Municipal Review,* 40 (Feb. 1951): 81–87, 99.

Ford, John Anson. Papers. Huntington.

Hill, Gladwin. *Dancing Bear: An Inside Look at California Politics.* Cleveland: World, 1968.

Kenny, Robert W. Papers. Bancroft.

McWilliams, Carey. *Southern California Country: An Island on the Land.* New York: Duell, Sloane, and Pearce, 1946.

Mead, William. Scrapbooks. Huntington.

Nadeau, Remi. *Los Angeles: From Mission to Modern City.* New York: Longmans, Green, 1960.

Nordskog, Andrae. Papers. Water Resources Center Archives, University of California, Berkeley.

Olson, Culbert. Papers. Bancroft.

Shaw, Joseph E. Papers. UCLA.

Stimson, Marshall. Papers. Huntington.

Story, Harold H. Papers. UCLA.

Wilshire, Logan. "Gaylord Wilshire, the Millionaire Socialist." Typescript, 1968. Los Angeles County Medical Association Library.

Index

In this index an "f" after a number indicates a separate reference on the next page, and an "ff" indicates separate references on the next two pages. A continuous discussion over two or more pages is indicated by a span of page numbers, e.g., "pp. 57–58." *Passim* is used for a cluster of references in close but not consecutive sequence.

cian in Philadelphia, 7–9, 188; as Episcopal church member, 8, 16, 28, 181, 198; illnesses suffered by, 9, 61–62, 72, 179, 206, 226, 251f; and family milieu in Los Angeles, 9, 11, 17, 128–29, 179, 233–34; business activities of, 11, 13–15f, 45, 61, 129–30; as physician in Los Angeles, 11–13, 16, 61, 72; social position of, 14ff, 18, 28, 44–45; social activities of, 15, 31, 61, 179, 227; and travel to England, 45–46; and San Francisco earthquake relief mission, 62–63; and travel to Europe, 63–64, 91, 131; and travel to Mexico, 63; and travel to Russia, 64, 66, 70; mansion of, 128; personal secretaries employed by, 129; wartime relief efforts of, 131–35; and avowal of atheism, 198f, 259; death of, 252, 253–54

—organizational roles: in Democratic party, 9, 16; in public health organizations, 13f, 48, 109, 132, 134; in Los Angeles cultural organizations, 15, 129; in Los Angeles social clubs, 15, 31, 61, 227; in municipal reform organizations, 21–24, 33, 48f, 80, 106f; in social reform organizations, 28–37 passim; in direct legislation organizations, 39, 43, 60, 89f; in Republican party, 47, 97, 151, 232, 238; as Los Angeles civil service commissioner, 48, 78–79, 109; in public ownership organizations, 54–55, 61, 70–71, 142; in Lincoln-Roosevelt League, 89–91; as California state prison overseer, 100–101, 109, 125–26, 153, 191; in National Civil Service Reform League, 109; as Los Angeles Board of Freeholders member, 113–14, 173–74; as Los Angeles Public Service Commission member, 125, 167–73; as Los Angeles Public Welfare Commission member, 125–26, 175; and wartime relief effort, 131–35; on federal draft board, 136–37; as labor dispute mediator, 136, 151, 188; in Morals Efficiency Association, 137; in California state government efficiency committee, 152; as University of California regent, 153, 156–57, 207–8; as California Constitutional Commission member, 206–10 passim; as California state tax commissioner, 206; as California State Unemployment Board member, 207; as Los Angeles Department of Water and Power commissioner, 214–26 passim, 242,

244–48, 253–54. See also Haynes Foundation

—political activism: and prohibitionism, 3, 96–97, 133, 193, 211; and child labor, 20, 144, 188; as "millionaire socialist," 44–45, 60, 76, 228; and Socialist party, 44, 55, 71, 139, 230; and English reformers, 45–46; and labor movement, 46–47, 94–95, 134–36, 174, 188, 258; and campaign to recall Councilman Davenport, 49–50; and saloon regulation, 59–64 passim, 109; and campaign to recall Mayor Harper, 66, 83–84; and William D. Stephens, 84, 132f, 136, 151–57 passim, 161f, 172; and Southern Pacific Railroad, 86–89, 92, 107; and Rudolph Spreckels, 90, 157f, 164f, 183, 204; and Hiram Johnson, 91–105 passim, 135, 148–54 passim, 194, 215, 240; and mining safety, 95, 135–36, 188, 200, 236, 258; and prison reform, 100–101; and Edwin T. Earl, 123–27; and patriotism, 131, 137–38, 140, 149; and tax reform, 137, 206, 241–42; and Upton Sinclair, 142–43, 146, 182, 195–96, 201; and Red Scare of 1919, 143–55 passim; and League of Nations, 148–49; and educational improvement, 153, 189, 208; and Better America Federation, 154–56; and Franklin Hichborn, 154, 156f, 161ff, 181f, 184, 187, 201–10 passim, 240; and La Follette's presidential campaign, 158; and Kent K. Parrot, 172–73, 177, 196, 204, 212–13, 217–18; and sterilization programs, 190–93; and Native American rights, 193–95; Clement C. Young, 205ff, 208; and New Deal, 230–33; and Frank L. Shaw, 243–51 passim. See also Haynes Foundation; and see under Municipal ownership; Municipal reform; Tax reform

—political philosophy: influenced by medical practice, 7, 9, 28, 188; and progressivism, 19–20, 98–99, 105, 228; and social reformism, 20, 28–31, 108, 141, 258–60; and Christian socialism, 26–29, 32, 44, 138–39, 198, 259; and evolutionary socialism, 26, 44, 46, 76, 99, 197; and William D. P. Bliss, 26–29, 33, 36; and paternalism, 46, 97, 193; and eugenics, 190–93; and racial segregation, 192–93

Haynes, Joseph (JRH's grandfather), 3
Haynes, Mary (JRH's sister), 3, 11, 17, 128, 177, 179, 183

Sage Foundation, 182, 235

Saloons: regulation of, 59f, 64, 91, 94, 106, 109

San Fernando Mission Land Company, 53

San Francisco: Union Reform League in, 27; direct legislation in, 38; streetcar safety in, 56; earthquake of 1906 in, 62–63; Union Labor party in, 67, 86; recall petitions in, 76

San Francisco Examiner, 56

Sanger, Margaret, 192

Santa Fe Railroad, 88, 174

Sartori, Joseph F., 15, 91, 206

Sartori, Margaret, 207

Saturday Post (periodical), 39

Scattergood, Ezra F., 120, 166, 168, 215, 220–25 *passim*, 244, 246f, 253, 257

Scharrenberg, Paul, 160, 163

Schenk, Joseph, 205

Schiesl, Martin, 118, 120

Schlesinger, Arthur M., 257

Scofield, E. M., 221ff

Scott, Joseph, 40

Sebastian, Charles E., 124, 127

Segregation, racial, 192–93, 257

Severance, Caroline S., 25f, 30, 32, 44, 63, 77

Severance Club, 63, 129, 146

Shannon, David A., 44, 110, 199

Shaw, Frank L., 242–51 *passim*

Shaw, George Bernard, 46, 190

Shenk, John, 118–19, 127

Shortridge, Samuel, 154, 204

Shuler, Robert, 219–25 *passim*, 239, 243, 250

Sinclair, Upton, 63, 129, 140, 228, 236; and JRH, 142–43, 146, 182, 195–96, 201; arrest of, 195–96; gubernatorial campaigns of, 204, 211, 239–40; and End Poverty in California program, 239–40

Single Tax Club, 24–25

Single Tax League, 163

Smith, Al, 211

Smith, Fred M., 40

Smith, George A., 69, 107

Snyder, Meredith P., 40, 48, 166, 167–68, 172, 177

Social Democratic League, 141

Socialism: and "millionaire socialists," 14, 44–45, 60, 76; as interventionism, 19f; and Los Angeles reform organizations, 24ff, 32; evolutionary, 25f, 44, 46, 76, 99, 197; Christian, 26–29, 32, 34, 44, 63, 138–39, 198, 259; JRH's advocacy

of, 26, 34, 44, 55, 76, 99, 138–39, 196f; postal censorship of, 77–78; and middle-class progressivism, 98–99

Socialist Labor party, 24f, 29, 36ff

Socialist Party of America, 25, 32, 44, 70f, 95; and direct legislation, 24, 36f, 90; founding of, 24; JRH's support for, 44, 55, 71, 76, 139, 230; in Los Angeles, 54f, 70, 76, 80, 84, 110–19 *passim*; and municipal ownership, 54f, 110; compared to Progressive party, 99; and Harriman's mayoral campaign, 110–12; labor alliance of, 110, 112; and city charters and amendments, 112, 114–17; and La Follette's presidential campaign, 158, 165; and single tax proposal, 159, 161; and Upton Sinclair's gubernatorial campaigns, 204, 211, 239; and Norman Thomas's presidential campaign, 230, 232

Social reformism: compared to structural reformism, 20; JRH's advocacy of, 20, 28–31, 108; in Los Angeles, 24–26, 108; nonrevolutionary character of, 24, 26, 44; and William D. P. Bliss, 28–31; and proportional representation, 116

Social Reform Union, 30–32, 38, 44, 115

Social security, 230

Southern California Civil Service Reform League, 109

Southern California Edison Company, 166–71 *passim*, 221, 245

Southern California Gas Company, 53

Southern California Practitioner (periodical), 12f, 18

Southern Pacific Railroad: political power of, 18, 22, 60, 68–69, 70, 83–92 *passim*, 102, 107, 187, 233; and harbor controversy, 22–23; and direct legislation, 42f, 69, 87; and JRH, 86–89, 92, 107; and Republican party, 88–89, 90–91. *See also* Parker, Walter F. X.

Southwick, Albert F., 223, 225, 244

Spain: civil war in, 231

Spalding, William A., 25, 37

Spanish-American War, 50

Spargo, John, 141, 182

Sprague, A. K., 31

Spreckels, Rudolph, 90, 98, 157f, 162, 164f, 183, 204, 211, 236

Sproul, R. G., 157

Stanford University, 162

Starr, Kevin, 25, 44

State Council of Defense, 132, 134, 151

Stead, William, 46

Library of Congress Cataloging-in-Publication Data

Sitton, Tom, 1949–
    John Randolph Haynes, California progressive / Tom Sitton.
        p.   cm.
    Includes bibliographical references (p.   ) and index.
    ISBN 0-8047-2067-3 (cloth : acid-free paper):
        1. Haynes, John Randolph, b. 1853. 2. Politicians—California—Biography. 3. Social reform-
    ers—California—Biography. 4. Progressivism (United States politics) 5. California—Politics and
    government—1850–1950. I. Title.
    F866.H3473S58   1992
    979.4'05'092—dc20
    [B]   92–7879
                                                                                                   CIP

⊗This book is printed on acid-free paper

DATE DUE

Demco, Inc. 38-293